# Lost Plays

## of the

## Harlem

## Renaissance,

## 1920–1940

# Lost Plays
## of the
# Harlem
# Renaissance,
# 1920–1940

Edited by
James V. Hatch and
Leo Hamalian

WAYNE STATE UNIVERSITY PRESS
DETROIT

### Library of Congress Cataloging-in-Publication Data

Lost plays of the Harlem Renaissance, 1920–1940 / edited by James V. Hatch
and Leo Hamalian.
    p.  cm. — (African American life series)
    Includes bibliographical references.
    ISBN 0-8143-2580-7 (pbk. : alk. paper)
    1. American drama—Afro-American authors. 2. American drama—20th
century. 3. Afro-Americans—Drama. 4. Harlem Renaissance.
I. Hatch, James Vernon, 1928–  . II. Hamalian, Leo. III. Series.
PS628.N4L67   1996
812'.52080896073—dc20                     96–29052

## African American Life Series

A complete listing of the books in this series can be found
in the back of this volume.

*Acknowledgments*

The editors wish to thank Dorothy and Reuben Silver,
formerly of Karamu House in Cleveland, Ohio, for providing
copies of several unpublished plays in this volume. We also
express our gratitude to the Schomburg Center for Research
in Black Culture, and to the Hatch-Billops Collection for
assisting our research.

"Harlem Renaissance" is actually a misnomer, because the rich surge of Black arts and letters during the 1920s was not limited to activities a few blocks south of 125th St. in New York, or even to New York City. "Negro Renaissance" gave way to "Harlem Renaissance" as <u>colored</u> gave way to <u>Negro</u>, <u>Negro</u> to <u>Black</u>, and more recently <u>Black</u> to <u>Afro-American</u> [now <u>African American</u>].

Bruce Kellner
*The Harlem Renaissance: A Historical Dictionary for the Arts*

# CONTENTS

▼▼▼▼▼▼▼▼▼

# INTRODUCTION
▼▼▼▼▼▼▼▼▼▼▼

James V. Hatch

## THE LOST TREASURES

During the 1980s and 1990s, scholars rediscovered two troves of African American theatre history, undocumented and even unsuspected treasures—unsuspected because the specter of nineteenth-century minstrelsy had hidden African American theatrical achievements beneath grotesque burnt cork. Nonetheless, the two caches of Black theatre history lay in wait—performance history and literary history.

The first treasure cache, Black popular entertainment, which African Americans initially created to please themselves, was christened "Jes' Grew" because, like Harriet Beecher Stowe's Topsy, it claimed no parents. We do not know who invented the Charleston or the Cake Walk, but African influences—including those from the Caribbean—on American theatre can be found.[1] The names of the Big Four white minstrel men—Christy, Rice, Emmett and Bryant—were widely known and written about, but who knows the slave musicians, street performers, church singers, and riverboat roustabouts whose songs and jokes and dances were stolen by the white minstrel men? It took us over one hundred years to learn that a Black family had composed the song "Dixie."[2] The "Jes' Grew" chameleon of Black popular entertainment appeared, was appropriated by whites who changed its color,

and then passed it into American theatre history as white performance.[3] With this new information and point of view, an exciting
reexamination of the turn-of-the-century ragtime musicals is
already in process.[4]

The second newly rediscovered cache, the literary history—
the one approached in this volume—has a more specific lineage,
making it easier to configure, because this group of writers published their plays and criticism. This became the literary drama
that African Americans created in order to "advance" themselves,
and from this cache, too, excellent research has been published:[5]

The Harlem Renaissance, which took place in the period
between the two World Wars, has been described as the time that
African Americans first defined themselves; however, the term
"Harlem Renaissance," is, in part, a misnomer because Black artists all across America created music, literature, and dance, and the
Renaissance was not a *re*-birth. The art born was a new child with
a new voice. To understand the plays written in that time, and
how they became "lost," some social history is pertinent.

## WHO ARE WE?

At the close of the Civil War, Black illiteracy exceeded ninety
percent. By 1880, thirty percent had learned to read; by 1890 half
the population read, and by 1910, two-thirds possessed literacy.
This development meant changes in newspapers, cultural taste,
aspirations, and political and economic access. The talented tenth
(those with good educations) often turned their backs upon "Jes'
Grew," at least in the presence of white people. A leader on the
cultural front, James Weldon Johnson, wrote in his preface to *The
Book of American Negro Poetry* (1921): "A people may become
great through many means, but there is only one measure by
which its greatness is recognized and acknowledged. The final
measure of the greatness of all people is the amount and standard
of the literature and art they have produced."

The mission to prove oneself "worthy" was fraught with
dangerous pitfalls: on the one hand, Black writers attempted to
"legitimize" their ethnic culture to Europeans by "elevating" it to
European forms ("we's risin'"). At the same time, they slammed
the cabin door on "Jes' Grew" folk culture, even while whites
demanded more and more because they found Negroes exotic:

(Wallace Thurman exploited white pruriency in his successful play *Harlem*). No matter which way African Americans moved, racism's double bind laid snares.

So while aspiring middle-class Blacks were warning their children against ragtime (as Eubie Blake's mother warned him), whites were desperately trying to "shake that thing." Boogeying to African drums while European violins played waltzes created a cultural tension. To further confuse things, debates flourished in the press concerning whether they should call themselves "Colored," "Ethiopian," "Black," "Africans," "Negroes," "African Americans." No matter which term, Du Bois insisted it should be capitalized in the same fashion as French, English, and Irish. "Negroes" were a people!" (see appendix, documents 2, 3).

### INFLUENCES OF WHITE ON BLACK

For evil or good, white participants in the Black 1920s and 30s influenced the Renaissance's development. They drew attention to African American life, art, and artists, brought the Negro into vogue. They even drew the larger Black community into an awareness of its own artists, and opened up markets for Blacks as performers, critics, and writers (although whites made most of the money). White playwrights often emphasized the exotic folk elements of Black culture; they did not place Black actors on stage in serious drama. White playwrights—Ridgley Torrence, Eugene O'Neill, Paul Green, Dubose and Dorothy Heyward, and Marc Connelly—brought attention to the Negro theatre, as did the white critics Carl Van Vechten (see appendix document 10), and George Jean Nathan. H. L. Mencken, who had been a sometimes friend of the Black arts movement, on July 17, 1927, in "Hiring a Hall" in the *New York World*, printed his version of the Negro's artistic contributions:

> The acceptance of the educated Negro removes his last ground for complaint against his fate in the Republic, and leaves him exposed to the same criteria of judgment that apply to everybody else. . . . Once we drop the notion of special consideration for the Negro artist, what do we find? So far, it seems to me, these accomplishments have been very modest. Even in those fields wherein his opportunities for years have been precisely equal to the white man's, he has done very little of solid value. I point, for example, to the field of music.[6]

Mencken then attributed the best jazz to George Gershwin and Paul Whiteman. He even asked, "Where is the Negro composer who is writing spirituals today—I mean good ones?" (Did Mencken know "Jes' Grew" had written that music?) Professor Nathan Irvin Huggins, in his widely read book *Harlem Renaissance* (1971), agreed that the art of the Renaissance had not been successful: "the race consciousness that is so necessary for identity most likely leads to a provincialism which forever limits possibility of achieving good art." The failure of both of these savants to recognize "good art" was caused by their unwillingness to acknowledge that the Negro art of that era was not created for them, but for a people with very different needs and agendas. (See appendix documents 1, 4, 5.)

## The Beginnings of Social Drama and the Folk Play

Bert Williams' prayer for serious Negro drama dawned in 1916 with Angelina Weld Grimké's *Rachel*, a story of a sensitive Black woman who after witnessing the brutality of racism refuses to bear children (See appendix, document 9). This powerful drama, commissioned by the NAACP to counter the virulent propaganda of D. W. Griffith's *Birth of a Nation* (1915), premiered at Minor Teachers College in Washington, D.C., and provoked controversy. Should Negro drama (as it was known then) be dedicated to propaganda for the race, as W. E. B. Du Bois urged (see appendix document 14)? Or should the dramatist eschew message in favor of art, as Alain Locke urged (see appendix document 13)? The decade of the twenties became a battleground for these two visions, and the plays in this volume reflect various aspects of that conflict.

On April 17, 1917, a day before the United States entered World War I, Ridgley Torrence, a white poet who had grown up "around Negroes" in Ohio, presented *Three Plays for a Negro Theatre* at the Garden Theatre in New York City. The plays, *Granny Maumee*, *The Rider of Dreams*, and *Simon the Cyrenian*, represented Negroes as serious folk characters. Ridgley Torrence's plays conclusively demonstrated the effective use of folk characters, who were soon welcomed on intimate stages of the Little Theatre Movement. Alain Locke, to avoid "the common handicap of commercialism," designated Howard University as a center where "race drama becomes peculiarly the ward of our college, as new drama, as art-drama, and as folk-drama." The wild bird called "the folk" would be given a nest in the ivory tower (see appendix, document 13).

## WHITE PLAYWRIGHTS AND CRITICS

White authors wasted no time in exploring Negro folk themes. Eugene O'Neill led off with *The Dreamy Kid* (1919) and *All God's Chillun* (1924). His triumph, *The Emperor Jones* (1920), became fodder for Langston Hughes' satire *Em-Fuehrer Jones* (included in this volume). Dorothy Heyward adapted her husband Dubose's novel *Porgy* (1926), which became *Porgy and Bess* (1935). Paul Green won the Pulitzer Prize in 1927 with a folk drama *In Abraham's Bosom*. Julia Peterkin's play *Scarlet Sister Mary* (1930) gave Ethel Barrymore her chance to play the lead in blackface with a pretentiousness that Langston Hughes ridiculed in his play *Scarlet Sister Barry* (included in this volume). Marc Connelly capped the folk tradition by adapting Roark Bradford's book *Ol Man Adam an' His Chillun* to the stage, renaming it *The Green Pastures* (1930). All of these commercial successes exploited stereotypes of Negroes as inherently impulsive—musical —naive—religious—and sexual. In a word, a natural subject for drama.

White playwrights appropriated theatrical gestures from Negro culture, but rarely detected the meaning and the soul behind the gesture. The racism that made them feel superior, also made them blind. For example, in church scenes which appear in *Mamba's Daughters* (1939), *Porgy and Bess*, and *The Green Pastures*, the music is exciting, the voices beautiful, and the action spectacular as men and women "get happy," throwing their hats, legs, and prayer books into the air, but the scenes remain superficial and have no deeper significance. By contrast, *Run Little, Chillun* (included in this volume) by Francis Hall Johnson, choir director for *The Green Pastures*, is a serious study of African and Christian religions, a startling contrast to Marc Connelly's fantasy of Negro heaven as a perpetual fish fry for darkies. Black writers, too, recognized the theatrical value of gospel music and movement, but they also knew how essential the Sunday church service could be for a people who had to face a week with no other salvation. Andrew Burris in *You Mus' Be Bo'n Ag'in* (included in this volume) wrote a bitter denunciation of a hypocritical church. African Americans recorded religious experiences about which white writers knew little.

A contemporary reader who searches for Euro-standards of the well-made play in these early African American dramas will be often disappointed. The reader must also learn to grasp the significance these dramas had for the Black community. Although very few writers had been trained in play "construction," they ventured boldly where no American playwrights had gone before.

W. E. B. Du Bois expressed the issue of courage-to-write-the-truth in "The Negro and American Stage," a short essay in *The Crisis* (June 1924): "The Negro today fears any attempt of the artist to paint Negroes. He is not satisfied unless everything is perfect and proper and beautiful and joyful and hopeful. He is afraid to be painted as he is, lest his human foibles and shortcomings be seized by his enemies for the purposes of the ancient and hateful propaganda." With this caveat before them, Black dramatists plied a number of different strategies.

## THE NEGRO PAGEANT

To commemorate the fiftieth anniversary of the Emancipation Proclamation, W. E. B. Du Bois conceived a pageant that would "put into dramatic form for the benefit of large masses of people, a history of the Negro race.[7] On October 22, 1913, at the Twelfth Regiment Armory on Columbus Avenue in New York City, *The Star of Ethiopia* begins with

> The lights of the court of Freedom blaze. A trumpet blast is heard and four heralds, black and of gigantic stature appear with silver trumpets and standing at the four corners of the temple of beauty cry:
> "Hear ye, hear ye! Man of all Americans, and listen to the tale of the eldest and strongest of the races of mankind, whose faces be black."[8]

Negro colleges followed Du Bois' lead and throughout the 1920s presented dozens of pageants, *The Masque of Colored America, Pageant of Progress in Chicago, Culture of Color, The Milestones of the Race*, and many more. Willis Richardson included four pageants in his anthology *Plays and Pageants from the Life of the Negro* (1930).

## The Little Theatre Movement in Black

As the Little Theatre Movement spread across America, amateur drama groups formed, met, produced, and disbanded. Schools, ladies' clubs, men's lodges, churches, "Y's," and settlement houses provided raised platforms for stages and "put on plays," one-acts which seldom required more than a single set. Since experienced actors were not available for amateur productions, characters were broadly conceived and generally few in number. A production rarely boasted of more than two performances, and royalties were left unpaid because they could not be paid (appendix, document 16).

## The Playwrights, the Social Issues

In 1919, one of the earliest and most prolific playwrights, Willis Richardson, wrote a manifesto "The Hope of the Negro Drama," (appendix, document 12). He pleaded for Negro plays by Negro authors. "I do not mean merely plays with Negro characters. . . . There is another kind of play—the play that shows the soul of a people, and the soul of this people is truly worth showing." The script included here, *A Pillar of the Church*, is a gentle and convincing attempt to promote equal rights for women in voting and education (appendix, document 6, 7, 8).[9]

World War I caused dissention. Some African Americans welcomed military service as an opportunity to prove their manhood, their loyalty. Randolph Edmonds in *Yellow Death* (1935) found reasons for optimism when the Black soldiers in the Spanish American War volunteered to act as hosts for mosquito larva in order to learn the cause of malaria. Joseph Cotter, Jr.'s *On the Fields of France* (included in this volume) dramatized two officers, a white and a Black, dying together on the battlefield and wondering why they had not been friends. Other authors, like Mary Burrill in *Aftermath* (1919), spurned patriotism as a disgrace.

Tens of thousands of southern Blacks migrated north for freedom and for work. Playwrights recorded this national drama in individual human terms. John Matheus, who taught the miners at West Virginia State College near the coal mines depicted in *Black Damp* (included in this volume), as well as the migrants described in *'Cruiter* (1926), the story of a poor family leaving the old southern homestead for war-time jobs in the north. Randolph Edmonds' *Old Man Pete* (1934) presented a similar migrant family, perhaps a few years later, living a middle-class life in Harlem, but at the expense of turning their backs upon their "down home" parents. Ralf Coleman's *The Girl from Back Home* (included in this volume) replays the theme of Dreiser's novel *Sister Carrie*—an innocent young country girl seduced by a city hustler. *Environment* (included in this volume) by Mercedes Gilbert portrays the destruction of an entire family by the brutal environment of the city slums. They save themselves only by returning to the South. Playwrights Black and white used the new sociological word "environment" to explain why "good" characters, when they moved to the city, become "bad."

## THE ANTI-LYNCHING PLAYS

No injustice touched southern Black writers more deeply than lynch mobs. After the Civil War, lynching came to mean vengeful, often public, executions, particularly by southern lynch mobs, who between 1889 and 1921 killed over 3,436 individuals. Most victims were Black, though some were white, some Native American, and some Mexican. Nearly eighty were women, some pregnant. Victims were hung, shot, burned, drowned, or beaten to death. Causes might vary from "insulting a white woman" to "wearing his soldier's uniform too long after discharge."

In 1892, Ida B. Wells, a Black woman from Memphis, initiated the first campaign to stop lynching, but a federal anti-lynch law, often proposed in Congress, never passed. In this collection, Conrad Seiler's *Darker Brother* (included in this volume) is a full-length anti-lynch drama which uses fantasies boardering on expressionism. A rarity in Lynch plays, Joseph S. Mitchell's *Son-Boy* (also in this volume) has a happy ending.

Most anti-lynching plays were written by women.[10] The passage of the Nineteeth Amendment in 1920 had empowered them to become social warriors on many fronts. Because no African American of the 1920s earned a living by scripting plays, it is no accident that many writers taught school—the three professions open to women were teaching, medicine, and dentistry (see appendix, documents 7, 8). Playwright May Miller, the daughter of the professor Kelly Miller, founder of the department of sociology at Howard University, taught high school English in Baltimore. Teachers Angelina Grimké, Mary Burrill, Eulalie Spence, Shirley Graham, Ruth Gaines-Shelton, and Myrtle Smith Livingstone all published plays. Their work kept them in touch with poverty. These teachers (whose purchasing power at the store was half that of their white counterparts) wrote compassionately about the poor. No play reveals this more clearly than Mary Burrill's *They That Sit in Darkness* (1919), a drama about birth control in which an impoverished mother literally dies after bearing too many children. Because women had so much at stake in the rapidly changing society, the issues of work, family, and education remained primary (see appendix, documents 6, 7, 8). In drama after drama, we see the woman not only in command of her house but also as a wage-earner, struggling to hold the family, and even the race, together.

"Miscegenation" (a term created in 1863 to express the white man's fear of a Black marrying his daughter) remained America's forbidden fruit. Georgia Douglas Johnson in *Blue Blood* presented two Black women who discover, when their children are about to marry one another, that they have the same white father—the governor of the state.

As the Great Depression transformed the Art Theatre Movement into a movement concerned with social problems and leftist politics, Langston Hughes wrote *Angelo Herndon Jones* (1936), a drama about a Black man sentenced to a chain gang for twenty years for leading a protest against unemployment. With the musician James P. Johnson, Hughes wrote *The Organizer (De Organizer), a blues opera* (included in this volume), an anthem dedicated to organizing the Black cotton pickers of the south. When Joe Louis knocked out Germany's Max Schmeling in the first round of the heavyweight title fight in 1938, Hughes seized the occasion to write *Young Black Joe* (included in this volume) about a new warrior erasing the old minstrel image.

Amid all the storm and stress of that twenties and thirties, a few playwrights permitted themselves the luxury of being playful. Alvira Hazzard in *Mother Liked It* (included in this volume) is a "silly" boy/girl comedy in the style of *The Boy Friend* and *Very Good Eddie*. George S. Schuyler, novelist and editor, turned melodrama into farce in *The Yellow Peril* (included in this volume) while satirizing the "bourgie" life of a "kept" woman. Shirley

Graham's *Track Thirteen*, the only radio play in this collection, is a farce with a satiric racial bite. African American playwrights wrote in every style and on every subject that white writers did, and more.

As the African American theatre burgeoned, Black critics proliferated because white critics either did not review local performances, or, when they did—some were syndicated—their opinions were uninformed. Among the new arbiters of performance arts, Romeo Dougherty, Lester Walton, Eulalie Spence, James A. Jackson, J. A. Rogers, Bennie Butler, and Tony Langston wrote regularly for weekly newspapers and monthly periodicals. At least one critic, Theophilus Lewis, with his flashing wit and elegant prose in *The Messenger, The Amsterdam News,* and *Inter-State Tattler* equaled any critic—white and Black—in perceptive judgment (see appendix, documents 16, 17, 18, 19, 20).

Fortunately for the theatre, "Jes' Grew" ignored European aesthetics and danced along its syncopated way. The great comics —Bert Williams, Flournoy Miller and Aubrey Lyles, Pigmeat Markham, Johnny Hudgins, Eddie Hunter, Harold Cromer, and Moms Mabley—continued to provide fresh materials and new styles from which white comics such as Eddie Cantor, Al Jolson, Jerry Lewis, and others, "borrowed."

Nine of the "lost" plays in this collection were never published; one play was printed privately, and the remainder appeared in magazines or literary journals. Possibly eight or nine saw one production. What then is the value of *re*-discovering these plays? First, they document the thoughts and feelings of African Americans at that time. The breadth of the plays' subject matter and their styles—ranging from farce to tragedy—wipe clean the blackface images smeared on African American performers by whites during those two decades. These plays also challenge the critics who claim that the Harlem Renaissance produced little of artistic merit; these plays demonstrate that the theatre could speak to and for African Americans. During those years, Black playwrights injected very serious business into amateur theatre with drama that embraced more than entertainment. "The theatre in its fullest sense, is created from the lives of the people and expresses the very foundation upon which the life is built. Each nation and each people has a contribution to make such a theatre of the people."[11]

The plays in this anthology—some are good, some less so—are all documents of African American persistence under extreme duress; they are witness to human hope and dignity, and in that sense, they were never "lost." The dream did not die.

## NOTES

1. Errol Hill, *The Jamaican Stage, 1655–1900: A History of a Colonial Theatre* (Amherst: University of Massachusetts Press, 1993).

2. Among recent articles and books about African American participation in minstrelsy in both the North and the South are Eric Lott's *Love and Theft: Blackface Minstrelsy and the American Working Class* (New York: Oxford University Press, 1993); Williams J. Mahar's "Ethiopian Skits and Sketches: Contents and Contexts of Blackface Minstrelsy, 1840–1890," *Prospects: An Annual of American Cultural Studies* 16 (Cambridge: Cambridge University Press, 1991); Thomas L. Riis's "More Than Just Minstrel Shows: The Rise of Black Musical Theatre at the Turn of the Century," I.S.A.M. Monographs: 33 (Brooklyn: Brooklyn College: Institute for Studies in American Music, 1992); and Mel Watkins's *On the Real Side: Laughing, Lying, and Signifying—The Underground Tradition of African American Humor that Transformed American Culture, from Slavery to Richard Pryor* (New York: Simon & Schuster, 1994).

3. John Graziano, "Sentimental Songs, Rags, and Transformations: The Emergence of the Black Musical, 1895–1910," *Musical Theatre in America*, ed. Glen Loney, (Westport, CT: Greenwood Press, 1984).

4. A sampling would include Thomas Riis' *Just before Jazz, Black Musical Theatre, 1890–1915* (Washington, D.C.: Smithsonian Institution Press, 1989) as well as highly specific and valuable articles including David Krasner's "The Mirror up to Nature: Modernist Aesthetics Racial Authenticity in African American Theatre, 1895–1900" *Theatre History Studies* 16 (1996), and Richard Newman's "The Brightest Star," *Prospectus* 18 (Cambridge: Harvard University, 1993).

5. Among the important, fresh contributions to the scholarship of nineteenth-century Black theatre are Errol Hill's *Shakespeare in Sable: A History of Black Shakespearean Actors* (Amherst: University of Massachusetts Press, 1984); Eileen Southern's "The Georgia Minstrels: The Early Years," *Behind the Minstrel Mask*, ed. Anna Marie Bean, James V. Hatch, Brooks McNamara (Middletown, CT: Wesleyan University Press, 1996); Samuel Hay's *African American Theatre: An Historical and Critical Analysis* (New York: Cambridge University Press, 1994); George A. Thompson, Jr.'s *William A. Brown, The African Theatre and James Hewlett: A Documentary Study*, a careful reconstruction of the African Grove theatre of 1821. This work is still in process.

6. Scruggs, Charles. *H. L. Mencken and the Black Writers of the 1920s* (Baltimore: John Hopkins University Press, 1984).

7. Professor Freda Scott Giles pioneered the research on *The Star of Ethiopia* in an excellent article "*The Star of Ethiopia:* A Contribution Toward the

Development of Black Drama and Theater in the Harlem Renaissance," *The Harlem Renaissance: Revaluations*, ed. Amritjit Singh et al (New York: Garland, 1989).

8. The scenario/text can be found in Hatch and Shine, eds., *Black Theatre USA*, rev. ed. (New York: The Free Press, 1996).

9. Professor Christine Gray's dissertation on Richardson and her editing and re-issuing of Willis Richardson's anthology *Plays and Pageants from Life of the Negro* (Jackson: University of Mississippi Press, 1993) have gone a long way toward the recognition of Richardson as an original thinker.

10. Professors Judith Stevens and Kathy Perkins have uncovered a large number of plays whose themes are anti-lynch. Their anthology is in press.

11. Introduction to the Constitution of the American Negro Theatre, 1940. Reprinted in "Those Were the Days," *Artist and Influence* 10 (New York: Hatch-Billops Collection, Inc. 1989).

# Joseph Seamon Cotter, Jr.
# (1895–1919)
▼▼▼▼▼▼▼▼▼▼▼

Known primarily for the innovative poetry that he wrote during his brief span of years, Joseph Cotter, Jr., was also a promising playwright whose untimely death from tuberculosis deprived the Harlem Renaissance of fully enjoying his unique voice.

Cotter was born on September 2, 1895, in Louisville, Kentucky, the son of Maria F. and Joseph Seamon Cotter, the educator and nationally known poet. Cotter senior says his son was born in the room where Paul Lawrence Dunbar read his poetry in the South for the first time while a guest in the Cotter home. Young Cotter had available his father's private library (poetry left a particularly deep impression on his imagination) and the attention of his older sister Florence Olivia, who taught him to read when he was very young, and who would become an important influence on Cotter's development as a poet.

Another significant relationship was with Abram Simpson, who would become the youngest Black army captain in World War I. Simpson probably inspired Cotter's war poetry and provided the model for one of the two characters in *On the Fields of France*, reprinted here. Cotter graduated with distinction from Louisville Central High School in 1911 and enrolled in Fisk University, where his sister was already studying. In his second year,

Cotter came down with tuberculosis—which killed his sister in 1914—and had to be sent home under doctor's care. Four years later, Cotter succumbed to the same disease, cutting short a brilliant career as "one of the young, modern American poets of genuine promise and achievement" (Payne 70). His talents and concerns are best reflected in the volume of poetry entitled *The Band of Gideon and Other Lyrics* (1918).

*On the Fields of France* was first published in *The Crisis* 20 (June 1920). It presents a dialogue between two dying American officers, one white and one Black. The irony is that they recognize their common heritage and their mutual estate when it is too late to act on that knowledge. In a sense, both have been deceived by the country that they presumably hold dear. Against that background, their final utterance must have a hollow ring for an audience of African Americans.

## REFERENCES

*Note:* Manuscript papers of Joseph Cotter, Jr., are housed at the Louisville Free Public Library, Western Branch, Louisville, Kentucky.

Cotter, Joseph, Sr. "Joseph S. Cotter, Jr." *Caroling Dusk: An Anthology of Verse by Negro Poets,* ed. Countee Cullen. New York: Harper Bros., 1927.

Payne, James Robert. "Joseph Seamon Cotter, Jr." *Dictionary of Literary Biography.* Detroit: Gale Research, 1986, 70–73.

Redmond, Eugene B. *Drumvoices: The Mission of Afro-American Poetry.* Garden City, N.Y.: Anchor Doubleday, 1976.

# ON THE FIELDS OF FRANCE

## Joseph Seamon Cotter, Jr.

CAST

### A WHITE AMERICAN OFFICER
### A COLORED AMERICAN OFFICER

*Time:* Present
*Place:* Battlefield of Northern France

*(Curtain rises on* WHITE AMERICAN OFFICER *and* COLORED AMERICAN OFFICER, *both mortally wounded)*

**WHITE OFFICER:** *(rises on elbow and sees someone across field. Speaks slowly as if in pain)* I say there, my good fellow, have you a drop of water to spare? The Boches have about done for me, I fear.

**COLORED OFFICER:** *(turns over)* Who calls?

**WHITE OFFICER:** *(sees that he is a fellow-officer)* It is I, a fellow-officer, my friend. A shell has gone through my body and the fever has parched my lips. Have you a drop to spare?

**COLORED OFFICER:** *(speaks in catches)* I am—about done for—myself. They've got me—through the lung. I've

---

First published in *The Crisis*, June 1920.

enough water—to moisten our—lips about as long—as either of—us will be here.

*(they drag themselves across toward each other. They get close enough to touch hands.* COLORED OFFICER *hands his canteen to* WHITE OFFICER, *who moistens his lips and hands it back)*

**WHITE OFFICER:** That is much better, my friend. I have been lying here for several hours, it seems, waiting for someone. We went over the Boches' trenches in a bombing squad and they got me coming back.

**COLORED OFFICER:** I was range-finding—and the snipers—got me. I have been dragging—myself towards our trenches —for an hour or so. I got this—far and decided to—stop and close my eyes—and wait for the—end here. It won't be—far off anywhere. *(*WHITE OFFICER*'s strength begins to fail and he slips back.* COLORED OFFICER *takes his hand and he raises himself up with an effort and speaks.)*

**WHITE OFFICER:** I thought I was gone then. My strength is going fast. Hold my hand. It won't feel so lonesome dying way over here in France.

**COLORED OFFICER:** *(takes his hand)* I feel much better —myself. After all—it isn't so hard—to die when—you are dying —for Liberty.

**WHITE OFFICER:** Do you feel that way too? I've often wondered how your people felt. We've treated you so bally mean over home that I've wondered if you could feel that way. I've been as guilty as the rest, maybe more so than some. But that was yesterday.—What is that I see? *(Rises with unbelievable strength and points toward the heavens)* Do you see it? It is a white-haired figure clad in the Old Continentals, standing there within the gates of heaven. And he is beckoning for me. It is Washington.

**COLORED OFFICER:** *(speaks excitedly and rapidly)* I see him, I see him. And who is that beside him with his swarthy chest bare and torn? It is Attucks—Crispus Attucks, and he beckons to me. *(He gasps for breath, fatigued with his rapid talk)*

**WHITE OFFICER:** They stand hand in hand. And there is Lee. He beckons to me. Those serried hosts behind him,—they're Forrest and his men. They call to me to join them.

**COLORED OFFICER:** *(speaks slowly now, gasping for breath all the while)* And there is—Carney with the Old Flag—still in the air. And back of—him, those swarthy—hosts, they're Shaw —and his black—heroes. And they—beckon to me.

**WHITE OFFICER:** *(slips back on elbow)* They stand hand in hand over there and we die hand in hand here on the fields of France. Why couldn't we have lived like this at home? They beckon to us, to you and to me. It is one country she will some day be, in truth as well as in spirit—the country of Washington and Attucks, *(speaks slowly and painfully)* of Lee and Carney. The country of the whites and the country of the blacks. *Our* country!

**WHITE OFFICER AND COLORED OFFICER:** *(together)* America! *(They fall back hand in hand as their life blood ebbs away)*

(Curtain)

# WILLIS RICHARDSON
## (1889–1977)
▼▼▼▼▼▼▼▼▼▼▼▼

During his illustrious thirty-year career in the theatre, Willis Richardson wrote forty-eight plays on subjects ranging from children's fantasies to Black historical figures to problems of family and marriage that continue to engage our interest. Perhaps his most prescient drama of conflicting views of a Black community, *A Pillar of the Church* (192–), is a crisp, convincing appeal for equal rights of another kind.

Richardson was born in Wilmington, North Carolina, to Willis Wilder and Agnes [Harper] Richardson and lived there until the riots over Blacks voting in the 1898 elections. His parents moved to Washington, D.C., where he attended the M Street School (later known as Dunbar High School). Among his teachers were Mary Burrill and Angelina Grimké, two of the earliest African-American playwrights. He was also encouraged to write by Carter Woodson, who taught Spanish and who would publish Richardson's first anthology of African-American drama, *Plays and Pageants from the Life of the Negro* (1930). After graduating from M Street School in 1910, he was awarded a scholarship to Howard University. His family could not afford to send him to college, so he continued to educate himself in poetry and drama through correspondence school while working as a clerk in the

27

U.S. Bureau of Printing and Engraving. In 1914, he married Mary Ellen Jones, and they raised three children, Jean Paula, Antonella, and Joel Justine.

Inspired by Angelina Grimké's play *Rachel* (which he saw in 1916), Richardson wrote a pioneering article for the magazine *The Crisis*,[1] entitled "The Hope of a Negro Drama" (Appendix, document 12). There he outlined the pitfalls he hoped to avoid and the values he wanted to dramatize in his own plays: "*Rachel* is a propaganda play and a great portion of it shows the manner in which negroes are treated by white people in the United States. Still there is another kind of play: the kind that shows the soul of a people; and the soul of this people is truly worth showing." He warmed up to the genre by publishing four dramatic sketches for children in W. E. B. Du Bois's *The Brownies' Book* (1920–1921). Richardson's first adult one-act play, *The Deacon's Awakening*, was published in *The Crisis*[1] in 1920 and produced in St. Paul in 1921. The action centers on a deacon who is determined to discipline the women in his parish who have the nerve to vote until he discovers something within his own family that changes his attitude.

During this period, Richardson attended the gatherings of the Saturday Nighters at the home of Georgia Douglas Johnson, a playwright and poet. The leading literary figures of the "New Negro Renaissance" met at her row house on S Street to discuss literature and read their work. It was also during this period that Richardson, with the help of E. C. Williams, his Latin teacher and mentor at the M Street School, was able to interest Alain Locke and Montgomery Gregory, co-directors of the Howard Players, in reading his plays. When the white president of Howard University forbade the group from performing the plays on the grounds that they were propagandistic and would hurt the school's reputation, W. E. B. Du Bois encouraged Richardson to try Raymond O'Neil's Ethiopian Art Players in Chicago. This was the break he needed. In 1923, he gained the spotlight when *The Chip Woman's Fortune* was performed by O'Neil's group, first in Harlem and then at the Frazee Theatre on Broadway, making him the first Black writer to have a non-musical play produced on The Great White Way.

After that, the Howard Players staged his *Mortgaged* in 1924; in the following year, that play, performed by the Dunbar Dramatic Club at a tournament held in Plainfield, New Jersey, won fourth place, That same year the Karamu House enacted his *Compromise*. In April of 1926, Du Bois, assisted by Zora Neale Hurston and others, organized the Krigwa Players. The New York group opened its first season with three plays, two of them by Richardson: *Compromise* and *The Broken Banjo*, which won the Spingarn Prize in a competition conducted by *The Crisis*. One of the judges, Eugene O'Neill, commented, "I am glad to hear the judges all agreed on *The Broken Banjo* and that the play was so successfully staged. Willis Richardson should certainly continue working in his field."

Richardson was again awarded a prize ($100) in 1926 for *Boot-Black Lover*. Shortly afterward, another one-act play, *Room for Rent*, was performed by the Negro Art Players. In 1929 he published a one-act domestic drama called "The Idle Head" in *The Carolina Magazine*. Wearing another hat, Richardson edited *Plays and Pageants from the Life of the Negro* in 1930 and co-edited *Negro History in Thirteen Plays* in 1935. His *Attucks, the Martyr* was performed in 1934 in Baltimore by the Morgan College Players. Little was heard from Richardson during the 1940s, except for the performance of *Miss or Mrs*, a one-act play (not yet published) about a group of busybodies who pry into the marital status of a woman teacher.

He continued to work as a clerk at the Bureau of Engraving and Printing until his retirement in 1954. In 1956, he brought out his third and final collection of plays (made up of five previously published), entitled *The King's Dilemma and Other Plays for Children* (typescripts of several of his unpublished works are preserved in the Hatch-Billops Collection in New York). He died in 1977 in relative obscurity, but recently his role as one of the prime movers in African American theatre has become recognized (see, for instance, Christine Gray's splendid introduction to the 1993 reprint of *Plays and Pageants* by the University Press of Mississippi and her dissertation on Richardson University of Maryland 1995).

*The Deacon's Awakening* is a brief but powerful play in which sexism intersects with racism. Martha Jones, a housewife, and her daughter Eva are determined to take advantage of the new laws granting women the vote. Martha's husband David, a deacon of their church, and his crony Sol are equally determined to prevent them from doing so. Horrified by the prospect of women's suffrage, the deacon threatens to take his daughter out of college as punishment for espousing the cause in public. He believes that a woman's place is at home, not at the polling booth, trying "to fill a man's shoes." It is significant that in the final confrontation his wife stands up to his bullying tactics. At the end, the men are forced to accept the new reality, but we sense that we may be witnessing only a lull in the battle of the sexes—which will not be resolved for the Jones family or any other until sexism is recognized as the mirror image of the racism that makes its victims victimize others with lesser power.

If *The Deacon's Awakening* may be viewed as a dramatic victory for the cause of women, then *A Pillar of the Church*, not published until now, must be regarded as a drama of defeat. In contrast to the women in the Jones family who close ranks to resist the tyranny of the patriarch, the mother and daughters in the Fisher family submit to the warped will of the father. Resistance against "the pillar" of the church appears to be unthinkable. In demeaning the humanistic education that the shining Ms. Knight offers to May and Geneva, Mr. Fisher may be unwittingly steering both girls towards another form of enslavement, which he typifies, this time to the rule of the "practical." In both plays, male authority figures oppose anything that might expand the horizons of their daughters' lives. Given the implied fact that they are resisting the racial stereotyping of Blacks, their insensitivity to their own stereotypes of women is ironic. Richardson hardly spared his own people when it came to dramatizing prejudice.

Richardson was among the first African American playwrights to realize that the European dramatic form itself had to be claimed and transformed to meet the needs of his people. He maintained an awareness of the larger stage tradition both as a measure of what ought to constitute theatre and as a genre degrading to Blacks. His plays deliberately countered the usual depiction of Blacks on the American stage and sought to create situations that addressed the true concerns of Black audiences. Sadly enough, American theatre was not ready for Richardson— he has commented bitterly that it only wanted plays "with prostitutes, dope-handlers, thieves, and criminals," although one of his early plays is called *The Amateur Prostitute*. In general, Richardson was loathe to present African Americans in a negative light, and for that reason, his work has become part of the movement to emphasize the constructive aspects of African American history.

## NOTE

1. *The Crisis* could properly be dubbed "the news magazine of the civil rights movement." Founded in 1910 by W. E. B. Du Bois as an analytical tool to represent the NAACP, *The Crisis* has survived eighty years of tumultuous social progress and backlash in the process of changing from a small-format black-and-white periodical to a glossy magazine with color photos. *The Crisis* has always reported on the crucial political, social, and cultural issues (such as the creation of a legitimate African American theater) that faced its readers.

## REFERENCES

Gray, Christine, ed. *Plays and Pageants from the Life of the Negro*. Jackson: University of Mississippi Press, 1993.
Perry, Patsy B., "Willis Richardson," *Dictionary of Literary Biography* 51. Detroit: Gale Research Company, 1987, 236–44.

# A PILLAR OF THE CHURCH

## Willis Richardson

CAST

> JOHN FISHER, *a pillar of the church*
> MARY FISHER, *his wife*
> MAY FISHER, *their daughter*
> GENEVA FISHER, *their younger daughter*
> MISS KNIGHT, *a school teacher*

*The sitting room of the Fishers is next to the dining room, to and from which a door at the upper left gives exit and entrance. Below the door stands a large old-style bookcase with a Bible on top of it, and below the bookcase is a chair against the wall. In the rear wall is a window below which is a sofa, and to the right and left of which are straight chairs. Against the right wall stands a new-style bookcase with a small statue of liberty on top of it. In the center of the room a square uncovered table stands with a Morris chair and a rocker at each side of it. This, on the whole, is the comfortable resting place of good-living, but extremely religious people. The pictures about the walls are so chosen as to keep Christianity constantly impressed upon the minds of those who sit here. When the curtain rises* FISHER, *his wife and his daughter,* GENEVA, *are kneeling before*

By permission of Joyce Richardson.

*their chairs at morning prayers. They have been on their knees for some time for* GENEVA *can be seen shifting her weight restlessly from one knee to the other.*

**FISHER:** *(with face averted and hands glasped)* And look down on us, O Father, on us and the evil men and things that surround us, we pray Thee with all our heart. And while we pray we will wait for years and years as we have waited for years and years for thy kingdom to come and thy will to be done on earth as it is in Heaven. Amen. *(When they rise we get a better view of them.* FISHER *is a stout man of fifty, with mixed gray hair and a black mustache. He is wearing a white vest but no coat. From every movement of the man one can see that he considers himself the supreme and unquestioned lord and master of this household.* MRS. FISHER *is a small woman about forty. Her thin face has once been pretty, but constant bullying has driven all away from it save a sad expression of effacement. In fact, her husband has bullied the soul out of her. She no longer expresses firm opinions, she is either silent or tries to gain points by persuasion when she knows she is right.* GENEVA *is a pretty brown girl of sixteen, with straight black hair and the brightest of eyes. When they rise,* GENEVA *moves across the floor stiffly with a frown on her face)*

**FISHER:** *(watching her)* What's the matter with you, Geneva, sick?

**GENEVA:** My knee is stiff from kneeling down so long.

**FISHER:** Oh, that'll never hurt you. Prayin' 'll never hurt nobody.

**GENEVA:** I'll be all right in a minute.

**FISHER:** The trouble with you young people is you don't pray enough.

**MRS. FISHER:** We did stay down quite a long time, John.

**FISHER:** *(in disagreeable tones)* I knew you'd say that; you always take sides with the children whether they're wrong or not. Do you want me to cut it shorter tomorrow? Did Ah asked God for anything you don't want?

**MRS. FISHER:** I didn't mean anything like that.

**FISHER:** Well, whether she gets tired or not she's goin' to get on her knees and say her prayers every mornin' the Lord sends. *(MRS. FISHER *is silent)* Where's May? Ain't she up yet?

**MRS. FISHER:** No, she's sleeping late this morning; she travelled so yesterday.

**FISHER:** Well, Ah won't say anything about it this time since she's just back, but Ah reckon Ah'll have to remind her that she's got to be down to these prayers every mornin'.

**MRS. FISHER:** *(trying to change the subject)* May won two medals last term but she was too tired to show them to us last night.

**FISHER:** What's the medals for?

**MRS. FISHER:** She didn't say.

**FISHER:** *(feeling his beard)* Ah'll have to run out and get a shave this mornin'. Ah'll go now and see May when Ah come back.

**MRS. FISHER:** I think I hear her coming down now. (GENEVA *starts towards the dining room as the door bell rings*)

**FISHER:** Answer the bell, Geneva. (GENEVA *turns and goes out through the hall*)

**FISHER:** Ah reckon that's the letter man.

**MRS. FISHER:** Are you expecting any mail?

**FISHER:** *(putting on his coat which has been lying on the sofa.* GENEVA *returns with a letter in her hand. She gives it to* FISHER*)* No.

**FISHER:** *(feeling for his glasses before handing the letter to his wife)* Ah left ma glasses upstairs. Here, Mary, you read it; it's for both of us.

**MRS. FISHER:** I wonder—Oh, it's from May's school. *(she opens the letter and reads)*

Mr. and Mrs. John Fisher,

Dear Sir and Madam,

On my way home for the vacation days I shall take the privilege of stopping in to see you for a few minutes concerning your younger daughter, Geneva. May, who is one of our most excellent and best loved students, has told us about her; and the principal and I thought that by my talking with you, you may be influenced to send her to us for the coming term.

I shall arrive in your city on Monday and shall have a few minutes to spare between trains.

Very sincerely,
C. J. Knight.

**FISHER:** So that's the Miss Knight May's been talking so much about.

**MRS. FISHER:** Yes, they seem to be great friends.

**GENEVA:** *(who has been an interested listener)* Do you think I can go, papa?

**FISHER:** Ah'll see about it. Ah'll have to talk to this lady first. I'll be back from the barber shop before she comes. *(He goes out of the door but comes back at once)*

**FISHER:** Tell May Ah want to talk to her when Ah come back.

**MRS. FISHER:** All right. (FISHER *goes out)*

**GENEVA:** Do you think he'll let me go, mama?

**MRS. FISHER:** I don't see any reason why he shouldn't.

**GENEVA:** I know May'll like it if he does let me go.

**MRS. FISHER:** Yes, she'll be glad to take you with her.

**GENEVA:** I'll tell her about it. *(She goes to the dining room door)* May! May!

**MAY:** I'm coming!

**MRS. FISHER:** Don't call her from her breakfast.

**MAY:** *(appearing at the door)* I've finished. I didn't want anything but a cup of coffee. I'm so glad to be home I haven't any appetite. (MAY *is twenty-two. She is slightly fairer in color than her mother and sister and her hair is brown and abundant. Her face is not as pretty as* GENEVA, *but her disposition is the most lovable. Both of these girls dress simply but neatly, and both have had the best of training.)*

**MAY:** What is it?

**GENEVA:** Miss Knight is coming here today.

**MAY:** She told me she was going to stop here on the way home.

**GENEVA:** Did she tell you she wanted me to start school there in the fall?

**MAY:** Yes, that's why she's coming.

**MRS. FISHER:** You didn't say anything about it, May.

**MAY:** I was so tired last night, mama—

**MRS. FISHER:** And your medals—you promised to show them to us.

**GENEVA:** Yes, May, get them.

**MAY:** I meant to show them to you last night, but one can't remember everything. I'll get them now. *(She starts out)*

**MRS. FISHER:** Wait a moment, May; let me tell you before I forget it. Your father wants to speak with you when he comes back.

**MAY:** What is it—anything wrong?

**MRS. FISHER:** I think he wants to tell you about coming down in time for morning prayers.

**MAY:** *(slightly displeased)* What, that again! Mama, papa is really too religious. People don't—

**MRS. FISHER:** Well, don't tell him that unless you want trouble.

**MAY:** I really think you let him have his own way too much in everything. He hasn't any consideration for anyone's feelings but his own.

**MRS. FISHER:** He's used to having his own way.

**MAY:** I know, but he ought to have some respect for others.

**MRS. FISHER:** You don't object to the prayers, do you?

**MAY:** *(putting an arm around her mother's shoulders)* No, it's not that; it's the way he goes around bossing everybody.

**MRS. FISHER:** It's a second nature with him now.

**MAY:** Then it's time for him to outgrow it.

**MRS. FISHER:** : Don't talk like that, May; you know your father. He'll be like that until he dies.

**MAY:** I suppose he will. He's hopeless. *(She goes out)*

**GENEVA:** Won't it be grand to go away with May, mama?

**MRS. FISHER:** Yes, it's the best thing that could happen. This is her last year and she'll have a chance to introduce you to all her friends so that you won't be so new when you go there next year.

**GENEVA:** I know we'll have the best time. If papa only agrees.

**MRS. FISHER:** I think he will agree.

**GENEVA:** But he has such strange ideas sometimes.

**MRS. FISHER:** I think you children criticise your father a little too harshly. (MAY *enters with two small boxes in her hand*)

**MAY:** What now?

**GENEVA:** I was saying that papa has such strange ideas sometimes.

**MRS. FISHER:** You know that when people have been holding certain opinions and doing certain things year in and year out for thirty or forty years they don't easily change, or take up new ideas.

**MAY:** I know, mama; but some of his ideas are so—so—they're really hundreds of years old. In some things he acts like an ancient dropped suddenly into the modern world.

**MRS. FISHER:** Well, we won't criticise too much behind his back. Let us see what you have, May. (MAY *opens the boxes showing two gold medals*)

**GENEVA:** *(enthusiastic)* Oh, aren't they beautiful, mama?

**MRS. FISHER:** They're just grand. What are they for, May?

**MAY:** *(taking up the medals one at a time)* This is for what they call artistic dancing which comes under physical culture; and this one is for leading my class in music.

**GENEVA:** And will I have a chance to win something like this if I go there?

**MAY:** Certainly.

**MRS. FISHER:** You must dance and play for us sometime, May.

**GENEVA:** Let us see you dance now. (MAY *looks to her mother for approval*)

**MRS. FISHER:** Yes, let us see it. I want to see what it is, because anything by the name of dance is a great sin with your father. (MAY *dances the rhythmatic and graceful movements of the dance delight her mother and sister who do not conceal their pleasure*)

**MRS. FISHER:** That was really pretty, May.

**GENEVA:** May, please dance the last part over again.

**MAY:** Let me get a breath.

**MRS. FISHER:** If you play as well as you dance no wonder they gave you medals.

**GENEVA:** I wonder how papa will like it?

**MRS. FISHER:** You must dance it for him, May; I'm sure he won't object to that.

**GENEVA:** But dance the last part over for us now.

**MAY:** Well, here it is. (*She dances again beginning at the last part of the dance. While she is dancing* FISHER *appears at the hall* *door, and he is so taken aback by what he sees that he can only stand and stare with open mouth and arms akimbo.* MAY *does not see him nor does* GENEVA; *but* MRS. FISHER *who is exactly in front of the doorway does see him, and her appreciation of the dance is chilled by the expression on his face. She sees that he is surprised, disgusted and angered; and she fears that trouble will come of it all.* FISHER *does not speak or make* MAY *otherwise aware of his presence until she finishes the dance.)*

**FISHER:** *(entering and speaking angrily)* What's this? Turnin' the house into a dance hall?

**MRS. FISHER:** *(to whom he has spoken)* That's May's artistic dance—the one she got the medal for.

**FISHER:** Ah don't care what kind o' dance it is; or what she won for it, Ah won't have it in this house. And another thing, if they can't teach you anything better than that there's no use of you goin' to that school any more. *(to Mrs. Fisher)* Ah'm surprised at you Mary for lettin' her dance in here.

**MRS. FISHER:** I didn't think there was any harm in it, John; since she learned it at school. *(showing him the medal)* Here's the medal she got for it.

**FISHER:** *(merely glancing at the medal)* Did you win any medals for anything besides dancin'?

**MAY:** That other one is for music.

**FISHER:** Is that all?

**MAY:** *(impatiently)* How many did you expect me to win, papa? I couldn't be first in everything.

**FISHER:** How about your books? Couldn't you win anything for bein' first in your real lessons?

**MAY:** I stood pretty well, but I wasn't first in anything else.

**FISHER:** Well, Ah sent you there to learn the book, and not a lot of sinful foolishness.

**MAY:** I had to have these things along with what you call my books, and I can't help it if I led my classes in them.

**FISHER:** It just shows that you wasted a lot of time from your books fooling with such stuff. *(MAY is silent)* And now they want to take Geneva and teach her the same things. Well, Ah don't know—Ah'll have to see about that. And this is another thing Ah want to say before Ah go any further. Ah want you to come downstairs every mornin' to prayers. Seems like Ah have to tell you the same things every time you come home from school. Now, Ah don't want to have to tell you this again. (MAY *picks up her medals and goes out silently*)

**MRS. FISHER:** You didn't treat her very kindly, John.

**FISHER:** Kindly? What did you want me to do, get down on ma knees and beg her not to dance in here any more?

**MRS. FISHER:** You might have appreciated her success a little.

**FISHER:** What success—winnin' medals for playin' the piano and dancin'? We've got too much of that foolishness goin' on now. No wonder we can't keep the young people in the churches. Teachin' such things in schools is just a waste of time.

**MRS. FISHER:** They have different ways of teaching from what they had when we came along.

**FISHER:** And they don't do it half as well.

**MRS. FISHER:** We've got to send them to some school.

**FISHER:** Not to some school where they won't learn nothin' but singin' and dancin'.

**MRS. FISHER:** You mean to say May isn't going back?

**FISHER:** Ah don't know, Ah've got to think about it. (*to* GENEVA) And don't you be too hopeful about goin' to that school; Ah've got to think about that to. (*Taking off his coat, putting it on the sofa and taking the Bible he goes out through the dining-room. Presently* MAY *returns*)

**MAY:** Isn't papa unreasonable?

**MRS. FISHER:** Where is he?

**MAY:** Upstairs.

**MRS. FISHER:** Don't let him hear you say that, May; it will only make trouble.

**GENEVA:** May, he talks like he's not going to let me go.

**MAY:** Where is he going to let you go? He'll have to let you go somewhere.

**GENEVA:** Maybe he'll want to send me to a church school.

**MAY:** For your sake I hope he won't.

**MRS. FISHER:** Don't judge too quickly now. He hasn't said you couldn't go. He only said he'd have to think about it.

**GENEVA:** He even talked as if he might not let you go back.

**MAY:** (*in surprise*) Me!

**MRS. FISHER:** Now, Geneva.

**GENEVA:** But he did, mother. You know he said he'd have to think about May.

**MAY:** I know he wouldn't be that unreasonable, that would be foolish. If he doesn't let me go back, all the money he has already spent will be wasted and you know papa never did believe in wasting anything. *(The bell rings)*

**MRS. FISHER:** I wonder if that's Miss Knight?

**MAY:** I'll go. *(She goes out)*

**MRS. FISHER:** Sit down, Geneva. (GENEVA *sits by the table and pretends to be reading a newspaper.* MAY *and* MISS KNIGHT *enter with their arms around each other.* MISS KNIGHT *is a tall, thin woman of thirty-five, brown in complexion, with long straight hair. She is very pleasant to talk to, and her visit to a house for that purpose has never failed to gain another student for her school)*

**MAY:** *(introducing her mother)* This is my mother. Mama, Miss Knight.

**MISS KNIGHT:** *(taking* MRS. FISHER'S *hand)* Oh, Mrs. Fisher, I'm so glad to meet you. I've heard so much of you during the past three years.

**MRS. FISHER:** And I have heard equally as much of you, Miss Knight. It's quite a pleasure to meet you.

**MAY:** And this is Geneva.

**MISS KNIGHT:** *(taking both of* GENEVA'S *hands)* So this is the sweet little girl? Your description was wonderful, May; I should have known her anywhere. How would you like to come to school to me, Geneva??

**GENEVA:** I'd be glad to, Miss Knight.

**MISS KNIGHT:** *(as she sits in a chair which* MAY *has brought forward)* You know, Mrs. Fisher, May and I are the greatest of friends.

**MRS. FISHER:** So she has been telling me.

**MISS KNIGHT:** She has been telling me about her little sister, too, and as I was passing this way on the way home, and knew I'd have a half-hour, I thought I'd stop in a moment and speak to you about her.

**MRS. FISHER:** Yes, we received your letter this morning.

**MISS KNIGHT:** May has been such an excellent student, that we should be glad to have her younger sister.

**MRS. FISHER:** Mr. Fisher and I were just talking it over a few moments ago.

**MISS KNIGHT:** Do you think you would like to send her to us?

**MRS. FISHER:** We hadn't quite decided. We will be glad to talk to you about it. Geneva, ask your father to spare us a few moments, please *(Geneva goes out)*

**MISS KNIGHT:** I think we shall enjoy having her as much as we enjoy having May. Of course, we haven't quite finished with May.

**MAY:** I'm glad you haven't. I wouldn't miss the coming year for anything in the world. *(*GENEVA *returns silently and carries her father's coat out to him)*

**MRS. FISHER:** When we were speaking of it Mr. Fisher seemed quite undecided about Geneva, but I think you can get a decided answer from him.

**MISS KNIGHT:** There will be quite an advantage in sending her while May is there.

**MRS. FISHER:** Yes, we had thought of that. *(*FISHER *enters with the Bible which he places upon the bookcase)*

**MAY:** Papa, let me introduce you to Miss Knight. You've heard me speak of her.

**FISHER:** *(bowing)* Ah'm glad to know you, Miss Knight.

**MISS KNIGHT:** *(bowing)* Mr. Fisher.

**FISHER:** Ah've heard ma daughter speak of you.

**MISS KNIGHT:** Yes, May and I are the best of friends. In fact, we're such great friends that I thought I'd stop in on my way home and ask if you would care to send your younger daughter to us.

**FISHER:** Well, Ah hadn't decided about Geneva yet.

**MISS KNIGHT:** May has done so very well, and aside from that there will be a great advantage in sending Geneva the year before May leaves, as that will give her the opportunity of knowing the other girls. First-year girls often have a very lonesome time of it.

**FISHER:** How is May in her lessons?

**MISS KNIGHT:** She is what I call a fine student in everything. Those medals were for excellence in music and physical culture.

**FISHER:** She wasn't so good in her other studies, was she?

**MISS KNIGHT:** Yes, but her music was exceptional.

**FISHER:** Ah'll be frank with you, Miss Knight; there's one or two things Ah don't like about your school.

**MISS KNIGHT:** I shall be glad to hear your criticism, Mr. Fisher.

**FISHER:** In the first place Ah don't like the idea of teachin' girls to dance.

**MISS KNIGHT:** Do you mean the artistic dance for which May won the medal?

**FISHER:** Ah don't believe in dancin' at all.

**MISS KNIGHT:** That dance was a part of her physical culture work.

**FISHER:** *(with a motion towards the smaller bookcase)* And the books she reads—Ah've been lookin' at some of them, and to tell the truth Ah don't like them a bit.

**MISS KNIGHT:** Which ones in particular?

**FISHER:** The novels. Ah don't believe in young girls readin' novels. The other books are all right, but—what do you have novel readin' for anyhow?

**MISS KNIGHT:** That's a part of the English course.

**FISHER:** The grammar ought to be enough. Don't you teach that?

**MISS KNIGHT:** Yes, we teach grammar, but grammar only gives the rules, so to speak, of the language. These other books broaden the mind of the student, give the student a clear idea of how the language is artistically used by masters of writing.

**FISHER:** These novels are nothin' but stories. Why don't you teach them facts, plain newspaper and Bible?

**MISS KNIGHT:** They get a fair share of newspaper and Bible, but each girl must read a certain number of books each year; and these books are written by men and women who really make the language.

**FISHER:** Ah wouldn't try to interfere with your school, but you ought to drop that novel readin' and dancin'.

**MISS KNIGHT:** I always thought our requirements were very conservative, Mr. Fisher.

**FISHER:** If you could take Geneva there without teachin' her one or two things Ah don't like, Ah'd be glad to send her.

**MISS KNIGHT:** I couldn't consent to teach her less than the other girls. We always try to give each student the best we can afford.

**FISHER:** Ah haven't decided yet, but Ah'll think over it.

**MISS KNIGHT:** I hope you will. *(she looks at her watch and rises)* Oh, I'm over-staying my time. I hate to rush from you, but I must catch my train. Good-bye, all.

**FISHER:** Good-bye, Miss Knight. (MRS. FISHER, MAY *and* GENEVA *rise and go out with her)*

**MRS. FISHER:** *(as they go)* After we have decided, May will write and let you know.

**MISS KNIGHT:** I hope your decision will be favorable.

**MRS. FISHER:** I think it will. *(They pass out of hearing.* FISHER *as he paces the floor, seems to be somewhat angry. He takes off his coat and throws it on the sofa.)*

**MRS. FISHER:** *(entering at the moment)* What's the matter, John?

**FISHER:** These new-fangled school teachers make me sick with their novel readin' and dancin'.

**MRS. FISHER:** I hope you don't mean to keep Geneva home another year.

**FISHER:** Ah said Ah'd think about it. Ah haven't thought about it yet. *(He goes into the dining room rudely leaving his wife standing by the table.* MAY *and* GENEVA *return.)*

**MAY:** How do you like Miss Knight, mama?

**MRS. FISHER:** I think she's just grand.

**GENEVA:** Do you think papa will let me go?

**MRS. FISHER:** I think he will. If he didn't intend to let you go he would have said so at first. He never would have taken time to think it over.

**MAY:** I don't know, mama; he didn't seem to be pleased.

**GENEVA:** I hope he won't refuse.

**MRS. FISHER:** *(sitting)* We'll wait and see. *(FISHER comes from the dining room and puts his coat on in silence.)*

**GENEVA:** *(as he pulls his coat on)* Papa—

**FISHER:** *(coming to the table)* Now, you're goin' to ask me again about goin' to that school. Ah told you Ah'd think about it. Well, Ah have thought about it; and Ah've decided that May can go back next year because that's her last year, but that's all. You sha'n't go.

**MRS. FISHER:** *(who, like the two girls, is surprised by the decision)* But she must go to some school, John. I don't see any reason—

**FISHER:** Then she'll go to some school where they teach something else besides music and dancin', and if Ah can't find a school to suit me she'll stay right home. That ends it. *(As he says this he strikes the table with his fist and goes out through the hall.* GENEVA, *whose eyes have been filling with tears, falls on her knees and rests her head on her mother's lap.)*

**MAY:** Isn't he mean? That was just like him.

**MRS. FISHER:** *(to* GENEVA*)* Don't cry, Geneva, don't cry.

**MAY:** Don't you think you can persuade him, mother?

**MRS. FISHER:** No, May, when he sets his mind one way he never changes.

**MAY:** I should have known that.

(Curtain)

# George S. Schuyler
# (1895–1977)
▼▼▼▼▼▼▼▼▼▼▼▼

A journalist and satirist who started his career as a radical and ended it as a conservative, George Schuyler was born in Providence, Rhode Island, and brought up in Syracuse, New York. In 1912, at the age of seventeen, he dropped out of school and enlisted in the army. He spent seven years with the Black Twenty-fifth U.S. Infantry until he was discharged as a first lieutenant just in time to participate in the first stirrings of the Harlem Renaissance.

Following a brief sojourn in Syracuse, he came to New York City in the winter of 1922–23 and for several months lived there as a homeless person before he was "discovered" by two African American socialists, A. Philip Randolph and Chandler Owen, who were then editing the radical magazine *The Messenger*. From 1923 to 1928 Schuyler helped them write and put out the publication, then left to join the staff of the popular Black weekly *The Pittsburgh Courier* as a regular columnist. During the 1920s and 1930s, Schuyler published numerous articles in both Black and white periodicals, the most famous of which was "The Negro-Art Hokum" in *The Nation* of June 16, 1926 (see appendix, document 4). In that article, Schuyler contended that the African American was "merely a lampblacked Anglo-Saxon" and therefore

45

should create art in the mainstream of the Western European culture which had shaped his consciousness. In the next issue of *The Nation*, Langston Hughes responded with a rebuttal of Schuyler's position, "The Negro Artist and the Racial Mounain" (see Appendix, document 5), urging African American writers and artists not to forget their racial heritage, but to look within themselves for inspiration rather than searching for it elsewhere. According to Bruce Kellner, Schuyler, in this debate and in general, tended to articulate the classic assimilationist view.

Schuyler wrote a number of pieces on racial themes for the influential *American Mercury* and published a series of articles in *The Pittsburgh Courier* based on his 1925 assignment to tour two hundred communities in the South and report on conditions. In 1931, he published his first and best-known novel, *Black No More*. Earlier, Schuyler had denied that "Negroes wish to be white"; yet he based *Black No More* on this very premise. In this novel, an early full-length satiric novel by an African American, Schuyler added a sophisticated dimension to the Harlem Renaissance by caricaturing most of the major Black figures of the 1920s. Fifty years later, George Wolfe's biting revue, *The Colored Museum*, taking a leaf from Schuyler, would also make mayhem of ill-conceived Black and white racial attitudes.

In January 1931, Schuyler was hired as a secret foreign correspondent by *The New York Evening Post* to investigate the slave trade in Liberia. On his return from Africa, he wrote a series of shocking revelations that became the basis of his second novel, *Slaves Today* (1931). In 1945, collaborating with his wife, Josephine, he contributed a piece to the June issue of the *Negro Digest* called, "Does Interracial Marriage Succeed?" Schuyler became increasingly conservative after World War II and an outspoken critic of Communism and the civil rights revolution. His critical essay in the May 1950 issue of the *Negro Digest*, "What is Wrong With Negro Authors?" suggests how far to the right he had moved. His last years were darkened by personal tragedy when Phillipa, his only child and a concert pianist, died in an air crash in Korea in 1968.

The subject of color distinction among African Americans— the pain of being too Black or being too white—has been dealt with in novels and plays, usually as tragedy. In *The Yellow Peril*, reprinted in this volume, the theme of being too white is buried in a bedroom farce about a con artist/madame who comes to a sad end. *The Yellow Peril*, a reference to her light skin, adroitly and overconfidently juggles her married lovers who underwrite her high style of life. When her duplicity is uncovered, they make sure to remove any evidence that could imperil them. The aspirations of The Girl become an easy mark for Schuyler's wit, but the "successful" African American men who treat her as a commodity are also targets of his sometimes obvious satire. The play first appeared in the January 1925 issue of *The Messenger*.

## REFERENCES

Bone, Robert. *The Negro Novel in America*. New Haven: Yale University Press, 1965.

Kellner, Bruce, ed. *The Harlem Renaissance*. Westport, Conn.: Greenwood Press, 1984.

Peplow, Michael W. *George S. Schuyler*. Boston: Twayne, 1980.

Schuyler, George S. *Black and Conservative*. New Rochelle, N.Y.: Arlington House, 1966.

———. "Theatre." *The Messenger*, November 1923; November 1924.

Schuyler, Philippa. "Meet the George Schuylers: America's Strangest Family." *Our World* 6 (April 1951): 22–26.

# THE YELLOW PERIL

## George S. Schuyler

CAST

> THE GIRL
> MARTHA, *the Maid*
> JOHNNIE, *the Rent Man*
> GEORGE, *the Shoe Man*
> FRANK, *the Coat Man*
> SAMMY, *the Dress Man*
> HENRY, *the Hat Man*
> CHARLIE, *the Jewelry Man*
> PHYLLIS, *the Dog*

> *Time:* All the time
> *Place:* The parlor of a Seventh Avenue apartment, North Harlem, New York City.

*It is about 7:00 P.M. The room is done in bright red. There are two windows backstage with lace curtains and green shades. Between them is a player piano with a neat pile of music rolls atop of it. A long bench is placed before it. On the left are two doors: the nearest to the audience leading into a hall, the other leading into the bathroom. Between these two doors is a library table covered with an imitation animal skin. On the table are several books and popu-*

---

First published in *The Messenger*, January 1925.

*lar magazines. On the right are also two doors exactly opposite those on the left. The one nearest the audience leads into the kitchen, while the other leads into a bedroom. Between the two doors is a writing desk. There is a chair on each side of the piano, before the writing desk and alongside the library table. There is a telephone on the library table behind an artistic screen. In the center of the room downstage there is a day bed. The head is nearest the kitchen door. Near the bed is a smoking cabinet. One of its doors are open, and inside can be glimpsed a quart bottle of a shape familiar before Prohibition, and several whiskey glasses. Behind the bed is a floor lamp.*

*On this day bed reclines an octoroon who could easily pass for white. She possesses lustrous black hair; a chubby, painted baby face; delicate hands and very shapely limbs. She is garbed in pink silk pajamas with baby blue ribbons. On her feet are a dainty pair of house slippers of the same color. She is reading a magazine of the "snappy" variety, and taking occasional puffs from a gold-tipped cigarette. A gold watch encircles her wrist. Asleep on a blue sofa pillow at the foot of the bed is a fluffy white poodle dog. There is no light except that from the floor lamp. After the curtain rises she glances at her watch, and noting the time, rises, casts the cigarette into the receiver, tosses the magazine onto the table, and yawns and stretches lazily.*

**THE GIRL:** Ho hum! . . . Martha! *(calling)*

**MARTHA:** *(opening the kitchen door)* Yes, Ma'am! *(She is a dark brown girl with rigidly straightened black hair. She wears the apron and cap of a maid)*

**THE GIRL:** Suppose you run over to the delicatessen store and get me a quart of rye—we're almost out of stuff. You'll find some money on my bureau. I may have some company tonight.

**MARTHA:** Yes, Ma'am.

**THE GIRL:** You'd better dust up the parlor a bit too, before you go. And don't forget to take Phyllis out for an airing. . . . Let's have some light here.

**MARTHA:** Yes, Ma'am! *(She switches on the lights and disappears into the kitchen)*

**THE GIRL:** *(suddenly starting)* Oh! the rent. I almost forgot it! *(She goes over to the telephone)* Give me Bradhurst 00077. No! Not Rhinelander—Bradhurst! Bradhurst 00077! Yes, that's the number I gave—Bradhurst 00077! Hello! Is Mr. Russel in? *(very sweetly)* May I speak to him, please? (MARTHA *re-enters with a duster and begins tidying up the room. She looks at* THE GIRL, *shakes her head and laughs knowingly)* Oh, Hello Johnnie!—Oh! I'm feelin' kinda bad tonight, sweetheart—no, nothing serious. Say, daddy, send me over fifty right away, please. Yes, for the rent—certainly—tomorrow's the fifteenth, ain't it? Now looka here, Johnnie, I don't want all that who—struck—John—I want that fifty dollars—now you're talking business—oh, I'm awfully sorry, Johnnie, but you can't come over tonight—my husband's coming in—no! I wouldn't dare take a chance—that's a good boy—Friday night, then—good bye, dearest. *(She kisses noisily into the mouthpiece, hangs up, and sighs heavily)* Well, Martha, that's settled. It takes me to make these men toe the mark. He tried to stall me for the rent. Can you beat that? Imagine tryin' to stall *me!*

**MARTHA:** You're a wonder alright. How do you do it? Don't they ever get wise, or anything?

**THE GIRL:** *(dropping into the chair near the library table)* Not a chance in the world. It's easy to handle men because they're *all* saps. All you gotta do is to treat 'em as if they were about ten years old. It's easy as rollin' off a log.

**MARTHA:** Well, you certainly know these Harlem men, alright. I wonder how you manage to get such big bugs: lawyers, ministers, newspaper men, and that bunch. *(she tidies the day-bed)*

**THE GIRL:** Oh, there's not much to know about them, except that they are the biggest boobs in New York—and that's saying a lot, too. Of course, the married ones are the worst of the lot; especially the so-called society leaders and business men. Once in a while a fellow gets rambunctious on my hands, but I know how to handle 'em. *(she laughs)*

**MARTHA:** *(going into the kitchen)* Well, I'd better get the liquor. *(calling from the kitchen)* Do you want anything from the delicatessen?

**THE GIRL:** No, the booze is enough. Musn't give these johns too much—it spoils 'em. "Treat 'em rough" is my motto.

**MARTHA:** *(appearing at the kitchen door dressed for the street)* Well, you can get away with it; you're a high yaller. I wish I was your color. I've used everything advertised in the Chicago *Defender,* but I'm just as black as I was when I came from Jamaica two years ago. Have you ever tried to "pass"? You could get by easy, anywhere. *(THE GIRL goes into the bedroom)*

**THE GIRL:** *(returning with a blue dressing gown which she lazily dons)* Sure. I lived downtown for a year or two; but there's better pickings up here. Downtown, I was only another white girl. Up here I am worshipped by all the successful business men, professional fellows and society swells, because I am a high yaller. Yes, it's lots easier up here because there's less competition. These college graduates and swell dames don't stand no chance with me, even if I didn't finish grammar school. All I've got to do is to wink and I can have a hundred black men running after me.

**MARTHA:** Well, I can't understand it myself!

**THE GIRL:** Oh, it's easy to understand. You see, all these darkies are crazy about white women, but when they get prominent and up in the world, and all that, they don't dare let the shines know it, and they're ashamed to let the white folks know it. So they kinda compromise and get the whitest colored woman they can find. Of course, they won't admit that, but you can judge by their actions. I know 'em from A to Z. *(She opens the smoking cabinet, pours out a drink and swallows it, lights a cigarette, and then reclines luxuriously on the day bed. The maid chuckles and enters the bedroom)*

**MARTHA:** *(coming out of the bedroom)* Come, Phyllis! *(she fastens the lead string on the dog and goes out by the hall door)*

**THE GIRL:** *(meditatively)* Now, if I can only get a new outfit for that party next week, I'll be sitting pretty. If that darky just brings that fur coat, I'll knock 'em dead. Put on airs with me, will they? I'll make all the dickties look like rag bags. *(The telephone rings. She answers it)* Hello! Hello! Mr. Russel! *(in surprise)* Alright, tell him to come up. *(hangs up the receiver)* Hell! I told him not to come up here tonight. Damn fool! *(She paces back and forth angrily. The door bell rings. She admits a well dressed, shrewd-looking, sleek, black fellow)* Oh, Hello, Johnnie!

**JOHNNIE:** *(kissing her)* Hello, sweetheart!

**THE GIRL:** *(shaking her finger reproachfully at him)* I thought I told you not to come up tonight? You're always doing something to jam me!

**JOHNNIE:** *(apologetically)* Well, I had to come, darling. You know I couldn't trust anybody in Harlem with that amount of money. And I didn't dare send one of my kids with it. Here! (*handing her several bills. He sits on the day bed*)

THE GIRL: (*counting the money*) Well, you could have sent a messenger boy with it. You're the dumbest real estate man I ever saw. You never think of my welfare at all. Here! what does this mean? You're five dollars short.

JOHNNIE: Well, you see honey, I . . .

THE GIRL: Aw, shut up! What do you mean; trying to hold out on me? I told you I wanted fifty dollars. Now if you can't give me what I need I'll get it somewhere else. You're not the only nigger in Harlem that wants a good looking mama! Put that in your pipe and smoke it. There's plenty of men who'll be glad to take your place. (*She throws the money on the library table*) If you're that cheap, I'll quit!

JOHNNIE: (*thoroughly alarmed, drops to his knees in front of her*) Oh, honey! you wouldn't quit me, would you? I wouldn't have anyone but my wife, then.

THE GIRL: (*pushing him aside, as she moves to the other side of the room*) Well, it would serve you right. (*The telephone rings. The girl answers it.*) Hello! Hello—Who?—Put him on the wire— Oh, hello! I wasn't expecting you tonight—Well—I suppose I can spare you a minute—Yes, come on up. (*she rings off*) See, (*turning to* JOHNNIE) I told you the old man would be here tonight. Come on, beat it! (JOHNNIE *jumps up and looks around wildly for a place to hide, finally he makes for the hall door*) Come back here, you damn fool! He's coming that way. I told you he was coming but you *would* stick around. (*she glances wildly around the room. The door bell rings*) Quick! go in the kitchen and lock the door! Quick! (*exit* JOHNNIE *into the kitchen. The door bell rings again*) In a minute! (*sweetly* THE GIRL *snatches his hat off the day bed and throws it into the kitchen after* JOHNNIE) Keep still in there now, you big sap! And lock that door! (JOHNNIE *locks the door. The bell rings again*)

VOICE IN THE HALL: What's the matter in there? Open the door!

THE GIRL: Just a minute, dear! (*She admits a tall brown-skin man dressed as a clergyman and carrying a brief case. He looks around suspiciously*) Well, why don't you kiss me! (*putting her arms around his neck*) Ain't you my little reverend?

**THE MAN:** Ss–h! not so loud. I don't want anybody to know I am here. I'm awfully glad to see you, honey! *(He embraces her)*

**THE GIRL:** Well, what did you bring me, Georgie, dear?

**GEORGE:** *(reaching into the brief case and extracting a bottle of liquor)* Look at this pre-war stuff, will you?

**THE GIRL:** *(putting the bottle in the smoking cabinet)* Is *that* all you brought? Where are the shoes I asked you for?

**GEORGE:** Now, now, don't be so quick to get on your high horse. *(He reaches into the brief case and brings out a pair of expensive shoes)* Here's your shoes.

**THE GIRL:** *(embracing him)* Oh, George! you're so good to me! You're worth a hundred of these other men!

**GEORGE:** That's the talk, honey! *(He starts to take off his coat)*

**THE GIRL:** Oh, George! I'm sorry, but you can't stay. You know my husband's coming tonight and you don't want to jam me, do you?

**GEORGE:** *(reluctantly rising)* Well, alright, but it seems like you're always hustling me off.

**THE GIRL:** Aw, quit cryin'! You make me sick. A whole lot you care about me. You wouldn't care if my husband cut my throat . . . you and your cheap shoes!

**GEORGE:** *(aroused)* Cheap shoes! What do you mean; cheap shoes? Them shoes cost me fifteen dollars!

**THE GIRL:** Well, what of it? Do you think this is a charitable institution? Come on, beat it! *(The telephone rings)* Good God! There he is now. *(She answers the telephone)* Hello! Hello!—Yes—Yes. Well, come on. Where are you now?—In about five minutes—yes—alright then. *(She hangs up the receiver and turns on* GEORGE *excitedly)* Come on—quick! I told you to get out of here. Go in the bedroom! Hurry up!

**GEORGE:** *(also excited)* Alright. Hurry up and get rid of him. I've got to attend prayer meeting tonight! *(Exit* GEORGE *into the bedroom)*

**JOHNNIE:** *(opening the kitchen door)* Is it alright now?

**THE GIRL:** *(savagely)* Shut that door, and lock it! *(Exit* JOHNNIE. *The door bell rings. She admits a small black fellow who carries a large bundle)*

**THE NEWCOMER:** Evening, old dear! *(embracing her)* Look what I brought you?

**THE GIRL:** Oh you dear! What is it?

**THE NEWCOMER:** *(unwrapping the bundle and displaying a long fur coat)* How do you like that, sweetie?

**THE GIRL:** Oh, Frank! You're worth a hundred of these other men! You're so good to me. How much did it cost?

**FRANK:** *(dramatically)* Six hundred berries!

**THE GIRL:** *(much impressed)* Nothing cheap about you? You must have made a touch.

**FRANK:** Well, I'm not treasurer of my lodge for nothing, you know. I handle all the funds, and I might as well spend it on you as to have them throwing it away on monkey uniforms and conventions.

**THE GIRL:** *(hopefully)* Have you got a meeting tonight, Frankie?

**FRANK:** Nope. I'm gonna stay right here with you.

**THE GIRL:** Oh! you can't, not tonight. My husband's coming home tonight. You'd better leave now. You don't want to jam me, do you?

**FRANK:** I don't see why I should run as soon as I get here. I ain't goin' nowhere!

**THE GIRL:** *(tearfully)* Oh, Frankie, you must! *(The telephone rings)*

**FRANK:** Naw I won't. I ain't spendin' six hundred iron men for nothin'. I wouldn't run for nobody!

**THE GIRL:** *(answering the telephone)* Hello! Hello! Yes, it's me—no, don't come up for a while yet—well—alright then.

**FRANK:** *(alarmed)* Who's that?

**THE GIRL:** Why it's my husband. I told you he was coming. Come on, beat it!

**FRANK:** : *(racing around the room)* Where shall I hide? Where shall I hide? *(He tries the kitchen and bedroom doors and finding them locked, opens the window on the right and steps out on the fire escape. The girl rushes after him, pulls down the sash and lowers the shade)*

**THE GIRL:** Oh, my God! what a mess! If I ever get out of this . . . *(The doorbell rings. She rushes to the door and admits a gigantic black fellow with a bundle under his arm.)* Oh, you dear boy! I wasn't expecting you so soon. I'm not even dressed yet. *(They embrace)* What have you got there, Sammy?

**SAMMY:** *(grinning)* Oh, I've got just what you want. *(He unwraps the bundle and displays a new dress)* Not so bad for seventy-five dollars, eh?

**THE GIRL:** *(rapturously)* Oh! it's so beautiful! You're worth a hundred of these other Harlem men, Sammy. Just what I wanted, too. Oh, you're a darling. *(she kisses him)*

**SAMMY:** *(boasting)* Oh, that's nuthin'. I can get a girl like you anything you want.

**THE GIRL:** Can you, dear?

**SAMMY:** I'll say I can! . . . Got anything to drink?

**THE GIRL:** Sure. Did you ever know me when I didn't have anything to drink! *(She pours both a drink)* I'm sorry you can't stay, Sammy. You see, my husband's coming in tonight.

**SAMMY:** *(huffily)* Say! what do you think I am? What do you think I'm buyin' this stuff for? I had to borrow twenty bucks off my old lady to help pay for that *(pointing to the gown)*.

**THE GIRL:** Now, Sammy, be nice! I can't help it 'cause he's coming in tonight. I didn't know it until this morning. You wouldn't jam me, would you? *(She looks fearfully at the doors and the right-hand window)*

**SAMMY:** *(suspiciously)* I ain't gonna move a step. So that's that. *(The doorbell rings. He glances wildly about)* Where'll I go?

**THE GIRL:** Oh God! Go somewhere. *(He rushes around to the doors)* Go out on the fire escape until I get rid of him! *(pointing to the left-hand window)*.

**SAMMY:** *(making a dive for the window)* Alright! Alright! *(He starts to raise the window, but it sticks)* What the hell's the matter with this damn window? *(The door bell rings again)*

**THE GIRL:** Quick! Quick! *(She helps him raise the window and pushes him out, lowering the sash and the shade. The bell rings again, supplemented by a kick at the door)*

**A VOICE:** Open up there!

**THE GIRL:** *(rushing to the door)* Alright, dear! *(She opens the door and admits a small, slender brown-skin man. His hair is slicked down, he sports a deep red necktie and wears a wrist watch. He has a soprano voice and a mincing walk. He carries a hat box)*

Hello! what you doing up here tonight? Why didn't you telephone?

**THE SLENDER ONE:** I just thought I'd surprise you, dearie. *(He drops the hatbox and embraces her.)*

**THE GIRL:** Kiss me on the cheek, dear. You know what I've always told you. . . . What have you got there; something for me?

**THE SLENDER ONE:** Oh, you know I have, sugar lump! *(He opens the box and brings forth a gorgeous hat)* Isn't it just perfectly beautiful?

**THE GIRL:** Oh, Henry! It's just what I wanted. You're worth a hundred of these *men* in Harlem. *(She embraces him, turning her head aside)* On the cheek, dear!

**HENRY:** Now we're going to have a perfectly lovely time, aren't we, darling? You see, I've worn a soft collar—I'm always looking out for you.

**THE GIRL:** Now, Henry, you can't stay.

**HENRY:** *(alarmed)* Oh, Honey! I got off from the "Y" early tonight especially for you. Won't you let me stay? *(He drops to his knees and placing his arms around her, pulls her toward him. She pushes him aside)*

**THE GIRL:** No, you can't stay! I'm not going to have my husband come in here and catch anything like you around!

**HENRY:** *(jumping up)* Now dear, that's terribly mean of you. I would almost say it's downright despicable, the way you treat me. I would, I would, I would. You have no idea what I went through in order to get the twenty dollars for that hat! *(He buries his face in his arms and sobs with much heaving of shoulders)* You treat me abominably, that's what you do. You're mean, mean, mean to me!

**THE GIRL:** *(revolted)* Come on, snap out of it, you little sissy! Get on back to your Y.M.C.A. before my husband gets here. Beat it!

**HENRY:** *(indignantly, hands on hips)* So that's the way you treat me, eh? I've a good mind never to come here again!

**THE GIRL:** Well, I've been expecting you to pull something like that. That's why I had you to get the dog for me. *(The door bell rings and* HENRY *jumps in alarm, glances wildly about.)* Quick! Under the bed! That's him now. (HENRY *dives under the* *bed. His feet tap the floor in fright)* Keep your feet still, you little fool. *(The bell rings again).* Alright *(loudly)*, just a minute. *(She opens the door and admits a big black man in policeman's uniform.)* Hello, dear! I've been so lonesome here without you.

**THE POLICEMAN:** *(kissing her)* I know you have, honey. *(He has a booming bass voice)*

**THE GIRL:** Why didn't you 'phone, Charlie? *(He sits in the large chair by the library table and tosses his hat aside. She sits on his knee)*

**CHARLIE:** I wanted to surprise my little girl.

**THE GIRL:** Well, you certainly did. I didn't expect you tonight. (HENRY, *under the day bed, can't make his feet behave.* CHARLIE *and* THE GIRL *both hear the tapping)* That's them kids up stairs, honey bunch. *(embracing him)*

**CHARLIE:** Oh! I was wondering . . . I see you gotta lotta new stuff. *(Glancing at the coat, hat and gown)*

**THE GIRL:** Yes, I was downtown shopping today.

**CHARLIE:** Well, I was shopping too. How do you like that? *(He produces a diamond ring from its box)* Ain't it a beauty?

**THE GIRL:** *(slipping the ring on her finger)* Oh, Charlie! You're such a *wonderful* daddy. You're worth a hundred of these other Harlem men! *(She holds her hand up to the light. The ring sparkles)*

**CHARLIE:** *(kissing her)* I sure had to shake down the bootleggers to get enough to buy that!

**THE GIRL:** Won't you have a drink before you go, Charlie?

**CHARLIE:** Waddaya mean; go? I'm stayin' right here, babe. *(producing a big flask)* Try some of this Scotch. I got it off that druggist on 135th Street. It's good stuff. (THE GIRL *pours both of them a stiff drink)*

**CHARLIE:** Well, here's excitin' times!

**THE GIRL:** They're exciting enough for me right now! *(They drink. Henry's feet misbehave again. The cop listens)*

**CHARLIE:** What's that?

**THE GIRL:** Oh, that's them kids upstairs, honey!

**CHARLIE:** Oh! I forgot. *(The door bell rings. The girl starts)*

**THE GIRL:** That must be Martha. *(She opens the door and* MARTHA *enters with a package and* PHYLLIS*)*

**MARTHA:** *(glancing at* CHARLIE *and handing the package to* THE GIRL*)* There's the stuff.

**CHARLIE:** More hooch, eh? Atta baby!

**MARTHA:** Yessir, more stuff. *(She unleashes the dog, who immediately makes for* HENRY'S *feet.* MARTHA *starts for the kitchen.)*

**THE GIRL:** *(quickly)* Martha, play a roll for us, won't you? Just put your things on the piano, or a chair.

**MARTHA:** *(wonderingly)* Yes, Ma'am! *(She walks to the piano. The telephone rings.* CHARLIE *and* THE GIRL *reach for it simultaneously.* CHARLIE, *being nearest, reaches it first. He answers.* MARTHA *takes off her things)*

**CHARLIE:** Hello! *(*HENRY'S *feet misbehave and* PHYLLIS *sniffs around him)* Yes—What's that?—On the fire escape! *(*THE GIRL *starts)*—Alright, I'll fix 'em! *(He replaces the receiver)*

**THE GIRL:** What is it? *(She is quite agitated)*

**CHARLIE:** *(reaching for his gun)* Two crooks on your fire escape, the janitor says. *(*MARTHA *runs to first the kitchen door and then the bedroom door.* CHARLIE *rushes to the window on the left and shouts out)* Come in here, you! *(*THE GIRL *sinks weakly into the chair.* SAMMY *raises the window and crawls into the room)* Put 'em up! Come out o' there, you other guy! *(*FRANK *raises the other window and enters, ranging himself alongside* SAMMY, *with hands pawing the air.* THE GIRL *tries to dart out the hall door)* Where you goin', Corinne? Come back here! I can handle these bums. *(Keeping the two men covered, he grasps her robe)*

**THE GIRL:** *(sinking back into the chair)* Oh, my God! Oh, my God!

**MARTHA:** These doors are locked from the inside; I can't open them! *(*HENRY *kicks at the dog.* CHARLIE *sees the kick)*

**CHARLIE:** Uh-huh! I thought there was something crooked here. Come out from under there! *(*HENRY *emerges)* Why, you dirty sissy! What are *you* doing here?

**MARTHA:** I can't get in the kitchen or bedroom.

**CHARLIE:** Come out o' them rooms or I'll shoot! *(The two doors open and* JOHNNIE *and* GEORGE *emerge with their hats on and hands elevated. The cop motions them over toward the piano)*

**MARTHA:** *(rushing over to* THE GIRL, *who has fainted across the table)* She's fainted! Call the doctor! *(She tries to revive her)*

**CHARLIE:** What are you guys doin' here?

**THE MEN:** *(in a chorus)* We came to see Corinne!

**CHARLIE:** *(turning to* CORINNE*)* Ah, hah! So! *Five* timing me, eh? *(*CORINNE, *revived by* MARTHA'S *ministrations, jumps up wildly)*

**CORINNE:** I don't know them, Charlie. Honest I don't. I never saw 'em before. *(becoming hysterical)* Really, I'm a good little girl. *(She drops on the day bed, wringing her hands and sobbing)*

**THE OTHER MEN:** *(in a chorus)* She's a liar; she's my gal! *(They point at her accusingly.* MARTHA *grabs her things and runs out the hall door)*

**JOHNNIE:** I pay her rent!

**GEORGE:** I buy her shoes!

**FRANK:** I buy her coats!

**SAMMY:** I buy her dresses!

**HENRY:** *(in his soprano)* I also purchase her millinery and I also gave her that dog to remind her of me. *(He places one hand on his hip and smooths his hair with the other. They all make a belligerent motion toward him, and glare. He wilts)* Now, now, gentlemen! Be yourselves, be yourselves!

**CHARLIE:** *(stuffing his gun in his pocket and reaching for his cap)* Well, I guess we're all a bunch o' saps. I'd wear this club out on her head, but my wife would hear about it.

**JOHNNIE**
**GEORGE**
**FRANK** } Mine, too!
**SAMMY**

**HENRY:** And I would just be *ruined;* positively *ruined. (They all make a belligerent motion toward him and glare. He wilts again)* Tutt! Tutt! I mean no harm, gentlemen. I mean no harm!

**CHARLIE:** Well, let's get our stuff off her. I guess we're monkey men, like the rest of the guys in Harlem. *(They all rush for their things.* CHARLIE *sits up dejectedly)*

**JOHNNIE:** *(sweeping his money off the table and rushing out)* My money!

**GEORGE:** *(following him, waving the shoes)* My shoes!

**FRANK:** *(following him, waving the coat)* My coat!

**SAMMY:** *(following him with the dress)* My dress!

**HENRY:** *(picking up* PHYLLIS *and the hat, and skipping out the door)* My hat! My dog!

**CHARLIE:** *(snatching the ring off* CORINNE'S *finger and swaggering out)* My ring!

**CORINNE:** My God!

(Curtain)

# Alvira Hazzard
## (1899–1953)
▼▼▼▼▼▼▼▼▼▼▼▼

Alvira Hazzard was born in North Brookfield, Massachusetts, to John and Rosella Curry Hazzard, a family of third-generation New Englanders. She graduated from Worcester Normal School, never married, and taught in the Boston public schools. In her free time, she wrote stories and poems, and two of her plays were published in *The Saturday Evening Quill*, the annual journal of a group of Black artists and intellectuals living in Roxbury and Boston. Members of the literary group included the playwright Joseph S. Mitchell, (see introduction to *Son-Boy*), the novelist Dorothy West, and poet Helene Johnson, as well as a dozen others. The group, founded in 1925, lasted about five years. Its noncommercial publication, *The Saturday Evening Quill*, was limited to 250 copies.

Hazzard's bio-note in the magazine states that she wrote one-act plays "which [had been] acted by amateurs." Only two are known: *Little Heads* (1929), which tells the story of a young Black woman who is invited to a party by a wealthy young white woman. She is delighted until she learns that she is to dress "old-fashioned" (plantation or minstrel style) and sing spirituals. *Mother Liked It*, reprinted here, is a two-act farce in the genre of the twenties musicals such as *Very Good Eddie* and *The Boyfriend*.

The "silly" plot is little more than an excuse to dress up and have fun—two young girls are excited by and infatuated with an Indian prince who turns out to be someone else.

Hazzard's play is included in this collection to demonstrate that African Americans wrote plays in all genres and on all subjects, including some which had nothing at all to do with "the problem."

# MOTHER LIKED IT

## Alvira Hazzard

### CAST

**PRINCE ALI KAHN,** *The problem*
**MEENA THOMAS,** *Who is in love with the prince*
**ALTA FIELDS,** *Whose practical jokes misfire*
**TESS,** *Who takes life as she finds it*
**JAY WINDSOR,** *Who helps to solve the problem*

### ACT ONE

SCENE I

*The lobby of a local theatre.* ALTA *is rather a spoiled, willful girl of twenty. She is pretty, but impatient and self-centered. Throughout the play she pays much attention to her nose and hat. As the curtain rises, she is seated near* TESS, *a pleasant, plain girl of twenty-two. They are both dressed for the street,* TESS *very plainly,* ALTA *smartly. They are seated Left.*

**ALTA:** *(rising and going to mirror to arrange her hat)* Are you sure you told her to meet us here?
**TESS:** Yes, in this lobby.

---

First published in *The Saturday Evening Quill*, June 1928.

**ALTA:** *(turning and looking at watch)* But we've waited twenty minutes! Meena is usually so very punctual.

**TESS:** Where are we going from here, to your home or to Crandall's?

**ALTA:** We can hardly make Crandall's if she doesn't hurry, and I must drive slowly today. I've paid two fines already this month.

**TESS:** *(powdering nose)* Well, Alta, my conscience is clear. I gave the message as you left it. Meena said that she already had a seat for the performance, but would meet us here at 4 o'clock. You haven't mentioned the show. Did you like it?

**ALTA:** All except that stupid Indian Prince. His stunts were all chestnuts, his make-up atrocious, and his manner entirely too artificial. He was condescending. Doubtless, by this time, he thinks every girl in town is penning him love notes. *(poses before mirror)* Let's go and leave Meena.

**TESS:** I thought the juggling act was exceptionally good. They usually bore me to distraction. I'm getting hungry. Alta, did you ever eat at the La Ming? The food is wonderful.

**ALTA:** *(visibly impatient, fixing hat)* Confound meeting an old maid! I suppose she's lengthening her newest gown, or hasn't come at all lest the Indian Prince shock her.

*(*MEENA *is a charming girl of eighteen years. One should get the idea that up to now she has been very retiring and reserved. She enters quietly with her hat in her hand.* ALTA *has her back turned and does not see her enter. She tosses the hat on* TESS' *lap, and, tipping up behind* ALTA, *covers her eyes.* TESS *rises)*

**ALTA:** *(embarrassed, turning as* MEENA *releases her)* You, Meena? We're out of sorts waiting!

**MEENA:** *(putting on hat before mirror)* So I judged by your last remark. *(laughs, with show of anger)* Cat!

**ALTA:** Oh, forgive me. I was a bit rude. But you yourself often admit that you are—

**MEENA:** *(with a dramatic gesture)* Practical—I've stopped calling myself an old maid. I'm sorry to be late, but I stayed over to see Ali Kahn again. For one mellow glance from him I'd—Oh, pshaw! Practically speaking, he's just another individual, but he *is* wonderful. Don't you think so?

**ALTA:** *(grimacing)* No, and we are late.

**TESS:** *(who, leaning against the wall, shows interest in the conversation)* And we are famished. *(general primping and powdering as* TESS *starts toward right)*

**MEENA:** *(dramatically, as she lags behind)* That adorable Prince! Practically speaking he is—

**ALTA:** Come to earth, Meena, let's move.

SCENE II

*The lobby of Crandall's fashionable Cafe. This scene is much the same as the first. Lounge chairs, and a mirror in the center of the back wall. There is a writing desk right. The girls enter right,* ALTA *going immediately to the mirror,* TESS *sitting and powdering her nose.* MEENA *perches on the arm of a chair.*

**ALTA:** *(without turning)* I know I'm a sight, and with this added excitement! Why I ever planned to come here is more than I can understand—now!

**MEENA:** Alta, I'm a bit worried. Don't you think we should have stopped? Did you notice how embarrassed that boy looked? I'm sure he has your number, and will report you to the Highway Commission.

**ALTA:** *(coming down center, and peering left)* Now I am disgraced! There's Mary Tallman in a gorgeous new wrap. Is that Tommy Boyle with her? And he has shaved off his mustache! Why *did* I go to that beastly show? I feel all awry.

**TESS:** *(happily rising)* Do we care about Tommy Boyle and Mary Tallman? Queen Elizabeth's ghost could not stop me now. I crave nourishment *(gesturing toward dining hall)*. Let us repair to the dining room and partake of the marvelous dishes that Monsieur Crandall has had prepared for us.

**MEENA:** I'll be satisfied to partake of the food. Tess, dear, you missed your calling when you didn't follow the stage. But I'm with you and famished. *(Turns to* ALTA, *who has slumped into a chair)* We're off to the victuals, Alta. *(They go into the dining hall)*

**ALTA:** *(rising reluctantly to follow them is attracted by something off right. She screams faintly, and drops back into the chair; rises again, goes quickly toward dining hall, then returns to center stage. She is very nervous, and her voice shakes)* The man, the very man I struck, and with Jay Windsor! Whatever shall I do? He'll surely recognize me! I—I—I'll— *(She turns from right to left sev-*

*eral times, and finally faces away from them.* JAY *and the stranger enter right. The stranger is limping. He has no hat, and his tie is twisted.* JAY *is a plain, modern young man of twenty-five. The stranger is the better looking and five years younger. His muddy clothes have a collegiate cut.* ALTA *is looking off left, but cannot, as they near her, resist looking at them)*

**ALTA:** *(facing them)* Jay, Jay, is he hurt! What can I do? Is it serious?

**JAY:** Why, it's Miss Fields. Don't be alarmed. This poor fellow had an accident, and I brought him here while I call a taxi. Some flapper nudged him and drove off. Traffic is very heavy just now. May I present Mr.—er—er . . .

**STRANGER:** Smith.

**JAY:** *(relieved)* Mr. Smith, Miss Fields.

**ALTA:** *(absently, with a rising inflection).* How—how—do you do, Mr. Smith?

**STRANGER:** *(ill at ease because of appearance)* How do you do, Miss Fields? Under the circumstances, I am sure you will pardon my disheveled appearance. Thought I could limp home, but it was a rather painful task.

**ALTA:** *(breathless)* You have their number—you will report them?

**STRANGER:** *(dreamily)* Unless—unless I meet the charming young lady who looked back so sympathetically as her companion drove ruthlessly away. I saw only her beautiful lustrous eyes . . . they seemed to say, "If I were at the wheel, I'd stop and be sorry." *(speaks more briskly)* You see, I was only side-swiped by the rear bumper. But there were no cushions on that bumper, nor where I landed. *(they laugh,* ALTA *weakly)*

**DOORMAN:** *(entering)* Cab for Mr. Jay Windsor.

**STRANGER:** *(backing out)* Happy to have met you, Miss Fields *(*JAY *is about to follow)* No, no, old man, it was enough for you to bring me here and get the cab . . . I insist. I'm all right. Good afternoon. *(He goes out)*

**ALTA:** *(about to cry)* Jay . . .

**JAY:** May I be of service?

**ALTA:** Jay, *I* hit him, and he's raving about Meena's eyes.

**JAY:** You're fooling!

**ALTA:** But I'm in dead earnest.

**JAY:** Well, I'm a son-of-a-gun! *(he laughs)*

**ALTA:** But, Jay, if they find out that I hit him it'll be dreadful. I would never have left him in the street, but *(she pauses)* why, you see, I've paid two fines recently for speeding. It would be awful *(her voice breaks)* to—to—go—to—jail. Couldn't you introduce him to Meena? Perhaps he really likes her.

**JAY:** Don't worry, Miss Fields, he'll not remember this after his bumps stop aching. He seems to be a fine fellow. And now, may I ask if you are dining alone at Crandall's?

**ALTA:** I'm not dining at all, I'm all upset. I wouldn't go in with the girls.

**JAY:** : Go in with me now, then. I tell you everything will be all right.

**ALTA:** *(firmly)* No. I shall *not* go in. Mary Tallman is in there with a new wrap on, and Tommy Boyle is with her. She's just showing off. I won't go in!

**JAY:** *(teasing)* Jealous?

**ALTA:** How absurd! I just won't have Mary see me so—so —upset.

**JAY:** Shall we go? May I take you home?

**ALTA:** *(sitting)* No, but you may talk to me while I wait for the girls, and if Mary Tallman is through before they are, I'll run out to the car. But perhaps you are hungry?

**JAY:** *(drawing up beside her)* No. I ate lunch late, and went to see Prince Ali Kahn at the Empire.

**ALTA:** Why, that's where I was this afternoon. I didn't like him. Did you?

**JAY:** Yes, immensely. Clever fellow. Thought his set was attractive, too. I sat through two shows—quite fascinated.

**ALTA:** *(surprised)* Why, Jay Windsor, how could you be so taken in by a mere grafter—an ordinary fraud? I'm distressed because I went to the old theatre instead of dressing for dinner, like a sensible person. *(She rises and walks left. Turning quickly, she addresses* JAY *as they sit)* Jay *(Pauses. He is all attention)*, will you assist me in a little practical joke? Say yes.

**JAY:** Don't you think it would be nice for me to know something about this joke before I commit myself?

**ALTA:** *(confidentially, leaning toward* JAY*)* It's this way. Meena is actually coming to life, giving up her prudish ways. I think a thrill, such as I have in mind, even though it is planned, will be a vital boost to her, and . . .

**JAY:** *(in mock seriousness)* Lady, lady, stop talking and tell me what I am expected to do! I cannot be party to anything . . .

**ALTA:** Meena is quite gone on your friend Ali Kahn. She kept Tess and me waiting ever so long while she gazed on his oriental beauty through a second performance. You are to impersonate Prince Ali Kahn, and make love to Meena. We'll arrange it somehow, if you'll consent to costume and ape the Prince. *(she is quite anxious)* You'll do it? Please? Just for fun?

**JAY:** *(outdone)* Never!! Why, Miss Fields! (ALTA *rises haughtily, obviously disappointed. She does not heed* JAY *as he follows her right)*

**JAY:** I'm so sorry, but I really couldn't. *(Enter* MEENA *and* TESS. JAY *walks back)*

**TESS:** *(to* MEENA*)* Look, Meena, she *is* here. Alta Fields, why didn't you come to your dinner? Meena bet me five that you'd driven home in a huff. *(mock tears)* And I've lost five. *(glances impishly at* MEENA*)*

**MEENA:** *(nudging* TESS *and motioning toward* JAY*)* They're together, and they've scrapped! Go ahead, say something else.

**JAY:** *(rather unhappily)* Hello, girls. Guess I'm just a buttinski. Good afternoon. *(He strides off)*

**TESS:** *(stepping about dramatically)* This awfternoon has been nothing if not eventful, my deahs. And now what is amiss with friend Jay?

**MEENA:** *(kindly)* Gee, Altie, I didn't think you would stay here so long waiting for us. Really, you shouldn't have, since you didn't have any dinner.

**ALTA:** *(haughtily)* If you are laboring under the impression that I waited for *you*, please let me tell you that I did nothing of the kind. However, if you are riding home with me, let's go. *(They go out.* ALTA *leads,* TESS *winking back at* MEENA*)*

## ACT II

*Crandall's. Dinner time. Several days later. (Same as Act I, Scene II.)* ALTA *is standing center,* TESS *is sitting left. They are both dressed for dinner. From three to six people may pass through to the dining hall.*

**TESS:** And how did you get Jay to finally agree?

**ALTA:** He promised only to walk through this lobby from a taxi, and right out again. I had to bully Meena into speaking to the Prince if she ever met him. Of course she hasn't the slightest idea that he'll ever cross her path. But I've her promise that she'll be here at five. If she speaks to him, Jay will say a few soft nothings and . . . Oh, it's all planned, and Meena's in for a good jolt.

**TESS:** Frankly, Alta, I don't get a kick out of your idea. Meena has a right to admire the Prince, and it'll be embarrassing for her to speak to him without first being introduced.

**ALTA:** *(impatiently)* But she will be speaking to Jay Windsor! What do you think, Tess? When I dropped in on her last evening, she was burning incense, and playing "The Song of India." Won't it all be funny? (ALTA *laughs*)

**TESS:** Very well, have your little fun. But remember that I'm not party to anything but Crandall's dinner. (MEENA *bursts in*)

**MEENA:** *(out of breath)* Don't chide me, Alta, please. I know I'm late, but only a few minutes. *(goes to mirror, as* ALTA *winks knowingly at* TESS)

**ALTA:** *(aside to* TESS*)*. If Jay is late I'll never forgive him. . . . Look, look, girls, do look! *(they crowd, looking right)* Prince Ali Khan, who is at the Empire. Isn't he adorable! See the profile, the turban. . . . Oh—o—o—o! *(All sigh deeply.* MEENA *is ill at ease)*

**TESS:** *(in earnest)* He does look good—like a real Prince!

**ALTA:** *(huskily)* Can you keep your promise, Meena? Do you dare?

**MEENA:** *(loftily)* Yes, I dare, but what will he think of me, Alta? I—I don't want to. *(Tess snickers)*

**ALTA:** *(in hoarse, tense, whisper)* You're afraid. You haven't the courage. Meena Thomas, I double dare you to speak to Prince Ali Kahn—double dare. . . . *(Enter* PRINCE ALI KAHN *in dress of Indian Prince. Girls back right, as he passes them walking slowly, sedately, looking straight ahead. As he passes center* MEENA *stammeringly addresses him)*

**MEENA:** I—I—you—how—Your Highness, may I not tell you how much I enjoyed your act at the Empire?

**PRINCE:** *(touching forehead with finger tips, and bowing low)* Such a pleasure it will be, charming lady. *(There is an awkward pause)*

**MEENA:** Such—such mystery! It is wonderful, the way you go into a—a trance and tell things. . . .

**PRINCE:** *(with another bow)* I present but the merest bit of the mystery of India for the approval of my illustrious American friends. *(Awkward pause. Girls in background talk in dumb show, not sure as to the identity of man talking to* MEENA.*)*

**MEENA:** *(more at ease)* Of course you will return next year. The Empire has never known such crowds. You have captivated the city.

**PRINCE:** I trust it will be my pleasure to return next year. *(He backs into the dining hall, bowing)*

**MEENA:** *(sighing deeply)* Well, smarty, I've done it, and I'm not disgraced. He was so kind and polite—and gracious. Say something, Alta Fields! Are you quite satisfied?

**ALTA:** *(fiercely)* That Jay Windsor to double-cross me!

**TESS:** Nothing to do but go in to dinner. Oh, Alta, you're a clever little fixer, you are. *(She laughs.* MEENA *and* TESS *go into dining hall)*

**ALTA:** *(hanging back)* As if I could have depended on Jay! I could swear real damns! *(She flounces after other girls. She is not quite off when* JAY *enters. He is ridiculously costumed: turban awry, trousers too large. He yoo-hoos to* ALTA, *who turns one fierce glance on him and turns again into the dining hall.* JAY *slumps into a chair.)*

**JAY:** Late, and all this tomfoolery for nothing. *(THE PRINCE enters.* JAY *does not see him. He studies* JAY, *and walking to him, speaks in perfect English)*

**PRINCE:** *(leaning over* JAY*)* What's this, old man, competition? You might have waited until I left town.

**JAY:** *(starting)* It's Mr. Smith, the man of the accident, or I lose my guess. And are you really the guy who has drawn such crowds to the Empire?

**PRINCE:** Soft pedal! I have two days more, and the public doesn't need to know the bare facts. You see, I'm a student and this act as a summer job pays my tuition at the University of Chicago. I begin my last year next month. But why the impersonation?

**JAY:** It's a long story, but fate must intend us to be friends. Why, this is the second unforeseen meeting in a week. I must get out of here at once. I say, how would you enjoy going home with me, where we may have a pleasant smoke-chat?

**PRINCE:** I'd like it, my friend, but there *(waving toward dining hall)* in that hall is the girl of the golden smile, the liquid eyes. The very girl I had never dared hope to meet.

**JAY:** *(with vim)* Well I'll be . . .

**PRINCE:** As I entered this lobby, she and two other young ladies were talking low and gesturing as if some conspiracy was afoot. As I came nearer, the girl of girls very timidly and reluctantly spoke to me. Never, never was I so distressed! This beastly make up! If I discard it she'll probably loathe me, but I *do* want to meet her as Jonas Smithly.

**JAY:** *(making a face)* Ye gods, man, is that your real name?

**PRINCE:** It is.

**JAY:** Well, I suppose that can't be helped, but I know the young lady. She is Miss Taylor, and a charming young lady, indeed.

**PRINCE:** *(in anticipation)* Can we dress and get back here by the time she comes out from dinner?

**JAY:** 'Fraid not. We've talked some time already. I can't be found here like this. *(He rises)* I'll arrange a meeting for tomorrow.

**PRINCE:** "No time like the present." "He who hesitates is lost." And so on. May I use your name?

**JAY:** *(moving toward exit)* Yes, use my name, but make it snappy. I'll wait out there in that taxi. *(*JAY *goes out.* THE PRINCE *sits at table where paper is provided. He writes and tears up six sheets. Finally he writes a note to his satisfaction. This he encloses in an envelope, kisses it lightly, and takes it with him out after* JAY. *The girls come out, and the doorman enters immediately and says, "Note for Miss Taylor." She opens it hurriedly, then gives a little scream. Others, who have been primping, turn.)*

**MEENA:** Listen to this! *(she reads)* "Dear Miss Taylor: I'm not an Indian Prince, but a husky college half-back and one-hundred-per cent American. My act is only a summer diversion. Can you like me the tiniest bit, just the same? Mr. Windsor promises to see that we are properly introduced. Despite the fact that my real name is Jonas Smithly, I trust that soon, very soon, we will be better acquainted.

"Very sincerely yours,

"J. Smithly.

"P. S.—If you can't stand the name, it *could* be changed, but mother liked it.

"J. S."

(MEENA *smiles to herself and holds the letter to her breast. The other girls stand in utter surprise and bewilderment.*)

(Curtain)

# JOSEPH S. MITCHELL
## (1891–195?)
▼▼▼▼▼▼▼▼▼▼▼▼

Joseph Mitchell's plays often dramatize the lives of African Americans victimized by racists who transgress the law, probably reflecting his early life in the Deep South at the turn of the century. If this theme seems overly familiar today, it is nevertheless one that is likely to endure so long as skin color remains destiny.

Born in Auburn, Alabama, to Solon and Elizabeth (Switcher) Mitchell, he was reared and schooled in the locale, graduating from Talladega College before moving north. He earned a degree in jurisprudence at Boston University and in 1924 married Lucy Miller of Daytona Beach, Florida. Together they raised two children, Laura and Joseph, Jr.

Mitchell supported his avocation as a playwright with his vocation as a lawyer. He served as executive secretary to the governor and the governor's council in Massachusetts during World War II and as the state's assistant attorney general between 1945 and 1949. While carrying out these duties, he worked with the Boston Center for Adult Education for many years. He managed to find time to write plays when not practicing law or serving the community. During the pre–Civil rights period, he was one of the few African Americans either elected or appointed to public office in a northern city.

*Son-Boy*, reprinted here, appeared in the June 1928 issue of *The Saturday Evening Quill*, a relatively conservative magazine published by a group of Black intellectuals with literary aspirations nourished by the Harlem Renaissance, which was then in full swing. Before it ceased publication in 1930, *Quill* could count among its contributors poet-composer Waring Cuney, ghetto poet Helene Johnson, Alvira Hazzard (see introduction to *Mother Liked It*), short-story writer Dorothy West, and W. E. B. Du Bois, who said that *Quill* was the most interesting Black publication of its time.

*Son-Boy's* title, if somewhat jaunty in tone, nevertheless suggests the serious nature of the conflict at the play's center. To his doting mother, Son-Boy is the "sun" as well as the heir of the family, but to the townspeople he is contemptuously known as "boy." His father represents the compliant Black male of the time, portrayed as a descendant of Uncle Tom, afraid to give his children "too much learnin' ter be a 'good nigger.'" The mother is ready to resist the would-be lynchers, with weapons if necessary. Her belief that African Americans equal whites in intelligence and that the town she lives in belongs to her no less than it does to whites makes her appear dangerously radical in the eyes of her docile husband (and perhaps to the townspeople). In the closing scene, we are left with the impression that no matter what virtues of courage and honesty the Johnsons exhibit alongside their fears, they may be powerless before the violently whimsical impulses of their tormentors. The hand of their tormentors stayed temporarily by mistaken identity, at the next alarm it will strike down the Johnsons without warning. Yet the play closed on a positive note, with Dinah singing her song of defiance and Son-Boy deciding to seek an education. *Son-Boy* is one of the very few "lynching" plays with a "happy" ending.

One of his early plays, *Help Wanted*, appeared in the second issue of *Saturday Evening Quill* (April 1929). Though like *Son-Boy* it is dated in its diction, the play has a surprisingly contemporary ambiance. It is included in the anthology *Roots of African American Drama* (Detroit: Wayne State University Press, 1991).

# REFERENCES

Johnson, Abby Arthur, and Ronald Mayberry Johnson. *Propaganda and Aesthetics: The Literary Politics of Afro-American Magazines in the Twentieth Century.* Amherst: University of Massachusetts Press, 1979.

*Who's Who in Colored America.* 7th ed. Yonkers-on-Hudson, NY: Christine E. Burckel & Assoc., 1950, p. 377.

# SON-BOY

## Joseph S. Mitchell

CAST

> **ZEKE JOHNSON,** *A middle-aged colored man*
> **DINAH,** *His wife*
> **SON-BOY,** *Their son*
> **SUSIE,** *A friend of the family*
> **JOE,** *Son-Boy's pal*
>
> *Time:* About 1900 A.D.
> *Place:* A village in the southern part of the United States.

*The scene is the bedroom of the Johnson family. There is a bed in the rear left-hand corner of the room; a table in the center; a fireplace at the right-side corner; a closet in the rear right-hand corner. In the middle of the mantle-piece is an old clock. A door leads outside at the rear center, and another into the kitchen at the left-side center. There are three or four old straight-back chairs arranged in different parts of the room. Several irons are heating on the hearth in front of the fire. There is a pile of clothes on the bed.* DINAH, *a woman of forty years, dressed in a calico dress and with a red bandana around her head, comes in from the kitchen singing:*

---

First published in *The Saturday Evening Quill*, June 1928.

Before I'd be a slave,
I'd be buried in my grave,
And go home to my father and be saved.

*As she is singing she goes directly to the closet, from which she takes an ironing-board. She places it on a table and a chair about the center of the room. She goes out into the kitchen and returns immediately with a pan of water. She begins sprinkling clothes, and continues singing:*

Weepin' Mary, Weepin' Mary, Weepin' Mary,
Weep no mo', weep no mo'.

Before I'd be a slave,
I'd be buried in my grave,
An' go home to my father an' be saved.

ZEKE, *who is about fifty years old, comes in from the kitchen, scraping his feet as he walks. He is shabbily dressed. He has a pipe in his mouth.*

**ZEKE:** (*going towards the fireplace*) Ain't Son-Boy come yit?
**DINAH:** (*looking up at the clock*). Naw; but it's time he's heah—it's seben o'clock.
**ZEKE:** I'se gittin' hongry now. I want 'im ter come on an' fetch in de wood fo' it gits too dark, an' make a fiah in de stove so y'kin cook my supper. (*He draws his chair up to the fireplace and sits down lazily*)
**DINAH:** Dere's some taters roastin' in de fiah.
**ZEKE:** I putty nigh fergit 'em. (*He takes a poker-iron and begins pulling them out of the fire. He lays his pipe on the mantle-piece, and begins peeling and eating potatoes*)
**DINAH:** (*continuing sprinkling clothes, singing*)

Doubtin' Thomas, Doubtin' Thomas, Doubtin' Thomas,
Doubt no mo', doubt no mo'.

Before I'd be a slave,
I'd be buried in my grave,
An' go home to my father an' be saved.

Fearin' Peter, Fearin' Peter, Fearin' Peter,
Fear no mo', fear no mo'.

Before I'd be a slave,
I'd be buried in my grave,
An' go home to my father an' be saved.

**ZEKE:** Looka heah, Dinah, don't yuh nevah gits tiahd o' singin' dem kin' o' songs?

**DINAH:** *(turning around and looking at* ZEKE*)* Tiahd o' what?

**ZEKE:** I mean skeered—

**DINAH:** Skeered o' what?

**ZEKE:** Y'kno' de whar fo'ks now kno's what y'mean when y'sing dem songs. One o'dem 'surance agents lakly ter come in heah any minit.

**DINAH:** I *want's* 'em ter kno'. Fuddermo', Zeke Johnson, de lawd ain't nevah made a man wid two legs dat I'se skeered uv.

**ZEKE:** I jes' thought I'd min' yuh fer yer own sake. Y'kno' we's got ter live in dis heah white man's town.

**DINAH:** *(raising her voice)* It's much mine 'tis his! My fo'ks come o'er heah 'fore his'n did. Me an' my fo'ks worked de fiel's so dey kin eat an' wear clo'es; us he'p buil' de sto'es an' houses fer 'em ter live in; an' us worked de streets so dey kin walk an' ride on. I've got jes' ez gooda right ter live heah an' sing, an' bring up my onlies chile Son-Boy ez anybody else is. De trubble wid *you* is, you's too skeered ter 'sert yer rights ez a man.

**ZEKE:** *(with his head lowered and still eating; he rolls his eyes at* DINAH*)* Who's skeered?

**DINAH:** You is! You's too skeered ter keep yer head up an' walk straight; you's too skeered to ax yer boss fer mo' pay *(ZEKE looks around at* DINAH*)* Deny it ef yuh dare. Y'kno' it's de truf. If it's a lie y'tol' it. You's too skeered ter 'fend yer fam'ly ef y'had ter —you's eben too skeered ter wash up and wear decent clo'es ter town.

**ZEKE:** Y'kno' de whar fo'ks don't lak ter see a nigger dressed up.

**DINAH:** I dresses up an' goes ter town, an' dey ain't nevah said nothin' ter me. Dey ain't stud'in' yuh ef y'tend ter an' min' yer own bizness.

**ZEKE:** Dey's thinkin' mighty hard.

**DINAH:** I thought I married a man what had guts in 'im— but you's de limit. I's glad dat Son-Boy ain't lak yuh ef you is 'sponsible fer 'im not havin' no learnin'. *(Leaving off the sprinkling she goes to the hearth and gets an iron. She tests the iron in the ordinary way to see if it is hot—She repeats this action several times during the play. She begins ironing at the board.)*

**ZEKE:** Dere yuh go ergin.

**DINAH:** Yeah, I said it, an' I'se sayin' it ergin. Now he'p yerse'f! Ef y'had took my advice an' let Son-Boy git some learnin' in his head when he wuz little he could now be takin' keer uv us both; an' y'wouldn't be sittin' 'roun' de fiah dis way mos' nigh froze ter def while I'se standin' on my feet all day washin' an' i'nin' de white fo'ks cl'oes. Son-Boy is jes' ez smart an' got jes' ez much guts ez any boy, white or black, an' always has. Don't yuh fergit it!

**ZEKE:** I recollects, ef y'don't, how de whar fo'ks took'n run ol' Aint Suckie's boy way f'om heah, 'cause dey says he wuz gittin' too much learnin' ter be a "good nigger." She ain't been right in de head since.

**DINAH:** Dey cain't run us all away. I'll see 'em when dey do. . . . Ef dey could dey wouldn't have nobody ter work fer 'em, an' we could work an' learn somewhere's else.

**ZEKE:** I'se gwine ter stay right heah, 'case I ain't gwine ter take no chance wid a place I don't kno' nothin' 'bout.

**DINAH:** Me an' Son-Boy ain't skeered ter, ef us wants ter.

**ZEKE:** Yuh better let well–'nuff 'lone. Son-Boy's makin' ten dollars a month now; an' he's got a chance ter make twelve, lak Sambo Jones done.

**DINAH:** What's twelve dollars a month? He's way f'om home all day an' ha'f de night. *(she glances at the clock)*

**ZEKE:** Dat's mo'en you's makin'! Fer all o'dem clo'es y'wash fer fo' fam'lies y'don't make mo'en two dollars a week.

**DINAH:** I don't 'spect ter get sich low wages all my life.

**ZEKE:** What you's an' Son-Boy's makin' is 'nuff fer poo' ignunt fo'ks lak y'all is.

**DINAH:** Ef Son-Boy be no count lak you an' stay 'roun' heah all his life he nevah will git ahead—he'll jes' be slavin' an' makin' dem same ten or twelve dollars er month all his life an' den li'ble ter be lynched by some poo' white trash. But dat aint lak my Son-boy! Naw! Naw! *(she shakes her head)* He's got too much uv de Battle fam'ly in 'im. He's got in his head ter git er edication.

**ZEKE:** Y'kno' dese whar fo'ks ain't gwine ter let 'im git nothin' lak dat 'roun' heah.

**DINAH:** He don't have ter stay 'roun' heah, crazy!

**ZEKE:** *(taking pipe off mantle-piece, cutting tobacco off a plug and putting it into his pipe)* De whar fo'ks ain't lettin' no niggers leave dis town; fer I heahed 'em say t'other day dat dey need all dey kin git ter work. *(he lights the tobacco)*

**DINAH:** Dey don't have ter let Son-Boy do a blessed thing. He do's what he wants ter do, thank Gawd! an' don't ax nobody no odds. He's got dat much o'de Battle fam'ly in 'im.

**ZEKE:** *(crossing his legs and puffing his pipe)* How's he gwine ter ride de train ef de whar fo'ks won't let 'im?

**DINAH:** He don't have ter ride no train! What's he got dem two big spreadin' atters fer? Dey'll take 'im anywhere's he wants ter go. Ef he evah gits away f'om dis one-horse town, an' gits some sense in his head lak he wants ter, he'll make a big man out o' hisse'f—he'll be a mail-carrier, or a school teacher, or a doctor.

**ZEKE:** What y'gwine ter let Son-Boy waste all o'dat time in school fer? Fer nothin'? Mr. Ross tol' me t'other day dat it took twenty years fer his son ter git ter be a doctor. He 'vised nevah let Son-Boy spen' so much time in school. It's too long fer Son-Boy, he said. An' Mr. Ross said Son-Boy'd be wastin' his time since he didn't eben kno' how ter write his own name now.

**DINAH:** *(cutting her eye at* ZEKE*)* Did Mr. Ross' boy waste his time learnin'?

**ZEKE:** Naw—but dat ain't de question. *(rears back in his chair)*

**DINAH:** An' he went ter school twenty years?

**ZEKE:** Dat what dey says.

**DINAH:** I betcha he didn't give his daddy an' mammy a red copper cent dem whol' twenty years.

**ZEKE:** How coul' he, ef he wuz in school?

**DINAH:** I betcha he didn't kno' "A" f'om bull-frog twenty years 'fore he wuz a doctor.

**ZEKE:** 'Course he didn't, 'fore he started ter school.

**DINAH:** An' look at HIM now!

**ZEKE:** But he's a white man!

**DINAH:** (*arms akimbo*) What does yuh mean ter set dere an' tell me, Zeke Johnson? Dat my Son-Boy ain't got de brains ter learn ter read an' write lak a white man? Le' me tell yuh now, Zeke Johnson, dat Af'ican brain o' Son-Boy Johnson is ez good a brain ez any othah man, whedder he be black or brown or white or yallow. An' don't YOU fergit it!

**ZEKE:** Don't git so 'cited; I jes' mean he's too ol' ter start now—

**DINAH:** Ef Son-Boy stays 'roun' heah an' lives ter be a hunderd years ol' he'll nevah 'mount ter nothin' workin' dis 'way. But ef he gits some learnin' in his head he kin have somethin', ef it takes 'im twenty years ter git it an' twenty years ter 'spose uv it.

**ZEKE:** Le' me see 'im git away firs'.

**DINAH:** He kin do dat; jes' leave it ter Dinah Johnson. (*she points to herself*) I'se tiahed o' seein' 'im workin' hisse'f ter def, leavin' heah 'fore sun-up an' comin' back 'way after sun-down. (*looking up at the clock*) Look what time 'tis now. (ZEKE *looks up at the clock. A knock is heard on door at rear*) Stop yer foolishness, Son-Boy, an' come on in heah. Yuh later 'nuff now. (*looking up at the clock*)

**SUSIE:** (*from the outside*) It's me, Aint Dinah.

**ZEKE:** Dat's Sister Suckie Jones, fetchin' yuh some mo' o'her troubles.

**DINAH:** Come in, Sister Suckie. (SUSIE *opens door at rear and comes in hurriedly, she looks scared*) Git close ter de fiah, Sister Suckie, I kno's yuh col'. (*gets chair and makes room for* SUSIE *at fireplace*) Move over fudder, Zeke. (ZEKE *moves back from fireplace*, SUSIE *sits down near fireplace. She warms her hands, blowing them at intervals*). Sister Suckie, y'mus' 'xcuse me fer speakin' dat away ter yuh. I thought yuh wuz Son-Boy cuttin' de foolishness. I don't kno' when he's been so pow'ful late comin' home ter he'p his mammy. I jes' feel lak blessin' 'im out. (SUSIE *stands up, shivering, then walks hurriedly towards rear door and returns*)

**ZEKE:** One o'dem spells comin' on yuh, Suk?

**SUSIE:** (*sitting down again near the fireplace and speaking with a quiver in her voice*) Naw sir, Uncle Zeke; but under de circumstances I jes' cain't he'p feelin' bad.

**DINAH:** (*going over to* SUSIE *and putting her arms around her*) Kin I he'p yuh, Sister Jones?

SUSIE: *(standing up)* No'm, Aint Dinah. *(wrings her hands)* 'Tain't nothin' de matter wid me—it's wid somebody else!

DINAH: *(standing straight up and placing her right hand on her right hip).* Do I kno' 'em?

SUSIE: *(moving farther away from* DINAH*)* Yeahs'm!

DINAH: *(going nearer* SUSIE, *and speaking rather excitedly)* Kin I he'p 'em, honey?

SUSIE: *(coming back to the fire and warming her hands)* I don't kno'm—yuh kno', Aint Dinah, when I wuz comin' down de road 'bout a mile away I saw a mob—de bigges' mob—

ZEKE: *(interrupting)* O'whar fo'ks?

DINAH: Y'aint nevah seen a mob o'niggers, is yuh? Dey cain't stick tergedder 'long enuff. *(turns to* SUSIE*)* Gwone, honey.

SUSIE: Dey wuz jes' lookin' fer some cullud boy.

ZEKE: *(smiling and speaking loudly)* I know'd it!

SUSIE: I slipped eroun' ter fin' out who 'twuz.

DINAH: *(coming nearer* SUSIE*)* Did y'fine' out, chile?

SUSIE: Yeahs'm.

DINAH: *(sympathetically)* Who wuz de poo' critter?

SUSIE: *(looking first in the fire and then at* DINAH*)* Er—er—er—I hates ter break de bad news ter yuh, Aint Dinah—

DINAH: *(interrupting excitedly)* Wuz it Son-Boy? *(kneeling down beside* SUSIE, *she looks up into her face inquiringly)* Wuz it my chile?* (*ZEKE *jumps up. He looks wild and puffs his pipe profusedly)*

SUSIE: Yeas'm. *(getting up excitedly, she pushes* DINAH *aside)* Dere, I'se done gone and spilled de beans an' tol' yuh ev'ything! I kno'd I hadn't oughter. Le'me go! *(she starts hurriedly towards door at rear)*

DINAH: *(getting between rear door and* SUSIE*)* Wait a minit, an' tell me somethin'!

SUSIE: Somebody heard 'im say he's gwine home an' git his gun. *(*ZEKE *goes out hurriedly through left side door)*

DINAH: *(looking at the clock)* Dey ain't gwine ter lynch my Son-Boy, is dey?

SUSIE: Dey said somethin' 'bout a necktie party.

DINAH: Good lawd, Sister Suckie! *(throws her arms around* SUSIE*).* What is dem white fo'ks murd'rin' my Son-Boy fer?

SUSIE: *(supporting* DINAH, *who weakly sits down in a chair)* Dey says he went an' gone in Miss Ann's room where he works.

**DINAH:** *(throwing up head and then bowing it)* Lawd have mercy! *(SUSIE pats DINAH on the shoulder and looks frightfully back at rear door)* Is dey cotch 'im yit?

**SUSIE:** No'm.

**DINAH:** *(throwing up her hands)* Thank Gawd! *(standing up)* Where kin dat boy be? *(She looks at the clock and begins walking up and down the floor. ZEKE comes in through left side door. He stands in middle of floor and looks at DINAH)*

**SUSIE:** *(keeping her eyes on DINAH)* But dey says dey ketches 'im dey's gwine ter do 'im worse'n dey done my boy. *(SUSIE goes out rear door. DINAH goes to closet and gets some clothes and begins changing them)*

**ZEKE:** Don't pay 'er no min'. She's on de way ter de bug house. She thinks dat dey's still lynchin' Sambo.

**DINAH:** Eb'n crazy fo'ks kno's what dey's talkin' 'bout sometimes. Somethin's de matter. Look what time 'tis. *(looks up at clock)*

**ZEKE:** *(looking up at clock)* Ef Son-Boy's bein' lynched what is yuh gwine ter do 'bout it?

**DINAH:** *(still dressing with her body half-way in closet and closet door half-way open)* What yuh axin' me fer? YOU'S a man— dat is, you's a piece o' one stuck up dere in dem britches! Is YOU too skerry ter he'p?

**ZEKE:** *(walking around room with pipe in his mouth upside down)* I would he'p, but I don't kno' where Son-Boy is.

**DINAH:** Y' don't want ter kno'.

**ZEKE:** I thought yuh'd kno'.

**DINAH:** Thought nothin'! How y'spect fer me ter kno'?

**ZEKE:** I thought yuh'd go out an' look fer 'im.

**DINAH:** Uv all de nerves—I ain't seen de lak in all my born days! Umph! Umph! Umph! ef dat don't beat all. Why don't yuh go out an' look fer 'im an' he'p 'im yerse'f? He's ez much yer Son-Boy ez he's mine.

**ZEKE:** I'se skeered de white fo'ks'll lynch me, fer when de mob gits mad dey's li'ble ter take any nigger dey see an' string 'em up.

**DINAH:** So dat's yer game! Don't min' 'em lynchin' me an' Son-Boy so long ez yer hide is safe. Well, take it f'om me, dis is one nigger dey ain't gwine ter lynch *(coming out of closet)*—an'

I'se gwine an' look fer Son-Boy, too. (*snatches irons from fire and leaves them on hearth*) I kin tell dat y'didn't come f'om a fightin' tribe (*putting on her hat*), an' dey ain't skeered o' nobody no time. Nobody ain't nevah beat 'em, neither. Dat's de stock I come f'om, an' dat's de stock I'se handing down ter Son-Boy (*looking around room hurriedly for shawl*).

**ZEKE:** De whar fo'ks got yuh lak dey did de othah niggers —I ain't seen no diff'ence.

**DINAH:** Dey didn't beat us. Dey fooled us on de boats. Heap uv us died ruther'n work fer somebody else fer nothin'. (*scatters clothes over bed, looking for shawl*)

**ZEKE:** I see YOU'S livin'.

**DINAH:** Y' kno' one thing, Zeke Johnson, me an' my fo'ks nevah wuz no slaves lak yuh an' yer fo'ks. (*finding shawl on bed, she fastens it around her shoulders*) My daddy bought our freedom on de 'stallment plan. His ol' master wuz tickled ter def ter git rid uv 'em dat way. Me an' Son-Boy is made out'n de same stuff. Ef I hafter buy Son-Boy's way f'om heah I'se gwine ter do it de same way.

(*In the meantime* ZEKE *has been standing in the middle of the floor, with his mouth wide open, listening to and gazing at* DINAH. DINAH *starts for door at rear. As she places her right hand on the door-knob,* SON-BOY *rushes in past* DINAH. *He is panting excitedly. His shirt is unbuttoned half-way down from the collar. His clothes are muddy. He is perspiring freely.* DINAH *stops and looks wildly at him.* ZEKE *drops his pipe.*)

**SON-BOY:** Dey's after me ma! Le'me git my gun! (*He runs out left side door into kitchen.* DINAH, *speechless, stands in center of floor and looks in the direction* SON-BOY *went*)

**ZEKE:** (*going towards rear door*) I'se gwine ter lock dis door right now. Where's de key, Dinah?

**DINAH:** (*going slowly towards left side door with her eyes set in that direction*) 'Tain't skercely dark; what y'lockin' de door fer?

**ZEKE:** (*looking around on the floor for the key*) De same reason dat Son-Boy's runnin' in heah so fas' fer.

**DINAH:** He's comin' heah ter pertect hisse'f. (*peeks through left side door at* SON-BOY)

**ZEKE:** An' dat's why I'se locking de do'—heah 'tis. *(picking up key off floor, he locks rear door)* Dat boy come in dis do' lak a streak o' lightin'. Don't tell me he ain't got no rabbit in 'im.

**DINAH:** Don't jedge 'im by yerse'f.

**ZEKE:** I ain't. I'se jedgin' dat black boy by de speed he makes.

*(*SON-BOY* comes in hurriedly through left-side door.)*

**DINAH:** I don't keer ef he is black—"fast black" nevah runs f'om nobody.

**SON-BOY:** *(disturbed)* I'se looked ev'ywhere! 'Tain't in dere! Where's it, Ma? Hurry! De bloodhounds on my tracks!

**ZEKE:** What is dey after yuh fer?

**DINAH:** *(going to closet to search for gun)* 'Tain't no time ter ax sich questions.

**SON-BOY:** *(looking under the bed and into different corners of the room)* Nothin'! Dey says somebody went in Miss Ann's room, an' cause dey sees me dressed up dey laid it on me. . . . Where's de gun?

**ZEKE:** *(sitting down and lighting his pipe)* I'se done took it out.

**SON-BOY:** *(astonished)* What fer, Pa?

**ZEKE:** *(with his head bowed)* I kno'd yuh'd come heah lookin' fer it—jes' lak yuh when y'gits in trouble. I ain't gwine ter let no whar fo'ks fin' no gun in heah when dey gits heah—an' den dey kills us all. I'se gwine ter pertect yuh dat much.

**DINAH:** *(taking off hat and shawl and throwing them on the bed)* Yuh's de bigges' coward in de worl'!

**SON-BOY:** Le'me git my razor den! *(He rushes out of left side-door)*

**ZEKE:** Y'kno' dey'll shoot us down lak dogs.

**DINAH:** Nobody nevah bothers a bitin' dog.

**ZEKE:** But dey shoots a mad dog, dough.

**DINAH:** Whilst dey's shooting' 'im he bites 'em, too. Nothin' badder'n a bite f'om a mad dog.

**SON-BOY:** *(coming in through left side door)* I cain't fin' dat razor! *(*ZEKE* drops his head and* DINAH *looks at him rebukingly)*

**DINAH:** *(rushing up to* ZEKE *and standing close beside him)* Where's dat razor, Zeke Johnson?

**ZEKE:** Don't y'think a person hafter shave?

**DINAH:** *(looking directly into* ZEKE'S *face)* Y'ain't shaved fer a month. Where's Son-Boy's razor? I ain't after a bit o'foolishness.

**ZEKE:** I lent it ter Uncle Remus ter shave wid, dis mornin'.

**DINAH:** Don't sit dere lying. Ef yuh's tellin' de truf, go an' git it.

**ZEKE:** Y'ain't tellin' me ter go out in dat dark an' git kilt. *(sauntering out through left side door)*

**DINAH:** *(standing in middle of floor with both hands on her hips she looks at* ZEKE *meanly as he goes out)* Hide in dat closet, Son-Boy. Yuh's too big ter hide under my dress lak yuh did when yuh's little an' de bouger-man wuz after yuh. . . . Yuh mammy'll go some where an' fin' yuh a gun. I ain't skeered o'de debbil hisse'f. *(*SON-BOY *starts into the closet)* Naw—don't go in dere; dat's de firs' place de mob'll look fer yuh. Le'me see! *(She stands thinking, holding her head in her hand. A few seconds later rapid, loud knocks are heard on door at rear)* Who's dat? *(*SON-BOY *runs towards left side-door and then comes back to middle of floor.* DINAH *speaks excitedly)* Zeke! Zeke! Come here! *(Rapid, loud knocks are again heard at rear door.* SON-BOY *runs towards closet.* DINAH *speaks nervously but softly)* Fer hev'ns sake, don't go in dere, I tol' yuh! *(Son-Boy opens his mouth as if to speak)* Don't speak ter me! Keep quiet! *(*DINAH *goes hurriedly to the bed and picks up clothes and a quilt)* Fall down on da flo'. *(*SON-BOY *gets down quickly on the floor and looks up questioningly at* DINAH. *In the meantime knocks have been heard again at rear door)* Zeke, come heah, I tol' you! *(covers up* SON-BOY *with clothes she took off bed and ironingboard)* Stay dere, an' don't move; dey'll think I'se gittin' ready fer ter wash.

**ZEKE:** *(coming in through left-side door and dragging his feet)* Where's Son-Boy? *(knocks are heard again at rear door, as if it is about to be broken open)*

**DINAH:** *(with her eyes on rear door)* None o'yer bizness.

**ZEKE:** What y'want wid me?

**DINAH:** *(pointing to rear door)* See who's at de do'.

**ZEKE:** Ain't yuh got two hands and foots?

**DINAH:** *(standing akimbo and staring meanly at* ZEKE*)* I didn't ax yuh dat. *(*ZEKE *starts towards left side door. She makes preparatory movements to go out)* Y'tend ter dis house whilst I goes out an' gets dem white fo'ks clo'es an' look for Son-Boy. *(*DINAH *having put on her hat and shawl goes to rear door and tries to open it)* Where's de key, Zeke?

**ZEKE:** *(standing on the sill of the left side door)* I ain't got it.

**DINAH:** *(coming towards* ZEKE*)* Gimme heah!

**ZEKE:** Fer what?

**DINAH:** What yuh reckon fer?

**ZEKE:** *(pointing to the rear door)* Ef y'go out o' dat do' yuh's gwine out lak a haint. Dem whar fo'ks waitin' out dere ter pounce yuh lak a dog do a rabbit.

**DINAH:** Dat ain't de onlies' do' in the de house. *(attempting to pass through left side door,* ZEKE *spreads himself out and prevents her)*

**ZEKE:** Ef y'goes out o'dis house now, yuh'll go over my dead body.

**DINAH:** *(giving* ZEKE *a hard push)* Dat won't be hard ter do. *(She goes out of left side door.* SON-BOY *grunts and turns;* ZEKE *looks at him)*

**ZEKE:** *(standing near left side door, looking at* DINAH*)* Ef y'gits kilt don't ax me ter bury yuh—*(softly)* Son-Boy, ain't dere no mo' dirty clo'es 'roun' heah?

**SON-BOY:** *(softly)* Hush, pa! De mob's standin' on de outside, listenin'.

**ZEKE:** *(softly)* I kno' dat mobs comin' in thu de back doo' now. *(*ZEKE *runs and gets into closet. A few seconds later* DINAH *and* JOE *come in through left side-door.* JOE *is a brown-skin boy and is about eighteen years of age. He is wearing overalls, an old felt hat, and dirty shoes. He looks older than his years)*

**JOE:** Good thing y'call me, Aint DINAH; I wuz goin' agin an' look fer Son-Boy. Y'all sho's hard ter hear. Y'aint seen Son-Boy, is yuh?

**DINAH:** I thought y'wuz col'. Git ter de fiah. *(*JOE *goes to the fireplace and begins warming his hands)* What y'want wid Son-Boy? *(impatiently)* Talk fast! I'se got ter go.

**JOE:** Nothin', Aint Dinah, I jes' had somethin' ter tell 'im.

**DINAH:** Tell me, I'se his mammy.

**JOE:** *(hesitantly).* Ef—er—de mob wuz after 'im ter lynch 'im.

**DINAH:** *(astonished)* What fer?

**JOE:** *(sitting down near fireplace).* Ol' Snow-Ball took'n lied on Son-Boy. De way dey tells it: Somebody went in Miss Ann's room ter steal somethin, an' she holloed. When she screamed a man 'bout Son-Boy's size run out de house. Snow-Ball wuz in de road, an' he seen de man run ter de barn. Den some white mens, dey comes out 'cause dey heard de screamin'. Dey ax Snow-Ball, "Who wuz it?" He says, "I don't kno', sar." Den dey ax 'im, "What did he look lak?" Snow-Ball says, "He had a black face an' black hands." Den one o'de white fo'ks says, "You's tryin' ter conceal a black nigger lak yerse'f." Snow-Ball den acts jes' ez skerred ez he coul' be! Anothah white man holloes at 'im, "Wuzn't it Son-Boy Johnson? Ef y'don't say it wuz we'll 'string' you." By dat time heap uv 'em had got 'roun' 'im, and Snow-Ball says, "Yaas-sar." Den dey runs ter de barn jes' ez fas' ez dey coul' go, but, ez de lawd woul' have it, dey didn't saw nobody. Dey den gits de blood-hounds.

**DINAH:** Did dey catch 'im?

**JOE:** Y'mean Son-Boy?

**DINAH:** Who's y'spect I means? He's de onlies' person I evah born in dis worl'.

**ZEKE:** *(creeping out of closet).* Dinah—

**DINAH:** *(interrupting)* Hush yer mouth, skerry. What y'doin' in dat closet?

**ZEKE:** I'se tryin' ter fin my jack-knife fer Son-Boy. I kno'd dat mob would git heah 'fore y'got back.

**DINAH:** Talk on, Joe—Don't pay 'im no min'.

**JOE:** No'm—Dey didn't ketch Son-Boy. He got away. Ef he didn't come heah he mus' be hidin' in de swamps. 'Taint no use uv'em bein' skeered no mo'.

**DINAH:** Skeered? 'Tain't but one sorry person skeered in dis house, an' dat's Son-Boy's ol' no 'count daddy. *(casts her eye at* ZEKE)

**ZEKE:** No, Dinah—

**DINAH:** *(interrupting)* Son-Boy's lak me—he kno's dey cain't do nothing' 'cept kill 'im, case he ain't got but one time ter die.

**ZEKE:** 'Tain't no use o'dyin' 'till yer time comes.

**DINAH:** Yuh's gwine ter be too skeery ter die when Gabriel blows his horn.

**ZEKE:** Don't cross de bridges 'fore y'git ter 'em.

**DINAH:** A person who's too skeered ter pertect hisse'f fer livin', is too skeered ter prepare hisse'f fer dyin'.

**ZEKE:** Don't worry; I'll be ready.

**DINAH:** Me an' Son-Boy's ready now. Ef y'don't b'lieve it let 'em bother us.

**JOE:** Dey ain't gwine ter bother yuh, Aint Dinah.

**DINAH:** *(courageously)* Y'ain't telling' me a thing I don't kno'.

**JOE:** Dey's cotch de right man.

**DINAH:** *(staring hard at* JOE, *with her hands on her hips)* Is yuh tellin' de truf, Joe Lincoln Washington?

**JOE:** Yeahs'm. *(raises his right hand)* I 'clare 'fore de lawd!

**DINAH:** You an' Son-Boy's buddies. Yuh wouldn't lie on 'im, turn traitor ter yer race an' git 'im kilt?

**JOE:** No'm. I tells de truf an' shame de debbil.

**DINAH:** Thanks Gawd! *(claps and throws up her hands)* Hallejujah! Praise de Lawd! My prayers done answered! Thank Gawd!

**JOE:** An' I tells a lie ef it saves Son-Boy. I sticks wid 'im ter de las'.

**DINAH:** *(glancing at* ZEKE*)* Dat's mo'n his ol' no 'count daddy would do fer 'im.

**ZEKE:** *(sitting down leisurely)* I he'p brung 'im in ter de worl'. Dat's mo'n anybody else 'sides you's done fer 'im. I didn't bargain ter he'p take 'im out.

**DINAH:** I kno' it wuzn't my Son-Boy! *(She is still clapping her hands)* He's a good boy!

**ZEKE:** Who did dey ketch?

**DINAH:** What y'want ter kno' fer? So y'kin go an' he'p 'im out?

**ZEKE:** Dat's my bizness.

**DINAH:** *(uncovering* SON-BOY*)* Come on out f'om yer hidin' place, Son-Boy. You'se safe. *(*SON-BOY *stands up,* DINAH *embraces him)* I kno'd yu' didn't done it.

**JOE:** *(embracing* SON-BOY*)* Shore is glad 'twuzn't you, Son-Boy!

**SON-BOY:** Betcha *I* is. Y'kno' I didn't do it, Joe. But ef dey HAD ter lynch me fer nothin' I wus gwine ter make 'em lynch me fer somethin'.

**DINAH:** *(taking off her hat and shawl)* Dat's right, Son-Boy; dat's right.

**ZEKE:** Yuh nevah did tell me what dey nigger did ketch.

**DINAH:** What makes y'thinks it hafter be a nigger?

**ZEKE:** 'Cause de white fo'ks says so.

**SON-BOY:** *(looking at* ZEKE *disgustedly)* Looka heah, pa, don't yuh nevah gits tiahed o'usin' dat word "nigger"? I gits tiahed o'hearin' it. Y'gits so mad y'could turn green ef a white man called yuh "nigger." Stop usin' it yerse'f, den.

**DINAH:** Perhaps, den, yuh stop bein' so skerry. *(She goes into closet to change clothes)*

**ZEKE:** Dat's my bizness. Where did dey cotch 'im, son?

**JOE:** In his own barn.

**SON-BOY:** I kno' who 'twuz, Joe.

**ZEKE:** Who wuz it?

**DINAH:** *(with her head out of closet)* Don't tell 'im nothin'.

**SON-BOY:** I ain't, fer he might tell de white fo'ks.

**JOE:** Dey caught de RIGHT one.

**ZEKE:** Don't no nig—(SON-BOY *looks cuttingly at* ZEKE*)*—I mean, don't no culled fo'ks own no barns 'roun' heah.

**JOE:** When dey caught 'im he wuz takin' de blackn' off'n his face an' han's.

**DINAH:** *(with her head out of closet)* What yuh say ter dat, Zeke Johnson?

**ZEKE:** Ef Son-Boy hadn't took ter his heels he'd been one dead cullud boy. Don't tell me dat a good run ain't better'n a bad stand. (DINAH *comes out of closet. She is dressed in her regular house-clothes)* I ain't got no time ter fool wid yuh. *(goes into the closet)* I'se got ter go an' see Mars Ross 'bout some work. *(puts his hat on)*

**DINAH:** It's dark out dere, *little culled baby.* Ain't yuh skerred?

**ZEKE:** Dat's my bizness. *(Going to rear door, he unlocks it)*

**DINAH:** Runnin' 'way lak a whip dog. Ev'rybody kicks a no-'count dog.

**ZEKE:** It's bes' ter be a no-'count dog dan ter be a dead dog.

**SON-BOY:** I'd ruther be a dead dog dan a kicked-eroun' dog. Dey cain't eben use a dead dog; ef dey do de dead dog don't kno' nothin' 'bout it. (ZEKE *goes out rear door.*)

**DINAH:** Y'aint gwine ter be no dog a-tall, Son-Boy. Yuh's gwine ter be a great big man! Dat yuh is! How ol' is yuh now?

**SON-BOY:** Y'all says I wus born when dat big storm come thu an' blowed down dat big hic'ry tree mos' nigh ter de creek.

**JOE:** Pa says dat'll be twenty years ago dis year when we starts ter pickin' cotton.

**DINAH:** It'll take yuh jes' er 'bout twenty years ter git de learnin' dat I wants yuh ter have. Yuh'll be how ol', den?

**SON-BOY:** (*counting on his fingers*) One, two, three, er—er —four—five, er (*changing the count from one finger to the other*). One, two, er—dat won't git it. How many, Joe?

**JOE:** (*counting*) Twenty an' twenty is er—is—er—

**SON-BOY:** Le'me see. Twenty an' twenty is—er—er—is— er—gi'me a piece o'paper an' a cedar pencil, Ma. (DINAH *looks in the drawer of the table, finds paper and gives it to* SON-BOY. *She looks on the mantel-piece for pencil, finds it and gives it to him.* JOE *comes and looks over* SON-BOY'S *shoulder, and they both begin to figure.* DINAH *looks on, also.*)

**JOE:** Forty.

**SON-BOY:** (*still looking down on the paper*) Dat's right.

**DINAH:** Den yuh'll have all yer life 'fore yuh ter be a big man an' have somethin'. I'll he'p yuh ef I hafter work my finger nails off takin' in washin' an' i'nin'.

**JOE:** I guess I'll be gwine now, Aint Dinah; Son-Boy's all right. (*Getting up to go.*)

**DINAH:** Stay ter dunner. I'se gwine ter fix somethin' good —somethin' yuh an' Son-Boy both laks. I kno' yuh an' Son-Boy's hongry, dodgin' an' runnin' f'om de white fo'ks. Yer daddy had ter go an' eat all dem 'taters up f'om yuh. Go in de kitchen, Son-Boy' an' make a fiah in de stove.

**SON-BOY:** Yeahs'm. (SON-BOY *goes out side door left, and* JOE *follows him.* DINAH *picks up the clothes off the floor, cleans up, and sings again*):

Before I'd be a slave

I'd be buried in my grave,
And go home to my father and be saved.

(Curtain)

# RALF M. COLEMAN
## (1898–197?)

▼▼▼▼▼▼▼▼▼▼▼▼

Ralf Coleman was born in Newark, New Jersey, to Meshack and Ellen (Johnson) Coleman. One of his high school teachers helped him to decide on his future career by making him memorize scenes from Shakespeare. He studied theatre at Harvard University under H. W. L. Dana and later at the Provincetown Wharf Theatre and the Boston Experimental Theatre. In 1918, he married Luella F. Burnett of Boston, with whom he had two children, J. Riche and Leona. He worked in the garment business for twenty-five years while he raised his children and became one of the pioneers of the little theatre movement that enriched the cultural life of New England.

About the time the Harlem Renaissance was sending out its early ripples, he joined the first Black community theatre in Boston, the Allied Arts Center. Supported by affluent residents of Beacon Hill, by 1926 it had become the showcase of Black artists in New England. Coleman directed studio plays and at least three productions a year. When the Center became affiliated with the Ford Hall Forum, Coleman was called upon to lead the Ford Hall Players. He made his professional debut as a director in a converted barn on Beacon Hill. The first three plays he directed were written with Black actors in mind: *Simon the Cyrene*, *Granny Maumee*, and *The Dreamy Kid*.

He then formed a new group called The Boston Players, composed mostly of former Allied Arts actors. He directed plays from Broadway at the Fine Arts Theatre for three or four years, introducing a program of technical training to develop his performers' skills. Around 1931, the Boston Players were doing *Scarlet Sister Mary* when Margaret Hughes, a play broker, came up to see their production and, impressed, told Coleman that she had an option on a play by Paul Green called *Potter's Field*. Would Coleman like to act in it on The Great White Way? With his years of experience in serious community theatre behind him, Coleman welcomed the chance to make his Broadway debut as the romantic lead in Green's play, renamed *Roll, Sweet Chariot*. When the play closed after a month's run, Coleman returned to Boston and was chosen in 1935 to direct the Negro Federal Theatre Project of Massachusetts, His brother Warren, an accomplished actor, remained in New York to create the role of Crown in *Porgy and Bess*.

Coleman wrote plays, acted, and directed, as well as managed a unit of 150 people during the FTP's four years (1935–1939). He did not have to contend with censorship, but pressure from the audience, black and white, and the FTP's response to the community, necessarily limited his freedom of choice. As a practical man of the theatre, he aimed his productions at his vision of the "average audience." His mission, he felt, was to entertain, not to teach or uplift. For example, when the play *Jericho* proved to be "too countrified" for Boston, he added music and New York nightclubs, adapting to his actors and his audience. His larger purpose was to please as many people as he could with good theatre. However, when FTP officials objected to his decision to put on the controversial play *Stevedore*, about a courageous Black man who dies defending himself against white bosses, he arranged to have his unit rehearse it on their own time in preparation for a non-FTP production. Frank Silvera, who would become one of the outstanding actors in the American theatre, played in most of the unit's productions.

During World War II, he produced and directed plays for the USO circuit and for the NAACP and the Negro College Fund in

Boston. He also acted as stage manager for the highly successful *Anna Lucasta* on Broadway, in Chicago, and on tour (1945–49). In the following years, he served as theatrical editor for *The Boston Sun*, *The Boston Times*, and the *New Boston Citizen* and was elected president of Saturday Night Quill Club, an organization of local creative writers that included Joseph S. Mitchell and Alvira Hazzard. From 1969 until his retirement, Coleman directed such Black plays as *Growin' in Blackness*, *Family Portrait*, *Happy Ending*, and *Tamborines to Glory* for the Negro Repertory Theatre, based in nearby Roxbury.

In 1972, after celebrating his 55th wedding anniversary, Coleman retired and began to write his memoirs, covering a varied career of half a century in the theatre. His eldest granddaughter taught mathematics at Princeton University and another granddaughter had her own TV show on Channel 5 in Boston.

*The Girl From Back Home* (also known as *The Girl from Bama*) was first published in *Saturday Evening Quill* of 1929 and first performed that same year. The action occurs in a Harlem apartment during the height of the bootlegging era (which, incidentally, coincided with the Renaissance). The Girl, the mistress of a Harlem racketeer who wants to escape from the desperate circumstances in which she is living, remains one-dimensional. The play really belongs to the man named Jazz, the prototype of the womanizing, swashbuckling, "bad ass" Black protagonists who became stereotyped in the Hollywood films of the seventies. Lacking the political context so essential for the contemporary playwright, Coleman's melodrama strongly implies that the individual rather than the social order is totally responsible for one's fate. However, a later play, *Swing Song* (1937), his full-length treatment of lynching, implies the opposite.

# THE GIRL FROM BACK HOME

## Ralf M. Coleman

### CAST

HENRY "JAZZ" BARRETT, *numbers "banker" and man about town*
DELLA HARVEY, *the girl*
DR. LEE MINOR, *also from "back home"*

*Time:* The present
*Place:* Barrett's flat, in Harlem

*"Right" and "Left" refer to the actor's right and left.*

*Living room, comfortably furnished. Victrola, table, center; flat topped desk with telephone, papers, etc., up left side. Two doors right; upper, bath room, lower, bedroom. One door down left. Window center, back. As curtain rises* DELLA *is discovered with negligee thrown carelessly around her, hastily packing suitcase. She glances ever so often at door, left, and at wrist watch. Packs last few things, goes into bedroom down right and appears immediately dressed for street. Sits at desk up left, writes note, addresses it, places it in upright position on desk. Takes handbag and suitcase, and with last look around, starts for exit down left. As she gets center stage, she stops in horror as key grates in lock and the door she is about to exit*

First published in *The Saturday Evening Quill*, April 1929.

*from slowly opens.* DELLA *looks around in confusion, as if for a place to hide.* "JAZZ" BARRETT *enters. He is about 35, tall, well dressed and good looking, but his face is hard and cruel and betrays his selfish, conceited nature. There is an awkward silence for a moment, during which they eye each other.*

**JAZZ:** *(quietly, as he advances to center)* Goin' away?

**DELLA:** *(in confusion)* Er—er—No.—*(Catching herself.)* (I mean—Yes.

**JAZZ:** *(as if he hadn't heard)*—Beg pardon?

**DELLA:** *(more firmly).* I said—yes.

**JAZZ:** *(calmly)* Taking French leave? *(He puts hat on table.)*

**DELLA:** *(bursting out)* No, dear—I—I was going to run by the club and tell you. I'm just running over to Newark for a few days. I called up Margie and she's terribly sick—wants me to come right over and look out for things. *(Looks searchingly at him.)* Really, dear. *(Setting down suitcase and taking note from desk.)* See—I wrote you a note—but you won't need it now. *(Puts note in handbag and goes to* JAZZ *and puts arms around his neck.)* How is it you're home so early, dear? Thought you were going to Jersey City.

**JAZZ:** *(looking straight into her eyes)* I've changed my plans —got to wait for a 'phone call. *(Slowly.)* I didn't know Margie was even sick.

**DELLA:** I didn't, either, dear. But you know we haven't seen her for days, so I just thought I'd call. Lucky I did, poor kid. She's pretty sick.

**JAZZ:** *(seemingly reassured)* That's tough. I'll drive over for you later on. Got a big deal on tonight, and I've got to meet Slim Henders at the Ebony Club in five minutes. *(*JAZZ *looks at watch and goes to desk, picking up a few papers.* DELLA *glances at her watch and then watches* JAZZ *for a moment.)*

**DELLA:** *(earnestly)* Listen, Jazz-boy. When are we going to be married?

**JAZZ:** *(coming down center, with half interested laugh)* Married? Say, what the hell!—Is that thing eatin' you again? You've got everything that money kin buy. Ain't 'cher? Clothes, automobile, jewelry—and ain't Jazz Barrett looking out for you? Ain't that enough? Married? People don't bother about that in New York. Forget it!

**DELLA:** *(hurt)* It's been a—a—year, now, Jazz, and I—I—

**JAZZ:** *(pulling her roughly to him and kissing her)* There—there, kid. You know I'm crazy 'bout you—and that's a whole lot. Why, every gal in New York envies you. When you pass along the street in that swell roadster, they all nudge each other and says, "There's Jazz Barrett's gal—Ain't she the lucky dog!" *(Pats her.)* You ain't got nuthin' to worry about, kid. I've taken care of you for over a year—that's as good as being married—ain't it? *(Kisses her.)* There. I'm goin' to run along. Might not get over for you at Margies 'till late, but I'll be there. *(Taking hat.)* If a call comes for me tell 'em I'm over at the Ebony. *(Puts on hat and crosses to door down left.)*

**DELLA:** *(running to him)* Jazz dear—'er—won't it be too late for you to drive over for me? You'll be awfully tired, too.

**JAZZ:** *(watching her)* Oh, I don't mind.

**DELLA:** All right. *(Kisses him.)* Goodby.

**JAZZ:** *(slowly)* 'Er—goodby, kid. *(He looks at her a moment, then exits quickly.* DELLA *leans against door, thinking deeply. Suddenly seems to remember, looks at watch, takes note from bag, places it upright on desk and exits hurriedly, left, leaving handbag on table and putting out lights. A moment later the door opens and* JAZZ *reenters. He snaps on lights, goes into rooms, looking around. Coming out, he sees note on desk.)*

**JAZZ:** *(reading note)* "Dear Jazz-boy: I can't stand it any longer. I'm going far away from it all. I've got to do it. With Milly Danvers and all the other women—you won't miss me. Please let me go, and wish me luck, as I do you with all my heart. Goodby forever—Dell." *(Bitterly.)* Just what I thought—Damn her. *(Laughs.)* There's a good joke on Jazz Barrett—a woman throws him over. Never been heard of before. I generally do all the throwing. *(More seriously.)* She can't do that to me. *(Throws hat on table. Sees purse and his face lights up as he takes it and starts to examine contents. 'Phone rings.)*

**JAZZ:** *(at 'phone)* Hello—hello. Yes, Jazz Barrett speaking. Oh, hello, Spike. What's up? Good! Forty cases. No, don't give him a cent more. Any hits today? What! Let them try and collect. Listen. Dell just gave me the air. Can you imagine it!—Well off and didn't know it. Sure. Say, but you know can't no one woman hold *me* down. *(Laughs.)* How's Julia? Tell her I'll see her tonight. She'll be glad to hear the good news—so will Milly. What? Sure, I was out with Milly the other night. What about it? Oh, he is, is he? Ha—ha! Milly's husband, Jim Danvers, looking for me with a gun! Say, that's a hot one. She's some kid, and with a husband like that, no wonder she wants a real man once in a while. Sure, he owes me two hundred bucks and needs more. I'll give him another loan and he'll forget it. Money talks, eh? Who, Della? Sure, I guess she's gone for good. Hope so. I've been trying to give her the air for a long time. Oh, I'm not worrying. You know me. Well, I'm going over to the Ebony. Say, they've put some new dicks on the force, so keep your eye open. See you later, Spike. so long. *(Hangs up receiver and sits back, looking at purse and envelope. Speaks bitterly.)* Only I'd like to have the chance to make up with her and then throw her over. The dirty little quitter. *(Noise of steps heard outside.* JAZZ, *taking purse, walks quickly across room to door down left, snapping out lights and standing behind door so as to be unseen when it opens.* DELLA *enters quickly, leaving door open. Light from hall streams in. She looks around, breaths sigh of relief, and goes to table, feeling for purse.)*

**DELLA:** *(softly)* Why, I'm sure—I must have left it here. Oh, I haven't got a moment to lose! Where?— *(*JAZZ *slowly closes the door, shutting off light, and stands against it.)*

**DELLA:** *(with scream)* Oh!—Who are you? Who is it?

**JAZZ:** *(quietly snapping on lights)* Are you looking for something?

**DELLA:** *(trying to conceal her surprise)* Why—yes—Jazz— My, you frightened me! Yes, I've—I've lost my handbag.

**JAZZ:** *(holding it out)* This one?

**DELLA:** *(eagerly going to him)* Why, yes, dear. Why, where—

**JAZZ:** *(throwing purse on desk and seizing her with both hands, hisses)* You dirty little quitter! Thought you could double cross the Kid, eh? After all I've done for you! *(Sneeringly.)* Just going over to Margie's for a few days, and if you hadn't forgot your purse, I'd never seen you again. *(Seizing her by the throat.)* Tryin' to make a fool out of Jazz Barrett, eh? I'll kill you for this!

**DELLA:** *(choking)* Please!—Jazz, for—God's—sake—don't!

**JAZZ:** *(releasing her)* No— No— I want to know a few things first. *(More quietly.)* Who's the bimbo you're running away with? Tom Hally?

**DELLA:** *(sobbing)* No—no. Not Tom.

**JAZZ:** Then who the hell is it?

**DELLA:** *(to herself)* I guess it's all off. I wouldn't been happy nohow. It's all up—

**JAZZ:** *(savagely)* You're damn right it's all up, and if you don't come clean *(leaning toward her)* I'll break your neck!

**DELLA:** *(hopelessly)* All right—all right. *(Sits in chair down center.)*

**JAZZ:** *(pulling one up beside her)* Well, shoot!

**DELLA:** *(nervously)* I don't know where to begin, now you're listening. I've tried a thousand times to tell you—and now you're listening, I can't remember a word—I—

**JAZZ:** *(cutting in)* This hadn't better be no framed up story.

**DELLA:** It's going to be the God's truth, Jazz. *(Pauses.)* Every time I asked you to marry me you laughed—just as if it was a joke. I was a decent girl once, back home. Maybe you don't believe me, but I was. And I had ideals once. Wanted to be a wife —a real one—with a home and kids—legitimate ones. See? *(Looks closely at him.)* Oh, I know I don't deserve it now,—cause—cause I ain't nothin now. But I had planned things different, Jazz. When I came here to Aunty from back home I was good—I was— er—er—

**JAZZ:** *(roughly)* Aw, you can't blame me for starting you wrong—

**DELLA:** I know it wasn't you. Aunty died and I just drifted into bad company. But I wanted life—lights—gayety—fun! *(Sobs.)* Things had been so tough—so dark and still back home, and I wanted to play enough to make up for it—and forget. *(Pleadingly.)* But I—but I didn't go the limit, Jazz. I—I—I stayed good till—'till I met you—

**JAZZ:** *(hotly)* What!

**DELLA:** Honest to God.

**JAZZ:** That's a lie! Why, you were Sam Connor's gal before I took you away from him, and—

**DELLA:** Yes, I know, but—

**JAZZ:** And Hip Brown's before that, and—

**DELLA:** *(with spirit)* Yes, and a dozen others' before him. *(More quietly.)* But I never really fell for them, Jazz. That's why I kept giving them the air.

**JAZZ:** 'Aw, a lot of boloney.

**DELLA:** Oh, I wish it was—but it's the God's truth, Jazz.

**JAZZ:** *(impatiently)* Well, go on.

**DELLA:** When we first started together I was as happy as I could be. I knew you were a big sport—had plenty of good looks and money, and that all the women were crazy about you. I knew, too, that you weren't a one-woman man. But you seemed to care so much for me that I was foolish enough to believe that I could change your ways. *(More softly.)* I hear all about your escapades—affairs—Julia Harris, Wenda Davis, even Margie, and Milly Danvers. I've been afraid, too, that some day you'd get into a lot of trouble with the men—Like Milly's husband, Jim Danvers. He's a bad actor when he's liquored up. But I'm not naturally jealous, and so long as you did everything for me I ought to feel pretty lucky. And it did flatter me to know you didn't want me to know about them, and didn't openly flaunt them in my face. But I felt, too, that if you married me I'd have a right to say something then. *(Slower.)* But I saw you didn't have no intentions of marrying me —and I couldn't help but worry. I'd been brought up different, and I can't do like these New York girls—and like it. *(Softly.)* Then, too, I—I thought—suppose something should happen. *(Hides face in hands.)* God, I'd rather die than become the mother of a nameless child. *(She sobs.)*

**JAZZ:** *(uneasily)* 'Aw—that ain't nothin'. Happens every day.

**DELLA:** *(with spirit)* But it'll never happen to me, Jazz. That's why I started thinking about going away. *(Dropping her voice.)* And then I—I met Lee.

**JAZZ:** Lee? Lee Johnson?

**DELLA:** No, Lee Minor. You don't know him. He was an old sweetheart of mine back home. We grew up together, and all our folks knew each other, and everybody in Clover thought we were going to be married. Well, I just up and went away—and didn't write back or anything, and I was hoping he would forget me. *(Sadly.)* And marry some one else. But he didn't—and he came way up here to New York—looking for me.

JAZZ: *(grunts disgustly)* Humph!

DELLA: *(continuing)* He's a big doctor now—back home —and he found me the other night on Lenox Avenue. I walked right into him—

JAZZ: Last Monday night, eh? So that's where you were until after three!

DELLA: At first I tried to hide my identity, but he knew me so well and seemed so glad to see me, that I couldn't freeze him out. So he took me to Martin's for supper and we had a long talk.

JAZZ: *(cynically)* And to make a long story short, you and him planned to run back to the sticks together, eh? *(Sneering.)* How romantic!

DELLA: *(pleading)* Oh, Jazz! I didn't know what to do. I —I do care a lot for you. I thought for a long time I really loved you. *(Pause.)* Maybe it's the life you represent—the fascination and all that *(Determinedly.)* But I couldn't stand for it any longer. *(She bows her head.)*

JAZZ: *(snapping)* Couldn't stand what?

DELLA: Not being married. *(Earnestly.)* I want to live decent, Jazz—like respectable people. Have a home—husband— babies. Live within the law. *(Sobs.)* Oh, I'm sick of this life. *(Buries face in hands.)*

JAZZ: *(lying)* Well—well, suppose I say I'll marry you.

DELLA: *(hardly believing her ears)* Really? I don't know— but I think I'd be the happiest woman in the world.

JAZZ: *(slyly)* And you'll forget this bozo from back home.

DELLA: *(jumping up—looking at watch)* Oh, I forgot. He's waiting for me—I must go and tell—

JAZZ: *(quickly)* No you don't. Where is he? I'll attend to him. *(Takes hat.)*

DELLA: No, no, dear. *(Pause.)* Wait, I'll get him on the 'phone. *(Goes to desk.)*

JAZZ: *(lighting cigarette)* Aw right, go ahead and tell him it's all off and to catch the next train far Bam alone.—'Cause you're going to marry Jazz Barrett. *(Under his breath.)* Maybe.

*(Loudly.)* And if he keeps hanging around New York, trying to see you, he's liable to go back in a box.

**DELLA:** *(at telephone)* Bradhurst 2671. Yes. Hello—waiting room, 125th street station? Will you please page Dr. Lee Minor? Yes, Lee Minor. He must be waiting there. Thanks. *(Looks at* JAZZ.*)* Hello, is that you, Lee? Della speaking. Yes—yes—I know. I'm sorry, but I can't go with you. No—never. I know—I promised—But please—

**JAZZ:** *(cutting in)* Aw, tell him to go to—

**DELLA:** *(raising hand)* Sssh! *(To 'phone.)* Listen, Lee. I've changed my mind. I'm not going back home with you. I can't. *(Sob in voice.)* Please, don't ask me why or try any more to see me. I'm sorry. Go back home and forget me. Goodbye—and good luck. *(Hangs up receiver sharply.)*

**JAZZ:** *(pleased)* Atta baby! You're showing some sense now. *(Putting arms around her.)* Want to go back home and starve to death with some hick doctor who don't know what it's all about? Why, you'd die of lonliness, down there behind the sun, for good old New York and Jazz Barrett. *(Brightly.)* Forget it, and we'll go to Stumble Inn and celebrate.

**DELLA:** I tell you, dear. You go out and get some eats— chop suey, ice cream and everything, and we'll celebrate here— just you and me.

**JAZZ:** *(putting on hat)* That suits me for tonight. *(Slyly.)* And tomorrow I'll spring a little surprise, eh?

**DELLA:** *(putting suitcase, hat, etc., in bedroom, she comes out and bustles about)* Now, hurry, and I'll get things fixed. *(*JAZZ *watches her closely with sneer, but when she looks up he smiles and exits left. When door closes behind him* DELLA *goes to desk and looks thoughtfully at 'phone. Gives deep sigh, gets up briskly, and starts victrola. She goes into bedroom down right, leaving door open. Knock is heard at door, left.* DELLA, *humming in bedroom, does not hear. Knock comes louder.* DELLA *comes out, stops victrola, and returns to bedroom. Knock comes much louder.)*

**DELLA:** *(at door arranging hair)* Come in, dear, the door's open. *(Goes back into room.)* *(Door opens and* LEE MINOR *enters. He is around middle age and, in direct contrast to* JAZZ, *is conservative in dress and appearance. He has a kindly, honest face—a typical* *"country gentleman." He looks around, then hesitantly advances to center stage.)*

**DELLA:** *(from inside)* Why, Jazz dear, you certainly made time. *(Comes to door, sees* LEE, *starts back in horror.)* Why—Lee—you—here?

**LEE:** *(brightly)* Why, what's the big idea, Dell? You didn't think you could shake me as easy as that, did you? After all these weary months I've spent looking for you! I couldn't go back home alone. *(Seeing her dismay.)* Why, what on earth has changed you so?—

**DELLA:** *(in tense whisper)* For God's sake, Lee, how did you know where to find me?

**LEE:** *(laughing)* Easy enough. I just called back and asked Central the number of the party that called me and the rest was easy.

**DELLA:** *(entreatingly)* Lee, you shouldn't have come. I asked you not to look for me again. I—I can't have you here. Please—please go at once!

**LEE:** *(bewildered)* Come, Dell. You've got to give me some reason. You didn't act like this last time I saw you, and we arranged to go back together tonight. *(Pleading.)* You'll never regret it, dear. You know I own my own place—cozy little farm—and I'm as good a farmer as a doctor. And then, too, I'm the only doctor in Clover, so, you see, I'll be able to take care of you right. You won't have to worry about anything. *(Softer.)* All the home folks will be tickled to death to see you, Dell. Just think!

**DELLA:** *(hysterical)* No—no, Lee! Please don't tempt me any more or stay here a moment longer. Go, for God's sake!

**LEE:** *(looking around and seeing desk and man's things, puzzled)* Why, I thought you lived here all alone. *(Looking at her closely.)* You aren't married, are you?

**DELLA:** *(confused)* No—er *(catching herself)*—I mean—Yes. Yes, I am.

**LEE:** *(surprised)* Why didn't you tell me? *(Pause.)* And you were going to leave your husband for me? *(Sternly.)* Then he can't be treating you right!

**DELLA:** *(more confused)* Yes—yes, he is—Oh, I can't explain. He might come in any moment. *(Looks in terror toward door, left.)*

**LEE:** *(desperately)* I don't care—I know you're not happy, and I won't go without you. *(Passionately.)* I love you, Della. Have always loved you. *(Forcibly taking her in his arms.)* You promised to go back home with me—and you're going! *(Door opens and* JAZZ *enters. He has several large paper bags in his hands. Upon seeing him,* DELLA *shrinks away from* LEE *up stage between them.* LEE *faces* JAZZ.)

**JAZZ:** *(sarcastically, closing door)* I've evidently messed up a party.

**LEE:** *(politely)* I beg pardon, sir. *(He looks at* DELLA *appealingly.)*

**DELLA:** *(timidly)* This is—Dr. Lee Minor, and he—er—

**JAZZ:** *(putting hat and the bags on the table)* Oh, the horse doctor from Bam, eh?

**DELLA:** *(quickly to* LEE*)* And this is—is my husband Henry "Jazz" Barrett.

**JAZZ:** *(in anger)* Like hell it is! *(*DELLA *hides her face.)*

**LEE:** *(loudly)* What?

**JAZZ:** *(hotly)* You heard me! I'm not her husband or any other woman's. *(Evil leer.)* Fact is, Mister Doctor, she's my—

**DELLA:** *(screaming)* No! No!

**LEE:** *(advancing to* JAZZ*)* Careful, sir. I love this girl, and I won't have you or anyone else say a word against her.

**JAZZ:** *(bitterly)* Oh, is that so? Well, she's changed a lot since you knew her, and when I get through telling you what she is now, you'll—

**LEE:** *(loudly, with face close to* JAZZ*)* You're not going to tell me anything, Big Boy. She's the same girl to me she always was, and if she's gone wrong, it's the fault of dirty, stinking yellow dogs like you, who go about like ravaging wolves corrupting and destroying the bodies and souls of womankind.

**JAZZ:** *(in astonishment)* Well, I'll be damned!

**LEE:** *(boldly)* Get your things, Della—we're going back home! *(*DELLA *hesitates a moment, then starts for bedroom, down right. The two men eye each other face to face, ready to strike.)*

**LEE:** *(loudly, fists clenched)* Well, have you any objections? *(*JAZZ *eyes him a moment, then slinks backward, afraid. He goes to desk with evil look and sits with one leg upon it.)*

**JAZZ:** *(lighting cigarette)* You're welcome to her.

**LEE:** *(mockingly)* Thanks. *(DELLA, with suitcase, etc., is ready to go.* LEE *goes to door, with hat, holding door open.)*

**DELLA:** *(mid stage, to* JAZZ*)* I'm glad I found you out before it was too late. I don't believe you ever intended to marry me.

**JAZZ:** *(coldly)* I wouldn't marry the best woman on earth.

**DELLA:** *(going to door)* And to think I was such a fool.

**JAZZ:** *(sneeringly)* Aw, blow! I got my money's worth. *(In a rage* LEE *rushes for him.)*

**LEE:** You—!

**DELLA:** *(holding* LEE *back)* Come, Lee, he isn't worth it. *(*LEE *continues to glare at* JAZZ *as* DELLA *pulls him toward door, and they exit left, closing door.* JAZZ *watches closed door with twisted smile. He shrugs shoulders, saunters to chair and takes telephone.)*

**JAZZ:** *(at 'phone)* Morningside 37922. Hello! Hello! That you, Milly? Jazz speaking. Got good news—I'm free. Sure, she's gone for good. I had to give her the air. What you doing tonight? What! Afraid of your husband? Say, I can handle Jim Danvers. He's just trying to scare you. Sure. Better look out, he'll shoot himself with that gun. He's hard up—as usual—ain't he? I'll let him have another loan and he'll forget it. Sure. Don't worry—I'll see you tonight. Some place. O. K. *(He hangs up receiver and leans back with a self-satisfied smile. Doorbell rings. He rises, adjusts tie, brushes self off, and goes to door down left. He opens it and his smile turns to horror as he sees the man before him, his visitor unseen by the audience.)*

**JAZZ:** *(gulping and trying to appear unconcerned)* Why— why, hello, Jim Danvers, Old Top. *(Dry laugh.)* Come for another loan? Sure thing. How much? *(He reaches for back pocket, but stops half way and raises both hands above head, his face distorted with fear. Whispers hoarsely.)* Why—Jim, what's the idea of the gat!—Be yourself! *(Cowering in fear.)* I ain't foolin' with Milly. Honest to—

*(Three metallic clicks of a silenced automatic ring out in rapid succession.* JAZZ *grasps his chest and reels forward, closing and locking the door. Gasping, he leans against it, trying to straighten up. With great difficulty he staggers to desk and sinks into chair. With last desperate effort to reach telephone, he sprawls face forward upon desk as* CURTAIN *slowly descends.)*

# John Frederick Matheus
## (1887–1982)
▼▼▼▼▼▼▼▼▼▼▼▼

Although he was not a major figure and did not live in New York, John Frederick Matheus was known in African American artistic circles during and after the Harlem Renaissance as the author of five original, provocative, and powerful one-act plays and an opera based on the life of Dessalines, the liberator of Haiti. In addition, he wrote many articles and twenty-four short stories, the most famous of which was "Fog," first published in *Opportunity* and included in Edward O'Brien's *Best Short Stories of 1925.* He travelled extensively (especially in Haiti, France, and Africa) and became acquainted with many important Black American artists of the 1920s and 1930s, including Willis Richardson, Alain Locke, and Countee Cullen.

Born in Keyser, West Virginia, to a farming family descended from slaves, Matheus grew up in Steubenville, Ohio. The earliest literary influence on him was his mother, who introduced him to books. After receiving a classical education at the local high school, he worked as a bookkeeper to a plumber. In 1906, he attended Western Reserve University in Cleveland, where he continued his study of the classics. After graduating *cum laude* in 1910, he met Martha Miller Roberts, a singer, and married her soon afterward. She introduced him to Negro theatre and made him aware of such performers as Bert Williams and George Walker. For a time he attended law school at the University of Pennsylvania, but decided that he wanted to become a teacher and creative writer. In 1911, he became a professor of Latin and modern foreign languages at Florida A & M College in Tallahassee (and apparently doubled as business manager for a short period), a post he held until 1922. While living in Florida, he heard about a pregnant Black woman, a tragedy which inspired him to write *Mr. Bradford Teaches Sunday School*. His short story "Clay" also grew out of his experience in the South.

In 1921, he resumed his education, and with an M.A. degree from Columbia University in hand, he returned to West Virginia to teach French at West Virginia State College for the next thirty years. Matheus believed in broadening himself through travel as well as study. He visited Cuba in 1924, and in the following year he took his first trip to Paris, where he studied briefly at the Sorbonne and came under the spell of both the legendary painter Henry Tanner and Alexandre Dumas, the French novelist of mixed ancestry (Matheus thought he himself had French blood through his great-grandfather).

In 1927, Clarence Cameron White, a colleague at West Virginia State College, persuaded Matheus to accompany him to Haiti to gather material for an opera about the Emperor Dessalines. He completed the libretto in collaboration with White, who wrote the score, and *Ouanga!* was performed at the Philadelphia Academy of Music. The influence of William Easton's earlier *Dessalines* is discernible, but does not detract from the overall effectiveness of the opera. It enjoyed a minor success in several limited productions, the most notable in 1949 at South Bend, Indiana. A theatrical "angel" was about to provide money for a full production when World War II broke out and the project was put aside.

His interest in human rights Matheus to spend six months in Liberia during 1929–30 as secretary to Dr. Charles S. Johnson, a professor of sociology at Fisk University and American member of the International Commission of Inquiry to investigate charges of slavery and forced labor in Liberia. On his second visit to Paris in 1930, he met Countee Cullen, who became his friend.

By the late 1920s, Matheus had already gained notice as a writer. About 1925, his story "Swamp Moccasin" won first prize in one contest sponsored by Charles Johnson and in another sponsored by Du Bois (whom he met at the latter contest). His one-act play *Ti Yvette*, about a Creole brother who hates his sister for dating a white man during Mardi Gras, was produced by Krigwa Players and was later included in Willis Richardson's *Plays and Pageants from the Life of the Negro* (1930). In 1929, *Tambour*, his one-act comedy about a Haitian peasant with a passion for his drum, was produced in Boston by Maude Cuney Hare for a mostly Black audience. It included a *meringue* dance written for the production by Clarence White. The script was published by Boston's Negro press. About his most popular play, *'Cruiter*, which won first prize in the *Opportunity* magazine contest of 1926, Matheus says: "It expresses my sympathy for the poor ignorant Negro who is a human being in travail and a victim of man's inhumanity to man." Alain Locke, the guiding spirit of the Harlem Renaissance whom Matheus had met in Cleveland in 1925, included it in his anthology, *Plays of Negro Life*.

During the 1930s, Matheus published several scholarly articles in journals such as *Modern Language Journal, Journal of Negro History*, and *Quarterly Review of Higher Education Among Negroes*. In 1945–46, he spent a year in Haiti as director for the teaching of English in the national schools. While there, he prepared and broadcast progressive lessons in English and lectures on American music. Eventually he was awarded the Officier de l'Ordre Nationale Honneur et Merite by the Haitian government. In 1950, he returned to his beloved Paris and visited the studio of the artist Beauford Delaney. He spent the last years of his life with his wife in Charleston, West Virginia, pursuing his new-found interests in theosophy, spiritualism, and Bahaism. Among the contemporary African American writers whom he most admired are Lorraine Hansberry, Amiri Baraka, and Ralph Ellison.

Inspired by a tragedy that he recalled from his childhood in an ethnically-mixed, coal mining town, *Black Damp*, reprinted in this volume, was published in *The Carolina Magazine* of April 1929 and performed in Cleveland by an educationally orientated theatre group in 1950. The idea for the play, with its West Virginia setting, came to Matheus from his youthful experiences. Several coal miners lived in his hometown and he came into contact with many different ethnic groups during his high school years. The play reminds us that the dirty, gruelling, and dangerous work of providing coal to warm American homes and fuel American industry was performed largely by Blacks, Italians, and Poles who had almost no stake in the prosperity they helped to create. This accounts for the relatively large cast of characters in such a short play. They are connected to one another by their mutual hardship in a fatal brotherhood of coal. This relationship is marked by a rough, boisterous, miner's comraderie that overrides racial differences. It is the minion of the law who introduces racism and devisiveness (". . . the coal gits everybody an' the laws is allus pickin on niggahs"). The violence of life in the mines is matched by echoes of ominous events connected to Prohibition and sexual revenge. Ironically, the self-confessed criminal is the one who is saved while the others one by one are claimed by the "black damp." The curtain descends on a symbolic heap of corpses on an empty stage. Matheus tries valiantly to reproduce the speech patterns of both European immigrants and American Blacks, but wisely refrains from having them use dialect when revealing their most intimate thoughts (all men speak the same inner language).

## REFERENCES

Perry, Margaret. "John F. Matheus." *Dictionary of Literary Biography* 51. Detroit: Gale Research, 1987, 196–200.

*Who's Who in Colored America*. 7th ed. Yonkers-on-Hudson, NY: Christine E. Burckel & Assoc., 1950, p. 358.

# BLACK DAMP

## John Frederick Matheus

CAST

> BIG STEVE JOHNSON, *a Negro miner*
> "FOOTS" WILLIAMS, *a Negro miner*
> "GOOSY" WOODS, *a white American miner*
> JOE DOMINI, *an Italian miner*
> MIKE, *a Polish track man*
> RAINFORD, *American fireboss*
> DAWSON, *police officer*
> LOPEZ, *Spanish motorman*
> RESCUERS

SCENE I

A *"room," running off from a long gallery in a present day West Virginia shaft coal mine, two miles from the entrance. In the rear an exit leads into the gallery. A row of wooden props runs the length of the stage at intervals of four feet with supporting beams to hold up the roof of slate and rock. Beyond the exit an electric light is visible above the mine electric railway track running along the gallery. Two spurs from this track branch into the "room," one to the right, the other to the left. On either side two piles of coal are heaped*

---

First published in *The Carolina Magazine*, April 1929. Reprinted with the permission of Ellen Matheus.

*up to be loaded into cars invisible to the audience, but into which the miners are seen to throw the coal. Shovels and picks lie around, and an empty keg of tin marked "Powder." The stage is in semi-darkness. It is 5:30 A. M. Voices are heard off stage.*

**VOICES:** Hello! That you Mike? Yah, Meester Rainford.— Gittin' thru early ain't yer?—Mebbe. I no stop lasr night. My woman, she seeck, my boy she seeck too. (RAINFORD *and* MIKE *appear before the entrance. Both wear overalls and miners' caps provided with safety lamps which are burning steadily)*
**RAINFORD:** How old's the boy?
**MIKE:** Thr-r-ee year.
**RAINFORD:** Well I betcha he's a chip off the old block and that he'll make a better miner than his daddy.
**MIKE:** Naw! I no want heem to work like me, under ground.
**RAINFORD:** Oh, I don't know. There's lots o' worse jobs.
**MIKE:** Mebbe? Anyway he find better.
**RAINFORD:** Everything all right?
**MIKE:** Fine.
**RAINFORD:** I noticed a couple o' bad ties about a quarter o' mile from the entrance elevator. Take your gang to-night and have it fixed.
**MIKE:** Sure thing.
**RAINFORD:** So long.
**MIKE:** S'long. *(Exit)*
**RAINFORD:** *(entering the "room" and looking around, examining the roof, supports, sides. The flickering glare from his single lamp sends lurid shadows across the room. At intervals he flashes a spot light from a pocket flash light upon the parts he is examining)* By God, if it ain't pretty tough, but dog gone ut, he ain't got no holler, the hunkey. All he's o fightin' fer. Minin' ain't no white man's job, but not so bad for niggers an' hunkies. *(Mechanically pushing posts to test their strength)* Humph! Now to git out o' this hell hole afore the gang gits here. *(Sound of a bell is heard ringing and the rumble of approaching cars)* May as well wait and ketch a ride back. *(Begins to whistle indifferently. Off stage the cars are heard coming to a stop. The sound of men's voices comes from a distance)*

**VOICES:** Hey! Cut it out!—Ha! Ha! (BIG STEVE *and* FOOTS *enter carrying between them a keg of powder and fuses which they throw on the floor.* GOOSY *and* JOE *follow. All have dinner pails, wear overalls and wear miners' safety lamps in their caps)*

**VOICE OF LOPEZ:** All r-r-right?

**FOUR MINERS:** *(loudly)* All right.

**RAINFORD:** Hello, boys.

**MINERS:** *(in concert)* Good mornin'.

**RAINFORD:** Goin' to shoot some today, eh?

**JOE:** *(pertly)* That's the beesness. We feenish heem *(Pointing to piles of coal)* to-day, an' then we shoota beega pile, make da mon'. Then—Carlotta an' Joe, sweet. *(He waves right hand to lips and throws a kiss in the air)*

**RAINFORD:** O hell!

**GOOSY:** Knockin' off, Rainford?

**RAINFORD:** In a few minutes. What's it doin' up above?

**GOOSY:** It was rainin' cats and dogs when we came down.

**RAINFORD:** That's luck fer you, when I had planned to go to town.

**BIG STEVE:** We all ain't studin' no rain, Mister Rainford.

**RAINFORD:** *(banteringly)* None o' yer kiddin' now. I ain't feelin' too right an' I wouldn't min' knockin' a coon in the mouth.

**BIG STEVE:** *(laughing)* Kayah! Kah! Hah!

**FOOTS:** *(sullenly)* An' ah ain't feelin' so pert mahself. Wouldn't mine bustin' a sager.

**GOOSY:** O go on, Foots! Can't you take a joke? Cripes! What's ailin' you?

**RAINFORD:** Well, I ain't takin' back nothin' an' pay day is Saturday.

**BIG STEVE:** Foots ain't been feelin' right sence las' night in town at the dance. Buck Pope done danced too much with his old lady.

**FOOTS:** Shet up. *(The men put down their pails.* BIG STEVE *yawns and stretches himself.* FOOTS *spits on his hands.* JOE *picks up a shovel and goes thru a pantomime of shoveling.* GOOSY *reaches in his hip pocket and pulls out a plug of black tobacco, biting off a chew)*

**RAINFORD:** You darkies drink too much red eye an' white mule at them dances. Where do you all git it?

**FOOTS:** None o' yer damn business.

**GOOSY:** By the way, Riley was found dead this mornin'. Passed by the crowd on my way to work. He raided that dance las' night, didn't he boys?

**RAINFORD:** So that's why it's none o' yer damn business? *(Silence)* Why don't you shoot off your lip? Go to it.

**BIG STEVE:** Fo' Gawd! Done found him dead?

**VOICE OF LOPEZ:** All r-right. *(Noise of electric motor is heard)*

**RAINFORD:** *(moving toward the exit)* Keep a watch on the ventilation. One of the fans wasn't working so well last night. *(Exit. The cars are heard rolling away)*

**FOOTS:** Well work's what we're cravin', so let's git at it.

**BIG STEVE:** *(in deep meditation)* What you know 'bout that?

**FOOTS:** What?

**BIG STEVE:** Riley dead.

**GOOSY:** A man's flirtin' with death, I says, when he takes one o' them Prohibition jobs.

**JOE:** Proheebeesh poleece *(shaking his head)* no good.

**FOOTS:** Ah' yo' workin' this mornin', Steve or ain't yo'? Let's eat up this pile of coal so we's kin shoot another. I allus likes the sounds of shootin'. Sort a fun. Makes yo' fergit yer troubles.

**STEVE:** Ah'm with yo', Foots. Almost fergot about Sis. You know *(to GOOSY and JOE) my sister. (sheepishly)* She is away in school an' ah got to keep her theah an' in plenty o' money. I couldn't stand her hangin' roun' any of these dance hall shieks. Ah ain't no angel, but ah gots some pride an' ambition fo' huh.

**FOOTS:** Lot a good it'll do. All Janes are alike. She'll come back an' marry one o' em, just the same.

**BIG STEVE:** How yo' know so much?

**FOOTS:** Ah means ef she wants to she will. Yo' can't stop 'em. *(bitterly)* Yo' can't stop 'em.

**BIG STEVE:** Well she won't want to. Heah, lissen to this— jes' one minute. I gots a letter from huh las' night. *(He fumbles in his pockets)* I put it in my work clothes to read it agin. *(Pulls out letter.)* Lemme see. Lemme see. Dog gone, I can't see. *(Takes off his cap and by the aid of his safety lamp reads)* "Dear, dear Brother."

**FOOTS:** Cut it out. What do you do when yo' get off a work?

**GOOSY:** Let's hear it, Big Steve. I got a girl in school too. My own. Her mother died when she was bo'n. How ol's yer sister?

**BIG STEVE:** She's about, 'bout, lessee, 'bout eight year younger an' me. She's 'bout eighteen, come July.

**GOOSY:** My kid's fifteen.

**BIG STEVE:** *(reading)* "I am learnin' to make cake and all the things you like. I am learning to sew, also. I can make all my own dresses now." *(smiling)* Ain't that fine? That's somethin' great—"My other"—What's that word *(looks hard and peers intently at all sides of paper)* O yes—"My other stu-studies are hard. We have to pay our board bill ond buy some books before we can go on." *(folding up letter hurriedly)* Shucks! What's the matter with me? Ah ain't got no time to be a losin', got to git busy 'round heah. That gal's got to go on.

**FOOTS:** Well git goin'.

**JOE:** We'll beat yo' loadin'. Bet yo' five cent.

**FOOTS:** Shet up, white fo'ks an' git a doin'. Talk ain't gittin' yo' nothin'.

**GOOSY:** *(Winking at* JOE *and pointing his thumb in the direction of* FOOTS*)* Gittin' mighty bloody.

**JOE:** *Si*—thinkin' beeg.

**FOOTS:** *(Disdainfully)* Uh huh! *(Both sides shovel manfully for a few seconds)*

**JOE:** *(singing)*

Giovanezza!
Giovanezza!
Primavera per Italia!
Mussolini!

**GOOSY:** What the . . . say, air you goin' crazy?

**JOE:** Yes—crazy—crazy, lika all Italians, crazy. I wanta sing, to sing to Carlotta. Ah, thay's the end of the Fascisti song. Mussolini—bigga man.

**BIG STEVE:** *(stopping his work in admiration)* Ah don't know what it means but it sounds mighty good.

**FOOTS:** Yo' all mek me sick.

**BIG STEVE:** Go hang crepe on yourself.

**FOOTS:** Ef yo' knows what good fo' yo', you'd let Carlotta stay over yander amongst them Eyetalians.

**JOE:** For what you think-a like that?

**FOOTS:** Say, Joe, what 'ud you do ef somebody would try to butt in atwixt you an' Carlotta?

**JOE:** *No capisc'*—me no onderstand "butt in."

**GOOSY:** He means if some other fellow would try to take Carlotta from you for himself.

**JOE:** Some other fallow! Take Carlotta?

**FOOTS:** Uh huh. That's what I mean.

**JOE:** Me keela heem—queeck with one stilletto. In my contree whar I come from in Sicilia, no lika here.

**BIG STEVE:** 'Ain't it so!

**FOOTS:** Jes' what I knowed. You'se all jes' nacherly fools about you'se all women.

**JOE:** *(excitedly)* But—*bene*—Carlotta—she mine—she no want to go with other fallow. Six month I work—I go back with planty mon', marry Carlotta.

**FOOTS:** Can't be too sure.

**GOOSY:** Seems like yo' got a grudge agin somebody, Foots.

**FOOTS:** Jes' like Big Steve done said ah'm sore. Ah got it in fo' Buck Pope. Ah don't bother nobody. I don't fight no mans what lemme be. But lemme be. Ef yo' don't ah don't keer who yo' is ner what happens. Buck Pope dances with my old lady an' she falls fo' his smooth tongue. Ah gives her all muh money an' treats her right. Am Ah goin' tek it? No, I ain't, an' Ah don't mean any maybe so promise either.

**BIG STEVE:** You don't know nothin' that's got any sense. 'Spose yo' kill that no count scalawag. What good would it do yo', when the electric cheer'll be burnin' fo' yo' or the pen'll have yo'?

**FOOTS:** Well he'll not be havin' her—I'll know that.

**BIG STEVE:** 'Taint worth it. No, 'taint worth it, Ah say. Too many womens in the world.

**FOOTS:** Ain't but one fo' me.

**JOE:** Ah, *Si*—oll right—only one!

**BIG STEVE:** Ah don't know.

**FOOTS:** Well yo' an' me is two diff'ent persons. *(The noise of approaching cars attracts their attention)*

**GOOSY:** Here comes some empties. Remind me of you fellows' heads, makin' a lot of racket an' nothin' in 'em. *(They all begin to shovel coal. The cars are heard coming to a stop. The* VOICE OF LOPEZ *sounds in the distance.)*

**VOICE OF LOPEZ:** Turn in first door—*a la derecha*, at the right, señor.

**JOE:** *(whispering)* Some inspector.

**GOOSY:** Must be a new one. (DAWSON *appears in the entrance dressed in blue uniform of a policeman)*

**DAWSON:** Good morning, boys. *(All look up in surprise)*

**ALL IN CHORUS:** Good mornin'.

**DAWSON:** You all know who I am an' you know I mean business. *(Turning toward* BIG STEVE*)* Are you Steve Jackson?

**BIG STEVE:** Yes sah.

**DAWSON:** And you're Bill Williams, known as Foots?

**FOOTS:** That's me.

**DAWSON:** *(pulling out warrant from his coat pocket)* You're under arrest.

**BIG STEVE:** Undah arrest?

**FOOTS:** Fo' what?

**DAWSON:** Fo' killin' Prohibition officer Riley last night.

**BIG STEVE:** Fo' Gawd, Cap'n yo' sho' got the wrong man.

**DAWSON:** Who said anything about the man. I said *men*, you coons.

**FOOTS:** *(defiantly)* We all ain't done nothin' to nobody, so go'long. Don't mess with me.

**GOOSY:** No use fightin', Foots. Go on peaceably.

**JOE:** They fine fallows, Steve an' Foots.

**FOOTS:** But we ain't killed nobody.

**DAWSON:** Tell it to the judge, boys. I ain't takin' evidence.

**BIG STEVE:** But Ah got to work man. I got to send some money away.

**GOOSY:** You can't beat the law.

**FOOTS:** Ah ain't skeered o' no law.

**BIG STEVE:** We been a fightin' coal together, Foots, an' we ain't beat yit. The coal's after us, but we've beat. I reckon we'll fight the law. There ain't much difference, 'ceptin' the coal gits everybody an' the laws is allus pickin' on niggahs.

**DAWSON:** *(pulling a Colt revolver)* Start something if you like.

**FOOTS:** We ain't got much chance, Steve.

**BIG STEVE:** We'll go, officer, ef yo' let us finish this job.

**DAWSON:** The devil I will. Yo'll go now. Think I'm goin' wait on yer convenience.

**FOOTS:** *(grabbing the can of powder which lies within reach)* My pardner says we'll go when we finish this work. *(Holds the powder before him as a shield)*

**BIG STEVE:** *(desperately)* Ah jes' gotta get some money.

**GOOSY:** They'll go, Dawson. I'll vouch fer it.

**DAWSON:** How long will it take.

**FOOTS:** Not long.

**DAWSON:** *(curtly)* All right. I'll wait. This gun's drawn; one false move an'—. Joe, tell Lopez, we'll take the next car. *(exit* JOE*)*

**BIG STEVE:** 'Course we ain't goin' to be long about provin' our innocence. But we're goin' as we said. (BIG STEVE *begins to shovel frantically;* FOOTS *aids him. The cars are heard noisily speeding on)*

**GOOSY:** Where'd they take the body.

**DAWSON:** The undertaker has it in charge. The coroner gave orders for it to be moved.

**GOOSY:** Where was he last seen.

**DAWSON:** He raided that darkey dance in town. After that he jumped in his car and he wasn't seen alive since. These two birds passed by the place he was found. Several persons on their way home saw them in a Ford car.

**BIG STEVE:** *(pausing in his shoveling)* We was comin' home from the dance.

**DAWSON:** *(waving the revolver)* Tell it to the judge.

**JOE:** *(returning)* Oll right.

**DAWSON:** Bring me that powder can, Joe.

**JOE:** Sure. *(fetches it)*

**GOOSY:** Say, Joe, you might as well bore your holes for the next shot.

**DAWSON:** No, you fellows stay right here. I may have to deputize you to help take in my prisoners. *(Silence, save the scraping of the shovels)*

**BIG STEVE:** Oh, Lawdy, Lawdy, Lawdy! *(Silence again. Only the iron tools can be heard. Suddenly a dull, thundering rumble is heard, followed by a sharp explosion. Immediately following this a sharp crackling echoes thru the gallery. The men cry out instinctively, "Gas! Gas!" The electric light at the entrance goes out and plunges all in darkness save for the unsteady lights on the safety lamps)*

**DAWSON:** *(excitedly)* I'll shoot the first one of you prisoners that tries to get away.

**GOOSY:** For God's sake, Dawson, there's been an explosion. Gas is burning down the gallery. Here it cracking.

**JOE:** Queeck! *Abbasso! A terra!*

**FOOTS:** Lissen! Them's flames roarin'.

**BIG STEVE:** Down, git down on the floor.

**GOOSY:** Hug the ground, Dawson, or you'll git your fool head burnt off. *(All fall precipitously to the floor. A dazzling wave of burning gas flashes over their prostrate forms)*

**BIG STEVE:** *(after a silence)* That's what Ah calls singein' yo'.

**GOOSY:** *(springing up)* Up! No time to lose. I've been in these gas explosions afore. The black damp's a comin'. We got to beat it two miles to the entrance. *(The others jump to their feet)*

**DAWSON:** My God! What do you mean?

**FOOTS:** Run fo' yo' life!

**GOOSY:** : Run, fool, afore the black damp gits yo'.

**JOE:** *(hystically)* Ah, *Madre Mia! Madre Mia!*

**BIG STEVE:** The black damp!

**DAWSON:** *(as the truth slowly dawns upon him)* The black damp! *(Runs to the exit of the "room" and looks out into the dark gallery)* God! It's pitch dark. I can't see.

**GOOSY:** The current's off. Connections broken. *(Pushing determinedly past him)* Follow me. My lamp will make a little light as long as it and me will last. *(Exit running; Dawson follows)*

**FOOTS:** Lemme out o' here, I kin outrun the damp. *(Exits running)*

**JOE:** *(singing)* Giovanezza! *(Dashes out madly)*

**BIG STEVE:** *(in calm deliberation)* Help me fight the coal, Lord, help me fight the coal and dust and black death damp.

*(Rushes from room) (The stage is empty for thirty seconds, when the sounds of the retreating footsteps have died away. The curtain falls.)*

## SCENE II

*One half mile from the entrance in the long gallery. When the curtain rises only the vague outline of black overhanging walls and low ceiling are visible. Sounds of footsteps grow louder and louder, approaching with uneven, slow tread. The faint beam from the light of the safety lamp is seen. Finally* GOOSY *appears followed at some distance by* DAWSON. GOOSY'S *lamp is burning very low.* DAWSON *of course has no light.*

**GOOSY:** *(Staggering like a drunken man. He speaks out in a clear, supernatural voice the inner thoughts that obsess him.)* I must watch out for live wires—the current may be on back here. May be it would be better to—to —my tongue wants to skip that word —to *die*—yes to die at once by electricity, sudden, killing volts, than to be smothered, choked this way by inches. O God! Do you hear me? Can you hear me? What will become of my poor child? Without mother, without father she will be so alone. I wonder if the Company will help her? Who is this behind me? He will have to help himself. He will have to go it alone, just as I am going it. Every man for himself. O yes. Maybe that is Foots. A good workman. *(Peers)* No. It is Steve. Too bad he's a nigger. *(Calls)* Hello. *(His voice sounds hollow and rechoes)* Hello, Steve.

**DAWSON:** I'm Dawson. Goosy! Thought you were Foots. *(To himself as in a trance)* O why did I come after those men? Why, why, why? Some air, some air. I wonder if I could suck his breath to keep me alive.

**GOOSY:** He's scared! So am I. Alone in the dark—God! "Sweet fields of Eden" my granddaddy used to sing when I was a boy on the farm in Pocohontas. Wonder if he's found them. Wonder if he's found his granddaddy, killed by the Indians. Wonder if I'll know. My wife used to teach the girl how to pray. Oh, I can't pray. I wonder if the entrance is near. It seem's to be receding. Maybe we're lost. Going the wrong way. O for the smell of pine trees, the sniff of the air from the West Virginia hills. Something's closing around my neck. *(Screams)* It's chokin' me. *(Staggers on)*

**DAWSON:** *(groans)* I'm thirsty. I want water, water! I want air. *(Follows Goosy.)*

**JOE:** *(Singing, as if out of his head, as he enters forcing each step)*

Giovanezza! Giovanezza!
Primavera per Italia!
Mussolini!

*(Speaks with low muffled voice, as though another were speaking thru him)* When I was a soldier in the army of Italy, I was proud to wear the uniform of the Fascisti, the black shirt. Now I wear the garb of the miner, black all over. These harsh speaking Americans call me Dago Joe, but my forefathers built Rome. Why did I not die in *Italia*, like a soldier. Now Carlotta will never know. She will wonder why no more letters will come bearing the likeness of Washington on the pink stamp *dei Stati Uniti*, or the face of Lincoln. My countrymen helped to make this America, her railroads, skyscrapers, fields of fruit. O Holy Mother, I belong to Youth, to the *Giovanezza*, I do not want to die, not yet, not now! *(He gasps, coughs, strangles)* I choke, choke, choke. *(Exit clutching his throat.)*

**FOOTS:** *(speaking naively, as if apart from his environment)* I remember my Alabama cabin. I first saw the hot sun there and smelled the honeysuckle and jasmin in the cool of the evening. There I grew up. My mammy was black and fat and her lap was soft and warm. I helped her pick cotton. I learned the songs of the mocking birds and the crickets at dawn, chirping when my bare feet plowed thru the dewy grass. I won't see or hear them any more. Mammy's dead. I can't see her, unless? I wonder if there is any truth in what the preachers say? I never did know my pappy. I remember the log school house—two terms, the big handed teacher an' the "white fo'ks" always wantin' work, more work, and givin' me things to eat out in the back yard with the dog. Then mines of Alabama, of Birmingham—Red Mountain, red whiskey, women, black, red, brown, yellow, red eyes. I see that long train pulling North, after the endless hours in Birmingham, fighting coal for them "white fo'ks'" steel mills to make guns to fight other "white fo'ks" across the ocean.

West Virginia! Mines of West Virginia! Another woman, different from other women, brown, wavy locks, sweet face—O memory of Buck Pope—robber, thief, I'll kill him! Prison—noose —chair! How can I get out of this. Ah, I'm chokin'! I'm chokin'. I don't want to die, I don't, an' leave Buck Pope. *(Exit moaning)*

**BIG STEVE:** *(staggering in and lunging, almost falls)* I wonder where they have all gone. Everything is so still—*(looks around)*—like a graveyard. Where am I? Where am I going? Oh, yes, the entrance. It can't be far away now. Wonder if I'll be late for dinner. They'll pay off Saturday. *(Pulls himself up with a start)* Oh, I've got to send that money to Sis, Saturday. *(Laughs to himself)* Huh! Making her own clothes now. Ain't that summin'. Must let that gal go on! Never had no chance muhself. Oh well— lots a worse jobs than minin'. Wonder why the lights are out. Wonder why everything smells so hot and close. My, how tight my head feels. *(Feels his temples)* What's that pounding? Oh! *(Starts)* It's the explosion. We must run for our lives. I must hurry I may be too late—too late—*(Staggers off choking)*

(Curtain)

*Five Minutes Later*
*(A point further on in the gallery. The five men are huddled together in a sitting posture on the floor. The lights in the lamps are almost out)*

**DAWSON:** Listen here, men. I've got to tell you all. *(Attempts to rise, but falls back)* Listen, I say—I came here to arrest two of you. Which two? *(He tries to look around at each man)* I can't see. It's getting darker and darker. Turn on the lights. Oh- yes—I will put it on the darkies. What difference does it make. They ain't got no come back. Who cares? But I'm going to tell it now. The niggers didn't kill Riley. Riley was a crook. He didn't play square. He pulled the poor cusses and let the rich go free. I used to tip him off, and he promised to divide the spoils. But he double crossed me and played me for a fool. He was in with the Bootlegger ring. Do you hear, fellows? If I've got blood on my hands, it's crook's blood. I killed Riley. Do you hear, niggers, I killed Riley. *(Tries to shout, but ends in a hoarse whisper.)* I KILLED RILEY.

**FOOTS:** (arouses himself) Yo' means Buck Pope! Ah killed him! Ah couldn't let her have him. *(Sinks back on floor.* JOE *and* GOOSY *keel over without saying anything)*

**DAWSON:** *(whispering)* Riley's after me. He's chokin' me. Hel-p ! *(Cries out and ends in gurgle. He falls back. The lights all go out one after the other. There is silence. Then noises are heard from the direction of the entrance and voices. Rays from a flash light are seen, as the sound of men walking resounds. Two* RESCUERS *appear wearing gas masks. They talk thru the masks)*

**FIRST RESCUER:** The others had to turn back.

**SECOND RESCUER:** *(holding the flash light)* Strike a match.

**FIRST RESCUER:** *(Strikes a match; it goes out immediately. He strikes another. It also refuses to burn)*

**SECOND RESCUER:** We can go no farther. *(The light falls on the men.)*

**FIRST RESCUER:** What's this?

**SECOND RESCUER:** Some of the boys.

**FIRST RESCUER:** Are they living?

**SECOND RESCUER:** *(kneels down and feels pulses)* Faintly beating.

**FIRST RESCUER:** We can take one and get out alive. There's a chance to save one.

**SECOND RESCUER:** Which one?

**FIRST RESCUER:** The one with no lamp in his cap

**SECOND RESCUER:** Yes, he's the smallest.

**FIRST RESCUER:** I'm feeling faint. Hurry. *(The* SECOND RESCUER *picks up the trunk of* DAWSON'S *unconscious form. The* FIRST RESCUER *lifts him by the feet. They march off. The other men lay motionless.)*

(Curtain)

*Note. The characters cease to talk dialect in the speeches purporting to tell their thoughts. The thoughts of all men speak the same inner language.*

# Andrew M. Burris
## (1898–c.1977)
▼▼▼▼▼▼▼▼▼▼▼▼▼

Andrew Marion Burris was born in 1898 in Helena, Arkansas, a small town on the Mississippi River below Memphis. He was raised by his maternal grandmother because his father was "a wandering man." He had one brother, William, who moved to Chicago. Young Andrew attended Hampton Institute, where he exhibited a passion for literature. Sometime between 1920 and 1925, he moved to Harlem, the mecca for African American artists and writers.

Burris compiled scholarly bibliographies on Charles Chestnut and Paul Laurence Dunbar for *Publishers Weekly* and *The American Collector* respectively. He wrote plays and songs and devoted much of his time to community service. He earned his livelihood as a librarian for the Century Association. In 1931, Loften Mitchell, at the age of thirteen, met Burris, who was then leader of a young "Y" group named the Panthers (not to be confused with the Black Panthers thirty years later). Burris left a lasting impression on the young Mitchell, which he described in his autobiographical novel *The Stubborn Old Lady Who Resisted Change* (1973):

Mr. Burris lived on the top floor of a walk-up on the corner of Lenox and 127th Street. The stairs turned and twisted as you climbed them. You had to ring downstairs bell to get into the building. . . . Mr. Burris invariably yelled down the stairs to you: "Yes?" He did so in a manner commanding the utmost respect. You had to answer quite politely, "Mr. Burris??"

I liked Mr. Burris. He was dogmatic, unrelenting, pigheaded, vociferous, critical, cynical, vitriolic, vituperative, snobbish and down-right cheap. On the other hand, he was generous, open-minded, quiet, considerate, encouraging, gentle, democratic, and downright brilliant. He was one of the first men I knew to go out and buy the work of Jacob Lawrence, the great painter. He bought and talked about the greatness of painter Romare Bearden. He sang the praises of Langston Hughes, Abram Hill, Canada Lee, Dick Campbell, Zell Ingram and a thousand other black artists. . . . Andrew Burris . . . served as a link in the Black Heritage between the past and the present.

While Loften Mitchell was attending City College of New York—then a mostly white school—Burris obtained a scholarship for Loften to Talladega College, an all-Black college in Alabama, where Mitchell earned his B.A.

Burris wrote one unpublished novel, *Up North*, a story of southern migrants; none of his plays was published and only four titles are known, three of which are *This Is My Destiny, You're No Man*, the story of a soldier who suffered castration in the war, and *Black But Comely*, the story of millionaire Mme. C. J. Walker, a play which the American Negro Theatre refused to produce. (Burris never wrote for the theatre again.) Earlier, he had written *You Mus' Be Bo'n Ag'in*, a comedy-drama produced by the Harlem Experimental Theatre circa 1929. The play was subsequently performed by the Gilpin Players of the Karamu Theatre in Cleveland, running from February 25 to March 1, 1931. The production was successful enough to be given a final performance on March 14th to the Interracial Committee, Women's International League for Peace and Freedom. The Federal Theater Project (FTP), (1935–1939) kept the play on its list of Negro plays, but no one produced it. Southern FTP units produced few plays, and northern units soon discovered that their audiences preferred stories of urban life.

Burris set *You Mus' Be Bo'n Ag'in* in the time and place of his own boyhood—1900 in Camdus, Arkansas, a place much like the small, gossipy town of his birth. The setting for the protagonist's home is recorded in such intimate detail that it could only be known by one who had lived there.

The plot centers around Clem Coleman, who has fathered two children with Eliza Coleman, the woman he lives with and supports but has never married. The Baptist community in the persons of the Piney Grove congregation bring constant pressure on Clem to join their church, marry Eliza, and make his children legitimate in the eyes of God. However, Clem considers the Baptists to be hypocrites (which the play bears out), and he knows they care nothing for his soul but lust for his money. Even when his own children return from school crying because the other children call them "bastards," Clem refuses to submit, until, during an emotional revival scene in the church, a maternal grandmother, whom he loves and respects, pleads with him "to be born again" while she yet lives. Clem submits, and there is great rejoicing in the church. This is the end of act two. Clem "comes to his senses" in act three.

According to the Gilpin Players program, the "spirituals, moans, shouts, and intonations are selected and arranged by Ulysses S. Elam," and certainly, the revival scene (although overly extended) is one of the better of many that have been written for the stage (*Mule Bone, Earth, Mamba's Daughters, Run Little Chillun, Porgy,* etc.). Unlike most other revival scenes, the one in *You Mus' Be Bo'n Ag'in* does not compromise the bent of "sinner's" essential nature. The play is a damning indictment of religiosity. One might speculate that in his childhood, Burris suffered similar mockery from the small town "Christians," and that the play itself is his own personal assertion that he need not be born again.

*You Mus' Be Bo'n Ag'in* lay in great danger of being "lost" forever. Reuben and Dorothy Silver, former directors at Karamu, are to be thanked for preserving the script.

# YOU MUS' BE BO'N AG'IN

## ANDREW M. BURRIS

CAST

>CLEM COLEMAN, *a farmer*
>ELIZA COLEMAN, *his wife*
>ELMER COLEMAN
>MAMIE COLEMAN, *their children*
>REV. OBADIAH TUKES, *a traveling preacher*
>MRS. DOSHIA BRAGGS, *a deaconess of Piney Grove Baptist Church*
>JOE SCRUGGS, *a deacon of Piney Grove Baptist Church*
>"MAMMY" CAROLINE LANE, *an old midwife*
>MRS. MAHALA TURNER, *a neighbor*
>MRS. CISSIE BROWN, *a church worker*
>JOHN GRAY, *an elder of Piney Grove Baptist Church*
>JIMMIE AMY, *a neighbor's son*
>NEIGHBORS, MOURNERS, AND MEMBERS OF PINEY GROVE BAPTIST CHURCH

ACT ONE

SCENE I

Scene: *The front room of the Colemans' home in Camdus, Arkansas, on an early afternoon in spring, about the year 1900.*

128

*(The room is indiscriminately furnished in the manner typical of rural southern Negro homes. The general effect is that of a room overcrowded with furniture picked up here and there, and of no particular design. There is no attempt at harmony in the various colors, yet a strange harmony persists, dominated by the blood red and white diamond-patterned quilt on the long box-couch beside the right wall. In the center of the upstage wall of the room is the front door, with a window in the wall to each side of it. To the right of this door is a plain old fashioned fireplace with a thick, unfinished board for a mantelpiece. In the center of the mantel is a fancy oak striking clock, and on each side of the clock a vase with paper flowers. Since it is spring there is no fire in the fireplace; the hearth is clean but there are the ashes from last winter's fire carefully swept back. To the left of the front door is a dresser covered by a plain white runner, and on it are the usual pin cushion and tray, small vases, photographs, and the like. In the left wall, near the corner, is another door, with a washstand to the left of it. On the washstand are a white runner, and a washbowl and pitcher set including a shaving mug, soapdish, and toothbrush holder. A hatrack hangs over the washstand.*

*Over the mantel is a tinted photograph of* CLEM *and* ELIZA *together. Elsewhere on walls are framed family portrait and one of Jesus. A center table, holding the family Bible and a fancy oil lamp, stands near the right wall, having been moved out of place for the quilt in the center of the room, which is stretched out over old fashioned X-shaped quilting horses. Straight chairs and rocking chairs placed about the room add to the general effect of crowding.*

ELIZA, *a plump, well built, dark brown-skinned woman about thirty-five years old, is sitting in the center of the room sewing on the quilt and softly humming a plantation melody.* ELIZA *is a woman of sound common sense, motherly, and ingratiating. She has had practically no education, but is appreciative of the rudimentary education that* CLEM *has had, and accepts his authority in their home. Nevertheless, in her dealings with him she is subtle and effective in the use of feminine strategy. In her relationships with members of the community, she is constantly torn between her devotion to* CLEM *and her desire for their approbation.*

*There is a knock at the front door.* ELIZA *sticks her needle in place, removes the scraps of cloth from her lap, tidies herself, and then opens the door, admitting* MRS. DOSHIA BRAGGS *and* MRS. MAHALA TURNER.

MRS. DOSHIA BRAGGS *is a corpulent, dark brown person of about middle age. Her attitude and appearance are those of a militant defender of the faith, willing to die for her God, and for Piney Grove Baptist Church of which she is a deaconess.*

MRS. MAHALA TURNER *is a slender, wrinkled, light brown-skinned woman of about the same age as* MRS. BRAGGS. *Her appearance and manner are passive: she is the kind of person who has no thought of her own, who willingly and thoughtlessly sanctions whatever anybody else says, particularly someone like* MRS. BRAGGS.

ELIZA *welcomes her visitors graciously with a seeming consciousness that she is being visited by her superiors, since being a deaconess is to her a mark of social superiority.*

**ELIZA:** *(bowing obsequiously)* Good mawnin', Miss' Doshia, an' *(with evident surprise)* Mis' Mahala Turnah. How is you? I ain' seen you foh de longes' kin' o' time. Come right in, y'all, an' set down. Let me move dis heah quilt out o' de way so—

**MRS. DOSHIA:** Good mawnin', chile. You jes' leave it right wheah 'tis. Go right on wid yo' quiltin', 'cause we ain' got long to stay no-how.

**ELIZA:** *(proceeding to move the quilt to one side anyway, and placing chairs in the center of the room for her guests)* Hit's about time foh me to quit anyhow. Clem an' de chillun'll soon be comin' home foh dey suppah.

**MRS. DOSHIA:** *(going over and looking at the quilt)* Das a mighty putty quilt you makin', ain't it, Sistah Turnah?

**MRS. TURNER:** *(who has taken her seat without giving any attention to the quilt, answering obediently)* Sho is, Sistah Doshia. Sho is a nice un.

**ELIZA:** *(modestly)* I'm glad y'all laks it.

**MRS. DOSHIA:** Now you see, honey, ef you was in de church, de quiltin' circle would come ovah heah an' git dat quilt out foh you in a little er no time.

**ELIZA:** *(meekly)* Yas'm!

**MRS. DOSHIA:** You sho misses a whole lot when you ain't in de church, Chile. All de good times we has on picnics, an' collations.

**ELIZA:** I knows it, Mis' Doshia. Dere's many a time I wished I was in de church.

**MRS. DOSHIA:** Thank de Lawd! How come you don' git in b'hin' Clem an' git him to jine de church? Is you said anything to him heah lately, since we been talkin' 'bout it?

**ELIZA:** No'm! Fact is he ain' been in sech good sperrets lately, an' when he lak dat dey ain' no use talkin' to him, 'bout nothin'. 'Specially 'bout some'm he don' lak.

**MRS. DOSHIA:** Lawd, chile, you don' know mens yit, long ez you been me'ied . . . dat is, livin' wid Clem. De bes' time to talk to men folks is when dey min's heavy wid trouble, 'specially sinnah mens. Hit's de Lawd what's workin' on dey conscience. Don' you lose no mo' time, honey. You talk to Clem dis very day. How 'bout it, Sistah Turnah?

**MRS. TURNER:** You is talkin' gospel words, Sistah Doshia, gospel words.

**ELIZA:** *(meekly)* Maybe y'all is right . . .

**MRS. DOSHIA:** *(dogmatically)* Maybe? Dey ain' no maybe to it. I knows I'm right. De Mastah speaks to me an' tells me what to do. You jes do what I says.

**ELIZA:** Well, Mis' Doshia, I'll try what you say, but I done foun' out de bes' thing to do when Clem's worried is to leave 'im alone.

**MRS. DOSHIA:** Honey, don't you worry. De Lawd will melt de heart o' de hardes' sinnah an' we gwine pray for de Lawd to melt de heart of Clem Coleman. Don't mattah ef yo' is livin' in sin. God uses sinnahs someties to do His biddin' ex well as us Christians. An' don't think God don't know yo' is a good woman an's wants to do what's right, and dat' it's Clem Coleman what won't let you. God knows it.

**MRS. TURNER:** Hit so is de truf, Lawd. Hit so is de truf.

**ELIZA:** *(reluctant to accept all the praise and let them make Clem responsible for the "evil" in their lives)* But don' y'all git de notion dat Clem is a bad, mean man, 'cause he 'ain'. Clem is one o' de bes'-hearted men dey is, but he's jes a little headstrung an' want to have his own way, lak mos' mens, das all. But he's a good man an' don' wrong nobody.

**MRS. DOSHIA:** We ain' said he was all bad, but he's a sinnah jest de same, an' you is a sinnah too, long 'ez you ain't ma'ied an' ain't a membah o' de church of God. Sistah Turnah, I reckon we bettah be movin' 'long.

**ELIZA:** Y'all ain' goin' so soon, is you, Mis' Doshia?

**MRS. DOSHIA:** Yas, honey.

**ELIZA:** Can't you wait jes a li'l while? I jes cooked some apple dumplin' for suppah. Maybe y'all 'd lak some. Clem's jes crazy 'bout apple dumplin's wid a plenty dumplin's in 'em. Y'all 'scuse me jes a minute an' I'll git you some.

**MRS. DOSHIA:** Well, I 'spec' we c'n wait a li'l spell longah, can' we, Sistah Turnah?

**MRS. TURNER:** Yas, I reckon we kin, Sistah Doshia. I laks dumplin's right well myse'f.

**ELIZA:** Y'all jes make yo'se'f at home, an' I'll be right back in a little er no time. *(She goes out left door)*

**MRS. TURNER:** *(walking around the room inspecting things rather closely and curiously, then sitting down and whispering audibly to Mrs. Doshia)* Got a right nice home, ain' dey?

**MRS. DOSHIA:** *(indifferently)* Kinda so-so.

**MRS. TURNER:** Ain' many in dese bottoms what got a parlor wid no bed in it, is dey?

**MRS. DOSHIA:** Naw, I reckon dey ain't.

**MRS. TURNER:** An' dey tell me dis heah place is all paid foh, too!

**MRS. DOSHIA:** *(Leaning forward in her chair and whispering maliciously)* Yas, hit's all paid foh, but Clem Coleman ain' paid foh it.

**MRS. TURNER:** *(eagerly sensing the rare morsel of gossip in this remark)* Sho 'nough, Mis' Doshia?

**MRS. DOSHIA:** *(knowingly)* Shor'n dat. How you think somebody lak Clem Coleman, what think he so good-lookin' eve'y woman jes nachly crazy 'bout 'im; how you think dat lazy, yallah man gwine work an' buy a big farm lak dis heah?

**MRS. TURNER:** *(agape with surprise and curiosity)* Lawd, how dey git it? How dey come by it, Mis' Doshia?

**MRS. DOSHIA:** *(bringing her chair closer to Mrs. Turner and looking about, listening to be sure that they are not overheard)* Ain' you nevah hyeahd how Clem is all mixed up wid ole Cunnel Thompson's folks?

**MRS. TURNER:** Naw, Lawd, I ain' knowed a thing about it.

**MRS. DOSHIA:** *(preening herself to tell her story)* Well, dey says dat Clem Coleman is ole Cunnel Thompson's daughtah May Belle's chile. De one what ain' nevah ma'ied an' what live up No'th mos' all de time. Dey say de pappy was de Cunnel's coachman, a big black man name' Dan. When Clem growed up to be a man, Cunnel Thompson give him dis heah lan' an' tol' him to git hisse'f a wife an' go to work. Now you got de whole story jes lak it is.

**MRS. TURNER:** *(blowing from the effect of the news)* Well, dat do settle it!

**MRS. DOSHIA:** Das how come Clem Coleman is so uppity. Hit's de mixtra in 'im. Hit's de white blood an' de black blood pullin' 'gin deyse'f. Any time dem two mixtras comes togethah, people, hit's trouble. De white blood say do one thing, an' de black blood say do som'n else. Das how come Clem ain' done ma'ied dis heah gal an' gi'n 'uh his name lak he oughta. De black blood in 'im won' let 'uh go, 'cause dey is de same. De white blood in 'im don' wan't ma'y huh 'case she black an' ain' good uhnough.

**MRS. TURNER:** Lawd, heish yo' mouf, Mis' Doshia! Ef dat ain' de beatines' I evah hyeahd tell of.

**MRS. DOSHIA:** Yassa, Clem go 'roun' heah braggin' 'bout how his farm's out o' debt, an' how he got de bes' crops in dese bottoms, but ef I evah hyeahs 'im a-blowin' off steam, I'm gwine take 'im down a button hole, 'cause I'm gwine tell 'im how he come by dis heah farm. I hopes we c'n git 'im to jine church, 'cause we sho will need his money when we sta'ts building' de new church. (ELIZA'S *footsteps are heard.* MRS. DOSHIA *and* MRS. TURNER *sit upright and try to assume attitudes of patient waiting.*)

**ELIZA:** *(as she enters the door)* Y'all musta thought I wa'n' nevah comin'. *(She carries the food on an improvised tray, evidently the cover of a large lard can, and places it on the center table.)*

**MRS. DOSHIA:** Naw, honey, we ain' hardly missed you. Me an' Sistah Turnah jes been talkin' 'bout what a nice home y'all got since you done had mo' room put on an' fixed it up.

**ELIZA:** Now y'all come up to de table wheah you'll be mo' comf'table. We is right proud of de house now. Clem say he gwine put some papah on de walls soon's he git 'roun' to it.

**MRS. DOSHIA:** *(tasting the food)* Um-umm, dis sho do taste good. You sho knows how to season yo' grub, chile. No wondah you an' Clem gits 'long so good all de time. Dey say das de bes' way to hol' a man . . . feed 'im good victuals, an' give 'im what he wants.

**MRS. TURNER:** Hit sho is good. Y'all's house'll look swell when you gits it all papered. An' dey tell me y'all don't owe nothin' on yo' farm.

**ELIZA:** No'm, we don' owe nothin', thank de Lawd.

**MRS. TURNER:** Das mighty nice. Dey ain' many in Camdus c'n say dat.

**MRS. DOSHIA:** You right, Sistah. But, 'Liza, wa'n' dis heah farm give to you an' Clem?

**ELIZA:** *(emphatically)* Naw ma'am, it sho wa'n't. Clem an' me worked hard an' paid ouah own money foh dis heah farm.

**MRS. DOSHIA:** I been hearin' dat Cunnel Thompson give Clem dish heah place. Co'se I ain' one o' dem dat b'lieves all dey heahs.

**ELIZA:** Well, Mis' Doshia, I don' mean to call you no lie, but I . . .

**MRS. DOSHIA:** Naw, chile, you ain' callin' me no lie. I ain' said it. I reckon you knows how you got yo' own farm—but don' you 'spec' Clem got a li'l he'p from Cunnel Thompson?

**ELIZA:** De only thing I knows de Cunnel give us was a plough hoss one time. You see Clem was de Cunnel's privey boy up at de big house. An' de Cunnel give us a dollah when Mame was bo'n, foh to put in de savin' bank. He wa'n' livin' when Elmer was bo'n. I 'spec' he'd a give him a dollah, too.

**MRS. DOSHIA:** Well, I sho Lawd hyeahd he give y'all dis heah farm.

**ELIZA:** No'm, Mis' Doshia. I done see Clem wid de money myse'f when he ready to go way down yondah to Gennessee to de bank house, an' sometime he stay a day er so payin' de money an' seein' 'bout sellin' de cotton.

**MRS. DOSHIA:** Is you nevah been down to Gennessee wid Clem?

**ELIZA:** No'm, I ain' had no cause to go.

**MRS. DOSHIA:** Well, 'tain' none o' my business, but I hyeahs dat when Clem go down yondah to Gennessee, he go on one gran' spree wid dem fas' girls.

**ELIZA:** *(with animation)* Who tol' you dat, Mis' Doshia? Who tol' you dat? Hit ain' so. Hit ain' so. I don' b'lieve nary word of it.

**MRS. DOSHIA:** I ain' tellin', chile, who tol' me, but I sho hyeahd it. Ain' you, Sistah Turnah?

**MRS. TURNER:** I is dat. I is foh a fac'.

**ELIZA:** *(almost losing control)* I don' keer who said it. Hit ain' true. Hit's a lie. I knows Clem don' run 'roun' wid no bad womens.

**MRS. DOSHIA:** *(calmly folding her arms across her lap, and gently pouring oil on the blaze she has started)* Dey ain' no use gittin' all riled an' het up 'bout it, honey. We is yo' frien's an' is tellin' you foh yo' own good.

**ELIZA:** *(bowing her head and speaking tearfully)* I jes can' believe it. I can' b'lieve Clem done lied to me lak dat. I jes can' b'lieve it.

**MRS. DOSHIA:** Honey, I see you sho is got a whole lot to learn 'bout men folks. Clem Coleman ain' no diffunt from mos' mens.

**ELIZA:** *(regaining her composure and speaking with spirit)* I don' keer what you says, Mis' Doshia. I don' b'lieve Clem done it. Clem ain' lak othah mens. He's de bes' man I evah seen. I don' b'lieve he done been lyin' to me all dis time an' I jes now findin' it out. He ain' had no cause to lie to me.

**MRS. DOSHIA:** Mens ain' got to have no cause to lie to womens, honey. Dey jes does it nachly. Hit's in 'em. Look lak de blessed Mastah jes give 'em a right to do what dey wants an' dey ain' nothin' much done 'bout it. Mens is got rights what us women ain' got somehow. Hit mus' be 'cause god is a man. He knows de ways o' mens bettah'n de ways o' womens. Well, I reckon we bettah be goin' Sistah Turnah. We is already stayed longah'n we oughta.

**ELIZA:** *(her spirit killed, but trying bravely to be pleasant to her guests)* I sho is glad y'all come by. You mus' come ag'in soon.

**MRS. DOSHIA:** *(rising to go)* Awright, honey, we will— but I'm 'bout to go 'way 'dout de rain thing we come by heah

foh. 'Liza, how 'bout us bringing de committee from de church—
de special committee foh de r'vival—to talk wid Clem an' try an'
git 'im to jine church? Rev'un Tukes is a pow'ful preachah, an' I
bet ef we c'n git Clem up dere he gwine come 'way a changed
man.

**ELIZA:** I don' know, Mis' Doshia, Clem's so funny sometime. I can' say 'tell I see what he say. I tell you, ef he say he don'
wan' y'all to come I'll sen' you word by de chillun. An' ef you
don' heah from me by sundown, you know it's awright an' y'all
come on ovah 'bout firs' night.

**MRS. DOSHIA:** Das good, honey. Das good. Now you do
jes lak I say an' trust in de good Lawd, an' you see ef He don'
bring you out mo' 'n conquer'. We ain' gwine say goodbye 'cause
we gwine see you ag'in soon, I hopes.

**ELIZA:** *(as she closes the door)* Yas'm. *(She returns and begins
removing the dishes and straightening things up. Suddenly he stops,
stands in a challenging attitude, and says)* Clem ain' lied to me.
Naw, he ain'. I don' b'lieve a word of it. Naw sah, I don' b'lieve . . .
*(She stops and reflects)* But it sho is funny how it take Clem so long
to go down yondah to Gennessee. It sho. . . . *(A noise is heard
from outside the left door.* ELIZA *listens, then goes to the door and
calls)* Who's dat?

**MAMMY CAROLINE:** *(from without, in a voice weak with
age)* 'Tain' nobody but me, honey.

**ELIZA:** *(recognizing the voice and its owner as she draws
nearer)* Lawd, ef it ain' Mammy Ca'line! Come on in, Mammy
Ca'line. I sho is glad to see you. You don' come roun' to see us no
mo' lak you sued to. How come you come in de back way?

*(*MAMMY CAROLINE LANE *enters, bent over with age, on her walking stick. Her close-fitting cloth bonnet with large wings on the sides
is tied underneath her chin and completely hides her face. Mammy
Caroline is the midwife of Camdus and surrounding villages. She is
about eighty-five or ninety years old; nobody, not even she, knows her
exact age. The nearest date she can give is that she was "a striplin' of
a gal when de stars come down." She is one of the few persons in the
bottoms who remembers that memorable event. She was never married and has no children—nor even relatives. She lives alone beside
Chaynee Creek, which overflows its banks with every heavy rain and
floods Mammy's two-room hut. But she will not leave the place.*

*There are many legends about why she stays, but like most legends no one can verify them. She lives from the produce of her fowls and of the garden around her house which is tended by some of her many "chillun," for all the children whom she has brought into the world are her "chillun." She goes about from house to house to see how they are getting along and to receive whatever they have to give her, but she asks for nothing. Mammy never knocks at the doors of her children's homes, but enters as she pleases. In some families there are as many as four generations of her children, and about each one of them Mammy remembers some little incident at the birth or in the early infancy which she delights in telling them as she meets them.)*

**MAMMY:** I comes up de back, chile, 'cause dey ain' many steps to go up. Mammy's gittin' ole an' feeble now, honey, an' can' git about lak she useta. Gittin' ole. . . . *(Grunting and groaning as she sits down in a chair which* ELIZA *has brought nearer, and throwing her bonnet back from her face)* an' feeble. Mammy ain' gwine be heah long, daughtah. She's tryin' to git 'roun' to see all huh chillun foh de las' time maybe 'fo' she go up yondah to glory.

**ELIZA:** Aw, Mammy, you been talkin' lak dat foh twenty yeahs er mo'. You got a long time yit.

**MAMMY:** Now, chile, you don' know lak Mammy. Mammy knows when she heah de Mastah's call. Ole Mastah been mighty good to me. Mighty good. Let me stay heah to see all my chillun grow up an' make fine men an' women. Wheah dat boy Clem, an' dem othah two saplin's?

**ELIZA:** Clem's down in de fiel' somewheah. I sho hopes he come in 'fo' you leaves 'cause I knows he'll be glad to see you. Mame an' Elmer ain' come home from school yit, but it's 'bout time dey was heah now.

**MAMMY:** Well, I gwine res' my weary bones a li'l while 'tell dey come, ef day ain' too long.

**ELIZA:** Yas, Mammy, don' you wan' some'm t'eat? I got some spare ribs an' new collard greens, an' some apple dumplin's, an'. . . . *(She is interrupted by the two children,* MAME *and* ELMER, *who run in the front door, both with clothes terribly disordered.* ELMER *is about eight years old. His recent tears stain his pouting face, and it is evident that he is on the verge of tears again.* MAME *is about ten.)* Lawd, y'all is a sight! What is you been doin'? *(As*

MAME *begins to tell her mother what has happened,* ELMER *begins crying and goes to his mother for comfort)*

**MAME:** Ma, dem ole chillun up to de schoolhouse was callin' us names ag'in today. Dey called us—uh-uh—bastards.

**ELIZA:** Shet yo' mouf, Mame! Yo' Pa tol' you he didn't nevah want to heah you say dat word ag'in.

**MAME:** But Ma, we didn' say it. Das what dey called us. Dat wa'n' so bad, but when dey started callin' Pa one too, me an' Bud hit 'em, but dey was more'n us. Jes de same I hit Johnny Amps a good lick right in de mouf, an' made it bleed.

**ELMER:** *(thru his tears and sniffling)* Ma, how come dey call us bastards?

**ELIZA:** *(patting him on the head)* Heish yo' cryin'. Don't you see who's heah? Go ovah dere an' see Mammy Ca'line. She been waitin' heah foh you. *(Both children forget their troubles and go over to* MAMMY CAROLINE*)*

**MAME:** Lawd, Mammy Ca'line, we didn' see you.

**ELMER:** *(still sulkin)* Howdy, Mammy.

**MAMMY:** How you do, chillun? So you been fightin', eh? Good boys an' gals don' fight.

**MAME:** But, Mammy Ca'line, dey called Pa a bad name, an' we wa'n' goin' to stand foh it.

**MAMMY:** Chile, yo' pa c'n take keer o' hisse'f bettah 'n you kin. You leave dem things to yo' pa.

**ELMER:** Mammy Ca'line, what's a bastard?

**ELIZA:** You Elmer! Didn' I tell you 'bout sayin' dat?

**MAMMY:** *(raising her hand to* ELIZA*)* Das awright, daughtah *(to the children)* Bastards is chillun what ain' got no ma an' pa. Now you knows you ain' none, 'cause you got a ma an' a pa, too.

**ELMER:** But dey say Pa's one. Ain' he got no pa an' ma?

**MAMMY:** *(vehemently, and striking her cane on the floor for emphasis)* Co'se he had a ma an' pa. Co'se he did. Ain' I brung his ma in dis worl' jes lak I brung him an' you too?

**ELMER:** Mammy Ca'line, tell us about Pa's ma an' pa. We ain' nevah hyeahd 'bout 'em, is we, Sis?

**MAME:** No'm. Mammy Ca'line, do tell us.

**MAMMY:** Set down heah, chillun, by Mammy's chair. You too big an' my limbs too feeble foh me to hol' you in my lap lak I use' to do when you was babies so high. *(indicating the height* *with her hand)* Set down heah on de flo' close to Mammy. Clem's ma, Nannie, was one o' de puttes' cullud gals I evah laid eyes on. She was de only one o' huh kin'. She had colah lak a ripe magnolia jes when it's ripe an' turnin'. She was built lak a 'oman in a pitchah book—tall lak Clem an' straight an' proud es a peacock. Clem is de spittin' image of 'is ma. Yassah, jes lak huh foh de worl'.

**MAME:** Mammy Ca'line, do I look lak Pa's ma what was so putty?

**ELMER:** Aw, shet up, Sis!

**MAMMY:** *(with an original or unusual chuckle)* He! He! Lawd, gal, you is a case! You chillun don' take much from yo' ma's side.

**ELIZA:** *(smiling and nodding agreement)* Dey sho don', Mammy.

**MAMMY:** Nannie, po' chile, wa'n' nevah no 'count attah she brung Clem in de worl'. She wa'n' strong an' built foh labor pains, no-how. When Clem's sistah, Ma'y Jane, was bo'n, she had a hard time. Ma'y Jane didn' weigh but sebben pounds, an' Clem weighed lebben pounds when he come heah. Boy chillun is allus mo' trouble'n gals is. *(*MAME *makes a face at* ELMER*)* But de main cause Nannie ain' got well no mo' was 'cause she grieve all de time 'bout Clem's pa, John. John was a hot-head niggah. He got all moxed up wid some o' dem Yankee folks what come roun' stirrin' up de slaves tellin' 'em to come up No'th wheah dey c'n be free. John ain' nevah wan' be no slave, an' one night he run away 'way pas' midnight. 'Tell dis day ain' nobody knowed what come o' him. Po' Nannie jes grieve huhse'f to death 'bout huh man. When Cunnel Thompson looked at dat fine baby, his heart was teched. When Clem growed up, de Cunnel laked 'im so much, he made 'im his privey boy, an' treat Clem almos' lak 'is own chile. Now y'all knows all 'bout yo' pas' ma an pa.

**ELIZA:** Y'all bettah be glad Mammy Ca'line was heah today. She done tol' you mo' 'bout yo' pa'n I could evah tell you.

**MAMMY:** Well, chillun, look lak dat boy, Clem, ain' comin'. Hit's gittin' 'long 'bout sundown an' Mammy can' see good nowadays. I got to be goin' home. *(She starts to rise)*

**ELIZA:** But Mammy Ca'line, you ain' 'had nothin' t'eat yit, an' Clem's goin' be comin' in any minute now.

**MAMMY:** Naw, honey, I ain' got no time to eat now. Jes gimme a li'l snack in a bag an' I'll eat when I gits home. I can' wait foh Clem.

**ELIZA:** Awright, you jes wait 'tell I fix you a little some'm. By dat time maybe Clem'll be heah. (ELIZA *goes out left door*)

**ELMER:** Mammy Ca'line, was you a slave, too?

**MAMMY:** Naw, chile, I wa'n' no slave. I was bo'n o' freedmen. My pa bought his freedom an' my ma's 'fo' I was bon'n. My pas was a Creole from n' O'leans. He used to make clothes foh de big, rich white folks. Dem was de days when clothes was gran' an' looked lak some'm. Dey wa'n' lak dese rags dey wears nowadays.

**ELIZA:** (*returning with a carefully wrapped package which she gives to* MAMMY) I don' see what's keepin' Clem so long. I knows he'll be sorry he missed you, Mammy Ca'line.

**MAMMY:** (*getting up slowly and grunting from pain*) Well, I reckon deah'll be anothah time to see Clem 'fo' I crosses ovah. Sun's a long way down now, ain't it, honey?

**ELIZA:** (*looking out of the window*) Yas, Mammy, I 'spec' you bettah let Mame an' Elmer go down de road a piece wid you. (*To children*) Y'all go out yondah on de back poach an' git a lantern so you c'n go 'long wid Mammy Ca'line, 'cause it'll be dark when you comes back. Wash yo' face an' straighten up yo' clothes whilse yo out dere. (ELMER *and* MAME *go out the left door.*)

**MAMMY:** (*sitting down again and speaking in a stern voice*) 'Liza, you an' Clem got to stop yo' way o' livin'. Das how come I wants to see Clem. I ain' said much to y'all b'fo' now 'cause I ain' want to meddle in y'all's business, but I sees some'm got to be done right now, adtah what I done seed today. You an' Clem got to jine de church an' git ma'ied lak you oughta, an' do right by dem chillun. Anothah thing, when I gits up yondah to hebben I wants my slate to be all cleah 'fo' de blessed Mastah. I wants to tell 'im dat all my chillun b'longs to God. I wants my heart to be free from sin. You tell Clem what I say.

**ELIZA:** I wants to git ma'ied an' jine de church so's Clem an' me an' de chillun c'n go 'bout lak othah folks. Das de one thing Clem an' me don' agree on. I used to try to reason wid 'im, but it didn' do nothin' but make trouble 'tween us, so I jes give it up. I loves Clem too much to let anything come 'tween us.

**MAMMY:** I know, chile! I know, chile!

**ELIZA:** I sho wished you'd stay heah an' talk to 'im, Mammy. Maybe it'd do some good.

**MAMMY:** *(looking up at* ELIZA *from underneath her bonnet, and speaking with determination)* Fight you' own battles, chile. Fight yo' own battles.

**ELIZA:** I done tried all I know how, Mammy, but it don' seem to do no good. You know Clem'll do anything foh you. I sho wished you'd talk to 'im dis ve'y night.

**MAMMY:** Clem's yo' man, 'Liza. Dey ain' no man bo'n o' woman what can be handled by a woman, ef she go 'bout it in de right way. Clem's ma, Nannie, was a God-fearin' 'oman. De las' words dat po' gal said to me on huh dyin' bed was, "Mammy, take good keer o' my chillun, an' bring 'em up in de feah o' God." When I meets dat chile up yondah in glory, I wants to tell 'uh I done done what she tol' me to do. You tell Clem dat. He ain' no fool, even ef he is lak 'is bull-head pa. *(The children return with lantern)* Come on, chillun, is y'all ready?

**MAME AND ELMER:** Yas'm. *(Just as they start out,* MAMMY *toward the left door and the children toward the front door —*MAMMY *stops suddenly and listens)*

**MAMMY:** *(in quick and bated breath)* Heish! Heish!

**MAME:** What you heah, Mammy Ca'line?

**MAMMY:** *(still listening intently)* Shet yo' mouf, chile, an' listen. *(All listen intently)* Don' you heah it? Don' you heah it? Das a screech owl—a death owl. (ELMER *and* MAME *look frightened and go over to their mother, nestling up to her for protection. The weird and fearful wailing of the owl can be heard in the distance.)* Lawd 'a' mussy, das death sho's you bo'n! Git a ole shoe, 'Liza, an' turn it down undah de bed. Any time you heahs dem owls cry hit's God callin' on somebody to come to jedgment. Go git one o' Clem's ole shoes an' turn it down, chile. (ELIZA *goes out left door with* MAME *and* ELMER *holding on to her dress in fright.* MAMMY *raises her hands and mutters prayerfully)* Lawd, gimme jes a lil mo' time. Jes a li'l mo' time, bessed Mastah. *(She bows her head over her walking stick as in silent prayer.* ELIZA *and the children return)* He done stopped? Heish, le's see. *(All stand and listen)* Yas, dat done it. Le's go, chillun. *(Children start out as before.)* Wheah y'all gwine? I ain' gwine out dat way. I don' wan' no bad luck to go 'way from heah wid me. I'm gwine out de same way I come in heah. 'Sides, I ain' so much on climbin' dem high steps. Mammy's ole an' feeble now. *(They all go out the left door)*

**ELIZA:** Goodby, Mammy. I'll tell Clem what you you say.

**MAMMY:** Goodbye, honey.

**ELIZA:** Mame, you an' Elmer hurry right back, an' don' you stop nowheah on de road.

**MAME AND ELMER:** Yas'm.

*(*ELIZA, *alone again, begins clearing away the dishes and other things as she had been doing when* MAMMY *came in. She takes the dishes out the side door.* CLEM *enters. He is a tall, rather good-looking mulatto, about thirty-eight years old. He has a mass of curly black hair which is badly in need of cutting, and he is dressed in field clothes—brown corduroy trousers, blue cotton shirt, and high-topped brogan shoes. His face shows strength and intelligence. Independence almost to the point of stubbornness, an inflammable temper, but beneath all a gentleness and kindliness—these are further marks of his character. He casually removes his hat and hangs it on the rack.)*

**ELIZA:** *(returning to the room and seeing* CLEM*)* Clem! Lawd, you is jes too late. Who you reckon been heah to see you?

**CLEM:** You puzzle me, 'cause I know dey an' nobody in dese bottoms what go'n' come to see me 'lessen dey wants some'm.

**ELIZA:** *(reproachfully)* Well, dey is, an' ef it wa'n' gittin' 'long 'bout dark dey'd a' been heah it, an' dey ain' wantin' nothin'.

**CLEM:** *(indifferently)* Don' know who't could 'a' been.

**ELIZA:** Well, it was Mammy Ca'line, das who 'twas.

**CLEM:** *(cheered)* Ah . . . Mammy Ca'line! Das diffunt. Why n' you call me? I been right down by de ole oak foh de las' hour uh so.

**ELIZA:** I didn' wan to bothah you, Clem, an' I kinda thought you'd be comin' in any minute.

**CLEM:** How's Mammy gittin' 'long?

**ELIZA:** She sho look feeble, Clem. I hates to see 'uh tryin' to git about. I wish dey was some way we could git 'uh to leave dat ole shack down by de ditch an' come heah an' live wid us wheah we could see aftah huh.

**CLEM:** Yas, I wish de same thing, but ain' no use'n wishin', 'cause you know Mammy ain' go'n' leave dat house. Some'm keep 'uh dere, I don' know what 'tis. You give 'uh sume'm?

**ELIZA:** Yas, I give 'uh a half a shouldah o' bacon, an' some coffee an' a dollah. Dat awright?

**CLEM:** Yas, 'ceptin' you might 'a give 'uh some mo' money.

**ELIZA:** Das all I had in change. Did de mailman leave a lettah dis mawnin', Clem? I seed y'all talkin' out by de box.

**CLEM:** Yas, dey was a lettah from Sis.

**ELIZA:** Is huh an' Jasper well?

**CLEM:** Yas, dey's well, but Sis says she gits mighty lonesome to see me an' you an' de chillun sometime.

**ELIZA:** What else she say? Say anything 'bout when dey's comin' down heah?

**CLEM:** She says she don' know when dey c'n come. She was jes wonderin' ef . . . seein' huh an' Jasper ain' got no chillun an' dey got plenty room in dey new house . . . ef it wouldn' be nice ef Mame an' Elmer come up dere to live wid dem an' go to school an' git a good ejucation.

**ELIZA:** *(visibly aroused)* Tell 'uh naw, Clem. Naw sah! I ain' wantin' Mame an' Elmer to go 'way up yondah to Sain' Louis. Dey c'n git plenty ejucation right heah in Camdus. Let Ma'y Jane an' Jasper git chillun o' dey own. You an' Mame an' Elmer is all I got to live foh, Clem, an' I wants y'all right heah by me.

**CLEM:** How come you gittin' all stirred up? I ain' said Mame an' Elmer was goin' nowheah, is I? You as' me what Sis said an' I'm jes tellin' you, das all. Wheah's Mame an' Elmer?

**ELIZA:** Dey gone down de road a piece wid Mammy Ca'line. Soon's dey come back, I'm go'n' put suppah on de table. *(ELIZA goes out with dishes. CLEM goes over to the front door, throws it open, fills his pipe, and stands with his back to the room, smoking and looking thoughtfully out over the landscape. ELIZA is heard singing from without. As she returns, a church bell is heard ringing in the distance.)*

**CLEM:** *(turning around)* Well, dere goes de church bell, callin' de hypocrites an' backslidahs togethah ag'in. Revival's goin' on now. Niggahs gittin' up confessin' dey sins, an' talkin' 'bout startin' a new life. An' soon's revival's ovah dey goes on doin' jest lak dey was 'fo' it started.

ELIZA: Clem, you ain't got no right to poke fun at othah folks goin' to church. You oughtn' talk lak dat nohow.

CLEM: Talk lak what? You sho is gittin' aueah dese days. Don' seem lak de same woman foh a week er so. What's de mattah? Ain' you feelin' good, er is you gittin' 'ligion too?

ELIZA: I'm awright. I jes don' lak to heah you talkin' 'gin de church so. Hit ain' right.

CLEM: 'Liza, when yo git so yo was de guardian angel foh de church? Dat don' soun' lak you talkin'. I knows what's wrong wid you. Settin' heah sewin' on dem quilts all de time. You needs some fresh aih an' outside work to liven you up, das what you needs.

ELIZA: Dey ain' nothin' 't all wrong wid me, Clem. I gits a plenty aih out lookin' aftah dem chickens an' cows. An' I ain' been quiltin' all day heah lately, 'cause lak today, some days comp'ny been heah.

CLEM: Comp'ny? What kin' o' comp'ny? You ain' callin' Mammy Ca'line comp'ny, is you?

ELIZA: Naw, somebody 'sides Mammy Ca'line been heah.

CLEM: Ef it was somebody else, dey must 'a been wantin' some'm. Das de only time dese Jesus-lovin' an' God-fearin' niggahs comes heah. We low-down sinnahs in dey sight, but dey don' nevah let dat stop 'em when dey wants come'm. What dey want dis time?

ELIZA: Clem, what you ravin' so 'bout? Don' nobody wan' nothin' foh deyse'f an' de church neithah.

CLEM: Well den, who been heah? How come you so secut 'bout it?

ELIZA: Dey ain' been so secut 'bout it, Clem. Mis' Doshia Braggs been heah two times dis las' gone week, an' today huh an' Mis' Mahala Turnah been heah. An' . . .

CLEM: Uh-huh! Now I knows how come you talkin' so righteous 'bout de church an' actin' so sanctified. Dem ole sistahs been 'roun' heah tryin' to put de feah o' God in you, an' tendin' to ev'body's business 'ceptin' dey own.

**ELIZA:** Clem, you oughtn' talk lak dat 'bout Mis Doshia. She's a good 'oman an' don' harm nobody. She ain' nevah stop comin' to see us lak de rest of 'em. She say you an' me . . .

**CLEM:** *(showing animation)* Yas, yas, I know what she say. It's de same ole chune. Repent, come to Jesus. You chillun is livin' in sin. Jes a whole lot o' fool talk, daa sll 'tis. All dem hallelujah niggahs c'n do is talk. Dey don' nevah try an' live by what dey says.

**ELIZA:** Clem, hon', don' talk lak dat. God go'n' punish you sho's you bo'n, you keep on jokin' 'bout His works lak yo is.

**CLEM:** I ain' jokin' 'bout God's work, no sech thing. I'm talkin' 'bout dem backbitin' niggahs up yondah to Piney Grove Church what won' let a hones' hard-workin' man an' his family live in peace.

**ELIZA:** But Clem, dey . . .

**CLEM:** *(with increasing animation)* Ain' no "but Clem" 'bout it. I been lookin' to heah some'm lak dis out o' you evah since I hyeahd 'bout dat pow'ful preachah ca'yin' on revival. Eva-wheah you goes now, you hyeahs 'em talkin' 'bout what a great preachah he is, an' how he go'n' git some o' dem hard-shell sin-nahs what thinks dey can' be got.

**ELIZA:** But Clem, all dey wants . . .

**CLEM:** Yes, all dey wants is you an' me to be liahs an' hypo-crites lak dey is; goin' 'roun' shoutin' hallelujah an' praise de Lawd wid ouah moufs lak dey do, whilse in dey hearts dey got uhnough sin an' dirt to fill de ocean. Dey can' stan' nobody who don' think an' ac' jes lak dey do. When you ain' lak dey is, dey's scared you gittin' some'm dey ain' gittin', an' dey tries to houn' yo' life out.

**ELIZA:** I knows dey's a whole lot o' truf in what you sayin', Clem. But dere's mo' 'n one side to it.

**CLEM:** 'Liza, looks lak when dem church sistahs gits aroun' you, you forgits ouah side an' b'lieves all dey says. Heah we been livin' togethah in Camdus foh twelves yeahs, an' jes 'cause we ain' as' no preachah could we live togethah, we ain' had no peace. You wanted me an' I wanted you. It wa'n't nobody's business but jes ouah own. Dey ain' been no mo' peaceful an' ten-to-yo'-own-business folks 'roun' heah 'n we is. We both worked lak hosses, saved all we could rake an' scrape, an' paid down on dis farm, an' now we got it all paid foh. An' jes 'cause we ain' got no ma'iage papahs, we ain' Christians. Dere ole Cassie Simmons had to go to co't to make Sam Phillips ma'y huh gal aftah he give 'uh a baby. Sam lef' de gal two days aftah he ma'ied huh an' ain' been seen nor hyeahd tell of since. An' dat gal an' huh Christian-talkin' mammy got de nerve to talk 'bout somebody livin' in sin an' 'dultry. Ef it was jes you an' me dey pestered, I wouldn' min,' but dey keeps aftah de chillun, callin' 'em out o' dey names to dey face an' 'hind dey backs.

**ELIZA:** (*eager to make her point here*) Den you hit de nail on de head, honey. You an' me don' mattah. We c'n stan' all dey says, but it's de chillun we got to think about mo'. 'Tina' fair to dem foh you an' me to go on lak dis. Mos' nigh evah day dey comes home cross an' frettin' 'cause some o' dem dev'lish chillun at de school house done hurt dey feelin's. Mos' time I don' say nothin' to you 'bout it, 'cause I knows how you loses yo' tempah. Jes dis ve'y day whilse Mammy Ca'line was heah dey come in from school wid dey clothes all messed up, an' Elmer was cryin' lak somebody done broke 'is heart, 'cause de chillun called 'em bastards ag'in. An' Clem, day as'es me things dat makes me sick to heah. I can' tell 'em de truf. Naw, I can' tell 'em we ain' ma'ied lak othah folks. De las' thing Mammy Ca'line said 'fo' she lef' was, "'Liza, you chillun got to stop yo' way o' livin'. You got to think least o' yo'se'f an' mo' 'bout dese heah chillun das growin' up an' go'n' be heah when you's dead an' gone."

**CLEM:** (*after a few moments of silence*) How come Mammy jes now gittin' so worked up 'bout de way you an' me livin'?

**ELIZA:** Mammy ain' wan' say nothin' to you an' me b'fo' 'cause she say it's ouah business, an' she don' want to be buttin' in jes 'cause we is huh chillun; but Mammy Ca'line love you, jes lak you was huh own chile. She proud o' you, too, Clem, an' she say she been prayin' to God foh to show us de way 'fo' she dies. She say yo' mas was a good Christian woman—a God-fearin' woman —an' de las' thing she said to Mammy Ca'line 'fo' she dies was "Mammy, take keer o' my chillun, an' raise 'em up to be good Christians. (*There is a change of expression on Clem's face. His independence and self-confidence desert him for a moment and he looks sad. The logic of all that* ELIZA *has said, together with this message from his mother, weakens him. He does not answer immediate-*

*ly, but walks about the room with his head bowed, his hands dug deep down into his pockets.* ELIZA *stands silently by, sensing the real situation. She realizes that this is the best opportunity for her to press her point home. She goes up to him, places her hands on his shoulders affectionately, as he stops walking with his back toward her. Gradually she moves around to face him and looks into his face with passionate affection and pleading, and bringing to bear all the feminine strategy at her command.)*

**CLEM:** 'Liza, ef we gits ma'ied, is dat go'n' make you mo happy?

**ELIZA:** You know I don' keer no mo' 'bout it den you, Clem, 'cause it ain' go'n'make me love you no mo', but it sho will bring mo' peace. An' Clem, I wants you to jine church an' go 'mongst dem folks up dere so's dey c'n see what a good man you is. I knows you a bettah man den a dozen o' dem what hangs 'roun' de church. Dey go'n' see. Dey jes can' he'p it. I was jes sayin' dat to Mis' Doshia today.

**CLEM:** *(trying to remain adamant, but even his voice shows a change, a softening, a weakening in his attitude)* What Mis' Doshia been comin' heah foh so much lately? She wan' money to he'p pay dat new preachah, I bet.

**ELIZA:** Naw, she ain' wantin' no money. She jes wan' know ef de committee c'n come ovah heah dis evenin' to git us to jine church.

**CLEM:** *(quickly)* What you tell huh?

**ELIZA:** I didn' tell 'uh nothin'. I jes said I'd talk wid you 'bout it, an' ef you said yas, it was awright wid me, an' I'd let 'uh know.

**CLEM:** Let 'uh know when?

**ELIZA:** Whenevah you say, hon'. Don't make no diffunce 'bout de time.

**CLEM:** I can' be bothered wid all dat stuff. *(As he talks, he seems to gain confidence in himself from the force of his own words and voice, but it is only a last and momentary stand which* ELIZA *skillfully breaks down)*

**ELIZA:** But Clem, you 'bout to forgit de chillun. You knows hit's dem we got to be thinkin' 'bout.

**CLEM:** Oh, yas! Wondah wheah dey is. Ain' dey been gone long uhnough to be back now? 'Spec' I bettah go an' see wheah dey is. Hit's gittin' mighty dark foh dem to be out by deyse'f.

**ELIZA:** *(divining his attempt to evade the issue by running away)* Naw, naw. Dey is awright. Dey got a lantern wid 'em, an' I reckon dey be heah any minute now. You set down a minute. I'm go'n' put suppah on de table, an' by dat time de chillun'll be heah. Suppah's all ready. Hit's on de stove keepin' hot, an' I got some'm you laks. *(She starts out, then stops suddenly at the left door)* But Clem, how 'bout de committee? C'n dey come?

**CLEM:** *(sharply)* Come when?

**ELIZA:** *(softly and pleadingly)* C'n dey come dis evenin', honey?

**CLEM:** *(hesitating, and answering sulkily like a spoiled boy)* My Lawd, yas, I s'pose dey may's well come dis evenin' as any time, but dey ain' go'n' make me do nothin' I don' wanna do. (ELIZA *comes up to him and embraces him. Clem, apparently, does not share her happiness and appears indifferent to her embraces.*)

**ELIZA:** Oh, Clem, I'm so glad! I knowed you'd see it de right way. You a good man, Clem, a good man. Now we go'n' hurry an' eat 'cause it'll soon be time foh de committee to be heah. Mis' Doshia said 'bout firs' night.

**CLEM:** *(visibly affected by the deception he thinks he senses)* Said what? An' you done tol' 'uh yas 'fo' you even as' me? Thought you was as'in' me could dey come. You done give 'em my ansah 'fo' I knowed what 'tas myse'f.

**ELIZA:** Naw, Clem. I jes tol' 'uh ef she didn' heah from me by firs' night to come on ovah, but ef you said naw, I'd sen' 'uh word. Dat saved a trip, das all. But I knowed you say yas. Now I'm go'n' put suppah on.

**CLEM:** Das awright 'bout suppah. You don' need to fix none foh me.

**ELIZA:** *(with sudden surprise)* What's mattah, Clem? You mean you ain' go'n' eat nothin', an' I done fix you a special dish? I got apple dumplin's wid a whole lot o' dumplin's, lak you lak 'em.

**CLEM:** Naw, I ain' go'n' eat nothin'. I wants to have all my senses cleah an' ready an' sharp when dese folks come. An' I sho can' think good an' cleah when my belly's full. A fully belly clogs de brain, I allus hyeahd 'em say. Any mo' dat soupnong wine lef' from las' yeah's makin'? *(He walks to the washstand and takes a jug from the lower part, pours out a glass of wine, and drinks it in one tilt. Then he gives a drinker's puff)*

**CLEM:** Dis is what I needs to sharpen my brains. Dis ole wine is gettin better and better. (ELIZA *looks at him anxiously, but refrains speaking, in the interest of peace.* CLEM *takes the jug and goes to a seat beside the table, lights his pipe and stretches out for a smoke.)*

**CLEM:** Now let de committee, de deacons, and de preacher all come. I'm ready for 'em all.

(Curtain: End of Act I, Scene 1).

SCENE 2

*Same as Scene 1. It is evening of the same day, about an hour later.* CLEM *is stretched out on the long box-couch beside the right wall, his head propped up on folded quilts. He is blowing smoke into the air and appears generally at ease. The room is dark except for the light of a brilliant spring moon shining in through the windows.* ELIZA *comes in with two lighted oil lamps, holding them far out from her body to avoid soiling her clean clothes. She is dressed in a plain white cotton shirt-waist, black skirt, and white apron. She stops with surprise when she sees* CLEM.

**ELIZA:** Clem! Lawd, you been dere all dis time? Ain' you go'n' put on yo' good clothes 'fo' de committee come?

**CLEM:** *(indignantly)* Put on my good clothes for what? Ef dey can' see me lak I is, dey c'n jes stay 'way from my house. You mus' think dey is Jesus hisse'f, wantin' me to dress up foh 'em. Naw, I ain' go'n' put on nothin'. I'm go'n' stay jes lak I is, so don't bothah me no mo'.

**ELIZA:** *(placing the lamps and noticing the jug and glass on the table)* Is you thoo wid dis heah wine, Clem? I hope to God you is.

**CLEM:** Naw, gimme anothah swallah, den put it back, 'cause ef dese niggahs what's comin' heah sees it, dey won' leave heah 'tell it's all gone.

**ELIZA:** *(pouring him another glass and taking it over to him)* Clem, ain' you had uhnough o' dis stuff? You know dis wine's ole an' strong es c'n be.

**CLEM:** *(taking the wine)* Das awright, I wish it was a whole lot strongah. I needs some'm strong to put dese heah niggahs in dey place.

**ELIZA:** I didn' want you to change yo' clothes jes foh de committee, Clem. I wan' you to do it mo foh yo' own sake.

**CLEM:** How you mean foh my own sake? What good's changin' clothes go'n' do me?

**ELIZA:** A heap o' good, Clem. You know clothes an' outside looks is got a whole lot to do wid makin' folks b'lieve what you says. An' I wants 'em to see you at yo' bes' from all sides. It ain' foh dem I wants you to do it, 'cause dey ain' nothin' 'side you, Clem. You looks bettah'n any o' dem any way you comes. But co'se ef you don' wan' do it, hit's awright. I jes wished you could make up yo' mind to. *(CLEM does not answer. He remains stretched out smoking, but not with the same ease and comfort as before. It is only a last-minute obstinacy . . . his masculine pride that keeps him from admitting defeat and telling ELIZA that he will dress. Yet he knows that he will. The most he will say is a long deep sigh and a grunt.)*

**CLEM:** Uh—huhn. Maybe so.

**ELIZA:** Well, Clem, since you ain' go'n' change yo' clothes, bring de chaihs in from de rest o' de house. I 'spec' we go'n' need one o' dem benches on de front poach 'cause we ain' go'n' have uhnough chaihs, so bring one o' dem 'long whilse you at it.

**CLEM:** *(sitting up suddenly)* Look heah! Is dey dat many niggahs comin' heah dis evenin'? Call de chillun an' let dem bring de chaihs in. I got some'm else to do. *(He rises)*

**ELIZA:** *(looking at him doubtfully, but deciding not to say what she is thinking)* Awright, dey's straight'nin' up in de kitchen now, but I reckon dey 'bout thoo. Tell Elmer to come heah when you goes thoo de kitchen, Clem. *(CLEM goes out left door. ELIZA continues to dust and arrange the room)*

**ELMER:** *(entering)* You want me, Ma?

**ELIZA:** Yas, y'all done cleanin' up?

**ELMER:** No'm, almos'.

ELIZA: Well, Mame c'n finish what's lef'. You go bring in de chaihs from de res' o' de house. An' soon's Mame git thoo, I wan' y'al to bring in one o' dem benches off de front poach. Be sho you gits de bes' un. Dat un on de side by de barn, 'cause de othah un's kinda rickety.

ELMER: What you fixin' up foh, Ma? You gonna have a party?

ELIZA: Now, don' stan' dere as'in' me a whole lot o' questions. Go on an' do lak I tol' you. An' go tell Mame to hurry an' git thoo what she's doin'. Y'all takes 'tirely too long to clean dem few dishes an' straighten up back dere. (ELMER *goes out and soon returns with a chair, then another. As he brings them in,* ELIZA *dusts them and places them around the table*)

ELMER: (*as he brings the third chair*) Ma, I knows what's gonna happen, I bet.

ELIZA: You don' know nothin'. An' guessin' ain' go'n' make me tell you fo' I gits ready, so jes go on wid what you doin'. (ELMER *goes out, crestfallen.* MAME *enters with her sleeves rolled up to her elbows*)

MAME: Ma, Pa say wheah his collah buttons. What you fixin' up foh, Ma? How come you all dressed up?

ELIZA: (*shaking her head and smiling as she realizes her victory over* CLEM) Don' as' so many questions, Mame. You wuss 'n yo' baby brothah. Come heah an' do dis dustin' whilse I go see what yo' pa wants. (*She goes out left door.*)

ELMER: (*re-entering, backing in with a large chair*) Dese all de chaihs, Ma. Anything else? (*Looking around and seeing his sister instead of his mother*) Wheah Ma, Sis?

MAME: She gone to see what Pa want. You foun' out what 'tis?

ELMER: (*shaking his head*) Naw, I don' know, but I becha I c'n guess.

MAME: What?

ELMER: I bet it's gonna be a party foh de new preachah up to de church. Das all you hyeahs talk 'bout now. Johnny Amps say dey give a party foh de preachah at dey house an' he seed de preachah drink some w'iskey what his pa give 'im.

**MAME:** I bet you is wrong. You know Pa don' go 'roun' church, an' you know what he say 'bout he ain' gonna fatten no preachah at his table.

**ELMER:** Daw awright; Mis' Doshia Braggs been heah to see Ma, an' you know Mis' Doshia don' study 'bout nothin' but de church. Say, Sis, I betcha my blue pencil 'gainst yo' long green un it's foh de preachah.

**MAME:** I ain' gonna betcha nothin'. Ma done tol' you 'bout bettin'. Hit's gamblin'. (ELIZA *returns, beaming with happiness. The two children gasp with surprise when* CLEM *comes in behind her dressed in his best clothes. He is quite uncomfortable, and looks it, in his black suit now grown too small and long out of style. It is plainly a relic of his younger days for which he has had little use on the farm, as he does not go to church. The high stiff collar adds to his discomfort. The shave and grooming of his hair and his changed mental attitude make his handsome face strikingly inconsistent with his ill-fitting garments.*)

**ELIZA:** *(as she enters)* Is y'all done, Mame?

**MAME:** Yas'm, jes about.

**ELMER:** *(eagerly)* Ma, come on, tell us what the meetin's about.

**ELIZA:** Boy, you mo' cur'ous 'n a woman! But y'all ain' brought de bench in yit.

*(*ELMER *and* MAME *rush out left door for the bench)*

**ELIZA:** Clem, don' you want to tell de chillun 'bout de meetin'?

**CLEM:** *(pulling at his collar)* Naw, it ain' none o' my meetin'. Tell 'em yo'se'f. You de one what's havin' it.

**ELIZA:** Awright, I jes thought . . . but daw awright. I'll do it. (MAME *and* ELMER *return with the bench)*

**ELMER:** Now we ready, Ma.

**ELIZA:** Well, I reckon I bettah tell you so I c'n have some peace. Set de bench right heah. Dis evenin' some folks from de church is comin' to see yo' pa an' ma.

**ELMER:** *(jumping with glee)* I tol' you so, Sis! I tol' you so!

**ELIZA:** Be quiet, boy! Now you knows, I wants you an' Mame to go on to bed wheah you b'longs.

**ELMER:** But Ma, can' me an' Sis stay up jes a li'l while an' see de folks? What dey comin' foh, Ma?

**ELIZA:** My Lawd, boy, you sho is nosey. You an' Mame go on to bed lak good chillun.

**ELMER:** Ma, please ma'am let us stay in heah Jes a li'l while, Ma. We won' keep no noise, will we, Sis?

**MAME:** Naw! Ma, please ma'am let us stay a li'l while.

**ELIZA:** Naw, you can' stay. Now dat settles it.

**ELMER:** Pa, you ain' tol' us ouah story yet.

**ELIZA:** Dey ain' no time foh no story tonight. Hit's 'bout time foh 'em to come.

**CLEM:** Ain' no time? 'Liza, dese chillun comes 'fo' all de committees. Ef I tells y'all a story, you'll go right to bed, won't you?

**MAME AND ELMER:** *(joyfully)* Yassah.

**ELIZA:** Well, I reckon you is got time foh a shawt one 'fo' dey comes. *(She looks about the room to see that things are in order, then goes out the side door.)*

**MAME:** Pa, tell us de one 'bout de rabbit an' de possum.

**ELMER:** Naw, Pa, tell us de one 'bout de lion an' de rabbit.

**CLEM:** *(raising his hand in mock protest)* Wait, wait! Now le's see. You wan' one story, Mame, an' Elmer, you wants anothah. Le's pull straws to see who wins.

**ELMER:** *(running out the left door to get the broom)* I take de long straw!

**CLEM:** Awright. *(He pulls the straws from the broom and turns from the children to arrange them, then holds them out.)* Now heah we is. You pull firs', Mame. Now you pull, Elmer. *(They compare straws and* ELMER *has the longer.)* Elmer got de longes' straw, so we'll tell about de lion an' de rabbit. Tomorrah I'll tell yo' story, Mame. *(*CLEM *sits down.* MAME *sits on the floor, leaning against her father's leg, her head resting on his knee.* ELMER *stretches out on the floor face down, the upper part of his body raised on his elbows, his face held between his palms, and his heels in the air.)* Mistah Lion is de king of all de animals in de fores'. He rules 'em all.

**ELMER:** Even de great big elephant?

**CLEM:** Yas, even de elephant got to bow to King Lion. Well, every night King Lion would go out to git his meal. Sometime he would take a bear, sometime a deer, an' when he was right hongry he would tackle a elephant. De rest o' de animals was gittin' purty skeered, so dey called a meetin' an' as' King Lion to come an' talk things ovah an' see ef some'm couldn' be done to keep all of 'em from gittin' et up.

King Lion said, "Sho I'll come."

At de meetin' dey argued an' argued an' argued, but didn' look lak dey was go'n' fin' no way to please King Lion. By an' by Mistah Wise Fox say, "I got a plan. How's dis, King Lion? You stay in yo' house an' ev'ry day somebody will bring you some'm t' eat."

King Lion say, "Das awright wid me, but be sho you comes ev'ry day, an' brings a plenty."

So somebody got picked out foh ev'ry day to take some'm t' eat to King Lion. Aftah while somebody said, "Look heah, ain' none o' dem what's been totin' grub down yondah to King Lion's house come back yit. Wondah wheah dey is. An' sho 'nough, nobody hadn't seen none o' dem what went down to King Lion's. So de rest o' dem commenced gittin' skeered.

When it come to Mistah Rabbit's time, he was as skeered sho, 'cause he knowed he was so little he couldn' tote much an' King Lion would eat him to make up de meal. So he thought an' he thought an' he thought how he could git away from de King. He took so long 'tell when he got to King Lion's house de King was real hongry an' mad. "What's de mattah, Mistah Rabbit, you so late wid my grub?"

Mistah Rabbit say, "King Lion, I'm right sorry to be so late, but it wa'n' my fault. Anothah lion stopped me on de way heah an' took all yo' grub."

King Lion got mad sho 'nough when he hyeahd dis, an' he roared, "Who dares take my grub? Jes show 'im to me. I'll fix 'im so he won' do it no mo'."

Mistah Rabbit took 'im right down to de edge of de rivah an' say, "Look down here, King Lion. Dere's de one what took you' grub." King Lion was so mad when he look ovah in de watah an' seed de othah lion, he jes jumped right down aftah it an' sunk to de bottom, 'cause he couldn' swim. Ef he'd a took time to think he'd seen it was his own shadow down in de watah. Mistah Rabbit went back home an' all de animals come aroun' as' in' 'im how he got away from King Lion. (ELIZA *returns to the room and looks out of the window.*) Mistah Rabbit stuck out his ches' an' strut about an' say, right proud lak, "Brains, brains! King Lion had de might, but I got de brains an' heah I is."

**ELIZA:** *(turning from the window)* Heah dey comes now. Y'all done hyeah yo' story, now run on to bed lak good chillun.

**ELMER:** *(getting up reluctantly and whining in a half-spoiled manner)* Aw shucks, Ma. Let us stay jes a li'l while.

**ELIZA:** *(reprovingly)* Don't you be shucksin' me, boy. You git out o' heah dis minute 'fo' I take dat strop to you. *(MAME and ELMER go out reluctantly, but stand at the doorway peeping in as ELIZA opens the front door and admits the committee of about 12 persons, led by DEACON JOE SCRUGGS. He is a pious old man of about sixty-five years, who looks as if his early indiscretions have taken good toll. He wears a frock coat and carries a worn Bible. MRS. DOSHIA BRAGGS is the deacon's first lieutenant in conducting the meeting and makes it evident by her general efficiousness. All members of the committee shake hands with CLEM and ELIZA, and there are exchanges of greetings, such as the following:)*

How you do, Sistah!

How you do, Brothah!

Good evenin', Miss 'Liza!

Howdy, Clem, how's yo' co'n comin' 'long?

*(CLEM is civil, but by no means cordial in his greetings. He holds himself aloof, indifferent, with a chip-on-the-shoulder attitude. He is the last to sit down, a bit aside from the group around the center table. When everyone is seated, there is a momentary quiet, then DEACON SCRUGGS rises and in a very pompous, solemn manner addresses the group.)*

**SCRUGGS:** Brothahs an' sistahs, we air come heah dis evenin', by de he'p o' de Lawd, to pray an' wait on ouah neighbahs an' see ef we c'n bring 'em into de fol' o' de blessed Mastah. Let us commence by as'in' de Lawd's righteous blessin' whilse we sets about His biddin'. Sistah Doshia, lead us in a shawt word o' prayah. *(All kneel except CLEM, who sits with his elbows on his knees and his chin on the palms of his hands.)*

**MRS. DOSHIA:** *(praying)* O Lawd, come down 'mongst us dis evenin' an' he'p dese chillun to see de light. Show 'em de way to de kingdom. Larn 'em how to bow down an' be humble to Yo' will, blessed Mastah. Make 'em know dat You is de way an' de light o' de worl' an' besides You dere ain' no mo'. Give 'em dat faith dat passes all undahstandin'. Humble 'em, Lawd, humble 'em. Foh Jesus' sake, Amen.

**COMMITTEE:** *(in unison, as the prayer is ended and all rise)* Amen! Amen! Save 'em, Lawd! Do, blessed Mastah!

**SCRUGGS:** Now, brothahs an' sistahs, le's listen to de words o' de Mastah hisse'f, how when he say in de good book . . . *(He takes his old Bible that is filled with bookmarks, opens it to the place, and gives it to one of the younger members of the committee to read)* Read dere, brothah, what it say. I done forgot to bring my specs, an' my eyes ain' so good ' out 'em.

**BROTHER:** *(reading haltingly, painfully, from John 3:7. All listen in rapt silence as if truly they are hearing "the word of God.")* "Jesus answered and said unto him, verily, verily, I say unto thee, except a man be born again, he cannot see the kingdom of God." *(He stops)*

**SCRUGGS:** Read on, brothah, read on.

**BROTHER:** "Nicodemus saith unto him, How can a man be born when he is old? Can he enter the second time into his mother's womb and be born? Jesus answered, Verily, verily I say unto thee . . ."

**SCRUGGS:** *(interrupting)* Listen to 'im, chillun. Listen to de Mastah's word.

**BROTHER:** *(repeating)* "Verily, verily, I say unto thee, except a man be born of water and of the Spirit, he cannot enter into the kingdom of God."

**COMMITTEE:** *(led by* DEACON SCRUGGS*)* Amen! Amen!

**BROTHER:** *(continuing)* "Marvel not that I say unto thee, Ye must be born again."

**SCRUGGS:** Praise de Lawd! Dat'll do, brothah. Ye mus' be bo'n ag'in. Des de firs' p'int we want to take up wid ouah neighbahs, Mistah Clem Coleman an' Miss 'Liza . . . uh . . . uh . . . *(He cannot remember* ELIZA'S *maiden name and refuses to sanction their life by calling her by* CLEM'S *name. Some one of the committee comes to his assistance)*

**SISTER:** 'Liza Hicks.

**SCRUGGS:** *(continuing)* Uh-huh, Hicks, Hicks, yaas, yaas. Mistah Coleman an' Miss Hicks, we wants to 'stend you de right han' o' de church o' God an' 'vite you to jine de church. we wan' you to own up to yo' sins 'fo' de Lawd an' be baptized . . . be bo'n ag'in.

**CLEM:** But, Deacon, I was baptized when I was a baby, down to Freedonia Church on Cunnel Thompson's place.

**SCRUGGS:** Naw, son, naw, you ain' been baptized. You been what dey calls sprinkled, an' dat by a white man. Des awright foh dem white folks mebbe. But you can' go to hebben on dat, son. You can' go to hebben on dat! You got to go down undah de watahs an' git yo' soul an' body washed clean by de blood o' de Lamb. You got to be bo'n ag'in, lak de good book say, wid watah an' de sperret o' God.

**CLEM:** I been readin' de Bible same ez you, even ef I ain' no deacon, an' I ain' nevah seed nowheah in it wheah you got to go down undah de watahs to be baptized.

**SCRUGGS:** Daw awright, son. Naw, I ain' seed it, an' dat ain' all . . . I ain' got to see it foh myself to b'lieve it's dere. I takes de word o' de man o' God. Dat preachah up yondah to Piney Grove got mo' sense 'n' ejucation 'n you got ef you lives 'tell jedgment day. He's God's messengah. He says hi'ts dere, an' I knows it mus' be so. *(He looks around for the approval of the committee and when they do not respond, audibly, he asks:)* Ain' dat right, brothas an' sistahs?

**COMMITTEE:** You right, deacon. Tell 'em 'bout it, deacon! You right, brothah.

**SCRUGGS:** *(continuing, seeming to imbibe courage from this hearty response, and becoming more vehement)* das de trouble wid you young folks nowadays, you thinks you knows it all. You don' b'lieve. You doubts . . . *(an afterthought, by suggestion)* Uh-huh, lak doubtin' Thomas. *(appearing pleased with the originality of his thought and proudly repeating it)* Das what you is, doubtin' Thomas, doubtin' Thomas. But we ain' heah to argah wid you 'bout what's in de Bible an' what ain', Clem Coleman, an' it don' make no diffunce ef you is done been baptized, you is done backslided, an' we is heah to save yo' soul. 'Nothah thing we wants you an' yo' wi . . . *(He catches himself about to call* ELIZA CLEM'S *wife)* Uh . . . uh . . . I mean Miss . . . uh . . . uh . . . Hicks, to do when you is done jined de church an' been baptized is to git yo'se'f some ma'iage papahs an' go to de preachah an' git ma'ied an' be 'spectable folks.

**CLEM:** *(vehemently)* We already ma'ied. We been livin' togethah foh twelve yeahs, got a . . .

**SCRUGGS:** *(shaking his finger vigorously at* CLEM*)* Yas, das jes de trouble. You been livin' togethah all dem twelve yeahs in sin and 'dultry. De good book say . . . What it say dere, brothah? *(He takes the Bible and carefully looks thru the various marks until he finds the mark he wants, then gives the book to the* BROTHER, *pointing to the place)* Read what it say dere, son.

**BROTHER:** *(unintentionally losing his place and beginning to read from John 8:7)* "So when they continued asking him, he lifted up himself, and said unto them, He that is without sin among you, let him first cast a stone at . . ." *(*DEACON SCRUGGS *and others are surprised and embarrassed.* DEACON SCRUGGS *stops him.)*

**SCRUGGS:** Wait dere, son, you ain' readin' from de right place, is you? *(He takes the Bible and turns to the right mark and carefully points out the place to the* BROTHER, *who reads from Hebrews 15:4)*

**BROTHER:** *(reading)* "Marriage is honorable in all, and the bed undefiled; but whore-mongers . . ." *(Members of the* COM-MITTEE *look at one another, a bit shocked or startled that such a word is in the Bible)* "and adulterers God will punish."

**SCRUGGS:** Das all, son. Did you hyeah it? God gwine pun-ish you, 'cause das what you is.

**CLEM:** *(rising indignantly)* I is what?

**SCRUGGS:** *(meekly)* I ain' callin' you nothin', son. I ain' callin' you nothin', I'm jes talkin' de word o' God.

**CLEM:** But dat Bible don' say you got to have no papahs to marry. Hit don' say you got to go 'fo' no preachah to marry. I done looked thoo dis heah book from back to back an' I ain' nevah seen nowheah wheah it say how yo got to marry an' who got to marry you. All it say is marry. Somewheah it say ev'y man mus' take hisse'f a wife, an' das jes what I done done.

**SCRUGGS:** *(scratching his head meditatively and looking about the room as if expecting an answer to* CLEM'S *defense, which leaves him puzzled for a while)* Clem Coleman, you knows too much, cut de sho 'nough truf is you don' know nary thing, 'spe-cially 'bout de Bible. How you 'spec' a hard-shell sinnah lak you gwine know 'bout de Bible when you ain' seed God, you ain' felt de sperret o' God in yo' soul? You can' see what's in dat good

book 'cause God ain' gwine let you. God don' trus' His word to
sinnahs lak you. You 'spec' all dese ejucated white folks 'roun'
heah gwine be buyin' ma'iage papahs an' gwine to church to git
ma'ied by de preachah ef it wa'n't de law o' God? Clem Coleman,
you got to change yo' way o' livin'. You got to git right wid God.
Kepp on livin' lak you is, in sin an' 'dultry an' temptin' de Lawd,
an' He gwine smite you one o' dese days when you leas' 'spectin'
it, an' de devil gwine take yo soul an' body right on down to
to'ment. An' you is takin' dis heah good, God-fearin' 'oman an'
dem two chillun right down wid you. You knows dey will come in
ef you will. God knows it, too, an' He gwine hold it 'gainst you
foh keepin' dem out o' de church.

    **CLEM:** *(still standing)* I don' see how come y'all botherin'
so 'bout me an' 'Liza an' how we's livin'. You ain' got to die foh
us, is you? Ef we is happy livin' lak we is, what y'all got to do wif
it? We goes 'long tendin' to ouah own business. We don't owe
nobody nothin' an' don' as' nobody foh nothin'. How come you
can' let us be? Dey's a whole lot o' y'all what's in de church, been
baptized, and got ma'ied by de prechah, an' you do mo' sinnin' 'n
I even thinks about.

    **SISTER:** *(turning to her neighbor)* Who he talkin' 'bout?

    **CLEM:** I ain' callin' no names, but I goes 'bout in dese bot-
toms, an' I don' fail to see what's goin' on. An' I knows 'tain' only
de sinnahs I sees goin' in Jim Duke's saloon down yondah in
Genessee. Dey ain' all sinnahs I sees a-flyin' 'roun' wid othah
womens what dey ain' ma'ied to . . . jes lak dey ain' got dey own
wife an' chillun back home. 'Tain' always de lowdown sinnahs
y'all Christians talks 'gainst so much what goes down back o'
alleys an' shoots craps wid de money dey oughta be takin' home
to dey family. Hit ain' no sinnah man, what live right heah in
Camdus, an' got a baby by a little gal an' he got chillun biggah 'n
huh. I ain' callin' no names, I tells you, but I knows a thing er two
'bout some folks what ain' s'posed to be sinnahs. Don' y'all come
heah talkin' to me 'bout Christians, jinin' de church, an' gittin'
ma'ied. I ain'. . . .

    **MRS. DOSHIA:** *(who has with great difficulty restrained
herself so far, rising and sternly interrupting* CLEM, *shaking her
finger at him)* Clem Coleman, you can' hide yo' sins by gwine
'roun' talkin' bout how othah folks sins. Dat ain' gwine save yo'

sinful soul an' body from burnin' in hell wid fiah an' brimstone. De good book says we is all human an' is lak to err sometime. Dey ain' but one man ain' nevah sinned, an' dat was de Lawd God Jesus Hisse'f, an' none o' us good ez He was, but dat don' keep us from tryin' to be, jes de same. Ef you is a chile o' God, God gwine listen to yo' prayers an' forgive yo' sins, but ef you ain' a chile o' God you is boun' to burn in to'ment.

**COMMITTEE:** *(speaking fervently, since* MRS. DOSHIA BRAGGS' *retort has so capitally answered* CLEM'S *charges, which had them all fearing that he might directly accuse them)* Amen, Sistah, amen! Tell it to 'im, Sistah Doshia! Preach it, Sistah! You knows it's de truf, Lawd.

**MRS. DOSHIA:** *(her confidence renewed by this whole-hearted support)* We is heah to show you de way to God so's when you does sin, you c'n go to God in prayah an' as' to have yo' sins wiped away. Jesus, de Son o' God, done said, don' do ez I does, but do ez I tells you to do.

**SCRUGGS:** *(who has listened with evident approval and some delight, as shown by his frequent exclamations, again assuming the charge)* Dem sho is gospel words, sho's you bo'n. God knows dey is. Now, Clem, we ain' come heah dis evenin' to try to convert you right off de bat. We is jes heah to show you dat you ain' livin' right in de sight o' God A'mighty, an' we wants to prepare de way foh you to git converted. All we wants is foh you an' yo' folks to come yondah to Piney Grove an' listen to de new preachah. He's de greates' man o' God I evah hyeahd in dese bottoms in dese sixty-odd yeahs.

**CLEM:** *(standing facing them, but speaking in a slow, tired voice and the manner of one who has tried hard and has lost his fight for the moment, but who still has some fight left in him and intends to use it in time)* I done listened to all y'all got to say. I ain' got no mo' to say. Maybe you is right. Maybe you ain'. *(After a moment's hesitation)* I don' make no promise 'bout what I'm go'n' do. I takes my own time, an' thinks things thoo 'fo' I acts, an' I'm sho goin' take my time 'bout this. Dey ain' no use foh y'all to bothah me no mo'. Ef I makes up my min' to come an' heah 'im, I'll come. Ef I don' wanna come, all de committees in Camdus can' make me. *(The church bell is heard ringing in the distance)*

**SCRUGGS:** Awright, son, we ain' gwine make you come, but don' take too long. Wrastle wid ole satan, an' show 'im you is de bes' man. Dere's de las' bell foh meetin' dis evenin'. Sistahs an' brothahs, we is done all we c'n do. We can' do nothin' now but hope an' pray an' leave de res' to God. God is righteous, an' His ways don' nevah change.

**COMMITTEE:** Amen, brothah! Amen! amen!

**MRS. DOSHIA:** (*going over to* ELIZA *and whispering audibly*) Honey, you keep aftah him. He's breakin'.

**COMMITTEE:** (*rising and going out the front door, as* ELIZA *and* CLEM *stand on either side of the door bidding them good night*)

Good night, Sistah.
Good night, Brothah.
God bless you, 'Liza.
Trus' in de Lawd, chile.

(DEACON SCRUGGS *is the last to go out. He shakes hands with* ELIZA *and then turns to* CLEM, *but* CLEM *has gone back to the center of the room*)

**SCRUGGS:** Good night, Sistah. God be wid you 'tell we meets ag'in.

**ELIZA:** Good night, Deacon. I sho is glad y'all come. (CLEM *is standing in the center of the room with head bowed thoughtfully, and* ELIZA *is looking out of the door as the curtain falls*)

(Curtain, End Act One, Scene 2)

## ACT TWO

*The auditorium of the Piney Grove Baptist Church, two days later. The church is a plain, crude structure, but unmistakably the house of God. There are two rows of unpainted benches facing the left, with an aisle between them. The benches are constructed of long boards nailed to short, round logs. In the rear left corner of the stage are about three benches facing front, which are the "Amen Corner" where the elderly deacons and deaconesses of the church sit exclusively. At the left front of the room is a platform raised two steps from the floor, on which the pulpit stands, with the usual Bible and hymnal on it. In front of the pulpit is a small table used for the collection. Behind the pulpit and against the wall is the preacher's large chair, with two smaller chairs on each side. Hanging over the minister's chair is a picture of the crucifixion, with two wall lamps a little lower down on the wall on each side. There are three or four similar lamps on the bare wall back-stage. Three windows in this wall are open. Entrance to the auditorium is by the door in the right wall.*

*The curtain rises on the gathering congregation, some of whom are already in their seats. There is a look of expectancy on all faces, evidenced by unusual interest in persons coming in the door. All heads turn toward the door as each person enters. On the first two benches on each side of the aisle, which constitute the "mourners' bench," are seated six mourners, some praying, some moaning a long, doleful moan . . . all "wrestling with their souls, trying to rescue them from the clutches of Satan," and to "come over on the Lord's side."*

**1st SISTER:** *(She enters the church hurriedly, her hat and her clothes disarranged, and sits near the center of the church. When she sits down, she looks all about the house excitedly and expectantly to see who is present, then exclaims to the woman beside her)* Lawd, Tildie, is you heah too? How you git heah so soon, an' you lives 'way down yondah on t'othah side o' me?

**2nd SISTER:** I sho is, gal. I ain' wanna miss nothin' dis evenin'.

**1st SISTER:** Me neithah, but look lak, I jes couldn' git away from dem chillun foh nothin'. 'Fo' I'd a stayed away from heah dis evenin', I'd a bundled 'em right along, but John said he'd stay an look aftah 'em. Martha ain' been so pert heah lately. She cuttin' huh eye-teef, an' you know how mean chillun is den. Jes cry, cry, cry, all de time. *(Looking around the church again)* Dey ain' heah yit, is dey?

**2nd SISTER:** Naw, not yit.

**1st SISTER:** I guess dey'll be heah t'recly. Sho glad I got heah 'fo' dey did, so's I c'n see it all.

**2nd SISTER:** Yas, I reckon dey'll be heah soon.

**1st SISTER:** I sho wants to see Clem Coleman brought down to his knees . . . de onnery devil.

**2nd SISTER:** Me too, chile, an' I b'lieve Rev'n Tukes c'n do it ef anybody kin.

**1st SISTER:** But, chile, he got to go some to humble Clem. He got to git 'im in dis church firs'.

**2nd SISTER:** Mis' Doshia say dey comin' tonight sho.

**1st SISTER:** Das waht Mis' Doshia say, but chile, you don' know Clem Coleman. Das de stubbo'nes' niggah I evah seed in my bo'n days.

**2nd SISTER:** I know, but Mis' Doshia one o' dese determined souls.

**1st SISTER:** Uh-hunh! Ef dat was some o' dese othah mens she was workin' on, I mought take some stock in what she say, but wid Clem Coleman, I ain' believin' she got him 'tell I sees 'im wid my own eyes. *(From without the church, there comes the voice of a man, evidently having trouble with his horse)*

**VOICE:** Whoa! *(louder)* Whoa, I tell you! *(The cracking of the whip on the horse's back is heard)* Git ovah dere! *(All heads turn in the direction of the door. Those nearest the door lean over in their seats and look out.)*

**VOICES:** *(scattered in church)* Is it dem? *(When three persons enter and they are not* CLEM *and his family, the members of the congregation turn around disappointedly and settle in their seats. The three persons who have just come in shake hands with some friends as they go to their seats. When they sit down, they look about to see who is present and whisper among themselves.)*

**1st BROTHER:** Sam, I betcha a good cigar Clem don' show up heah dis evenin'.

**2nd BROTHER:** I ain' bettin', Tom, 'cause I got de same kin' o' feelin' myse'f . . . even ef Sistah Doshia do say she know dey comin', an' she oughta know ef anybody know, 'cause she sho been workin' hard on Clem an' 'Liza.

**1st BROTHER:** Clem liable to say anything jes to git rid o' Miss Doshia. Was you on de committee dat went to see 'em?

**2nd BROTHER:** Yas, I was right dere.

**1st BROTHER:** Did Clem say right out straight he was comin' or did he beat roun' de bush an' say he mought come?

**2nd BROTHER:** Now I come to think about, Tom, I b'lieve dem is his ve'y words. He said . . .

**1st BROTHER:** Uh-hunh! Now I'll betcha a whole box o' cigars, dey ain' comin! *(Three more persons enter, led by* MAMMY CAROLINE LANE, *who walks, bent over on her walking stick, slowly and laboriously up the aisle. The others walk slowly behind her watching her carefully as if they are expecting her to fall any minute. Everyone in the church looks at* MAMMY CAROLINE *as she goes up the aisle to the Amen Corner.)*

**1st SISTER:** *(As* MAMMY *is about half way up the aisle)* Well, Lawd bless my soul, ef dere ain' mammy Ca'line Lane!

**2nd SISTER:** Well, ef it ain't!

**1st SISTER:** I ain' seed dat ole crittah to church since I can' tell when.

**2nd SISTER:** I hyeahd las' week she was so feeble dey was lookin' foh huh to cross ovah any time.

**1st SISTER:** Cross ovah de vevil! Chile, Mammy Ca'line got life lak a cat.

**2nd SISTER:** Now I know Clem's comin'.

**1st SISTER:** I reckon you right, Tildie. Ef Mammy's heah, Clem mus' be comin!

**MRS. DOSHIA:** *(going over to* MAMMY CAROLINE*)* How you do, Mammy Ca'line. I see you got my message. I sho is glad to see you heah dis evenin'.

**MAMMY:** I'm po'ly, chile, po'ly. Is Clem an' 'Liza heah yit?

**MRS. DOSHIA:** No'm, I was jes comin' ovah to as' you ef you is seed er hyeahd anything of 'em. I thought maybe you'd be comin' 'long wid 'em.

**MAMMY:** Naw, chile, I come wid Alex an' Minnie Amps, an' it was all I could do to git heah. Did Clem say he was comin'?

**MRS. DOSHIA:** Yas'm, but you know how Clem is 'bout de church. I hope he ain' changed 'is . . .

**MAMMY:** Ef Clem said he was comin', das all I wants to know. Clem don' make no habit o' lyin'.

**MRS. DOSHIA:** *(returning to her seat)* I hope you right, Mammy. *(As a group enters the door, there is the usual craning of necks and whispering)*

**3rd SISTER:** Naw, chile, I ain' missed a night since dis r'vival been goin' on.

**4th SISTER:** Sho 'nough. You mus' be stuck on de new preachah.

**3rd SISTER:** Ain' nothin' diffunt. He c'n put his shoes undah my bed any time he wants to.

**4th SISTER:** Well, from all I hyeahs, he done had his shoes undah many a bed in Camdus an' abouts, an' sometime he have to git undah dere hisse'f. Did you hyeah 'bout what happened ovah to Cissie Brown's house las' week?

**3rd SISTER:** Naw, chile. You don' mean Cissie Brown what's captain of comp'ny F on de buildin' committee?

**4th SISTER:** I sho do. Huh ole man come in dere one day when she wa'n't expectin' him, an' huh an' Rev'un Tukes was . . .

**5TH SISTER:** *(an elderly, beligerently righteous* SISTER *who sits nearby, turning to them angrily)* You two devils shet yo' mouf! You oughta be shame' o' yo'se'f settin' heah in de house o' God scandalizin'. (She folds her hands before her and sits up righteously indignant; content in the satisfaction that she has so completely squelched them)*

(REVEREND OBADIAH TUKES *enters thru the door that leads to the pulpit. He is a tall, dark-brown-skinned, generously proportioned person about forty-five years old, sleek and well fed and well preserved for his age. His black ministerial coat hangs well below his knees. He places his Bible on the pulpit, turns around and falls to his knees before the large center chair and prays silently. When he has finished his prayer, he rises and shakes hands with the elders, looks over toward the Amen Corner and bows to the deacons and deaconesses. As the* REV. TUKES *enters,* DEACON SCRUGGS, *from his place in the Amen Corner, starts a song in which the congregation joins . . . "I can't stay away")*

*(The general effect of this entire act may be likened unto a symphony in music, whose theme is announced as the movement opens, or soon afterwards, is developed by various instruments as it proceeds to its close, when all instruments are combined for the great moment . . . the climax. As in the symphony, there will be moments when one level is maintained longer than others; nevertheless the movement is always upward, never declining. The bits of dialogue, the various ejaculations . . . amens and hallelujahs . . . the clapping of hands, patting of feet, moans, screams, and shouting should increase in frequency, intensity, and volume as the service proceeds to its climax and close)*

**SONG:**

Lord, I can' stay away,
I can' stay away,
I can' stay away,
I can' stay away.

I got to go to hebben to stan' mah trial,
I got to go to hebben to stan' mah trial,
I got to go to hebben to stan' mah trial,
I can' stay away.

Lord, I can' stay away, (etc.)

I got to go to hebben to pay mah vow,
I got to go to hebben to pay mah vow,
I got to go to hebben to pay mah vow,
I can' stay away.

Lord, I can' stay away, (etc.)

*(During the singing* MRS. DOSHIA *is ill at ease. She avoids looking at the minister and keeps her eyes anxiously on the door. When some latecomers enter a vacant seat up front, she comes to them and orders them to find another seat, since she is reserving that one for* CLEM *and* ELIZA. *When about the third verse of the song has been sung,* REV. TUKES *rises and stands behind the pulpit, singing, more or less casually, and looking over the congregation. He looks questioningly at* MRS. DOSHIA *but she does not look toward him, since her eyes are still on the door. This first song is merely a signal for order, so only a few "amens" follow the end. As it is concluded, the* REVEREND TUKES *turns to one of the elders.)*

**REV. TUKES:** *(in a solemn voice)* Eldah Gray, lead us in a shawt word o' prayer.

**ELDER GRAY:** *(rising from his seat and falling on his knees beside the pulpit)* Oh! Lawd an' blessed Mastah, we comes dis evenin', head bowed an' body bent befo' yo' th'one o' grace, to as' yo to be wid us heah whilse we yo' humble servants bows b'fo' you to do yo' biddin'. We knows, O Lawd, dat we's done strayed from de way lak los' sheeps, but blessed Jesus, you tol' us to as' an' it shall be given. We as' you to fohgive ouah sins dis evenin'. We as' you to be wid him who come to bring us de message from on high. Sheathe 'im wid de wisdom o' Solomon, an' de powah o'

Golia'h. He'p 'im to git into de hearts o' dese po' sinnahs, an' show 'em de way to glory. We thanks you, O hebbenly Fathah, dat we is still in de land o' de livin'. . . .

VOICES: Thank you, Jesus, thank you! Yas we do!

ELDER GRAY: *(continuing)* . . . an' is not numbered 'monsgst de dead er de damn . . . dat we's in a cool worl' safe fah from de fiahs o' hell. We is glad, O Fathah, dat whilse we was sleepin' las' night dat de bed wa'n't ouah coolin' boa'd an' dat de kivers wa'n't ouah windin' sheet . . .

VOICES: Yas, Lawd! Glory to God!

ELDER GRAY: . . . O Lawd an' mastah, sometimes we has to chew hard bones an' swallah bittah pills, but you tol' us to b'lieve in you an' all will be well. Sometimes we ain't got no wood, sometimes we ain' got no food . . .

SOPRANO VOICE: *(in a singsong)* Yas, Lawd, we sho ain'!

ELDER GRAY: Sometimes ouah backs is at de mussy of de wind an' de sun. Sometimes, lak yo' son, Jesus Chris', we ain' got no place to lay ouah heads down. Sometimes we is jes got yo' name to call on, Lawd, but we is trustin' on you . . . we is trustin' on you.

VOICE: *(singing)* Yas, we is!

ELDER GRAY: *(after a slight pause)* An' now, hebbenly Fathah, when ouah work in dis worl' is done, when we done sung de las' chune, when we is done said de las' word, we as' you to give us a home up yondah, wheah dey ain' no mo' pain . . .

VOICES: Umph! Umph!
Glory to God!

ELDER GRAY: . . . dey ain' no mo' sin, an' wheah death can' bothah us no mo', wheah we is safe from thieves an' corruption, wheah all de streets is paved wid gol' . . .

VOICES: Hallelujah!
Praise 'is name!
Glory to God!

ELDER GRAY: . . . an' milk an' honey flows all de time. Foh Jesus' sake. Amen.

VOICES: Amen! Amen! Amen! *(All rise from their knees and resume their seats)*

**REV. TUKES:** Praise de Lawd! Amen! *(DEACON SCRUGGS starts a song, "He said He would calm de ocean"* . . . *a bit more spirited than the first)*
**SONG:**

Come down, Jesus, stan' by me;
He said He would calm de ocean, He said He would.
I know you done gi'n me d' victory;
He said He would calm de ocean, He said He would.
(Refrain)
He said He would calm de ocean,
Oh, yes, He said He would:
He said He would calm d' rollin' seas,
He said He would.

Everything abides His will;
He said He would calm de ocean, He said He would.
He talked to de sea an' de sea stood still;
He said He would calm de ocean, He said He would.

(Refrain repeated)

*(During the second verse of the song,* ELMER *and* MAME *enter the door just ahead of their parents.* MRS. DOSHIA, *ever watchful for them, beckons the children to come up front to the seat she has reserved for them.* CLEM *and* ELIZA *stand in the doorway for a moment looking about for a seat, since the seats are practically all taken by now. There is one vacant near the back of the church.* CLEM *leaves* ELIZA *and goes up the aisle, where* MRS. DOSHIA *has seated* ELMER *and* MAME *and is beckoning* CLEM *to be seated there too. He calls the children out, ignoring her and her invitation, and returns with them to the back where they all sit down. When* CLEM *and his family enter, all members of the congregation look intently at them. There is some snickering behind hands at* MRS. DOSHIA'S *little setback. The* REVEREND TUKES, *who has been sitting down until* CLEM *and* ELIZA *enter, rises, smiles broadly and rubs his hands together gladly, and takes the lead in the singing which has almost ceased with the attention of the members of the congregation becomes centered on the principals of the little drama.* REVEREND TUKES *looks at* MRS. DOSHIA *and she at him; they smile broadly and approvingly. When the song is concluded, the* REVEREND TUKES *stands silent for a moment, as the congrega-*

*tion becomes quiet and settled, then he speaks in a slow, heavy, ominous voice.)*

**REV. TUKES:** Brothahs an' sistahs, we's gittin' 'long to de end o' dis r'vival. We been goin' on now foh ten nights. But dey's still a heap o' work to do. Dere's still some sinnahs in Camdus.

**WOMAN'S VOICE:** Dey sho is!

**REV. TUKES:** I done tol' you when I come heah dat when Tukes leave dey ain' go'n' be a sinnah in Camdus. I means dat, too. I means ev'ry word of it. Now dis evenin' I'm go'n' change my tactics. You know, dey say, ef you can' beat de devil one way, try anothah. Change yo' tactics.

**VOICES:** *(in unison)* Yas! Yas!

**REV. TUKES:** Now dis evenin 'stead o' startin' off preachin' myse'f lak I always do, I'm go'n' let y'all do de startin'. I wants dem what's already followin' de Mastah . . . dem what's been washed in de blood o' de Lamb an' is saved . . . I wants you to stan' up heah dis evenin' an' talk foh Jesus. I wants you to blaze de way foh de sinnahs; tell 'em how you come to be saved, an' what Chris' is done foh you. Now come on, ole an' young, git up. Let whosomevah will git up an' speak foh Jesus. *(Several rise together, but an elderly deacon begins speaking first.)*

**DEACON:** Sistahs an' brothahs, I wants to tell you, I'm a chile o' God, an' I don' keer who knows it. Jesus come to me when I was a boy knee-high to a duck, whilse I was pickin' cotton' way down yondah in de fiel' by myse'f. An' he say to me jes ez plain ez I'm talkin' to you. *(Mournfully, raising his right hand with his fist clenched.)* "'Lijah, 'Lijah, pick up yo' cross an' follah me." An' Lawd hab mussy, my soul was so glad 'tell I th'owed down my bag wheah I was an ' run out shoutin' an' a-singin' foh joy, an' singin' de name o' Jesus wheahevah I go. I been wid Jesus since dat day. He ain' nevah failed me. When I'm sick, he stay by my bed. When I'm in trouble, Jesus takes me out. Jesus been my shiel' an' bucklah evah since dat day to dis. I been servin' 'im, an' I'mm gwine keep on servin' 'im 'tell I dies.

**VOICES:** Amen! Amen! Tell 'em 'bout it, Brothah 'Lijah!

**ELDERLY SISTER:** *(rising from the body of the church, and throwing both arms up and clapping her hands as she cries in a high, shrill voice)* Hallelujah! Hallelujah: I'm a chile o' god. I been servin' in the Mastah's vineyard foh goin' on forty-odd yeahs an' I ain' nevah got tiahd. It was forty yeahs dis las'-gone June I went down in de woods an' stayed sebben days an' sebben nights 'dout eatin' an' sleepin' . . . naw sah, I wa'n' doin' nothin' but wrastlin' wid my soul tryin' to git it outen ole Satan's grip. An' when I done been down dere de las' day I see de light fro hebben, an' Jesus come walkin' down out o' de sky an' showed me de way. An' Lawd bless mah soul, I come out o' dem woods a-shoutin' an' a-praisin' God, an' I been praisin' 'im since dat day, an' I'm gwine keep on praisin'. *(shouting)* Yas, I'm gwine keep on praisin' 'im, hallelujah! Hallelujah! *(She throws her arms up and strides up and down the center aisle swinging her arms and shouting)* Hallelujah! Hallelujah! My soul's happy! *(Some others rise, but seeing* MAMMY CAROLINE *coming out of the corner to the front of the church, they sit back down and everyone watches her. Some rise in their seats to get a better view.* CLEM *seems absorbed in his own thoughts.* ELIZA *recognizes* MAMMY *and speaks to* CLEM*)*

**ELIZA:** Lawd, Clem, yon's Mammy Ca'line! *(*CLEM *looks up and sees* MAMMY CAROLINE, *then bows his head as she speaks.) (There is absolute silence and intense interest on the part of all, while* MAMMY *speaks in a feeble, cracked, but distinctly audible voice.)*

**MAMMY:** I'm a ole 'oman. Ole an' feeble. I done seed might nigh all y'all chillun come into dis worl' . . . Ca'line Lane ain' got long to stay heah, an' when she goes up yondah to Jesus she wanna tell him dat ev'y one o' huh chillun is a chile o' God. I'm feeble, an' dis night air ain' good foh my bones, but I come heah dis evenin' brothahs an' sistahs, to pray wid y'all an' to he'p my chillun cross ovah on de Lawd's side. I wants y'all to pray, chillun, wid me. Pray lak you ain' nevah prayed b'fo'. Pray foh de Lawd to send His sperret down heah 'mongst us dis evenin' an' save my chillun.

**SCRUGGS:** *(in a solemn, stentorian voice)* Pray, church, pray! *(Some kneel, others bow their heads.* MAMMY *goes back slowly to her seat.* DEACON SCRUGGS *starts a singing prayer in which all the congregation takes part. This song has a dirge-like effect, not being in the lively, spirited manner of the others.* CLEM *remains with his head bowed thru the prayer)*

**SONG:**

Prayer is de key of hebben,
Prayer is de key of hebben,

Prayer is de key of hebben,
Prayer is de key.

You go down in de valley,
Get down on yo' knees,
An' ask yo' Lawd
To have mercy please.

Prayer is de key of hebben, (etc.)

I went down in de valley,
Got down on my knees,
An' asked my Savior
To have mercy please.

Prayer is de key of hebben, (etc.)

*(When the song has ended, the* REV. TUKES *comes to the pulpit and stands for a moment until they are all settled. The congregation becomes silent and all attention is centered on him)*

**REV. TUKES:** Now; brothahs an' sistahs, we wants to see jes wheah we got to go dis evenin'. I wants all dem what's Christians an' b'longs to de church to stan'. *(All stand except* CLEM *and his family and about four others scattered thruout the congregation)* Ain' dat beautiful? Ain' dat gran? Jesus' army! Standin' foh Jesus! Amen! Amen! Dat'll do. God bless you, chillun! Now all dem dat ain' Christians stand. *(The Christians sit down again.* ELIZA *and the children and the four others stand.* ELMER *has gone to sleep and is leaning against his mother, but she rouses him and holds him up as he leans against her sleepily.* CLEM *remains seated. Members of the congregation look back at* CLEM *and at one another, incredulously whispering)* Now we wants all y'all what's standin' to come up heah on dese front seats wheah we c'n talk wid you heart to heart. Come right on up, ain' nobody go'n' hurt you. *(*ELIZA *looks at* CLEM, *waiting for him to go up. The members of the congregation are also looking back at* CLEM *to see if he is going up, but he remains seated and motions* ELIZA *to sit down. The other sinners who are standing go up to the mourners' bench.* REVEREND TUKES, *seeing that* CLEM *and* ELIZA *do not come up, holds out his hand to them)* Won't y'all come up to de front?

**CLEM:** *(looking up boldly and calmly)* Naw, dis is awright. We c'n hyeah heah jes de same.

**REV. TUKES:** *(standing silently for a moment, then speaking in a deep, ominous voice)* Chillun . . . I'm troubled dis evenin'. *(absolute silence in church)* I say I'm troubled dis evenin'. I'm troubled 'cause whilse I was down on my knees dis mawnin' communin' wid de Holy Sperrit, I had a vision. I had a vision, I say . . .

**VOICES:** Yas! Yas!

**REV. TUKES:** . . . an' in dat vision I saw uhnough to shake de gates o' hell loose on dey hinges an' make ev'y sinnah man an' woman run out cryin'. Holy, holy, holy, Lawd God o' host', all de earth is full o' thy glory. Listen, brothahs an' sistahs, let me tell you what I saw. Listen close, 'cause I don' wan' you to miss a single word. *(He stops a moment. There is absolute silence in the church and an eager, anxious look on all faces)* I seed God A'mighty settin' in de midst o' de hebbens, holdin' a council o' war . . .

**SISTER:** *(from Amen Corner, making three sudden grunts with simultaneous taps of her foot)* Ump! ump! Ump! Do Jesus! Do Jesus!

**REV. TUKES:** I seed God dere wid de billowy clouds all 'round 'im, a-settin' on 'is white marble throne. On 'is head was de golden crown a-shinin' and' a-sparklin' wid diamon's. He was shod in 'is golden slippahs. In 'is right hand was de rod o' thundah an' in 'is left hand was a shaft o' lightnin'. 'Round his waist was buckled 'is mighty sword dat wid one stroke c'n slay thousan's on thousan's.

**VOICE:** *(fearfully)* Lawd have mussy!

**REV. TUKES:** On 'is right side was settin' Jesus Christ de Son o' God, lookin' calm an' quiet an' peaceful lak he always do. On 'is lef' side was de Holy Ghost wid blood an' fiah in his eyes, an' 'is teeth an' fist clenched lak he's ready to tear de worl' in two. I says . . . brothahs an' sistahs, dey was settin' in a council o' war.

**VOICE:** *(joyfully, jubilantly)* Preach it, son! I hyeahs you! I hyeahs you!

**REV. TUKES:** An' God stood up in all 'is glory an' said in a voice lak de roarin' thundah dat shook de hebbens lak a mighty earthquake; an God said, "You see I got on my war garments 'cause I'm go'n' into battle. I'm go'n' down yondah on earth an' wage a battle on sin. Ole Satan been reignin' down yondah long

ahnough. Hit's my time now . . . *(intoning each word)* Hit's . . .
my . . . time . . . now . . . an' I'm ready to hold my own. . . .

**SISTER'S VOICE:** *(quickly, with emphasis)* Yas he is! Yas
he is! He sho is!

**REV. TUKES:** An' God said, "I'm goin' slay de chillun o'
de devil right an' lef'. I ain' a-go'n'-to miss a livin' sinnah. Dey
ain' a-go'n' a be but two sides, mine's an' de devil's. All what's on
my side 'scapes my wrath an' comes wid me into de Kingdom . . .

**SISTER'S VOICE:** *(joyfully)* Oh! Glory hallelujah!

**REV. TUKES:** . . . but him dat is not on my side . . . him
dat is not on my side, I says . . . him will I cast down into a burnin'
hell to burn in tawment forevah. Dey ain' go'n' be no halfway
groun'." Den I saw God A'mighty as He turned to His son, Jesus,
an' He said, "Son . . . *(intoning)* son . . . son . . . you go down
yondah an' make de way ready foh Me an' tell 'em I'm a-comin'.
tell 'em, tell 'em all what wants to be saved to rise up an' follah
Me." An' sistahs an' brothahs, I seed Jesus . . . dat same Jesus
what suffahed an' died on Calv'ry's cross dat we mought have
evahlastin' life . . . I seed Jesus as he bowed 'is head an' tears come
a-streamin' down 'is face, 'cause Jesus is tendah-hearted. He don'
want to hurt nobody, but Jesus know bettah 'n to disobey his
fathah. So Jesus, he rose an' he said, "Yas, Fathah, I will go an' do
yo' biddin'." Den God turned to de Holy Ghost an' He said,
"Tarry yo' wid Me, 'cause I needs you by My side in battle." Brothahs an' sistahs, can' you see 'em . . . Jesus, God, an' de Holy
Ghost . . . as dey starts out on de warpath? Oh, brothah, can't you
see 'em? Oh, sistah, can't you see 'em as dey walks side by side
down de milky white way?

**SISTER'S VOICE:** *(shouting joyfully)* Yas, Lawd, I see 'em!

**REV. TUKES:** *(intoning)* . . . Oh . . . sistahs an' brothahs,
I'm troubled . . . in mind. I'm troubled in mind dis evenin' 'cause
I'm skeered dere's somebody in Cambus, somebody right heah dis
evenin' settin' undah de spell o' my voice what ain' saved an' won'
be ready to meet de Mastah when he sets out on de warpath. I'm
come heah dis evenin' to tell dat brothah, to tell dat sistah, dey
bettah git ready, dey bettah git on boa'd de gospel train 'fo' it's
too late. She's a-steamin' up now, gittin' ready foh to make dat
long journey right up to de pearly gates. Dey bettah git on now
'fo' it's too late. I'm come heah to warn you sinnahs. Warn you to

flee from de wrath o' God's fire. *(calming down)* Come ovah on de Lawd's side. Come ovah on de Lawd's side an' be saved. God bless you . . . Amen! *(changing to a more conversational tone)* Now chillun, we is go'n' open de doors o' de church, an' whilse we sings we wants y'all to wrastle yo' souls from de devil's grip an' come ovah on de Lawd's side. All you got to do is trust in Jesus an' he will save you. Jes b'lieve an' you is saved. Won't you trust 'im whilse we sings? *(He starts a song more spirited and with greater feeling than any previous one, "I will trust in de Lawd.")*

> **SONG:**

> I will trust in de Lawd,
> I will trust in de Lawd,
> I will trust in de Lawd
> 'Tell I die.

> (Repeat)

> Go down, go down in yondah's worl'
> An search among de sheep;
> You'll find Him dere, so I am tol',
> Wid dem He loves to keep.

> (Refrain)
> I will trust in de Lawd, (etc.)

> I thank you frien', foh yo' advice;
> I'll find Him ef I can,
> An' ef I do, I will rejoice
> In Chris', de frien' to man.

> I will trust in de Lawd, (etc.)

**REV. TUKES:** *(as soon as the song is well started, beckoning to those in the Amen corner)* Some o' you brothahs an' sistahs come ovah heah an' he'p dese chillun wrastle wid dey souls. *(*MRS. DOSHIA *and others from the Amen Corner come over to the mourners' bench and talk and pray with the sinners. Meanwhile the* REV. TUKES *sings and pleads for them to come thru. His singing, pleading and gestures are all directed more at* CLEM *and* ELIZA *than at those on the mourner's bench)* Won't you come, sistah! Can' you trust Jesus? All you got to do is b'lieve in Jesus! Won' you come, brothah! Jesus calls you! Oh, brothah, can' you trust Him? Oh, sistah, can' you trust Him?

**YOUNG GIRL:** *(one of the sinners on the bench, "comes thru." She throws up both arms, yelling and shouting)* I'm saved at las'! Thank God A'mighty I'm saved at las'!

**REV. TUKES:** *(going to her, and taking her shouting and screaming form into his arms)* God bless you, chile, God bless you. *(He takes the girl back to the mourners' bench and gives her to one of the sisters, then returns to his pleading)* Won' you trust Jesus? Jesus calls you! Jesus'll stan' by you when you is sick. When you hongry he'll feed you. *(drifting into a singsong)* When you naked he'll hide yo' nakedness. When you is in trouble, an' de whole worl' done turned ag'in you, when yo' fathah an' yo' mothah an' yo' sistah an' yo' brothah forsakes you, de Lawd Jesus will take you up. *(A shrill soprano scream rends the air, followed by one or two other happy, shouting sisters. Another sinner, a man, "comes thru," and rises to go to the minister. The* REV. TUKES *takes his hands and adds his blessings verbally, but not with the evident affection he lavished on the former convert. The other two sinners are converted almost together. The shouting in the church has become general. Some clap their hands frantically, some walk up and down the aisle, some weep, all others sing with the greatest fervor. When the last sinner on the mourners' bench is converted,* REV. TUKES *returns to the pulpit. The singing has ceased and the fervor is abating.* REV. TUKES *raises his hand for silence)* Now, brothahs an' sistahs, we done fit de devil a good fight. We done snatched one, tow, three, fo' sinnahs out o' his hands an' brung 'em ovah on de Lawd's side, but de battle ain' ovah yit. We is still got a long ways to go. Dey's still some amongst us what thinks dey don' need God, but de time 'll come when dey'll wish dey had a listened to de voice o' God dis evenin'. *(holding up the Bible)* Dis heah good book says, "Be ready, for ye know not de time when de Son o' man cometh." Now foh de las' time, church, foh de las' time, let us pray. Pray foh God to save dese po wayfarin' sinnahs. *(*REV. TUKES *falls to his knees on the platform beside the pulpit, and begins to intone his prayer fervently, with his clasped hands hanging before him, and his face raised)* Oh, Lawd, you tol' us to call on you when we was in trouble, when de way was dark an' we couldn' see how to go on. You tol' us you'd be ouah shiel' an' bucklah in de time o' trial. Oh

Lawd, didn' you delivah Daniel from de lions' den? You went down into de belly o' de whale an' brought ole Jonah out on dry land. *(At this point a soprano voice starts a humming accompaniment. The tune is picked up by many other voices and there is a constant humming accompaniment to the minister's steady, roaring bass voice. Also there are occasional ejaculations at pertinent points of the prayer . . . just as there were in the sermon. Thru it all, the* REV. TUKES *continues without pause. He pleads with his voice, his hands, the expression on his face . . . his entire body becomes one deep, fervent, ecstatic plea to God for the granting of his prayer . . . the conversion of these last sinners)* You said to de waves, "Be still!" An' you walked from shore to shore jes lak you was on dry land. You tol' de win's to cease, an' dey obeyed yo' voice. You said to de sun, "Stop wheah you is!" an' dat hot ball o' molten lead stood still. An' oh . . . Lawd, didn't you command ole Moses to go down yondah in Egypt an' tell ole Phar'oh foh to let yo' people go? An' didn' Moses lead de Hebrew chillun thru de wilderness foh fo'ty days an' fo'ty nights? An' you stood on de banks o' de Red Sea an' raised yo' hand to hebben an' commanded de rollin' watahs to part so de chillun o' Israel moght cross ovah on dry groun'. An' when dey got ovah on de othah side, you tol' de waves to *(intoning)* ro . . . ll . . . on . . . roll on, thou deep an' mighty ocean, roll on, an' de army of ole Phar'oh was caught in by de rollin' watahs an' ev'ry man destroyed. *(calming down)* Oh, Lawd, Lawd, Lawd, we call on you dis evenin' to git into de hearts o' dese po' sinnahs, make 'em know dat you is God, dat you is de way an' de light o' de worl', an' besides you dere is no othah. Den on dat blessed jedgment day *(becoming animated again, as if by sudden inspiration)* when ole Gabriel, mounted on a white chargah wid de golden trumpit in 'is hand, rides down thru de pearly gates an' raises dat trumpit up to hebben an' *(intoning, with four notes for the first "blow," three for the second, two for the third and one for the fourth)* blow . . . o . . . o . . . o, blow . . . o . . . o, blow . . . o, blow . . . right slow an easy foh de firs' time to wake up de people; den he gonna blow it anothah time a little loudah so dey c'n git up an' git ready; den he's gonna blow de las' time wid all his might. He's gonna blow it so loud dat ev'ry ear an' ev'ry heart shall heah de soun'. 'Cause it's de las' signal. Hit's God's las' warnin' foh all dem dat believes in Him to git up an' follah, follah Him up de bright an' narrah way right up to de gates of hebben. An' on dat day, Lawd, on dat blessed jedgment day, we will meet all dem dat's gone b'fo' . . . mothahs an' fathahs, *(loud scream from some sistah)* sistahs an' brothahs. *(more screams)* An' down on de earth . . . Lawd save us! . . . dere'll be a mou'nful sight. Dem dat was shame' to come to God, dem what has lived in sin an' 'dultry, dem dat has been gamblin' an' partakin' freely of worldly things . . . I see 'em, Lawd, a- wailin' an' a-cryin' ez dey loved ones ascends to hebben on a white an' billowy cloud . . . O Lawd, won' it be a mighty day? I see de chillun o' sin an' darkness ez dey holds dey hands up to hebben cryin' in a mou'nful voice, "Lawd, have mussy on me a sinnah!" But it'll be too late, too late. An' jes ez de hebbens closes an' de las' Christians done went in, I sees old Satan an' his devils a-sweepin' down 'cross de earth, brin-gin' fiah an' brimstone in dey path. O . . . brothahs an' sistahs, what a awful sight! I see de chillun o' sin runnin' foh covah, tryin' to find a place to hide from de blazes o' hell, but *(singing)* dey ain' no hidin' place down dere; dey ain' no hidin' place down dere. An' now foh de las' time, foh de las' time, we calls on you, Lawd to save dese po sinnahs. Come down from above, Lawd, an' lead 'em . . . *(intoning)* lead . . . em, lead . . . 'em in de path o' righteousness foh Jesus' sake. *(calming down)* An' now, Lawd, when we is done fit ouah las' battle, an' de vict'ry is won, an' dey ain' no mo' foh us to do down heah below, we as' you to give us a home in yo kingdom wheah we c'n spend ouah days praisin' yo' name, foh Jesus' sake. Amen. (REV. TUKES *rises and walks down from the pulpit. As he does,* DEACON SCRUGGS *starts a soul-stirring, shouting song: "Sinnah, you know you boun' to die."*

**SONG:**

Sinnah, you know you boun' to die,
Sinnah, you know you boun' to die,
Sinnah, you know you boun' to die,
Sinnah, you know you boun' to die.

Jes so de tree fall, jes so it lie;
Jes so de sinnah live, jes so he die.

Sinnah, you know you boun' to die, (etc.)

Lightnin' will flash an' thundah will roll;

God's wrath gwine shine down on yo' naked soul.

Sinnah, you know you boun' to die, (etc.)

*(For a while,* REV. TUKES *stands in the front and pleads to* CLEM *and* ELIZA *as before, but finally he goes back to them and pleads directly from the aisle. At this point* ELIZA *cannot contain herself longer and wipes away the tears from her face. As the minister continues to plead her body shakes with sobbing.* MAME *shows concern over her mother's crying and begins weeping out of sympathy.* ELMER *is awakened by his mother's sobbing. He sits up sleepily and seeing his mother and sister crying, also begins to cry from sympathy and fright.* CLEM *sits stoically as before. He looks at* ELIZA, *but says nothing. The congregation are carried away with the song and do not give so much attention to* CLEM *and* ELIZA *as to expressing their own emotional fervor in singing, clapping hands, patting feet, and swaying their bodies to the strong rhythm.)*

**REV. TUKES:** Won' you come to Jesus, brothah? Won' you trus Him? Don' you want to meet yo' mothah in glory? . . . dat same mothah dat stayed by you when you was sick . . . she is standin' up yondah waitin' to take you in huh arms. Won' you make huh happy now an' come to Jesus? Won' you trust 'im, sistah? *(When he has repeated those and similar supplications,* REV. TUKES *finally gives up and returns to the pulpit, in an attitude and a feeling of having fought a good fight and lost. As he returns to the pulpit, the singing begins to die down and* MAMMY CAROLINE *rises from her seat and goes back to* CLEM *and* ELIZA. *The congregation seem to realize the significance of this move, and under the renewed and vigorous leadership of* REV. TUKES *they again increase the fervor of their singing.* MAMMY *places her arm about* CLEM'S *shoulder and talks to him and* ELIZA. CLEM *bows over and listens to* MAMMY *patiently, but does not speak.* MAMMY'S *words to them are not heard, but it is evident by the way* CLEM'S *body slumps and his head is bowed that she has broken* CLEM. *Finally* CLEM *looks up at* MAMMY *tenderly and nods his head, then straightens up, rises and looking at* ELIZA *(as if to say, "Come on, 'Liza"), goes up the aisle to the front followed by* ELIZA *and the children.* MAMMY *remains behind, seated and bowed over in prayer. When* REV. TUKES, *who has been watching the scene closely, sees* CLEM *rise, he comes down from the pulpit and meets them, clapping his hands jubilantly and crying, "Amen, amen!*

*Praise de Lawd!" At the same time, he gives the signal to stop the song they are singing and quickly starts another more jubilant and triumphant song.)*

**SONG:**

> *Hallelujah now!*
> *De angels are shoutin' 'roun' in hebben!*
> *Hallelujah now!*
> *De angels are shoutin' 'roun' in hebben!*

*(The congregation all rise and join heartily in singing, shouting, clapping hands and shaking hands with each other. As de curtain falls, dey files 'roun' an' shakes han's wid* CLEM *and* 'LIZA, *still singin'.)*

(Curtain, End of Act Two)

## ACT THREE

*Same as in Act One. It is early afternoon, two weeks after Act Two. From the distance,* ELIZA *can be heard rubbing clothes on a washboard and singing as she works.* CLEM *enters the front door. It is evident from his appearance and manner that he is angered at something. He throws his hat down on a chair and calls to* ELIZA *somewhat harshly*

**CLEM:** 'Liza! Uh, 'Liza!

**ELIZA:** *(answering from the distance)* Hoo-oo! Heah I is, Clem. *(She comes in left door, wiping her wet hands on her apron)* What you want, hon'?

**CLEM:** Is you seen my buck saw? It ain' hangin' ovah de corcrib wheah I allus keeps it.

**ELIZA:** Yas, hon'. Mistah Milt Brown come ovah heah dis mawnin' an' borrahd it.

**CLEM:** *(quickly)* Milt Brown . . . ain' dat de niggah dat tol' his chillun he'd skin 'em alive ef he evah so much ez caught 'em talkin' to Mame an' Elmer?

**ELIZA:** *(placatingly)* Now, Clem, can't you let bygones be bygones? Mistah Milt was jes sayin' how glad he is we done jined church an' is ma'ied an' livin' respectable . . .

**CLEM:** Livin' r'spectable? We ain' livin' no mo' r'spectable now'n we evah was.

**ELIZA:** You know what he mean, Clem.

**CLEM:** Naw, I don' know what he mean, but I know what you sayin'.

**ELIZA:** Mistah Milt say he wants us to come ovah an' see dem sometime. An' dey go'n' . . .

**CLEM:** Naw, 'Liza, we ain' go'n ovah dere, an' he ain' welcome heah.

**ELIZA:** *(in a placating manner)* Awright, hon', awright, you ain' got to go.

**CLEM:** *(snatching his hat and carelessly throwing it on his head, and starting out the front door talking angrily to himself as well as to* ELIZA*)* Ev'ytime you turn aroun' nowadays dese heah folks wants to borrah some'm. Hit's lemme dis, an' gimme dat.

**ELIZA:** *(looking at* CLEM *anxiously as if she wants to speak and is not certain whether she should or not)* Clem!

**CLEM:** *(with his hand on the knob of the open door)* Yas, 'Liza.

**ELIZA:** Shet de do' an' come back jes' a minute.

**CLEM:** *(talking back toward* ELIZA*)* Awright, heah I is, hon'.

**ELIZA:** Set down, you ain' in no hurry, is you?

**CLEM:** Not partic'lah, but 's 'bout time I was gittin' on down yondah to Genessee, ef I'm goin'.

**ELIZA:** I ain' go'n' take long. Clem, how come you lookin' so worried? Look lak some'm heavy on yo' min' all de time. I ain' wanted to say nothin' to you 'bout it, but I jes can' shet my eyes to it no longah. *(She sits down near him and places her hand on his in a tender, almost pleading manner)* What is it, Clem? I know you knows what you wants to do, but sometime, hon', when you talks things ovah wid somebody what's close to you, hit kinda makes you feel bettah. Look lak it he'ps take some o' de burden off yo' shouldah. Don' you wanna tell me what 'tis, hon'? Maybe I c'n he'p, an' maybe I can', but 'tain' go'n' do no harm to talk it ovah.

**CLEM:** *(He rises and walks about a moment with his head bowed in silence. He sits down again, with his elbows on his thighs, rubs his hands together slowly, and then begins to speak in a slow,* *deliberate manner)* 'Liza, I is got some'm on my min', an' it's been dere since de day we j'ined de church. I been tryin' hard to figure out how come, an' I done come to de conclusion dat we ain' done de bes' thing when we changed ouah way o' livin'.

ELIZA: How you mean, Clem? Look lak das de bes' thin's happened to us in a long time.

CLEM: Heah's how I mean. It look lak me an' you done said to dem, "Now, folks, foh twelve yeahs me an' 'Liza been wrong, an' y'all is been right; y'all is bettah 'n we is, an 'we wants to be lak y'all is." Now I don' b'lieve dat, 'Liza, an' I don' b'lieve you b'lieves it no mo' 'n I do.

ELIZA: I know de church ain' perfect' jes lak you do, Clem, but ev'rybody got to git r'ligion an' jine de church ef dey wants to go to hebben when dey dies.

CLEM: Gittin' 'ligion an' jinin' de church ain' de same, 'Liza.

ELIZA: How come dey ain', Clem? All de preachahs I evah hyeahd says dey is.

CLEM: Oh, yes, de preachahs says dat, an' dey tries to make us b'lieve it, 'cause das dey bread an' buttah. *(raising his head, looking at* ELIZA *and speaking with decisiveness)* 'Liza, you mean to tell me dat ef a man b'lieves in God, an' tries to live right, but don' b'long to de church, he can' go to hebben when he dies? *(He pauses briefly after this rhetorical question then goes on)* If I thought so I'd stop servin' God right now.

ELIZA: Lawd, I do declare, it makes me tremble to heah you talk lak dat.

CLEM: You know, de mo' I thinks about de church, de mo' I wondahs how all dem what ain' jined church an' ain' got no kind o' 'ligion gits along jes ez good, an' sometime a whole lot bettah 'n dem what spends all dey time prayin' an' singin' in de church.

ELIZA: Yas, Clem, God's ways is strange, but he don' nevah fail. You know what happened to ole Cap'n Jim Moore. He used to go 'roun' talkin' 'g'in de church an' 'ligion, he wouldn' let a preachah come in his yeard, an' didn' nevah let his wife an' chile go to church. Call hisse'f some kin' o' 'nostic or some'm lak dat. An' look how he treated de share-croppahs on his farm . . . shoot 'em down lak dogs ef dey didn' do what he say. But God come an' took his only chile, an' right on de back o' dat took his wife, an' lef' him paralyzed. Dey say cripple ez he is now, he's at de church ev'ry time de doors open.

**CLEM:** Yas, I know 'bout ole Cap'n Moore. But how 'bout Fred Green an' his folks? He was deacon in de church. Dey ain' killed nobody, an' dey was church-goin', God-fearin' folks ef evah dey was any, an' look how dey house burned smack down to de groun' an' burned dem all up. An' when dat Mississippi ovah-flows, it don' make no diffunce 'tween dem what's in de church an' dem what ain'.

**ELIZA:** It do look kinda funny, Clem, but le's don' bothah 'bout dem things now. Leave 'em to God. *(forcing a smile in an effort to cheer* CLEM*)* I got good news foh you.

**CLEM:** Good news?

**ELIZA:** Yas, hon'.

**CLEM:** Been a long time since I hyeahd any good news.

**ELIZA:** You ain' s'posed to know yit. But I wants to tell you so bad, I can' keep it no longah.

**CLEM:** Awright, what is it?

**ELIZA:** When you heah it ag'in, you jes make lak you ain' nevah hyeahd it b'fo'.

**CLEM:** I see!

**ELIZA:** Mis' Doshia was heah dis mawnin'.

**CLEM:** Thought you said you had good news.

**ELIZA:** Wait, Clem, wait, you ain' hyeahd de news yit. She say dey is 'lected you a deacon o' de church.

**CLEM:** *(with scornful surprise)* Deacon? You know any mo' jokes?

**ELIZA:** Naw, Clem, das de truf, so he'p me God. Ain' you glad, Clem? Ain' it jes lak I say dey was go'n' see what a good man you is.

**CLEM:** *(after a thoughtful silence)* I ain' so stuck on dis heah deacon business, 'Liza. Dey ain' makin' me a deacon 'cause dey thinks I'm sech a good man, lak you thinks. Folks don' change so quick; dat is, sho 'nough change. 'Cause dey grins at you now, an' says how-you-do when dey passes, ain' no sign dey done changed. Inside dey is de same, an' it's de inside what counts. De reason dey makin' me a deacon is plain ez yo' nose on yo' face. Hit's my money dey wants foh de new church dey talkin' 'bout buildin' das all. *(There is a knock at the front door, up-stage.* ELIZA, *who is nearest, opens the door.* CISSIE BROWN *enters. She is a slender mulatto woman about the same age as* ELIZA. *She is a very loquacious, gossiping and malignant type of person. In her attitude toward* CLEM *she is familiar and flirtatious. There is a coarseness about her suggestive of a woman who has lived a fast life.)*

**CISSIE:** *(rushing past* ELIZA *to* CLEM *and shaking his hand, then turning casually and speaking)* Hello, Clem. I sho is lucky to ketch y'all heah togethah. How you do, 'Liza.

**CLEM:** Howdy, Mis Brown!

**CISSIE:** Mis' Brown? When you start callin' me Mis', Clem Coleman?

**ELIZA:** Set right down heah, Mis' Brown. (ELIZA *places a chair left of the center table and sits on the right side herself)* I have to as' you to 'scuse my looks. I was jes gittin' my washin' done.

**CISSIE:** Honey, don' min' me. I oughta be washin' myse'f, but I got to git out an' git dis church work done. But I jes can' git ovah Clem callin' me Miss, good a frien's ez me an' him is.

**CLEM:** Aw, we is? An' dis de firs' time you been in my house?

**CISSIE:** Co'se! You ain' been a church membah 'tell now. An' I ain' wantin' to loose my good name an' git turned out o' de church foh 'sociatin' wid don'-believahs. You was a hard un, but dey humbled you at las', didn' dey, Clem?

**CLEM:** *(giving* ELIZA *a look)* Humbled who? Ain' nobody humbled me.

**CISSIE:** You allus was too proud to say you was wrong, Clem. I used to tell you dat when you was keepin' comp'ny wid me. We sho used to have some good times, didn't we? But ef I gits to talkin' 'bout dem ole courtin' days, I won' nevah stop. I come to see y'all on some church business. (CLEM *looks at* ELIZA *knowingly and smiles cynically.)* I wants y'all to jine my Buildin' de Temple Club. You see all de membahs o' de church is divided up in comp'nies lak in de army. We's God's army. Das what Rev'n Tukes say. I'm captain o' my comp'ny. Dis is Rev'n Tukes' plan. He sho is a sma't man. Well, ez I was sayin', I wants y'all to jine my comp'ny.

**CLEM:** *(sardonically)* Uh-hunh! I thought dat was what you wanted when you come in. Well, I reckon we got to tell you lak we tol' all de res' what's been heah.

**CISSIE:** *(with surprise)* All de res'? Is dey been anybody else heah tryin' to git y'all . . .

**CLEM:** Dey sho is. Jes about fo' mo' 'sides you.

**CISSIE:** Well ef dat don't beat all! An' dey all promised me dey was go'n' let me git y'all in my comp'ny, 'cause I tol' 'em dat Clem got mo' money 'n any cullud man in dese bottoms, an' bein's he's a ole beau o' mine, he mogght give me mo' 'n de rest of 'em foh ole time's sake. An' now Clem done been . . . He, he! *(She sniggers and places her hand before her mouf like a silly child.)* Lawd shet my mouf! I come might nigh tellin' it!

**CLEM:** Tellin' what?

**CISSIE:** Well, I reckon I may's well tell ez some o' de rest of 'em. Dey didn' keep dey promise to me 'bout lettin' y'all 'lone so I could git you in my club. Now don' y'all tell I tol' you, 'cause you ain' s'posed to know yit. Clem done been 'lected deacon o' de church.

**CLEM:** Dat all you got to tell me?

**CISSIE:** Dat all? Ain' dat uhnough? Now I know you go'n' jine my club, foh tellin' you, ain' you, Clem?

**CLEM:** You ain' tol' me nothin' I didn' know awready.

**CISSIE:** What! Who tol' you?

**CLEM:** I ain' tellin' dat part.

**CISSIE:** Well, ef dat don' beat all! You wait 'tell Rev'n Tukes fin's out you done been tol' 'fo' de time, he sho is go'n' give it to somebody. Dese folks don' know how to 'tend to dey own business. *(There is a knock at de do'. Clem opens it and admits* JIMMIE AMY, *a neighbor's boy of about 8 or 10 years)*

**JIMMIE:** Howdy, Mistah Clem. Howdy, Mis' Liza. Howdy, Mis' Cissie.

**CLEM:** Howdy, son.

**ELIZA:** Howdy, Jimmie.

**CISSIE:** Hello, Jimmie, is yo' ma home? I wants to stop by an' see huh whilse I'm down dis way.

**JIMMIE:** Yas'm, she's home. Mis' 'Liza, Ma say c'n you spare huh a little coal oil 'tell she gits some mo' an' she'll pay you back.

**ELIZA:** *(looking knowingly at* CLEM*)* Yas, Jimmie, I reckon I c'n spare a little. Come right out dis way. *(*ELIZA *and* JIMMIE *go out right door)*

**CLEM:** Well, das one mo' star added to ouah crown, since we been in de church.

**CISSIE:** *(coquettishly)* Clem, you sho don' change a bit. De same ole hard Clem. I'm mighty glad you ain' jined none o' dem othah comp'nies, 'cause I'm figurin' on you bein' my lootenant. Me an' you could work togethah an' win de bannah foh raisin' de mos' money, I bet. You go'n' be in my comp'ny, ain' you, Clem?

**CLEM:** I ain' jinin' nobody's comp'ny.

**CISSIE:** You sho do lak to make folks beg you, Clem. Jes lak when we was goin' on dat picnic long time ago. You remembah, Clem? I jes begged an' begged you to go, an' you said naw all de time. Den when we was all ready to go, who should come up wid a big box o' chocolate candy, but you. Lawd, we sho did have good times dem days, didn' we?

**CLEM:** *(dryly)* I reckon so.

**CISSIE:** I sho useta lak you a whole lot den, Clem. I ain' nevah laked nobody lak I did you. *(She looks up at* CLEM *in an appealing manner as* ELIZA *returns and observes* CISSIE'S *manner much to* CISSIE'S *embarrassment.* CISSIE *blushes and stutters in her attempt to control her confusion. She quickly changes the subject)* Uh, uh, uh, how much you go'n' give on de new church, Clem?

**CLEM:** I tol' you I ain' go'n' give nothin'.

**ELIZA:** I reckon I bettah be goin' down to Gennessee ef I'm go'n'.

**CISSIE:** Guess I bettah be goin' too. Clem, c'n I ride ez fur ez Minnie Amps' wid you?

**CLEM:** *(going out the front door)* Sorry, I ain' goin' dat way. 'Scuse me, won't you? You want anything from town, 'Liza?

**ELIZA:** Naw, Clem.

**CISSIE:** Clem sho don' change a bit. Always want to have his way. Ef I hadn' a got Sam, I spec' I'd a ma'ied Clem, but he was always too headstrong foh me. He's dat way still, ain' he?

**ELIZA:** I don' know.

**CISSIE:** You don' know? My Lawd, you was livin' wid 'im long uhnough b'fo' you ma'ied to know ev'ything about 'im.

**ELIZA:** Clem ain' dat kin' o' man what you c'n know ev'ything about.

**CISSIE:** I sho wouldn' let 'im live wid me lak dat, draggin' my good name down. He'd a had to ma'y me right off. Das one thing me an' him nevah did git 'long about when we was keepin' comp'ny. I nevah would a stood foh what you did. Naw, not me, chile! An' people talkin' lak dey was.

**ELIZA:** Stood foh what?

**CISSIE:** Uh, huh! You know de way Clem was livin' wid you 'fo' y'all was ma'ied!

**ELIZA:** (*vehemently*) Look heah, Cissie Brown, how come you settin' heah diggin' up all dem dead bones? You ain' hyeahd me complainin' 'bout de way Clem done me, an' ef I'm satisfied all de rest o' y'all oughta be tickled to death. (*There is a knock at the front door.* ELIZA *rises and admits* REV. OBADIAH TUKES. *She pulls her apron up before her and is embarrassed to be found in working clothes by the minister. He bows ceremoniously and smiles broadly as he extends his hand. He does not see* CISSIE BROWN *because her back is to the door and the high back of the rocking chair in which she sits hides her. When* CISSIE BROWN *recognizes* REV. TUKES' *voice, there is an expression of surprise on her face. She smiles cynically and nods her head knowingly*)

**REV. TUKES:** How you do, Sistah Coleman!

**ELIZA:** Right well, thank you, Rev'n. Come in an' set down. You'll please 'scuse me a minute whilse I puts on some decent clothes to talk to you in.

**REV. TUKES:** (*raising his hand ministerially*) Naw, naw, Sistah. Naw indeed, don' you do no sech a thing. I likes to find God's chillun at work. It shows dey's out o' mischief.

**ELIZA:** (*going out left door*) I won' take but jes a minute, Rev'un. You set down heah an' talk to Mis' Brown.

**REV. TUKES:** (*who has not seen* CISSIE *before, tries to hide his painful surprise behind a deep, ministerial bow. A distinct uneasiness is shown in his manner*) How . . . how you do, Sistah Brown?

**CISSIE:** (*sitting up rigidly and speaking austerely*) Howdy, Rev'n!

**REV. TUKES:** It's a surprise to see you heah.

**CISSIE:** Yas, I reckon 'tis, Rev'un. 'Specially since you tol' me you was leavin' town yestiddy.

**REV. TUKES:** *(whispering and looking back at the door fearing* ELIZA'S *return)* But you . . . you see . . . I . . . I had to git some business settled wid . . .

**CISSIE:** Yas, yas, business you calls it. Well, ef you ain' keerful, Obadiah Tukes, you ain' go'n' be able to do no mo' business.

**REV. TUKES:** *(leaning over and patting her hand placatingly)* Naw, naw, Cissie, you know I don' lak nobody but you, but I got to go to see de membahs o' de church 'fo' I goes. *(They sit erect as* ELIZA *returns with a clean gingham dress)*

**CISSIE:** *(rising)* Well, I reckon I bettah be goin' 'cause I don' wanna be in de way o' y'all's business. Good day! *(She goes out)*

**REV. TUKES:** What's de mattah wid Sistah Brown? Was y'all havin' words, Sistah Coleman, 'fo' I come in?

**ELIZA:** I reckon you'd call it dat, Rev'un. Look lak folks tries to make mo' trouble now'n dey did 'fo' we was in de church.

**REV. TUKES:** Don' let dem little things bothah you, Sistah Coleman. Jes hol' yo' head high, an' tell yo' troubles to God. He'll take keer of 'em. Is Brothah Coleman heah?

**ELIZA:** Naw sah. He went to town jes 'fo' you come in. He ain' no mo' 'n hitched up de wagon an' got out de gate by now. You'll 'scuse me whilse I sees ef I c'n ketch 'im.

**REV. TUKES:** Naw, sistah. Don't you bothah. I ain' got long to stay nohow. I jes thought I'd drop in to see y'all b'fo' I leaves Camdus. I allus tries to see de membahs o' de church, an' specially de new converts, 'fo' I goes away.

**ELIZA:** Das mighty nice of you, Rev'un.

**REV. TUKES:** I ain' got so fur today ez I planned 'cause look lak I jes can' git away when I stops sometime. I says to myse'f, "Now I'm go'n' look in on Sistah So-an'-so, foh jes a minute foh to say how-you-do an' God-be-wid-you-'tell-we-meet-ag'in," but somehow I gits in an' starts talkin' an' 'fo' I know a thing about it, I done passed a whole hour away.

**ELIZA:** Yas sah, time sho do fly, when you gits to talkin'.

**REV. TUKES:** It do dat! Well suh, ef Brothah Jim Proffitt hadn't a lent me his hoss an' buggy, I wouldn't a got fur ez I is, 'cause ev'ywheah I goes dey gives me some'm to remembah 'em by an' to kinda show how dey 'preciates my preachin'. An' now, bless me, de buggy's might nigh full, but I jes had to come by an' see you an' Brothah Coleman, 'cause y'all my star converts.

**ELIZA:** I'm glad you come by, Rev'un. 'Tain' much, but I wants to give you a little some'm, too. *(She starts out.)*

**REV. TUKES:** Das awright, Sistah Coleman. Dey's plenty o' time foh dat. Wheah's de chillun today? Is dey well?

**ELIZA:** Oh, yas sah, dey is jes fine, thank you. Dey is down de road playin'. I hopes dey comes 'fo' you leaves.

**REV. TUKES:** Yas, I hopes so, myse'f. Dem is sho two fine chillun, Sistah Coleman. You an' Brothan Coleman mus' be mighty proud of 'em.

**ELIZA:** Yas sah, we is kinda proud of 'em, Rev'un.

**REV. TUKES:** Brothah Coleman is sho one lucky man.

**ELIZA:** How you mean lucky, Rev'un?

**REV. TUKES:** He got a good farm heah, an' dey tell me it's all paid foh, an' y'all's cotton gits de prize ev'ry yeah at de county fair.

**ELIZA:** Yas sah, das right.

**REV. TUKES:** He got two up-an'-comin' chillun. An' dat ain' all. He got one o' de bes' womens in Camdus foh a wife.

**ELIZA:** *(blushing and bowing her head)* Lawd, Rev'un, you don' mean dat las' you say.

**REV. TUKES:** 'Deed I does mean it. I means ev'ry single word of it an' mo' too. Dat makes me think o' de good news I got foh y'all. What you reckon 'tis?

**ELIZA:** I'm sho I don' know what it c'n be, Rev'un.

**REV. TUKES:** Naw, an' you wouldn' guess ef you live 'tell jedgment day. I knowed it 'ud be a surprise to you, das how come I wanted to come heah an' tell you myse'f. I wanted to see de glad look on yo' face.

**ELIZA:** I'm mighty anxious to heah it.

**REV. TUKES:** I know you is, Sistah. An' de news I has foh you proves what I jes said. Brothah Coleman sho is lucky he got you foh a wife, 'cause ef it hadn' a been foh you it nevah would a happened. *(hesitating and smiling broadly)* I know you is on pins an' needles to heah it, ain' you, Sistah Coleman?

**ELIZA:** Yas sah, I sho is.

**REV. TUKES:** Well, git yo' yeahs all ready, 'cause I know you go'n' be deaf wid surprise. *(hesitating again to prolong* ELIZA'S *suspense and to enjoy his advantage)* We is 'lected Brothah Coleman on de deacon boa'd of Piney Grove Church . . . *(with emphasis)* on my recommendation.

ELIZA: *(appearing surprised)* Well, well, Rev'un, I'm mighty glad y'all seen fit to use Clem.

REV. TUKES: *(throwing off some of his ministerial dignity and becoming more natural and familiar in his manner)* But don' you think we go'n' let you waste away, Sistah Coleman. De church o' God needs good womens lak you.

ELIZA: Me, Rev'un? I don' know what you means, 'cause I ain' got nothin' much to waste away.

REV. TUKES: Das awright, Sistah Coleman, you needn' be 'preciatin' yo'se'f now. I jes got a nachul-bo'n gif' foh pickin' out good church workahs, 'specially 'mongst de sistahs. *(assuming a self-important, boasting manner)* You see, Sistah Coleman, I goes about from place to place carryin' on camp meetin's an' r'vivals . . . bringin' souls to de Mastah . . . an' I has a good chance to see what's goin' on in all de churches. I been tellin' 'em up yondah to Piney Grove dat what dey needs is some young blood 'mongst de deacons an' 'specially de deaconess'. I knows all I got to do is to say de word an' dey'll make you a deaconess, an' das what I got in min' today.

ELIZA: *(with incredulous surprise)* Lawd, make me a woman deacon, Rev'n? I ain' nevah had no larnin' 'bout de church lak it take to be a deacon. You mus' be jokin', Rev'un . . .

REV. TUKES: Naw, Sistah. Obadiah Tukes don' nevah joke 'bout God's business. All I wants to know is does you want to be a deaconess. You don' need to worry 'bout de larnin'. You jes say you wants to be one, an' leave de res' to me.

ELIZA: Well, Rev'un, ef you says I c'n do it, I'll sho be glad to try. I'll do my bes'.

REV. TUKES: Das all I wants to heah you say. I know you'll git 'lected, cause ain' none o' my recommendations nevah been turned down yit. An' das sayin' a whole lot, seein' how many churches I preaches at, an' all de kin' o' folks I deals with. An' you knows, Sistah Coleman, ouah folks is sho hard to suit.

ELIZA: Dey is dat, Rev'un.

REV. TUKES: *(looking up at the ceiling and around the room, and tapping his foot on the floor)* Yas sah, I sees a whole lot o' folks ez I goes about, but I ain' seed many what beats you foh looks.

**ELIZA:** *(embarrassed, bowing her head and playing with her dress)* Lawd, Rev'un, you is jes teasin' now, foh fair. Dey ain' no looks worth talkin' 'bout on me.

**REV. TUKES:** I ain' teasin', no sech a thing. I been thinkin' 'bout you since de firs' day I seed you. Sometime I even dreams about you.

**ELIZA:** Lawd, Rev'un, you sho is a great tease.

**REV. TUKES:** *(bringing his chair nearer to* ELIZA *and leaning over toward her, trying to look into her eyes)* I ain' teasin', no sech thing. I means eve'y word I says. You looks good uhnough to make any man lose his head. I been wishin' foh a chance to tell you so.

**ELIZA:** *(showing greater embarrassment and uneasiness as she senses the approaching trouble)* Many womens ez you sees in all yo' goin' about, you sholy is seen a whole lot bettah lookin' 'n me, Rev'un.

**REV. TUKES:** Hit ain' de looks dat counts so much, Sistah. You is got looks an' some'm else too. Dere's a whole lot of 'em got looks, but dey ain' got dat some'm else you got. *(He takes her hand.* ELIZA *draws away from him and stands up. She holds back. His voice is deep and soft with increasing passion)* 'Liza, I been wantin' you foh a long time. Don' be skeered, I ain' go'n' hurt you. Dey ain' nobody heah but jes you an' me.

**ELIZA:** *(excited, but trying to remain respectful)* But Rev'un, dis ain' right. You is a preachah. An' . . .

**REV. TUKES:** Ain' us preachahs got nachul feelin's jes lak othah folks? *(He tries again to embrace her)*

**ELIZA:** Don', Rev'un! Don' do dat! Hit's wrong.

**REV. TUKES:** Dey ain' nothin' wrong 'bout it. De Lawd give us dese heah feelin's, ain' He? An' He meant foh us to use 'em, else He wouldn't a gi' 'em to us.

**ELIZA:** *(Backing away from him, trying to get the table between them. He follows her in a ravenously passionate manner)* But it's sinnin'. I'm ma'ied woman, an' I couldn' nevah look Clem in de face, ef I done some'm I ain' got no business wid some othah man.

**REV. TUKES:** *(standing still for a moment and speaking in a challenging, harder voice and manner)* I bet he looks you in de face when he go down yondah to Genessee an' run 'roun' wid dem fas' womens. I done seed 'im down deere wid my own eyes. *(resuming his passionate manner and starting again in pursuit)* How come yu an' me can' be frien's?

**ELIZA:** *(Shocked at his accusation, she stops.* REV. TUKES, *feeling that he has scored a strong point in his own favor, takes advantage of her momentary bewilderment by taking her suddenly in full embrace)* Naw, Rev'un, don't! Don' do dat!

**REV. TUKES:** *(Pulling* ELIZA *to him passionately, and trying to kiss her. He seems to have forgotten all else and all his senses are intent upon one aim . . . the possession of* ELIZA*)* Liza, I loves you. I loves you, 'Liza. Ain' you go'n' kiss me, jes once? 'Liza, 'Liza, I . . .

**ELIZA:** *(She has been mildly but consistently repulsing the minister's advances, but now suddenly becomes furious and takes a definitely antagonistic stand. She breaks away from him)* Stop, Rev'un, Stop! I done stood all dis I kin. I'm s'prised at you. Heah you is a minister of de gospel tryin' to make me do wrong. You oughta be shame' o' yo'se'f.

**REV. TUKES:** *(a bit taken aback by this sudden change in* ELIZA, *but still trying to gain his objective)* But 'Liza, don' you see . . .

**ELIZA:** Stan' wheah you is, Rev'un. Don' come nigh me. Now I see you foh what you is . . . a backbitin', low-down hypocrite.

**REV. TUKES:** *(at last realizing the hopelessness of his situation and trying to regain his ministerial front)* But you know, Sistah Coleman, we is all lak to err sometime, so de good book say. An' God forgives dem what sins, ef dey repents an' . . .

**ELIZA:** Yas, but I'm go'n' pray He makes you rue de day you tried to make 'Liza Coleman sin.

**REV. TUKES:** But you forgit. I'm go'n' make you a deaconess . . .

**ELIZA:** You ain' go'n' make me no deacon er nothin' else.

**REV. TUKES:** *(looking about for his hat and backing to de do')* I'm go'n' make you a deaconess all de same, Sistah, 'cause I knows good stuff when I sees it. I knows you is a chile o' God, 'cause you done been put to de firey tes', an' you is come thoo wid yo' wings unsco'ched. I sho fooled you dat time, Sistah Coleman. You thought I was tryin' to make you sin. Naw sah, I was jes puttin' you thoo de tes' an' you is done stood up undah it lak a true soljah o' de cross. Good evenin', Sistah Coleman, an' God bless you. *(He bows sanctimoniously and goes out grinning broadly.)*

ELIZA: *(Bewildered by this sudden change in the minister's argument, she stands looking aghast at the closed door for a moment, then raises her hand to her head and turns about, still looking dazed. She then speaks in a distressed, confused manner)* Lawd have mussy! What he mean? Puttin' me thoo de tes'. What tes'? An' he say he seed Clem down yondah to Gennessee, too, runnin' 'roun' wid fas' womens. *(emphatically, in a challenging manner)* I don' believe it. I don' keer who said it. *(doubtfully; returning to the confused manner)* Lawd, I don' know what I do b'lieve. What am I gonna say to Clem? All dis time I been gittin' him to jin church an' dis is what it come to. Unh, unh, unh! Ef I tells him . . Lawd, how'm I go'n' tell Clem dis? *(falling to her knees in despair)* O Lawd, what mus' I do? What mus' I do? *(She remains on her knees in silence a moment. Then, hearing footsteps without, she rises and tries to assume a normal appearance. Thinking it is the children without, she calls)* Mame! Is dat you?

CLEM: *(entering, looking very dejected)* Naw, 'tain' Mame.

ELIZA: *(greatly surprised at seeing* CLEM*)* Clem! Lawd, I thought you was half way to Gennessee by now. *(She looks nervous and her voice trembles from the excitement thru which she has just passed, but she tries desperately to put up a good front to keep* CLEM *from perceiving her condition)*

CLEM: Naw, I was all ready to go when I saw Milt Brown's cows in my new corn wheah dey done broke down de fince. By de time I got 'em out an' fixed de fence, it was too late to git down to Gennessee b'fo' de stores all closed.

ELIZA: An' you been out dere ev'y since you lef' out o' heah?

CLEM: *(noticing* ELIZA'S *strange manner for the first time)* Yas. What's wrong wid you?

ELIZA: Oh, nothin'.

**CLEM:** Dey is some'm wrong wid you. You shakin' jes lak a leaf on a tree. What's mattah 'd you, 'Liza?

**ELIZA:** *(trying hard to brace up and appear natural, but unable to)* Nothin', Clem. I'm awright. We had comp'ny an' . . . an' I thought you was gone to Genessee er I'd a sho called you.

**CLEM:** Comp'ny make you ac' lak dat? Who was it?

**ELIZA:** *(She hesitates a moment, still trying to decide whether she should tell* CLEM. *When she starts to speak, she stutters, takes a deep breath and a swallow, and then speaks as if the name chokes her)* Rev'un Tukes.

**CLEM:** What he want?

**ELIZA:** Uh . . . uh . . . nothin'. He jes come to see us an' say goodbye fo' he leave town.

**CLEM:** 'Liza, you stop right now an' tell me what's wrong wid you. I ain' nevah seen you lak dis b'fo'. You ain' even de same cullah.

**ELIZA:** *(raising her hand to her forehead and closing her eyes as if to collect her thoughts)* Awright, Clem, awright. Wait jes a minute. *(She stands silently a minute holding her forehead, as* CLEM *looks at her anxiously)* First, I thought I wouldn' say nothin' to you about it, but it's too much foh me. Le's set down, 'cause whilse I'm at it I may's well tell de whole thing. *(They sit down in the same seats* ELIZA *and the preacher sat in.)* B'fo' you an' me jined church, folks was sayin' you was Cunnel Thompson's gran'chile. Said de Cunnel give us dis heah farm an' all we got.

**CLEM:** *(angrily)* Who said it? What folks?

**ELIZA:** Don'make no diffunce who said it, Clem. Jes wait 'tell I gits thoo. An' dey says when you goes down yondah to Gennessee to sell cotton an' pay on de farm, you don' pay on de farm, but you takes de money an' spen's it havin' a good time wid dem spo'tin' women . . .

**CLEM:** *(with an angry start)* What!

**ELIZA:** Wait, Clem, wait. I don' b'lieve a word of it, 'cause long ez I been livin' wid you, I ain' nevah knowed you to tell me no lie, an' I prays to God I nevah will. An' I sho ain' nevah lied to you.

**CLEM:** I jes wanna know who it is dat's tellin' all dese lies. Ef I evah gits my han's on de low-down, dirty niggah, I'll, I . . . I . . . *(In his anger he stutters and clenches his fists furiously)*

**ELIZA:** Dey ain' no use gittin' all het up, Clem. Das how come I ain' tol' you long ago. Couldn' nobody make me b'lieve dat you runnin' 'roun' wid spo'tin' womens an' comin' back heah to me, hon'. But dat ain' all I got to tell you. De wors' is got to come, an' I 'clare 'fo' God I hates to tell you, but I jes got to. *(She hesitates for a moment, as if to gather the courage to go on.)* When Rev'un Tukes come heah, Cissie Brown was heah talkin' 'bout de way you an' me used to live in sin. When he come in I was givin' huh a piece o' my mind. She lef' soon's he come. Me an' him sot heah talkin' 'bout firs' one thing an' anothah. By an' by he started talkin' 'bout how good I looks to him an' a whole lot o' othah funny talk. Den 'fo' I knowed it, he caught a-hold o' me an' tried to kiss an' hug me, talkin' 'bout, "Dey ain' nobody heah but jes you an' me, an' ain' nobody go'n' know what go on 'tween us." But I put him in his place, an' when he foun' I wa'n' no loose woman, he tried to 'scuse what he done by sayin' he jes want to tes' me to see ef I was a good Christian. But I done been 'roun' too many mens in my day not to know when dey's playin' an' when dey means what dey says. Das all, Clem.

**CLEM:** *(Who apparently has complete control of himself, sits looking at the floor in a blank, fixed gaze. They are both silent for a moment, and* ELIZA *looks at him anxiously awaiting his reaction. When he does speak, it is in a firm voice and the manner of one who has made up his mind as to his course of action)* 'Liza, how come you didn' tell me all dis 'bout what folks was sayin'?

**ELIZA:** I thought a whole lot 'bout it, an' I prayed to de Lawd to show me de right way. I was thinkin' mo' foh de chillun's sake. Das how come I didn't tell you. I thought ef we could jes get in de church 'fo' you hyeahd all dat stuff, maybe somehow dey'd stop talkin' an' ev'ything 'd be awright. Maybe I done wrong, but I sho Lawd didn' mean to, Clem. Hit's hard to tell, sometime, jes what is right an' what ain'.

**CLEM:** Wheah's dem ma'iage papahs, 'Liza?

**ELIZA:** Dey's in de dressah drawah. How come you as'?

**CLEM:** Han' 'em heah.

**ELIZA:** *(going over to the dresser and looking for the papers)* Dey oughta be right heah in dis top drawah wheah I put 'em soon's we come from de church. Yas, heah dey is, right wheah I put 'em. *(She gives them to* CLEM*)* What you go'n' do wid 'em, Clem?

CLEM: *(taking the papers)* Jes wait an' see. *(He goes to the fireplace, strikes a match to the paper, and throws it into the fireplace.)*

ELIZA: *(trying to stop him)* Lawd, Clem, what's ailin' you? Is you losin' yo' min'? *(She tries to recover the burning paper, but* CLEM *restrains her, and together they watch it burn.)*

CLEM: Ain' nothin' ailin' me.

ELIZA: Burnin' de papahs ain' go'n' keep us from bein' ma'ied, Clem.

CLEM: I knows dat, 'Liza. I jes don' wan' nothin' 'roun' dis house dat low-down preachah had his hands on. An' what's mo', I ain' go'n' have dem folks at de church an' nobody tellin' me how to live. I don' wan' none of 'em comin' 'roun' heah no mo'.

ELIZA: Clem, you done clean forgot de main thing we done all dis foh. It wa'n' foh you an' me. It was foh dem two chillun.

CLEM: I done listened to yo' reason long uhnough, 'Liza. From now on I follows my own min', an' ef I goes wrong I ain' got nobody to blame but Clem Coleman. I been thinkin' 'bout Mame an' Elmer an' I got plans foh 'em.

ELIZA: What is dey, Clem?

CLEM: Long ez Mame an' Elmer is heah in Camdus, dese pryin' niggahs is go'n' pestah 'em. Dey done it befo', an' dey go'n' keep on doin' it. I done made up my min' we got to sen' Mame an' Elmer away from heah.

ELIZA: Lawd, I knowed it. I knowed it no soonah'n you sta'ted talkin' 'bout yo' plans. Clem, dey ain' no need o' all dat. Things is go'n' come out awright. It jes take time. Naw, Clem, I'd ruthah see 'em livin' heah lak dey is'n to sen' 'em 'way up yondah to Ma'y Jane. I knows das wheah you wanna sen' 'em.

CLEM: Das jes wheah I'm go'n' send 'em.

ELIZA: Naw, Clem, I can' see my chillun go 'way from me lak dat.

CLEM: 'Liza, you is de one what's allus talkin' 'bout we got to think mo' bout de chillun. Don' think 'bout you an' me, you says. Now das jes what I'm doin'.

**ELIZA:** But Clem, when I thinks 'bout dey goin' 'way up yondah to Sain' Louis hit's jes too much.

**CLEM:** Much ez I hates to see 'em leave, I knows hit's de only way foh 'em to live in peace. I wants 'em to grow up wid mo' learnin' 'n you an' me got. I wants 'em to be big, an' proud, an' free. You an' me c'n stay heah an' work, 'Liza, an' give dem de chance dey can' nevah git heah in Camdus.

**ELIZA:** *(sorrowfully, but convinced)* I reckon you right, Clem. You allus is. But all dis come so quick 'tell I ain' had no time to think it out. Hit's go'n' be mighty hard to see dem chillun leave us. Even now when you jes talks 'bout it, Clem, I gits weak. How soon you wan' 'em to go?

**CLEM:** Soon ez dey kin. De quickah dey is away from dese niggahs, de bettah. When I gits dem chillun up yondah wid Sis, we c'n tell dese Camdus folks wheah to go, an' I c'n go out yondah in de fiel' an' work in peace.

**ELIZA:** When you go'n' tell Mame an' Elmer, Clem? *(There is a knock at the front door.* ELIZA *and* CLEM *look at each other in surprise.* ELIZA *goes to the door.)* I wondah who in de worl' dat c'n be!

**CLEM:** *(starting out the side door, sardonically)* Mo' sistahs an' brothas wanna borrah some'm, I reckon. Well, I ain' heah.

*(As* CLEM *goes out the left door,* ELIZA *opens the front door and is amazed to see* DEACON SCRUGGS *smiling broadly and bowing unctuously. Behind him are* MRS. DOSHIA BRAGGS, MRS. MAHALA TURNER, *and other deacons and deaconesses of Piney Grove Baptist Church. They all come in and are given seats, grouped about the center of the room. The members of the board are in quite a happy mood in contrast to the mood of their former visit to* CLEM. *They are exceedingly gracious . . . almost deferential . . . in their attitude toward* CLEM *and* ELIZA. *They particularly stress the titles "Brothah" and "Sistah" when they address* ELIZA *and* CLEM, *each of whom is civil, but by no means glad to see the deacons and deaconesses.)*

**SCRUGGS:** Howdy, Sistah Coleman! You kinda s'prised to see us heah so soon, ain' you? *(He extends his hand to* ELIZA *as he comes in the door, as do others of the board.)*

**ELIZA:** Howdy, Deacon! Come in, y'all!

**MRS. DOSHIA:** Well, 'Liza, how do it feel to be a membah o' de church 'o God an' ma'ied an' livin' lak de rest of us?

**ELIZA:** *(dryly)* Awright, I reckon, Mis' Doshia.

**MRS. DOSHIA:** You reckon, chile? You oughta say, "I knows!" . . . long ez you lived in sin.

**SCRUGGS:** We got a great su'prise foh y'all, Sistah Coleman. Wheah's Brothah Coleman?

**ELIZA:** Clem's out in de fiel', Deacon.

**SCRUGGS:** I reckon we got to as' you to call 'im, 'cause de news is 'specially foh him.

**ELIZA:** Can' I give it to him, Deacon? Clem don' lak to be bothered when he's busy workin'.

**SCRUGGS:** Naw, Sistah, we got to tell 'im. He'll be so glad when he heahs it, he won' min' ef you do stop 'im.

**ELIZA:** Yas, he do min', too. Clem's work come firs'.

**MRS. DOSHIA:** *(rising)* Chile, you talks lak you skeered o' Clem. I'l go git 'im. *(As she starts out the door,* CLEM *enters. There is a hard, cold, dispassionate expression on his face and in his attitude toward the board. He stands in the doorway.)* Heah he is now.

**SCRUGGS:** You is jes in time, Brothah Coleman. We is got a great su'prise foh you. An' de su'prise we got foh you is some'm dat don' happen to ev'rybody. Hit shows you lak de good book say, "God works in a mysterous way His wondahs to puhform." Now who would a thought dat when we was heah de las' time dat we'd a been heah dis evenin' foh what we is . . . to tell you de good news, Brothah Clem Coleman, dat you is done been 'lected deacon o' de Piney Grove Baptist Church. *(The members of the board look expectantly at* CLEM *for an expression of happy surprise, but he faces them with a superior and disdainful calm, and remains silent. Mistaking this silence,* DEACON SCRUGGS *continues.)* Yo so su'prised you don' know what to say, ain' you, Brothah? We jes knowed you'd be glad to heah de news, so we come by to give it to you official so's you could come on ovah to de church wid us now to de first' meetin' o' de boa'd since you been 'lected. *(looking about at his fellow board-members)* I . . . I 'spec' hit's 'bout time we was gittin' along, sistahs an' brothahs. Is you comin', Deacon Coleman?

**CLEM:** *(It is evident that all the troubles of the past weeks are seething within* CLEM *and come gradually to the surface as he talks. But he speaks firmly)* Naw, Deacon. But b'fo' y'all goes I wanna tell you how come I ain' comin'.

**SCRUGGS:** Well, maybe ef yu can' come dis time, you c'n come de nex' time we meets, on de secon' Friday.

**CLEM:** Naw, Deacon, I ain' comin' now an' no othah time. When y'all was heah b'fo' I tol' you I wa'n' go'n make you no promises 'bout jinin' de church . . . but dey ain' no use goin' ovah all dat. Now I want you to know dat I didn' jine church foh my sake. Ef it had a been lef' wid me I'd a stayed out 'tell jedgment. *(The members of the board appear shocked.)* I did it foh 'Liza' an' dem chillun, an' foh my ole Mammy Ca'line what's in huh grave now. Since de day we jined church, we done caught mo' hell one way er anothah den in all de yeahs we was out. Ev'ry day some-body comes heah foh money to build de new church. You makes me a deacon, 'cause you thinks I'll give you a whole lot o' money. You sets aroun' plannin' how to git mo' money out o' me. Ef it ain' dat, somebody wanna borrah some'm. You goes 'roun' tellin' lies 'bout my folks, sayin' Cunnel Thompson was my gran' pa. Some o' y'all been tryin' to make 'Liza b'lieve I runs aroun' wid spo'tin' womens when I goes down to Gennessee. All I got to say 'bout dem bare-face' lies is, ef dey's anybody heah what c'n prove 'em er ef dey knows anybody anywheah what c'n prove 'em, let 'em come out heah an' say so now. (CLEM *stands in a challenging attitude a moment. There is absolute silence. No one even whispers. All sit with lips pressed close and with pious faces.)* Well, don' look lak nobody go'n' speak.

**ELIZA:** An' de ones what said it is right heah in dis room, too, Clem. *(Members of the board look about at each other question-ingly.* MRS. DOSHIA *and* MRS. TURNER *look straight ahead into space.* MRS. DOSHIA *squirms uneasily in her seat, with her arms piously folded.* CLEM *waits a moment longer and no one speaks.)*

**CLEM:** I reckon dis is one time when dey don' b'lieve in tel-lin' de truf an' shamin' de devil. But I got some mo' news foh you. De bes' of all. Whilse I'm go'n' 'bout my business tryin' to make a decent livin' foh my folks . . . soon's my back is turned an' I gits a little ways away from home . . . dat low-down preachah, Obadiah Tukes, y'all calls such a man o' God, comes heah tryin' to make my wife do wrong. *(Great surprise on the faces of the dea-cons and deaconesses.)*

**SCRUGGS:** *(rising hurriedly and angrily starting out, turning to his fellow board-members)* Le's git away from heah, brothahs an' sistahs.

**MRS. TURNER:** De devil's got dis boy ag'in.

**MRS. DOSHIA:** He oughta be shame', slandahing a man o' God lak dat.

**ELIZA:** *(rising and going over beside* CLEM*)* He ain' slandahin', no sech a thing. You de one oughta be shame' foh all dem lies you been tellin' *(*MRS. DOSHIA *is unprepared for this direct accusation from* ELIZA. *She appears indignantly shocked, but for once has no further answer.)*

**CLEM:** *(He walks over and stands in front of the door. Members of the board are standing in their places transfixed. Then with incisive command he continues.)* But you ain' goin' nowheah 'tell you heah all I got to say. I done had uhnough o' y'all church-goin' niggahs. I ain' go'n' be no deacon, an' what's mo', I ain' go'n' put my foot inside dat church ez long ez I lives an' *(throwing the door open and standing aside)* when you goes out dat do' dis time, I don' want none of you to come in it no mo'. Dis heah house is my church an' my religion is right heah. *(Led by* DEACON SCRUGGS *and* MRS. DOSHIA, *the members of the board file out hurriedly, looking sheepishly and bewildered. When the last one is out* CLEM *closes the door forcefully, turns front, and bursts into a hearty laugh.)* Ha, Ha, Ha!

**ELIZA:** *(looking at* CLEM *joyously)* Das de way I likes to heah yo laugh, Clem. Now you mo lak yo'se'f.

**CLEM:** *(stretching both arms out, opening and closing his hands, and raising his head high)* Now I feels lak m'se'f ag'in.

(By Dis Time De Curtain Done Fell)

# MERCEDES GILBERT
# (18??–1952)
▼▼▼▼▼▼▼▼▼▼▼

Versatile performer and writer Mercedes Gilbert was born in Jacksonville, Florida, where she was educated at Edward Waters College. She had prepared herself to enter the nursing profession, but turned to song-writing when she was unable to find employment as a nurse (she later wrote "Decatur Street Blues" and "Also Ran Blues"). For a time, she played in silent films such as the *The Call of His People*, *Secret Sorrow*, and *Body and Soul* (starring Paul Robeson). She also appeared in Broadway productions of *The Lace Petticoat, Lost, Bambola, The Green Pastures,* and *Mulatto*. In addition, she contributed to the Associated Negro Press, published poetry, wrote a novel called *Aunt Sara's Wooden God* (1938), and penned two dramatic pieces, *In Greener Pastures* (date unknown) and *Ma Johnson's Harlem Boarding Room* (1938). She died in Jamaica, New York, not far from the scene of her most notable triumphs.

*Environment* first appeared in her anthology called *Selected Gems of Poetry, Comedy, and Drama*, published in Boston in 1931. A family drama of life in Harlem and North Carolina that opens like *Old Man Pete*, it soon explodes into violence, deception, chicanery, and dope dealing. When the Williams family moves to a rural area in the South, things change. In contrast to

Harlem, Mary Lou's North Carolina home is peaceful, secure, and unthreatened. Though we are more often told about developments rather than shown them in this domestic melodrama, the audience realizes that the Williams family is returning to its rural roots in the South where it truly feels at home. The ominous mood of Harlem life that dominates the first part of the play gives way to a benign ambiance that transforms even the villainous Mr. Jackson into a decent citizen. This final-curtain conversion of villains was not uncommon in African American drama (see, for example, *Peculiar Sam* in *Roots of African American Drama* [Detroit: Wayne State University Press, 1991]). Perhaps the need to forgive injury by "one's own" reflected the community's wish for unity in the face of constant racial harassment.

## REFERENCES

Obituary. *New York Times*, March 6, 1952.

Stewart, Harry T. "The Poet-Actress: A Personal Interview with Miss Mercedes Gilbert." *Education: A Journal of Reputation* 2 (September 1936): 7.

# ENVIRONMENT

## Mercedes Gilbert

## CAST

MARY LOU WILLIAMS, *The mother*
EDNA MAY WILLIAMS, *The daughter*
CARL WINTERS, *Edna's sweetheart*
HENRY WILLIAMS, *A son*
JAMES WILLIAMS, *The father*
ELIZA LOUDER, *A neighbor*
A DETECTIVE,
A POLICE OFFICER,
TEDDY SMITH, *Henry's friend*
ROSA LEE, *Henry's girl*
MILLIE BROWN, *Rosa's friend*
CHARLES JACKSON, *A disbarred lawyer and realtor*
MARGARET JACKSON, *His daughter*
ALICE ROSS, *A stenographer*
SAMUEL BLACKWELL ⎫ *Jackson's handymen*
RICHARD MOONEY ⎭

## SCENES

Act 1

Scene: The dining room in the Williams's basement apartment.
Time: At present. Around 9 P.M.

ACT 2

> *Scene 1:* The same as Act 1. Four months later.
> *Time:* Early evening.
> *Scene 2:* Jackson's office, in a downtown section. The next day.
> *Time:* Afternoon.

ACT 3

> *Scene:* Mary Lou's home in Durham, N. C.
> *Time:* Two years later, early afternoon.

## ACT I

SCENE 1

*(A poorly furnished combination dining room and kitchen, in a basement apartment. A delapidated table in the center of the floor. A few chairs, a small stove in one corner, and a cupboard with dishes in another corner.* MARY LOU *is discovered wrapping up a bundle which she is trying to conceal, as* EDNA *and* CARL *enter room. She has on hat and seems anxious to make her exit)*

**EDNA:** Oh! here is mother.

**CARL:** How are you Mrs. Williams? *(Crosses to shake her hand)*

**MARY LOU:** Just fine Carl. I'm going out for a minute.

**EDNA:** Let me go for you mother. I know you must be tired.

**MARY LOU:** No dear, I'm not tired and I think a little air will do me good. I'll be right back. *(Exits quickly with bundle under coat)*

**EDNA:** *(Looking thoughtful)* Gee, mother acted queer. I wonder what was in that package, that, she seemed so anxious to hide.

**CARL:** Goodness only knows. Edna I do wish you would listen to reason. I'm leaving tonight, and I have talked to you for three whole days, and haven't been able to make you see that it's all wrong, your staying here and—

**EDNA:** Now, Carl, please don't start all over again. I've told you it's impossible for me to leave them like this, when they need me so much.

**CARL:** But don't you see dear, that, there is no earthly reason for you, to sacrifice yourself like this.

**EDNA:** What would become of mother? Father has spent every cent we had, he can't get work.

**CARL:** You mean, won't stay sober long enough, to try.

**EDNA:** I won't deny that, but, mother wouldn't admit it, and she wouldn't leave him. And then she has her pride.

**CARL:** Pride? in these environments. How long will pride last? It will effect you too Edna, just as it has your father and brother. Even your mother has changed, she left home a beautiful woman, full of hope, and now; she is broken in health and mind.

**EDNA:** Oh! I know Carl, haven't I seen it all. We came here with money, we received from the sale of our farm, and for awhile lived in a better neighborhood. Then, when father could not get work, and the money was all spent, father started drinking and then, this. *(Indicating surroundings with her hand)* I don't know how it will end.

**CARL:** Let me take you out of it Edna. You promised to marry me. Say, that you will tomorrow, and then go home with me.

**EDNA:** No Carl, I can't, oh! can't you see that I can't leave mother now, like this.

**CARL:** Very well, I will go now, my train leaves within an hour. If you need me, you can just wire. I've got our home all finished, and a nice business, and no matter what happens, I will be waiting. I love you sweetheart. Oh! so much. *(Embraces her, and turns to go, as door opens and* MARY LOU *enters with arms full of packages)*

**MARY LOU:** Leaving so soon Carl? I was going to fix you some lunch. *(Places packages on table)*

**CARL:** *(Taking out watch)* Yes, Mrs. Williams, I must catch my train, which leaves within an hour. I will write as soon as I get home.

**EDNA:** I'll go to the station with you Carl. Wait until I get my hat. *(She exits into bedroom left)*

**CARL:** Mrs. Williams, I've just been trying to persuade Edna to marry me tomorrow, and go home to Durham, but she won't consent.

**MARY LOU:** Oh! I wish she would Carl. Sometimes, I feel so afraid for her here. I don't know why; but, this dreadful place has done us so much harm. Just think, only one year ago we came to this city, and since we have been here, just look how our lives have changed. My poor James, he is no longer the man he was, and Henry, why, I hardly know the boy. He keeps all kind of late hours, and his companions are just street ruffins, and I am so tired. Oh! *(She reels as if about to fall,* CARL *catches her in his arms)*

**CARL:** Are you better now? Let me get you a chair.

**MARY LOU:** I'm alright, just a weak spell. *(*EDNA *enters)*

**EDNA:** "I'll be back soon mother. You lie down and rest." *(Kisses mother and takes* CARL'S *arm and exits)* (MARY LOU *seated at table, drops her head on table and sobs. Door opens and* HENRY *a boy of eighteen enters, walks over to table, and places hand on mother's shoulder)*

**HENRY:** Mother, are you ill?

**MARY LOU:** No dear, I'm only tired.

**HENRY:** Has father been home, mother? *(*HENRY *busies himself over stove, looking for food, turns and looks at mother)*

**MARY LOU:** Yes Henry, your father was here, an hour ago.

**HENRY:** And was he—

**MARY LOU:** Don't say it Henry, I know, yes, he was drunk.

**HENRY:** And?

**MARY LOU:** Oh! he didn't do any harm. I had to give him money, that's all.

**HENRY:** Give him money, or take a beating. I know, I can't believe that he is my father nowadays. He is so different. But, mother, I have decided to quit school and go to work

**MARY LOU:** What! No Henry you cannot, you must not! I want you to finish, you will need your education, and you have only one more year. I will not hear of it.

**HENRY:** But, mother, I can't stand to see you working like this, night and day. I must help you.

**MARY LOU:** No Henry, I won't let you do that, and suppose you did not get work. It was not being able to get work that first started him doing as he does, that and these environments. Nothing to do, job after job, turned him down, he became discouraged, and then this.

**HENRY:** But, what about you? You have grown twenty years older, and you're working yourself to death.

**MARY LOU:** Oh! I'm alright, I don't mind it a bit, as long as I know that, I have you to fall back on, some day. *(Embraces boy)*. Now, you run along to bed, and Henry promise me, that you will always, be a good boy.

**HENRY:** I certainly will, mother. *(Starts toward bedroom door)*

**MARY LOU:** Henry, there's something that, I want to ask you. Why, do you keep company with that boy Teddy? He's not the kind of a boy that I like to see my son with.

**HENRY:** Why, mother, what has he done? He's my best pal, and he's promised, to help me find a way to make some money after school. Big money, not the dimes I make now.

**MARY LOU:** I've never seen him do anything Henry, but, he's no good. I know it. I've always been a good Christian Henry, and some how God! always shows his children, where there is danger. I feel it Henry, he will get into trouble.

**HENRY:** Mother you are excited and suspicious. Teddy is alright, and besides, I must have some friends, and he lives in the same house. So how can I shun him. But, I must go to bed, good-night mother. *(Kisses mother and exits into bedroom.* MARY LOU *starts sewing, seated at table)*

*(Knock is heard at door)*

**MARY LOU:** Come in! *(Woman enters)*

**ELIZA:** Oh, here you are, I just dropped in for a little chat.

**MARY LOU:** Glad to have you come in Eliza. *(Continues to sew)*

**ELIZA:** Well, you don't seem to like it. You're still sewing. Say, Mary Lou why don't you snap out of it. Come on upstairs, we're having a party, and I want you to join us.

**MARY LOU:** Thanks Eliza, but, I have some work to finish.

**ELIZA:** That's all you know, work. Cut it out and have some fun, for a change. There's a bunch of good boys, up in my flat, and plenty of good liquor, and the night is young; who knows what might happen.

**MARY LOU:** I don't care for liquor, and I don't want to meet any boys.

**ELIZA:** Alright, Salvation Army Ann, I guess your old man wouldn't turn none down though.

**MARY LOU:** I think I can sew better alone.

**ELIZA:** Now, don't be upish, it don't become your basement surroundings. You're just a fool to sit here and sew, while that man of yours makes whoopee, on the money you make.

**MARY LOU:** Please leave my affairs alone.

**ELIZA:** Affairs, you ain't got no affairs. That's what I'm trying to start for you. An affair that will get you more than that sewing will. Why, one of the boys is dying to meet you, on the strength of what I told him, how you looked.

**MARY LOU:** Please go!

**ELIZA:** Oh! well if you are dumb, it ain't my fault. But you've turned down a good time and money.

**MARY LOU:** (*goes over to door, and opens it*) Now, get out. I mean it.

**ELIZA:** Alright. But say, Mary Lou, won't you lend me a cup of sugar, to make some punch? I'll give it back tomorrow.

**MARY LOU:** (*goes over to cupboard, fills cup*) Here it is, good night.

**ELIZA:** Well, Mrs. Prim, here's how. (*Lifts hand as if taking a drink, laughing, exits*)

**MARY LOU:** Oh! Lord! how much longer, will I have to endure this? (*Goes over to stove and starts to pour cup of tea, as knock is heard on door, opens door,* JACKSON *enters*)

**JACKSON:** Good evening, Mrs. Williams. I was in the neighborhood, I thought I would drop in. How are you?

**MARY LOU:** (*looking frightened*) I'm alright, but is there anything wrong with the work?

**JACKSON:** No, everything is O. K. I just dropped in, as I was on this street.

**MARY LOU:** That's nice of you, Mr. Jackson.

**JACKSON:** Mrs. Williams, I wish you would take one of the upstairs apartments. I don't think it's healthy for you here. I could arrange it.

**MARY LOU:** But, my husband is the janitor, and this is the apartment, we are supposed to occupy. Isn't it?

**JACKSON:** You mean, you are the janitress. I know that you do all the work. You are a fine woman, and I want to help you.

**MARY LOU:** Thanks, but, I don't think we can afford it. It would cost some rent, wouldn't it?

**JACKSON:** I could fix that for you. *(Walks over and puts hand on her shoulder intimately)*

**MARY LOU:** I'd rather not, Mr. Jackson. *(Looks frightened)*

**JACKSON:** Very well, but you think it over. I'd like to help you, and you may see it different some day. These are my houses, and I could do a lot for you.

**MARY LOU:** Please, don't say any more about it, Mr. Jackson.

**JACKSON:** Well, if you should change your mind, or need my assistance, here is my card. Let me know personally.

**MARY LOU:** The agent tries to get me everything to work with, and is very nice.

**JACKSON:** Oh! the agent's alright. But, this is between you and I. Good night, my dear. *(Exits)*

**MARY LOU:** Insults, insults, everywhere. Oh! God, how can I bear this. *(Walks up and down floor in despair, door opens stealthly, and* JAMES WILLIAMS *enters, looks very much frightened, stands with back to door, and places finger on lips.* MARY LOU *startled, speaks)* James! for God's sake, tell me quickly, what has happened?

**JAMES:** Hush, don't talk so loud—hide me,—they are after me,—do you hear,—they are after me.

**MARY LOU:** Who? what do you mean?

**JAMES:** The police, I haven't much time, I must hide, a man was killed, in the place where I was. Before God, I didn't do it. Don't look at me like that. I was asleep, and when I awoke, the cops were there, and I had the gun, in my hand. Before God, I do not know how it got there. I got away in the excitement, and I must hide. They will be here any minute now, do something, don't stand there and look.

**MARY LOU:** No, James you must go away. It would never do for them to find you, it would mean imprisonment, or maybe death. Think of daughter and son, disgraced for life. Here, take this money and go. *(Goes over to stove, takes from coffee pot, a small roll of money. Gives it to* JAMES, *who, takes it hurriedly and puts it in pocket, they embrace. Starts apart frightened, as a loud knock is heard on door.* JAMES *exits on opposite side of stage.* MARY LOU *opens* *door, two cops enter, pushing her aside, and she starts toward other door, she to delay them, knocks cup off of table. They turn and address* MARY LOU)

**POLICE:** Well, where is that husband of yours?

**MARY LOU:** I do not know.

**DETECTIVE:** Now, listen here, you had better come clean. We saw him come in this house, and if you are hiding a murderer; it will go hard with you,—see.

**MARY LOU:** I tell you. I do not know where he is—

**POLICE:** Well, we will get him, and when we do, you had better look out—let's search the place. *(Starts toward bedroom,* MARY LOU *strikes cup from table, causes crash, also police and detective to turn)*

**DETECTIVE:** What, was that?

**POLICE:** I thought it was a shot. See, it was a ruse of this woman's. *(Walks over to* MARY LOU *catches her wrist and twists her arm, until she drops to her knees)* You devil, you know where he is, now, come through with it.

**MARY LOU:** *(cries out from pain)* I swear, I don't know. Oh! you are hurting my wrist, please stop.

**POLICE:** Not until you tell us where he is. You search the place. *(to detective)* Now, will you talk or not. We'll take you to headquarters.

**MARY LOU:** I don't know where he is. *(Crying)* (HENRY *comes out of bedroom, rushes toward mother)*

**HENRY:** Mother!

**POLICE:** *(to* HENRY*)* Get back there, you.

**DETECTIVE:** *(enters room)* It's no use. He's made his escape. What are we going to do with her?

**POLICE:** I won't take her down, I've got a better plan. We'll station a man here.

**DETECTIVE:** Well, you helped him to get away, and you will pay for it. (POLICE *and* DETECTIVE *exit)*

**HENRY:** *(rushes to mother's side, catches her in his arms)* Oh, mother this is terrible.

(Curtain)

## ACT II

SCENE 1

> *Time:* Afternoon four months later.
> *Place:* Same as First scene, in Act 1.

(HENRY *enters the Kitchen with bag, crosses over to bedroom door, leaves bag in bedroom. Comes out with books, takes a seat at the table. Opens book and tries to study. Gives gestures of impatience and brushes books to floor*)

**HENRY:** Oh! How can I put my mind on lessons, when my conscience is worrying me to death. Why, did I do it? How could I ever have brought myself to listen to Teddy. It would break my poor mother's heart. If she knew, oh!— (*Lays head on arms at table, door opens and* TEDDY *a boy of a few years* HENRY'S *senior enters, with cap in hand whistling*)

**TEDDY:** Oh! there you are, mamma's little school boy. How is tricks? (HENRY *starts as* TEDDY *speaks, but, looks away*) Is mamma's boy getting ready for night school, ha, ha, night school, and some school eh, Henry?

**HENRY:** Don't bother me, haven't you done enough harm? Oh! I'm sick of it all.

**TEDDY:** Now, there you go blame me if you want to. I didn't make you do anything. I only tried to do you a favor, when I got you in with the gang. And now, what you squawking about. Don't you get your share?

**HENRY:** Oh! I didn't mean anything, forget it.

**TEDDY:** Now, you are talking turkey. I met a girl, that is just nuts to meet you. You old shiek, she's coming here this afternoon. Works downtown in a small night club, and makes money to burn. (TEDDY *makes a few steps in imitation of girl, turns and extends hand to* HENRY, *laughs, then* HENRY *bows and laughs*)

**HENRY:** But, Teddy I don't want to meet any girl, that is, that kind of a girl. Some day I mean to get out of all this stuff. I met a girl last week, that, has made me feel ashamed of what I am doing, and these surroundings and everything.

**TEDDY:** Say, cut the sermon. How you do talk. You said that the law had run your father off, and that you was going to get your revenge. Now, you are squawking your head off, because everything is coming your way.

**HENRY:** Yes, but sooner or later, the law triumphs, it always does.

**TEDDY:** Oh! you make me sick. *(Goes over to bedroom, returns with bag, just as knock is heard on door. Rushes back to bedroom with bag and comes back on stage, just as* HENRY *admits two girls. Girls loudly dressed and too much makeup on their faces, smoking. Shakes hands with* TEDDY *who in turn introduces them to* HENRY, *nods head toward one and winks)* Well, Henry, here are the little dolls. Now, what can we do to make them happy?

**ROSA LEE:** I am more than pleased to meet you, Henry. For my part I suggest a little party, with everything that goes with a party, eh, Millie.

**MILLIE:** Suits me, right down to the ground. *(Takes out vanity case, begins to put on more paint, hands* TEDDY *a small mirror to hold)*

**ROSA LEE:** Of course, I want it understood, I stand the expenses. So here. *(Pulls out roll from purse, and starts to hand it to* HENRY, *who waves it aside.* TEDDY *steps between her and* HENRY *and takes money, gives* HENRY *a kick on the foot)*

**TEDDY:** Why certainly Rosa Lee, it shall be just as you desire. *(Starts toward door)*

**HENRY:** Teddy, you know I cannot pull any party here. Why, mother and Edna will be here soon.

**ROSA LEE:** Well, boys I'll tell you what we'll do. Come on over to my little shack, and we can have all the fun that we want, and the skies for the limit, eh, Millie.

**MILLIE:** You said it Rosa, and besides it's so exclusive. So let's go. *(They all exit.* HENRY *takes books from floor and hides them in oven)*

*(*MARY LOU *and* EDNA *enter)*

**EDNA:** Mother, you sit down. I'll fix you a bit to eat. I know you are tired.

**MARY LOU:** No more tired than you are, dear. Why, you look like a ghost. My poor baby. Pounding on an old typewriter all day is harder than sewing.

**EDNA:** Oh! I don't know about that. But, you see, I've got to go back and do some extra work. I only ran up here to let you know where I would be, so that you would not worry.

**MARY LOU:** Why, Edna! it's after ten o'clock. I won't let you do that.

**EDNA:** Now, mother this will mean five dollars more, and goodness knows we need it.

**MARY LOU:** But child, your health. Why, you are not well.

**EDNA:** Oh! I feel fine. I did have a headache. But one of the girls, who goes around with the boss, gave me a pill of some kind, and bingo, my headache went, just like that. (*Waves hands and both laugh*)

**MARY LOU:** Well, be careful Edna. I don't know what I'd do if I didn't have you to cheer me up. Henry's so wrapped up in his books.

**EDNA:** Yes, his books and Teddy. Mother, I don't like that boy, and Henry's been acting very queer lately. Ever since that night he said he met that girl that he rescued in the night club. By the way, what became of her?

**MARY LOU:** Henry, said that she went south. She and her mother. He says that she was a very nice girl. But I can't see how she can be nice, and in a place like that.

**EDNA:** (*placing foot on table*) My dear old fashioned mother. The best people go to night clubs here.

**MARY LOU:** But you mustn't, Edna. I just couldn't stand to have you go. You won't, will you? (*Sits at table*)

**EDNA:** (*kissing her*) Of course not. But I must hurry back, to the office, see you later, bye.

**MARY LOU:** Bye, bye, dear, hurry home as soon as you can. I'll be lonely with you out, and Henry at night school. (*Starts eating*) Well, Henry's gone to night school. I didn't know it was so late. (*Looking at clock, nearby*) I have so much ironing to do. (*Gets up, puts up ironing board, and starts ironing*) (*Knock is heard at the door*) Come in. (ELIZA *enters, takes seat at table, helps herself to a cup of tea and other food, eating with great gusto*)

**ELIZA:** This is good tea, Mrs. Williams. (*Sips tea*) I was just going to borrow some from you, but you've got some already made. It will save me the trouble of making it.

**MARY LOU:** Just help yourself, don't mind me.

**ELIZA:** Do you happen to have any more biscuits around? (*Takes last one from plate*)

**MARY LOU:** I have only one, for my son's supper.

**ELIZA:** Now, that's too bad. Say, you'd better watch that son of yours. He's running in some mighty bad crowds. I saw a gal down here this afternoon, that was in court the same time I was there for fighting, for peddling dope. She's a bad egg.

**MARY LOU:** I know Henry would not touch dope. But, I'll speak to him about that.

**ELIZA:** Well, I'm just wising you up. Of course, I ain't no angel, but I'd hate to see anybody on that stuff. I tried it once myself, but, I didn't go far that way. By the way, I saw Jackson down here last week, and what's he up to. Sweet on you or Edna.

**MARY LOU:** These houses belong to Mr. Jackson. I guess he can come around whenever he wishes. As to anybody being sweet on me, you should know better than that by now. I'm still married.

**ELIZA:** Oh! that ain't nothing, and besides old Jackson's got money and the Lord knows that's what you need.

**MARY LOU:** Let's talk about something else.

**ELIZA:** Alright, how about lending me a little tea.

**MARY LOU:** (*goes over to cupboard and puts some tea in a small paper*) Here you are, Mrs. Louder. (*Hands her tea*)

**ELIZA:** Thanks, pay you back soon. Good-bye. (*Exits*)

**MARY LOU:** Oh! but I'm tired. I worked hard today, but I must work hard, to just barely live. I could write home to father for aid, but, I do not want the folks at home, to know about James. (*Knock is heard at door,* MARY LOU *opens door and* HENRY *staggers into room, and sinks to floor. There is blood on his sleeve,* MARY LOU *rushes to him and starts to bathe his forehead. He is shaking with pain and fright*)

**MARY LOU:** Oh! my poor boy. How did this happen? Are you badly hurt? Tell mother all about it.

**HENRY:** (*brokenly*) They told me to watch, while they went inside. The cops came, I didn't see them, and when I did, I ran. They shot. I am not hurt much, only my arm. (*Loud knock is heard at door, two cops enter*)

**POLICE:** Well, here he is. So it's you again. I told you we'd get you. Now, it's your son, a gangster. But what can you expect, with such a father. (*They address these remarks to* MARY LOU, *who gathers* HENRY *in her arms*)

**MARY LOU:** You can't have him, he is mine! mine! I tell you. He hasn't done anything, he's hurt.

**DETECTIVE:** That's what they all say. *(Calls to police)* Come on help me here, let's get him to a hospital. He's our prisoner. *(*POLICE *and* DETECTIVE *starts picking boy up,* MARY LOU *still on her knees, holds on to him, they try to push her away and she fights back, crawling to keep up with them)*

**MARY LOU:** Oh! please don't take him, leave him here until he is well. Let me nurse him. I'll turn him over, when he is better, I swear it. For God's sake, don't take him away like this, he's my baby! Oh! my boy! my boy! *(*MARY LOU'S *voice rises higher and higher, until it is all a scream. The two officers push her away and take boy out of door. Her voice dies away into a sob, as she falls prone on the floor)*

(Curtain)

## ACT II

SCENE 2

*Time:* The next morning.

*Place:* Lawyer Jackson's office, furnished with upholstered easy chairs and a mahogany desk.

**JACKSON:** *(seated at desk dictating a letter to stenographer)* Mrs. Smith, this is to inform you that the mortgage, that I hold on your home, is past due. And I am giving you until tomorrow to either pay the same, or vacate the premises. Respectfully yours.

**ALICE:** Mr. Jackson, please don't send that letter. I know that Mrs. Smith is in trouble, and her husband is in the hospital, not expected to live another day.

**JACKSON:** Well, what has that got to do with me? I must have my money, that's my business. I'm not here for my health, hand me the letter, I'll mail it. From now on, you do as I tell you, or someone else will. See, who's in the outer office?

**ALICE:** Yes sir. *(*ALICE *leaves the room,* JACKSON *turns to desk,* ALICE *enters room)* There's a woman out there, seems sort of crazy. Says, that she must see you at once. A matter of life and death. *(*JACKSON, *looking up from paper he is reading)*

**JACKSON:** Is that so? Does she look as if she has money?

**ALICE:** No, sir.

**JACKSON:** Tell her, that I can't see her. I'm in a conference. By the way, Miss Ross, my wife's gone away for a short time, and I want you to send her a check every Saturday. Don't bother me with it, I'll make out a few. If you should hear anyone saying anything about her leaving, just say that she is in a Sanitarium in North Carolina, for her health. That's all. Oh! yes, Miss Ross, you can go to the bank now. Finish these briefs, that you are doing, and then go. (ALICE *crosses room to typewriter and starts writing.* SAMUEL BLACKWELL *and* RICHARD MOONEY *enter, walk over to* JACKSON'S *desk, all shake hands)*

**JACKSON:** Glad to see you. You are on time, what's up boys?

**SAM:** Oh! there's plenty stirring.

**RICHARD:** You bet your boots there is

**JACKSON:** Just a moment. *(Turns to* STENOGRAPHER*)* You may go to the bank now, Miss Ross. *(Puts up hands to men to be quiet until she leaves)* Have a cigar boys. *(Offers them box of cigars, the men each take one and light them.* STENOGRAPHER *leaves room)* Well, boys, shoot the works. You're first Dick.

**RICHARD:** Well, to start with, that woman you had taking care of the flat, took on too much of the stuff, and ran wild. This morning the bulls got her, and of course, they tried to make her tell, where she got the stuff, but, she wouldn't. Then they searched the flat, but they didn't find a thing. She's in the jug.

**SAM:** There's about five thousand dollars worth of the stuff, in that flat. The bulls are watching the place.

**JACKSON:** We've got to figure out a way, to get it out of there. Let me think. *(Meditatively)*

**RICHARD:** I don't believe we are going to get Scotty in again. The people have found out that our gang is back of his election.

**SAM:** Yes, and boss, you are none too popular with folks around here.

**JACKSON:** You two get busy and round up the others. Get around to my tenants, promise them things, anything, until after election. I've got to run this district, and with Scotty on the bench, everything is turkey.

**RICHARD:** What's going to be done about the girl in jail?

**JACKSON:** I've got a plan: Get Jones on the phone. *(SAM goes over to telephone, calls Monument 6253, gets number and hands receiver to* JACKSON, JACKSON *speaking over phone)* Hello, Jones. I want you to go down to the jail and see about Rosa Lee: what's that! oh, yes, she got charged up, and they canned her. Get her bonds for her, and send the girl, I just put there with you, over here. I can use her. That's none of your business, just do as I say, and be quick.

**SAM:** *(aside to* ROSA LEE*)* The boss is tight today.

**RICHARD:** Yes, and Jones ought to know better than cross him. What he's got on that fellow, could get him the chair.

**JACKSON:** You boys, clear out. *(*MILLIE *rushes into office)*

**MILLIE:** Gee, I had a time getting in here. How you guys feeling? *(Sits on desk)*

**JACKSON:** How did you get up here?

**MILLIE:** Used the stairs. You don't catch little Millie taking any chances. I guess you know Rosa Lee's canned.

**JACKSON:** Yes, you lay low for awhile. Take a few days out in my place. Long Island.

**MILLIE:** Alright, but, say Jack.—

**JACKSON:** Mr. Jackson.

**MILLIE:** Mr. Jackson, some stew. I want to know why do you want me to slip the stuff to that girl over at Jones office? What's your game?

**JACKSON:** I don't want none of that sob stuff, from you. I can use the girl and her mother, and I mean to do it. Now, all of you, get out.

**MILLIE:** Yes, you can use everybody, and God! how you do use them. But, some day, you'll get yours.

**RICHARD:** Cut it out Millie. It's our living and the boss is good to every one of us, and you know it.

**SAM:** Oh! she's just sentimental, over that kid Rosa Lee's been tagging around, some Henry. He's in the hold-up racket.

**MILLIE:** He's not in any racket, and you know it. It's these environments that's got him. Just like it got me. Then there is Teddy to push him on. God, I'm tired of the whole business. When I think of that innocent girl whose very soul I've damned with dope. *(Pacing floor)* Some day, I'm going to turn on all of you! *(Shakes finger in* JACKSON'S *face)* And when I do, God, help you.

**JACKSON:** *(catches her by shoulders and shakes her, both men spring to their feet)* Shut up, you little fool, don't you know if you try any of that stuff, I've only got to say the word, and you go out like a light.

**MILLIE:** Oh, don't worry, I know that. Give me the keys to the Long Island place. *(*JACKSON *hands her keys, she turns and leaves the office)*

**RICHARD:** She's alright now. I guess she took one pill too many.

**SAM:** I don't know about that. She's dangerous.

**JACKSON:** Just keep your eyes on her boys. Now, you both had better go.

**RICHARD:** Alright, we'll take the back stairs out. *(They exit, just as* MISS ROSS *enters other door)*

**ALICE:** Mr. Jackson. That woman is still out there.

**JACKSON:** Send her in. *(*MARY LOU *enters shabbily dressed and in great distress.* JACKSON *gets up, and meets her, places her in chair)*

**JACKSON:** My dear Mrs. Williams. What has happened?

**MARY LOU:** Oh! Mr. Jackson, I'm in so much trouble. *(Bursts into tears)*

**JACKSON:** *(patting her on the shoulder)* Now, calm yourself, tell me what is the trouble?

**MARY LOU:** My boy's a prisoner, and in the hospital.

**JACKSON:** What happened?

**MARY LOU:** Oh, Mr. Jackson, he's been running with a bad boy named Teddy. I warned him, but he would not listen. Last night, he was with a gang, who was robbing a store. He was outside watching for them.

**JACKSON:** And the cops got him.

**MARY LOU:** He tried to rum, when he saw them coming. They shot him.

**JACKSON:** Bad, bad. *(Shaking head)*

**MARY LOU:** Yes, and it will go harder with him, because they suspected his father of murder, and he got away.

**JACKSON:** Yes, the law never forgets.

**MARY LOU:** You'll take the case, won't you Mr. Jackson?

**JACKSON:** Well, it depends.

**MARY LOU:** What do you mean?

**JACKSON:** I can clear your boy, and put him on the street. What of my pay?

**MARY LOU:** Oh, I'll work night and day and Edna's working. We'll pay anything you ask.

**JACKSON:** I don't want money.

**MARY LOU:** Oh! *(Looking frightened)* How can I pay you then?

**JACKSON:** Listen, Mary Lou. You may have guessed that I love you. Now, don't interrupt me. I'm not trying to make love to you. I have a business proposition, for you to consider.

**MARY LOU:** Oh, I'm so glad it's that. Of course I'll accept.

**JACKSON:** But, you don't know what it is yet. I might as well tell you now. It's outside the law.

**MARY LOU:** I can't do anything, that would be breaking the law Mr. Jackson.

**JACKSON:** Well, you don't want your boy out.

**MARY LOU:** Oh, yes I do. Please Mr. Jackson, let me pay you. I do not want to do anything wrong.

**JACKSON:** It's all up to you. I have an apartment in one of the best parts of the city, and must have a nice quiet woman to keep it. I keep stuff there. I don't want the police to suspect the place.

**MARY LOU:** If they do find it there, then what. Oh, I can't do that, I can't.

**JACKSON:** Well, there are other lawyers.

**MARY LOU:** Yes, but, I haven't got a penny right now. They want their money in advance. Oh, I thought you were a friend.

**JACKSON:** And so I am, you are acting foolish, you get a good home and everything. What am I getting out of the bargain? Maybe some day you'll let me' be real nice to you, eh? *(Gets up and puts arms around her shoulder)*

**MARY LOU:** Please don't. What is it you keep in this apartment?

**JACKSON:** Thousands of dollars worth of dope and liquor, and my name must never be connected with the place, no matter what happens.

**MARY LOU:** My God! I don't want to be a criminal. I must get my boy out, I must.

**JACKSON:** I'll have Jones take you to the place. I'll pay all bills, and he will visit you there. You are to pose as a widow and Rosa Lee's mother. Rosa Lee is in jail, Jones will take care of her case.

**MARY LOU:** Oh, Mr. Jackson, I do not want to get mixed up in this. I'm in bad enough now, then there is my Edna. What about her?

**JACKSON:** I am giving her a job here, as my stenographer. She will bring the stuff here to me. Then I will pass it out to the boys, who will sell it.

**MARY LOU:** No, I can't, I won't.

**JACKSON:** There's no risk in it for people like you. I can just say the word to Scotty, the district attorney. Then your boy goes free, otherwise he can go up for several years.

**MARY LOU:** Oh, my God! that would kill me.

**JACKSON:** Well, will you accept my proposition, or not?

**MARY LOU:** Yes, for his sake. *(Spoken in tense whisper)*

(Curtain)

## ACT III

SCENE 1

*Time:* Two years later.
*Place:* Durham, North Carolina.
*Setting:* Living room in home of Mary Lou Williams.
*Furniture:* Large settee, comfortable chairs and living room table, piano, and a general air of comfort, and prosperity.

(HENRY *is discovered, hanging up hat, takes off coat and calls*)

**HENRY:** Mother, mother dear, where are you?

**MARY LOU:** Coming, dear. (MARY LOU *enters room, neatly dressed, they embrace, and* MARY LOU *holds* HENRY *at arm length, looking at him lovingly*) How is my big baby? Just look what a fine man you are. Then to think just as mamma has really gotten acquainted with you, she is about to lose you. Oh, well, that is the way, we mothers just raise you for some other woman to take.

**HENRY:** There, there, mother of mine. To hear you, one would think you were jealous of Margaret, you need have no fear. You will always hold first place in my heart, every day you grow dearer and dearer to me. When I think of all the trouble that I have caused you, and how you have suffered. It makes my heart ache.

**MARY LOU:** Don't Henry, it is just opening an old wound for both of us.

**HENRY:** You know mother, I've been here just six months, and have had two raises in salary. All of this, this home, sometimes, mother I feel as though I should tell Margaret about the time I spent in that terrible place. I hate making a new start, and still living a lie.

**MARY LOU:** Don't do it Henry. Some things are better untold. Just imagine that you are beginning life, and let it rest there.

**HENRY:** I guess you are right, mother. Oh, I wish Edna would come home. Sometimes I feel mother, that I am the cause of all the suffering, she is going through.

**MARY LOU:** Henry, don't say that, it's my fault. Had I not consented to keep that awful apartment for Jackson, my darling child wouldn't be what she is today. Oh! it's too dreadful to believe, my lovely baby, a—dope fiend. It's my fault!

**HENRY:** Mother, do not say that, you know—

**MILLIE:** (*standing in doorway, very pale and shaking*) Mrs. Williams and Henry. I have a confession to make. I hope you will forgive me. (*Comes into room*)

**HENRY:** Here, sit down Millie. You're still very weak and sick.

**MILLIE:** Well, I don't deserve the kindness you two have shown me. I am the one,—who gave Edna, her very first—dope.

**MARY LOU:** You! why! Millie.

**MILLIE:** That devil made me do it. He's got so much on me until I dared not disobey him. Oh, I wish you had left me where you found me to die. I ought to be dead. Before God, I had to obey him.

**HENRY:** God! I'd like to kill that man.

**MARY LOU:** Henry, don't say that.

**HENRY:** But, I mean it. Look how he's treated me, Edna, this girl and how he lied about getting me out of jail. I even found out, he used his influence, over that district attorney, to get me a year.

**MILLIE:** I'm so sorry, will you ever forgive me Mrs. Williams?

**MARY LOU:** Of course I will. Didn't I risk my life to save you, when I heard them plotting to take you out,—and kill you. I put you wise and scared them away. They'd killed you, but I slipped in blanks.

**MILLIE:** Jackson would kill us both, if he knew, where we were.

**MARY LOU:** Well, we don't have to worry. We are safe here. (HENRY *helps* MILLIE *from room.* MARY LOU *sits at table very thoughtful.* HENRY *returns immediately*)

**HENRY:** Mother, I am going over to call on Margaret. How are the rehearsals coming on? I saw our preacher downtown, and believe me, he is expecting your concert to be a big success. You know the church needs a lot of money, to finish the Community House.

**MARY LOU:** They shall have it. I am having just a few here tonight. Just the ones that need to rehearse most, as some know their parts so well. Tomorrow night is the big night. Henry is Margaret going to sing for us?

**HENRY:** Why yes mother. I am going over to get her now. She is expecting her father on the midnight train. (MARY LOU *looking into space wistfully*)

**MARY LOU:** Her father, oh, Henry, are you going to ask him tonight?

**HENRY:** I don't know, mother, I've got to see how he looks first. He might be a bear (*laughs*) and eat your little boy's head off, just like this—(*both laugh, as he imitates how bear would bite, as he growls and springs at mother*) (HENRY *moves over to door*) So long, mother, I'll be right back. (MARY LOU *busies herself round room, as* HENRY *throws her kiss, and exits meeting* CARL *at door*)

**CARL:** How are you, Mrs. Williams?

**MARY LOU:** Very well, Carl. You don't look so well yourself.

**CARL:** I'm not sick, just almost crazy with grief.

**MARY LOU:** You poor boy. I know, you mean about Edna.

**CARL:** Yes, I've made up my mind, to go to New York and find her, and bring her home. No matter what she is doing, or what she has done, I love her.

**MARY LOU:** I wish you success Carl, with all my heart.

**CARL:** Pray that God, will help me to find her Mrs. Williams. If I am not successful, I will never come back again.

**MARY LOU:** God bless you, my boy. *(Crying, starts towards door, meets* HENRY *with telegram, who comes in joyously)*

**HENRY:** I met the boy at the corner with this telegram. Listen, mother and Carl, it's from Edna.

**MARY LOU:** Read it, quick! *(They both collapse into chairs)*

**HENRY:** Haven't written because I've been West, found father he is cleared, guilty man caught, will be home tomorrow safe, well and cured. Edna.

**CARL:** Thank God.

**MARY LOU:** God is indeed good. Oh! I am so happy.

**HENRY:** So am I. *(Catches mother and* CARL *by the hands and dances around,* MARGARET *enters looks on happily)* Oh, Margaret, my sister and father will be here tomorrow. We are so happy.

**MARGARET:** And I'm happy, because that you are, I just ran over for a few moments. I've got to hurry back, to be at home, when father comes. Do you want me to sing, Mrs. Williams?

**MARY LOU:** No Margaret, I will not have any rehearsal tonight. Everybody knows their parts, and then, I am just too happy to bother.

**CARL:** Well, I'll go home and try to realize this happiness. Goodbye, folks. *(They all bid him goodbye.* CARL *exits)*

**MARY LOU:** Excuse me, children. *(*MARY LOU *exits into bedroom)*

**MARGARET:** It's all so strange, Henry. Father coming here, I haven't seen him in over two years. Mother and I have tried to forget all about him. That's why, I never mentioned him. As we have only been in Durham a few months, we don't know many people. No one here knows him, so mother was taken for a widow. We let it go at that.

**HENRY:** Will he and your mother become reconciled?

**MARGARET:** I guess they will.

**HENRY:** What if he objects to our marriage?

**MARGARET:** But, I know he won't. He'll think you are just grand.

**HENRY:** I do hope so.

**MARGARET:** Then when I tell him, how you saved my life in New York, when that terrible man got after my cousin and I. Well, he will say *(pokes out chest and puts thumbs in waist, as though it was a vest)* take her boy, she's yours.

**HENRY:** Margaret, you never lived in New York, did you?

**MARGARET:** Why no, I always lived over on Long Island. Mother and I went to New York seldom. Why, is it such a terrible place?

**HENRY:** Oh, no. Some parts are a bit rough, I was just wondering, why I didn't meet you before I did. *(Starts to embrace her, knock is heard at door)* Come in— (JACKSON *enters. He and* HENRY *stare at each other angrily.* MARGARET *runs to her father and embraces him)*

**MARGARET:** Oh, father! I'm so glad to see you. *(Looks from one man to the other)* Why, what's the matter? Do you know Henry father? *(Father pushes her away)*

**JACKSON:** Go home, Margaret.

**MARGARET:** But, father.—

**JACKSON:** Don't argue with me. Go— *(Points sternly to door,* MARGARET *exits)* (JACKSON *turns to* HENRY, *just as* MARY LOU *enters from bedroom, and as he raises his cane to strike* HENRY, MARY LOU *steps in between them)*

**MARY LOU:** So it's you, Jackson.

**JACKSON:** Yes, my wife told me I'd find Margaret at this house. To my surprise, I find her with this thief and ex-convict, son of yours.

**MARY LOU:** Be careful, Jackson.

**HENRY:** Yes, you had better be careful. You have caused my mother and sister enough trouble.

**JACKSON:** Not near as much as I will cause you, if the whole bunch of you don't clear out of this town. When I get through telling these people who you are, it won't be big enough to hold you.

**MARY LOU:** (*pushing* HENRY *away and facing him*) Now, you've had your way and say. I'll have mine. Mr. Jackson, you say one word to anyone about me or mine, and I'll start telling the world and your wife, what I know about you. You! hypocrite, you unspeakable beast, how you ruined my daughter's life and tried to ruin mine. Tried to make me do things, that I would be ashamed to mention. You dope peddler, I should kill you, where you stand. (*Her voice rises hysterically*)

**HENRY:** Let me do it, mother.

**MARY LOU:** No, let me handle this Henry.

**JACKSON:** And who do you think you are, that people would believe your word against mine.

**MARY LOU:** Oh! I've got proof enough. Edna worked in your office, she has duplicates of your code messages and Rosa Lee's signed confession before she died or how she smuggled the dope in for you, and how you tricked her and other girls into selling it.

**JACKSON:** Yes, Edna's dead, so what good can she do.

**MARY LOU:** She is not dead. She will be here tomorrow, and I'm telling you Jackson, if you want peace, it shall be peace. If you say one word, if you try to disgrace my boy and I, and send him back to the life, he has just got away from, I'll kill you.

**MILLIE:** (*entering quietly from the other room*) If you don't kill him, I will. (*Points gun at* JACKSON, HENRY *takes it from her*)

**JACKSON:** Millie, I thought.—

**MILLIE:** That I was dead. I know you did, but I'm not. You know I've got a plenty on you. I am beyond caring what becomes of me now. I will see that you get yours.

**MARY LOU:** Now, Jackson, what shall it be? Peace or war.

**JACKSON:** (*walks away, stands thinking, turns to* MARY LOU) Peace, you win Mary Lou. Henry do you still love Margaret, now that you know she is my daughter.

**HENRY:** Yes, that is not Margaret's fault. She's an angel. (MILLIE *sits down feebly*)

**JACKSON:** Go and find her boy. May God bless you. (HENRY *extends hand,* JACKSON *takes it and they shake.* HENRY *exits*) Mary Lou, can you and Millie ever forgive me. (*Goes over and takes* MARY LOU'S *hand, places other hand on* MILLIE'S *head*)

**MARY LOU:** Yes, Jackson. Maybe God will forgive you, and the rest of us. We can all start life anew.

**JACKSON:** Yes, in better environment.

(Curtain)

# Francis Hall Johnson
# (1888–1970)
▼▼▼▼▼▼▼▼▼▼▼

Composer and playwright Hall Johnson, as he was known, wrote one of the most successful musical dramas in the history of the Harlem Renaissance. Incredible as it may seem, the script of *Run Little Chillun* did not appear in print during the author's lifetime or after it until now.

Johnson was born in Athens, Georgia, the son of an Episcopal minister. As a boy he showed musical talent; fortunately, he had an older sister who could tutor him on the piano. After hearing a recital by Joseph Douglass, he became interested in playing the violin but was unable to study formally until he entered college. He studied music at Knox Institute in Knoxville (1903); Atlanta University (1904); Allen University in Columbia, South Carolina, where his father was president; the Hahn School of Music in Philadelphia; the University of Pennsylvania, where he took composition with Hugh A. Clark; and the Institute of Musical Art (later part of Julliard School of Music) in New York (1923–24).

Johnson made his debut as a professional violinist in a New York concert about the time of his graduation from the University of Pennsylvania in 1910. He soon settled in New York and became part of the Black music establishment. He played with

James Reese Europe's band that toured with Irene and Vernon Castle. In 1918, he performed with Will Marion Cook's New York Syncopated Orchestra. During these early years in Harlem, he conducted a music studio, played regularly in local concerts, and performed with theatre pit orchestras, including that of Noble Sissie/Eubie Blake's musical, *Shuffle Along* (1921). In 1923, he organized and led the Negro String Quartet. However, his interest was shifting to choral music, and in 1925, he organized his first permanent choral group. The Hall Johnson Choir gave its initial professional performance in February 1928 at the Pythian Temple and sang again in Town Hall the following month. During the next decade, the choir appeared on radio and in theatres, sang with major orchestras, and performed in Marc Connolly's play *The Green Pastures* (1930), for which Johnson was musical director. The Choir also sang in films such as *Lost Horizon* (1937), *Way Down South* (1939) and *Cabin in the Sky* (1943).

In 1933, Johnson produced his folk opera, *Run Little Chillun*, on Broadway. The musical was revived by the Federal Theatre Project at Los Angeles in 1935–37, with the Hollywood actor Clarence Muse as director. Because the production was judged to be successful—and controversial by those who thought that the voodoo scenes were inauthentic—it was produced again in San Francisco as a WPA exhibit in the Golden Gate Exposition of 1939. In 1938, he moved to California and organized the 200-voice Festival Choir of Los Angeles, where he restaged his folk opera. In 1946, he resettled in New York and organized the Festival Negro Chorus of New York City. The next year he began his annual concert series, entitled *New Artists*, featuring such young artists as cellist Kermit Moore and baritone Robert McFerrin. In 1951, the United States State Department sent the Hall Johnson Choir of twenty-seven singers to the International Festival of the Fine Arts in Berlin. The group toured Europe for several months.

Johnson is regarded as one of the most important choral directors of his period and, in recognition of his unique talent, received many awards and honors (including an honorary doctorate from the Philadelphia Academy of Music in 1934). His compositions became immensely popular with concert artists and groups, especially his arrangements of Negro spirituals (The title of his folk opera is from a spiritual: "Run, little chillun, run!/ Fo' de devil's done loose in de lan'"). In addition to single pieces, he published two collections, *The Green Pastures Spirituals* (1930) and *Thirty Negro Spirituals* (1946). His Easter cantata, *Son of Man* (1946), was well-received in New York.

Bouyant in spirit, *Run Little Chillun* (no comma in the original typescript) ran for four months on Broadway in the spring of 1933 despite the devastating depression. The play enacts the conflict between the two major faiths of the early African Americans of the rural South, so-called pagan and Baptist. Johnson, like his protagonist, Jim Jones, the son of a minister, believed that there was an African side to his people that could not be reconciled with their acquired mode of Christian worship. He also felt that religion, whatever form it took, had always been central in the daily lives of African Americans. Throughout their enslavement, they had used religious institutions to shout and sing out against injustice and to ask for release from the troubles of the world. *Run Little Chillun* is Johnson's attempt to reveal the sustaining power of folk religion, with its heavy dependence on vocal structure. Its story line is relatively simple: will the soul of the minister's son, who is an African American version of Everyman, be saved or will he burn in hell as a sinner? The ending is ambiguous, as though Johnson himself cannot decide between the conflicting creeds.

The play won qualified acclaim during its Broadway run of four months. The critics were of two minds: one group loved the music but only liked the libretto, while another group had severe reservations about the script. The noted writer Kenneth Burke remarked that audiences were witnessing on the stage the power that made it possible for African Americans to survive in a society that has continually oppressed them. In this play, says Burke, one sees a Negro genius, an attractive positive ability, exemplified with a conviction and gift of spontaneous organization.

## REFERENCES

"Johnson, Francis Hall." *Biographical Dictionary of African and Afro-American Musicians*, Ed. Eileen Southern. New York: Greenwood Press, 1982.
Troup, Cornelius V. *Distinguished Negro Georgians*. Dallas: Royal, 1962.

# RUN LITTLE CHILLUN

## Francis Hall Johnson

### SYNOPSIS OF SCENES

ACT ONE
> *Scene 1:* The Parlor of Rev. Jones' House
> *Scene 2:* Brother Moses' Meeting

ACT TWO
> *Scene 1:* Back Porch of Sulamai's House in Toomer's Bottom
> *Scene 2:* Interior of Hope Baptist Church

### CAST

> **ELLA JONES,** *Daughter-in-law of Rev. Jones*
> **JIMMIE JONES,** *Son of Rev. Jones*
> **REVEREND JONES,** *An elder of the Hope Baptist Church*
> **SISTER FULLILOVE** ⎱ *Members of the Hope congregation*
> **SISTER STRONG** ⎰
> **BROTHER BARTHOLOMEW LITTLE,** *A member of the Hope congregation*
> **SISTER FLOSSIE LITTLE,** *Wife of Bartholomew Little*
> **SISTER OCKLETREE,** *A member of the Hope congregation*
> **SISTER HICKS**
> **SISTER SUSIE HUNT** ⎱ *Members of the Hope congregation*
> **SISTER LULU HUNT** ⎰
> **BROTHER JENKINS,** *An elder of the Hope congregation*

230

SULAMAI, *Sweetheart of Jim Jones*
BROTHER MOSES, *Leader of the Pilgrims cult*
BELLE ⎫
MAME ⎬ *Members of the community*
MAG ⎭
MOTHER KANDA, *Courier for the Pilgrims*
REV. EBENEZER ALLEN, *A local preacher*
BROTHER BROWN, *A member of the congregation*
MINNIE WILLIAMS, *A recent convert*

# ACT I

Scene 1

*Scene:* The Parlor of Rev. Jones' house. "Parsonage." Simple old-fashioned furniture.
*At Rise:* Sister Ella Jones is rehearsing the choir. Song, "Come to the Church in the Wildwood."

**ELLA:** *(interrupts, clapping her hands together)* Chillun, Chillun, tain't no need fer yo'all to git slack in yo' choir practice jest 'cause the revival is goin' on. *(Cries of protest from children)*

**JIMMIE:** Tain't us, it's Bessiola. She always singin' the wrong note.

**ELLA:** *(turns to* BESSIOLA*)* Now, Bessiola, I done gib you dat alto toon three times. Now you git it in yo' head. *(She sings the alto part of Bessiola)* Yo'all ready? *(They nod assent—some say "Yes'm* MISS ELLA*." Children sing again, interrupted by* SISTER MATTIE FULLILOVE*)*

**SIS FULLILOVE:** *(enters)* Fer de Lawd's sake, Sis Ella! I got somethin' to tell you. Git dese chillun out of here. *(She starts to shoo the children out)* Gid dem out. Git on outta here! *(She shoos the children out and sees* SISTER STRONG. *An embarrassed pause)*

**SIS STRONG:** *(Rises. As she does so, she knocks pillow on floor)* Ef you two sisters will jest excuse me, I'll run upstairs and git ready for church.

**SIS FULLILOVE:** Certny, Sis Strong, certny. *(As* SISTER STRONG *disappears through archway which leads upstairs,* FULLILOVE *seizes* ELLA *quickly by the arm and pushes her into a chair which she has pulled a little offstage from table)* Here, set down honey. I ain't got but a minute.

**SIS ELLA:** (*frightened*) My Lawd, Sis Mattie. Don' skeer me lak dat. I hope nothin' terrible ain' happened.

**SIS FULLILOVE:** Well, it ain't happened yit, but it's gonna happen in a few minutes. (*Looks around*) Where Rev. Jones?

**SIS ELLA:** He's upstairs gittin' ready to go to de meetin'. Fer de Lawd's sake, Sis Mattie, what is it?

**SIS FULLILOVE:** Well, you go right up dere an' tell him dat a lot of de members an' a few of de deacons is been havin' a little business meetin' dis evenin', down at Brother Allen's house an' a committee is stoppin' by here on de way to church to talk to him about it.

**SIS ELLA:** Stoppin' by here? What dey want? Gonna cut his salary 'count o' de fallin' off in de membership?

**SIS FULLILOVE:** No. It's about dese here Outdoor Pilgrims. Dey claim dat de Pilgrims meetin' is takin' all our Hope Baptist members an' dat Rev. Jones is got to do somethin' to stop it.

**SIS ELLA:** (*rises*) But what kin he do about it? He's got all he kin do to keep up our own meetin's—specially wid de revival goin' on. 'Tween dat and worryin' about Jim we's jes' 'bout—

**SIS FULLILOVE:** (*interrupting*) Dat's jes' what dey gonna talk about. Dey think de Pilgrims is de cause of all de trouble an' dey is comin' here to talk it over. I know how worried and upset you been dese late days, an' I didn't think you wanted to be took by surprise, so I run on ahead of 'em to let you know dey was comin'.

**SIS ELLA:** You is right, Sis Mattie. I don't feel lak bein' bothered with none of dem folks, right now— (*Crosses to pick up pillow*) I declare! Folks always bother you at de wrong time. (*Returns to C.*)

**SIS FULLILOVE:** Dey do dat fer a fac'! But hurry up, Sis Ella. (*Sounds of voices offstage.* ELLA *realizes it is the committee and starts to hurry to go upstairs*) Dey'll be here any minute. Dey'd jes' love to ketch you unexpected lak. *You* know how dey is—specially dat ol' nosey Sis Little and dem two Hunt gals. Dey would jes'— (ELLA *has stopped D. S. of archway to hear this. The street door opens to admit* MR. *and* MRS. BARTHOLOMEW LITTLE) Oh, come on in, folkses. I was jes' tellin' Sis Ella yo'all couldn't be far behin'. (*Embarrassed, she crosses to L.V.S. of door*)

**SIS ELLA:** Yes, walk right in, Brother Little, Sis Little. (BROTHER LITTLE *enters. Crosses to* ELLA *and shakes hand*)

**SIS LITTLE:** (*a huge woman with a tiny handbag and a tiny hat*) Good even', Sister Ella. (*Then suspiciously to* SISTER MATTIE) You sho' must a hurried to git here so far ahead o' us. I thought we all started out together. I declare. Some folks will be first ef it kills 'em.

**BROTHER LITTLE:** You must remember, my dear, Sister Mattie travels a little lighter than you do. (SISTER LITTLE *crosses to husband.* ELLA *crosses down and says:*)

**SIS ELLA:** How are you, Sis Little?

**SIS LITTLE:** (*to* ELLA *with a keen look*) Well, how've you been, Sister Ella, and how's yo' husband?

**SIS ELLA:** Oh, I'm right smart, I thank you, an' Jim's well an' busy.

**SIS LITTLE:** *Yes*, I heard he was *very* busy. (*Voices of people are heard off L.*)

**SIS ELLA:** 'Scuse me, I'll go upstairs an' tell Pa you're here. Yo'all jes set down. (*Exits hastily through hall door as* SISTER STRONG *enters through same. At same moment new groups come in from street.* SIS STRONG *greets them all in her grave ministerial tone and there is much handshaking and babble of voices*)

**DEACON REDD:** (*crossing to table C., raps for order. Pompously*) All right now, ladies and gentlemen, let's come to order. (OCKLETREE *continues talking and he calls her to order with:*) Can't you keep yo' mouth shut fer a few minutes? Now then, jes as soon as Rev. Jones comes down we kin git right into our business without losin' no time. (*Takes out huge watch on a heavy chain*) It's most time fer de fus' bell a'ready. Brothers, let de sisters have de chairs. We's all still young enough to stan' up fer a few minutes. (*He hastily grabs chair at L. of table just in time to get it away from* BROTHER JOHNSON. *The women take seats, passing through the crowd to do so. The men drape themselves in various places.* SIS LITTLE, *as secretary, as an important location and the spinster sisters, the* MISSES HUNT, *find themselves together on the sofa in a conspicuous place*) Jes as soon as de pastor comes in, I will call on Sister Little to read de resolutions dat we resolved, den we can all hurry on to de meetin' an' praise God wid a freer min'.

**SIS OCKLETREE:** I hopes so indeed; 'cause I ain' drawed a free breath sence de fus' day dese her Outdoor Pilgrims got here.

**SIS HICKS:** How kin you? I'm so skeered I'll run into a passel of 'em I don't even go to Newtown to visit my sister no mo'.

**BROTHER LITTLE:** Dey tell me dat 'roun' near dey camp dey goes 'roun' without a stitch o' close on. (*Suppressed titter from the* HUNT SISTERS)

**SIS LITTLE:** I'd hate to be crossin' Newtown Bridge some evenin' an' run into one o' dem big Africans wid no close on—I'm sure I'd faint right on de spot.

**THE HUNT SISTERS:** (*to each other*) She would—of course.

**SIS LITTLE:** (*overhearing*) Oh, I suppose you two would try to convert him right den an' dere. (*General laughter*)

**BROTHER JENKINS:** Ladies, ladies! But I must say I caught sight of two of 'em downtown one Sad-dy and dey had on short robes—somethin' like a night shirt.

**MISS SUSIE HUNT:** A night shirt?

**MISS LULU HUNT:** A night shirt ain't come through our wash in fifteen years.

**SIS LITTLE:** An' of cose, *you'd* never git a chance to see one outside de wash tub. (*Laughter at* MISS HUNT'S *discomfiture*)

**DEACON REDD:** (*rises*) Chillun, chillun. You see we got to get shed o' dese Pilgrims. Look how much argument dey causes right here in de flocks. (*Sits*)

**SISTER HICKS:** Oh, dat been goin' on way fo' de Pilgrims got here. (*Laughter which dies away as stair door opens to admit*)

**REV. JONES:** (*typical Negro country preacher—dignified and rather well dressed*) Well, well, what a surprise? I ain't seen dese many people in de parsonage sence de las' poun' party. (*Shakes hands around. All immediately assume a proper demeanor*) I'm glad to see you as usual. Whatever brought you all here? (*Crosses to L. and stands by door. Everybody has strained look*)

**DEACON REDD:** We ain't got much time, so we jes' better git right into it. It's something lak dis, Reverend. (*Clears his throat and proceeds more slowly*) 'Course you know—we all know how de 'tendance has drapped off dis summer at Hope Baptis'. *Every* summer we 'spect it to drap off some. Dere's always a certain number of house servants dat have to go North wid dey white folks and dere's boun' to a reasonable amount o' backsliden' anyhow as soon as de picnic, and excursion season starts. But it ain't never been like dis summer an' we all know whar de backsliders kin be foun'. Dey ain't no use pretendin' we don' know.

**SIS HICKS:** 'Cause we *do* know. (*Remarks of assent from groups and slow nod of head from* REV. JONES)

**DEACON REDD:** We all been gittin' madder an' madder every time de devil would step in an' toll off one of our lam's—besides de fac' dat we soon won't be able to pay out bills on time an' purty soon we jest won't have no mo' church-a-tall. (*Grunts of assent*) So dis evenin' some of de deacon bo'd an' a few of the Ladies Auxiliary got together and drew up some resolutions. (SIS HICKS *to* SIS LITTLE)

**SIS HICKS:** Is you got 'em?

**DEACON REDD:** An' 'pointed a committee to wait on you wid 'em on de way to church, an' here we is. Sister Little, will you read de resolutions? (SIS FLOSSIE LOU LITTLE *rises ponderously, fumbles in her diminutive handbag and produces a paper. She thrusts her bag into* BROTHER LITTLE'S *hands who clumsily drops it and picks it up again*)

**SIS LITTLE:** (*reading*) Minutes of de business meetin' of de Deacon Boa'd an' de Ladies Auxiliary of Hope Baptis' Church, held at Brother Ebenezer Allen's house dis 3rd day of August in de year of 19 hundred thirty two. We, de undersigned, hereby an' forthwith draws up dis set of resolutions believin' dem to be fer de good of de community and de furderment of de True Gospel.

**BROTHER JENKINS:** Amen, Amen.

**SIS LITTLE:** Resolved—Dat inasmuch as it have come to our ears dat a ban' of people callin' demselves Pilgrims has come into our midst wid a lot of heathenish notions sich as holdin' meetin' in de woods, singin' unknown tongues, (*Turns to* BROTHER LITTLE) dancin' half-naked, playin' guitars, banjers an' sich, an' doin' all other sorts of things dat ain't fitten fer civilized folks to do; be it resolved dat a move mus' be made to put a stop to sich carryin's on. We further resolve to ask our dear Brother Pastor

Rev. Jones, to do somethin' 'bout gittin' dese heathen pilgrims to move their meetin's to some other place besides Newtown.

**SIS HICKS:** Dat's de truth.

**SIS LITTLE:** So as we kin be free to enjoy de workin' of de Holy sperrit en durin' de res' of our revival services.

**DEACON REDD:** Praise de Lawd.

**SIS LITTLE:** *(in a more conversational tone)* Now jes' to be sure all de members of de committee is present, and willin' to go thru with dis, I want you all to stan' an' answer to yo' names as I reads 'em off. *(Reading again)* Brother Esau Redd, chairman of de Deacon Boa'd.

**BROTHER REDD:** Here.

**SIS LITTLE:** Brother George W. Jenkins.

**BROTHER JENKINS:** Present.

**SIS LITTLE:** Brother Jerermiah Johnson.

**BROTHER JOHNSON:** Here.

**SIS LITTLE:** Brother Goliath Simpson.

**BROTHER SIMPSON:** Present.

**SIS LITTLE:** Brother Bartholomew Little. *(Before he can answer* SIS LITTLE *says:)* He's here.

**BROTHER LITTLE:** Right here, mah dear.

**SIS LITTLE:** Sis Lulu Jane Hunt an' Sis Susie May Hunt.

**HUNT SISTERS:** Present.

**SIS LITTLE:** Sis Mahalie Ockletree.

**SIS OCKLETREE:** I'm hyar.

**SIS LITTLE:** Sis Mattie Fullilove.

**SIS FULLILOVE:** Here.

**SIS LITTLE:** Sis Flossie Lou Little, Secretary fer de business meetin' an' President of de Ladies Auxiliary. *(Takes her bag back from* BROTHER LITTLE *and seats herself fussily)*

**BROTHER REDD:** *(resumes with great deliberation)* Now, Brother Pastor, dese is de resolutions dat was drawed up an' signed dis evenin' wid de hope of yo' 'proval an' suppo't. We is now waitin' to hear yo' 'pinion of de same.

**REV. JONES:** *(slowly and carefully)* Well brothers and sisters, I must admit dat all de points in yo document have been brought to my attention befo' an' I has spent many a prayerful moment tryin' to figure out de answer—

**SIS OCKLETREE:** Answer? Dey ain't but one answer—dey got to go—dat's all. *(Murmurs of approval)*

**REV. JONES:** That's very easy to say, Sister Ockletree. But even ef we could fin' de way to move them, has we de right?

**BROTHER JOHNSON:** I think we has de right, Rev. Jones. Ain't dey seriously interferin' wid our work?

**SIS FULLILOVE:** Amen!

**REV. JONES:** Our work is de Lawd's work and no man kin hinder Him. We must continue to gather lam's into his fol'.

**SIS HICKS:** *(sarcastically)* Yes, so dey kin jump over de back fence an' go gallopin' off to de Pilgrims. *(Murmurs of assent from crowd)*

**REV. JONES:** Dat also is de Lawd's affair. He will bring dem back in His own time an' way.

**SIS STRONG:** Yes, yes, de Lawd will take keer of His Own.

**BROTHER JOHNSON:** But, Sis Strong, here you is preachin' every day of yo' life dat it's a sin to dance, play games, sing worldly songs, an' wear fancy close, an' here right across de river is a bunch o' people tearin' it down jes' as fas' as you kin build it up.

**BROTHER SIMPSON:** It's a shame—de *Law* would stop it if dey knowed what was goin' on. *(Burst of approval from crowd)*

**BROTHER LITTLE:** *(approvingly)* Dat is right, Brother Simpson. De mayor is one of de bes' frien's we got.

**BROTHER JENKINS:** Yes, indeed, I 'member at de layin' of de cornerstone, Mayor Jimmerson made de fines' speech of de evenin' an' said dat at *any* time—

**SIS LITTLE:** *(interrupting)* An' you know when we hel' de rally to burn de secon' mortgage, Mis' Jimmerson went 'roun' to all her white lady frien's an' collected a heap o' money fer us. I think it muster been almos' four dollars.

**SUSIE MAY HUNT:** It was three dollars and sixty-nine cents.

**SIS HICKS:** Dat's a heap o' money. *(Argument among crowd)*

**REV. JONES:** *(quiets them with a gesture)* I has no doubt dat de mayor would give us his suppo't if we had any real complaint to bring against dese people, but dey is so fur across de river dat we can't truthfully say dey is a public nuisance.

**SIS OCKLETREE:** But de way dey go on is undecent, they ought to be—

**REV. JONES:** Listen, has any of you *here* ever *seen* 'em go on? *(Pause)* Has you? *(Pauses, looks around, no one budges)* Den I reckon tain't nothin' but hearsay, an' you got to have mo' than hearsay to go to de law.

**SIS OCKLETREE:** *(menacingly)* Look here, Brother Paster, anybody would think you was takin' up fer dese people. Is dat part o' yo' work too? *(Wild excitement prevails)*

**REV. JONES:** After all, Sister Ockletree, dey are people ain't dey?

**SIS OCKLETREE:** Maybe, but I ain't good enough yit to stretch my 'ligion over all dat mess. *(Murmur from crowd, then* OCKLETREE *says meaningly)* You gointer feel different too when you fin' out dey done sent fer Jim, yo' own son. *(*ELLA *appears in the stair doorway just in time to hear this last remark. She stands petrified.* REV. JONES' *face is blank with astonishment)*

**REV. JONES:** *(after collecting himself)* Sister Ockletree, did you—er—did I understand you to say dat dey have sent fer Jim? *(Pauses)* How do you know dey did?

**SIS OCKLETREE:** Why, everybody in town knows it but you.

**SIS LULU HUNT:** Everybody.

**SIS OCKLETREE:** An' I was standin' right dere when Sulamai made de brag an' heard it wid my own ears. *(Excitement in group increases) (Warn 1st Bell)*

**REV. JONES:** Well, I mus' say dat er—who did er—

**SIS OCKLETREE:** Now, Rev. Jones. I don't wanter hurt yo' feelin's, but everybody knows Sulamai's been a regular 'tendant over at de Pilgrims fer weeks, an' everybody knows she is Jim's—

**REV. JONES:** *(raises his hands to silence her)* Sister Ockletree!

**SIS OCKLETREE:** —Well—er—a good frien' o' Jim's. So ain't she de mos' natural pusson in de worl' to sen' fer im?

**REV. JONES:** *(visibly perturbed)* Oh, I can't believe it! It ain't possible.

**SIS OCKLETREE:** I wouldna believed it myse'f, ef I hadn't been in de sto' when she made de brag to Sue Scott.

**HUNT SISTERS:** We both were there.

**SIS OCKLETREE:** Everybody dere heard 'er.

**REV. JONES:** *(struggling)* But he wouldn't go—he wouldn't listen to her.

**SIS OCKLETREE:** *(snorts)* Ef he don't, it'll be de first time. (ELDER JONES *drops his head*) Look here, Brother Paster, we don't want to make you feel bad, but we thought you ought to know an' we'd rather you hear it from us den jes' pick it up in de street. De res' of de committee jes' didn't have de nerve to come out wid it, an' dass why I spoke up lak dat. Somethin' has jes' *got* to be did. *(Wild excitement in crowd)*

**BROTHER REDD:** Naturally, Reverend, you would feel a little broke up over dis, but it will be revealed to you what to do. The Lord will. *(Bell—all rise very much relieved)* De first bell is ringing, folks. I spose you'll be right over, Reverend.

**OTHERS:** So long Rev. Jones. See you in de meetin', I reckon, etc., etc. *(They all start for the door when* ELLA *bursts in suddenly. Everybody shows surprise)*

**ELLA:** Wait a minute, Brothers and Sisters—*I* wanter say somethin' befo' yo'all go. I don't thank yo'all fer bringin' all dis low down street talk in here to upset Pa when he's got too much on his min' already. I ain't so sho' dat Sulamai meant dat de way yo'all take it, an' ef she *did* I ain't so sho' she's 'oman enough to do it.

**SIS OCKLETREE:** Well, she did.

**ELLA:** Jim is *Pa's* son, but he's also my husband. He ain't always done to please us, but I believe he's too good a boy to do dis thing widout talkin' it over wid me an' pa. So let *us* worry 'bout de whole thing. I guess yo'all might a meant good comin' here lak dis, but I don't think you done much good. *(Little cries of protest)* Dat's all right—me an' Pa'll be along by de second bell. *(Crowd exits uncomfortably, leaving* SIS FULLILOVE *and* SIS STRONG *behind.* SIS ELLA *goes to hallway and gets* REV. JONES' *hat and stick)*

**SIS STRONG:** *(remaining behind a little)* Now, Brother Jones, don't let all dese reports shake yo' faith. You an' Sister Ella ain't sowed nothin' but good and nothin' but good kin you reap.

**SIS FULLILOVE:** Yes, indeed, chile. I bin tellin' Ella not to let dese long-tongue women upset her—specially Sis Little an' Sister Ockletree. Dey both hates peace.

**ELLA:** Thank you, sisters. I does my bes' to hol' up my head —no matter what I feels, but Pa ain't gettin' no younger, an' I hates to see him worried.

**REV. JONES:** Thanks for yo' kind words, sisters. I'm sho' everything's gonna work out all right. *(To* ELLA*)* Ella, I'd lak to say a word to you private befo' we start to church.

**ELLA:** *(to* SISTER STRONG*)* Sister Strong, ef you don' mind will you walk on wid Sister Fullilove. Me an' Pa'll be 'long ter-reckly.

**SIS STRONG:** Certny, Certny.

**SIS FULLILOVE:** Deys quite a few minutes yit—you got time. Come on, Sister Strong. *(They exit unhurriedly. As soon as the door is closed behind the visitors,* REV. JONES *releases the mantel and staggers toward a chair.* ELLA *rushes to support him. She is visibly alarmed at his condition)*

**ELLA:** Oh, Pa! Pa! You mustn't give down now. Set down here an' res' a minute. Dere, dat's better. *(Seating him)*

**REV. JONES:** *(feebly)* I'll be all right in a minute, daughter. Right now, de very thought of it makes me sick.

**ELLA:** It don't make me sick, it makes me mad. To think of all we've put up wid from dat boy an' den he go an' git hisse'f in a mess lak dis.

**REV. JONES:** But do you believe it, Ella? Do you think we would do that—after de way I brought him up?

**ELLA:** I ain't had much time to do no thinkin'. Jim had been *out so much* here lately an' a 'oman kin git *sech* a hol' on a man. *(In a brighter tone)* But I know one thing, Jim is de straight-forrardest boy in de worl'. He wouldn't lie to save his own neck an' he will tell me anything I ask 'im.

**REV. JONES:** *(weakly)* An' suppose he says he's goin'.

**ELLA:** *(stumped for a moment)* He can't do dat to you, Pa.

**REV. JONES:** An' what about you, Ella?

**ELLA:** Dat's de trouble. Ef I had a made more fuss 'bout him runnin' 'roun' wid Sulamai in de beginnin' all dis might not a happened.

**REV. JONES:** You've been too good to her, Ella. I can't understand how people kin be so hard.

**ELLA:** Well, wid sich a Ma, an' she's got an' no Pa at all, I reckon Salumai coulda turned out a sight wusser. Anyhow, Pa, it's time fer you to be startin'. Lemme git you' walkin' stick.

**REV. JONES:** *(pulling himself together)* Ain't you comin', Ella? It'll soon be time for de secon' bell.

**ELLA:** *(giving him his hat and cane)* No, I'm goin' to wait awhile till Jim comes in. I'm gonna have a understannin' wid him dis night. Now, you git yo'se'f together, pa, an' go on. After all, Jim ain't gone yit. *(She hurries him out and then drops into a chair L. of table and weeps. After a few moments sounds are heard from the hallway. It is* JIM *coming in. He hangs up hat and starts upstairs when he glances at* ELLA *and sees there's something unusual in the air)*

**JIM:** *(entering room and crossing to R. of table)* What's the matter, Ella? Don't you feel good?

**ELLA:** *(stares at him a moment, then)* Feel good? You 'speck me to feel good when you runnin' roun' here gittin' yo'se'f into all kinds o' mess? Jim, how's anybody gointer feel good? Poor Pa!

**JIM:** *(alarmed)* Poor Pa? What is it, Ella? Ain't he gone to church? I thought you'd a been gone too.

**ELLA:** I 'spose you tried to give both of us plenty time to git out. But I *waited* fer you.

**JIM:** What has happened, Ella for God's sake! What's the matter?

**ELLA:** Plenty's done happened. *(Coming closer to him with searching eyes)* Look at me, Jim. Don't you know what every-body's sayin' 'bout you now?

**JIM:** No.

**ELLA:** Ain't you heard what Sulamai's done?

**JIM:** *(with sincerity)* I ain't heard nothin' special—jes' the regular ol' gossip like all the time.

**ELLA:** *(rises)* Den you don' know dat Sulamai's done made a public brag dat she's goin' to git you over to de Pilgrims' mee-tin' an' of course everybody's done put two and two together and figgered out dat de Pilgrims is done sent her out to git you.

**JIM:** A bunch of these ol' women ought to have their tongues—

**ELLA:** Dat ain't all. A crowd o' Hope Baptis' people got together dis evenin' had a meetin'—drawed up resolutions an' everything. Dat wa'nt so bad, but dey got so full o' Christian duty dat dey called here in a body jes' fo' church time an' tol' yo Pa de whole thing.

**JIM:** An' what did Pa say?

**ELLA:** He was too broke up to say much, 'specially after dey drug yo' name in it. Jim, yo' heart woulda bled ef you coulda seed 'im when he went out o' here. He looked ten years older. (JIM *drops his head without a word,* ELLA *seizes this opportunity*) Jim! Jim! Yo ain't goin' to de Pilgrims meetin' is you, Jim. (*Silence*) Pa will never git over it ef you do. (JIM *preserves silence*) Jim, tell me, honey, tell me either way jes' like it is—

**JIM:** (*crossing away R. Brokenly*) I don' know, Ella, I don' know.

**ELLA:** (*with increasing anger*) Jim, don' let dat 'oman make you lose yo' soul. Ef you want to stay out with her night after night, I can't stop you. After all, I'm a 'oman, and she's a 'oman, an' it ain't de fus' time two women wanted de same man. But don' let 'er off straight to hell—followin' up these African devils.

**JIM:** (*crosses to* ELLA—*in outburst*) I ain't skeered o' hell no mo', Ella. It can't be no worse than what I've been through.

**ELLA:** It ain't no Christian religion, Jim and that ought to be enough for you—the way you was raised.

**JIM:** That's jes' it—I was raised like I was—born and brought up in Hope Baptist Church. When I come outa school I stepped right in de pulpit an' preached to these people I'd been brought up with. Now, I jes' (*Crosses to chair up R.*) can't do it no mo'. I can't do the things I tell them to do. I ain't never goin' preach agin'.

**ELLA:** (*crossing to him—soothingly*) Ain't nothin' de matter wid you, Jim. The congregation loves you an' looks up to you. They wain' gointer turn against you jes' because you got tangled up with a 'oman. They all know Sulamai.

**JIM:** If it wasn't her it would be somebody else.

**ELLA:** (*alarmed*) What do you mean, Jim?

**JIM:** I mean—I mean that my religion don't seem to support me no mo' like it used to.

**ELLA:** Why, Jim—why you never talked like dat befo'; even sence you been goin' wid Sulamai. What's de matter?

**JIM:** I don't feel wicked goin' wid Sulamai. I feel like a man that wants a man's life. An' it don't fit in with no sermons.

**ELLA:** It's jes' dat woman, an' the things she mus' be tellin' you all de time.

**JIM:** Maybe so. *(Crosses to chair R. of table)* Somethin' must' be wrong somewhere—or else God made me wrong to start with. But there's other things I want to know for my own peace, things I've got to know since I feel so different. *(Sits)*

**ELLA:** You got to pray mo'—have mo' faith. It will change all roun' after a while, honey. *(Warn—2nd bell)*

**JIM:** I ain't so sure I want to change back. I don't see why I can't be like I am an' still look God in the face.

**ELLA:** Don' go on like dat, Jim. Pray—pray, boy.

**JIM:** I been prayin' for years—an' then *this* thing come on me. It ain't jes' Salamai.

**ELLA:** No, maybe she didn't put it *in* yo' head but she sho' helped bring it out. Jim, did she ask you to go to de Pilgrims' meetin'?

**JIM:** *(slowly after a moment's hesitation)* It may be they can tell me what I want to know.

**ELLA:** *(contemptuously)* Tell you how to talk to evil sperrits an' do all other kin's of devilment.

**JIM:** Well, I ain't promised nobody to go to this meetin'; and I ain' gonter promise nobody not to go; but I have got a lotta curiosity about it.

**ELLA:** Well, I ain't got no curiosity about it. I'm jes' worried 'bout you, Jim.

**JIM:** Well, I ain't gone yet.

**ELLA:** *(flaring up)* No, wait till that woman gets through pesuadin' you. Ef you don' look sharp she'll lead you straight to hell. *(Second bell is heard ringing)*

**JIM:** There goes the second bell. You gointer be mighty late if you don' go on to church.

**ELLA:** *(crosses to back of* JIM*)* Second bell or third bell, I don't want to leave dis house till you tell me what is in yo' min' 'bout dem Pilgrims. When I git to church I got to see all dem folks dat hes' lef' here an' dey all gointer be watchin' *me*. Jim, I can't face 'em 'less I know.

**JIM:** I wish I could tell you, Ella, but I ain't sho myself.

**ELLA:** Yer Pa tol' 'em dat he didn't *believe* you would do it, an' I faced 'em all down an' tol' 'em dat I *knowed* you wouldn't. Is you gointer let us down now, Jim. Is you, honey?

**JIM:** *(turns away brokenly)* Oh, my God!

**ELLA:** *(grasping at the last straw)* Dey's one *sho'* way you *can* save yo'se'f—stay away from Sulamai. If you can't do *dat*, anything kin happen. I know you puts her befo' me, but you hadn't oughter put her befo' yo Pa. You'll miss *him* mo' 'en you would her. *(Pauses)* Don' you want to come to the meetin' tonight? I ain't gointer talk to you 'bout it no mo'. But I'm gointer start prayin' all over agin! Dey ain't *no* problem *God* can't solve, an' I specks to fas' an' pray. *(Crosses to door)* till He shows me de answer. *(She goes out the door L. JIM turns around, sees she is gone, starts after, stops. Goes to hallway then crosses to chair up R places it against wall—SULAMAI enters from L. backing in evidently watching to see that ELLA is out of sight. JIM does not see her at first)*

**SULAMAI:** *(calling softly)* Jim!

**JIM:** *(turns in surprise)* Sulamai! *(Sternly)* What are you doing here?

**SULAMAI:** *(crossing to him)* Well, you didn't show up down in de woods, an' I come up here. I jes' seed Miss Ella go out to church so I knowed you was alone—so I come on in. *(She snuggles up to him)* Ain't you gonna kiss me? *(JIM throws her off roughly and turns and faces her sternly) (Speaks hesitantly)* Why—why Jim! Wha' de matter?

**JIM:** *(angrily)* Matter? You know what's de matter. You probably *enjoy* the way de whole town talks about us all the time. You always say you ain't got nothin' to lose. *(Crosses to door L. and looks out, then closes it—SULAMAI shrinks back)* And when you start talkin' too much, I'm through.

**SULAMAI:** Me? Talkin' too much? What you mean?

**JIM:** I mean you ain't been careful enough what you said and who you said it befo'.

**SULAMAI:** *(looks puzzled)* What's dis now, Jim?

JIM: *(spacing out his words)* Didn't you make a brag to somebody 'bout me?

SULAMAI: No–o–o–o. I ain't made no brag.

JIM: Think. Think good.

SULAMAI: *(slowly)* No. I ain' called yo' name to a soul dis week—'cepn', oh, yes, yestiddy I did 'low to Sue Scott dat I thought you'd los' a little weight since de big meetin's been goin' on.

JIM: Is that all? Jes' that I'd los' a little weight?

SULAMAI: Yes. No. Den she up an' said, you ought to know—a black ugly heifer, she's jes' jealous, dat's all. *(Crosses R.)*

JIM: *(follows her)* Yeah—An' then what did you say? It ain't like you to let a woman git away with a jab like that.

SULAMAI: *(turns to* JIM*)* Lemme see—now—what did I say? Oh, yeah. I says, 'When I see Jim at church tomorrer, meaning today, I 'spec to tell him jes' what you said.' *(Sweetly)* An' Jim jes' to show you how *keerful* I was, I took extry special pains to say "at church" so she wouldn't git de idea dat I was meetin' you no wheres else.

JIM: An' then what did she say?

SULAMAI: *(imitating)* Den—she put 'er head—on one side an' kimboed an' said—"At church, eh, what ol' church? You know you ain't showed up at *our* church in God knows when; you too busy hangin' out wid dem Outdoor Pilgrims to remember to tell 'im anything. Pretty soon he'll be skeered to speak to you at all." An' date made me hot. So I drawed up an' I 'lowed—"Is dat so, Miss Scott? Well, ef I don't git a chance to tell 'em at yo' church, I jes' might git a chance to tell 'im at *mine*." An' wid dat I switches off. *(Crosses to D. S. of table)* An' lef' her stan' in' grinnin'.

JIM: Yes. I can see you switchin' now. It's one of the bes' things you do. So. So *that's* the way it started.

SULAMAI: What, Jim? What a started?

JIM: Well, you make a crack to keep Sue Scott from havin' the last word—an' she goes off and tells *everybody* that you're makin' brags about me.

SULAMAI: Brags? About you?

**JIM:** That's jes' what I said. An' she's done put it out all over town that you say you're goin' to have me over to the Pilgrims' meetin' befo' the week is out.

**SULAMAI:** Lor—dee! How kin dat 'oman *live*—an' lie like dat? Jesus! *(Crosses to L.)*

**JIM:** *(sits in chair R. of table)* Well, I can see now where she got it at. You jes' been talkin' too much. Jes' like I said.

**SULAMAI:** *(crosses V S of table to R.)* Oh, Jim, I ain' said nothin'. You know how women looks when dey tryin' to git into yo bus'ness. She was smilin' all nosey lak an' she says, "Don't you think Jim looks a little thin?" *(Crosses to him)* An' right there was where I walked in de trap. De dirty low-down—Oh, Jim, I didn't mean no harm.

**JIM:** Well, don' bother. It's too late now. *(Pulls her to him)*

**SULAMAI:** But, honey, you *is* goin' to de meetin', ain't you? Tonight dey's gonna have some kinda special service to de moon. You know what I was tellin' you 'bout; when de full moon comes up. Please, Jim, come on wid me. You as good as promised me las' night.

**JIM:** *(hesitatingly)* Yes, I know I did. That was *las' night*. But it's different now since Pa and Ella heard about it.

**SULAMAI:** Miss Ella? Miss Ella done heard about what Sue Scott said?

**JIM:** Ella was the one that tol' me.

**SULAMAI:** Oh, Jim, I'm terribly sorry. I'd rather anybody to hear dat but Miss Ella.

**JIM:** Ella *knows* you an' *understan's* you. But Pa! He's all broke up about it.

**SULAMAI:** *(sobs a little)* Oh, Jim—

**JIM:** *(rises)* If I go it'll jes' kill 'im, that's all. And he'd rather see me dead than for me to leave the church.

**SULAMAI:** Lawd, ain' dis a mess? I'm jes' beginnin' to see you, Jim, what it'll mean to *dem* ef you go over to de Pilgrims. *(Turns to* JIM *)* Yo' Pa may be *hurt* de baddes' but I feel de baddes' over Miss Ella. She's always been *so* sweet to me, Jim, even since—since everything. She ain' never turned up her nose at me an' Ma 'cause we lives down in Toomer's Bottom, an' I know dey woulda put me outa Hope Baptis' Choir long ago ef she hadn'ta took up fer me. In fac' dey never woulda had me in dere in de fus' place if she hadn'ta stood up fer me in de bo'd meetin'. She wuz de only 'oman in dis town dat ever had de nerve to stan' up an' say a good word fer me fo' a crowd. *An' now*—look what I'm doin' to 'er! Oh, Jim! Jim! *(Cries. Crosses to sofa and drops on it)*

**JIM:** *(crosses and sits U. S. of her)* Don' cry, Sulamai, that don't make it no better.

**SULAMAI:** I ain't cryin' 'bout dat. I'm cryin' 'cause I *want* to give you up an' *can't*. I ain't dat good. An' I'm cryin' caused I hates to hurt Miss Ella. Oh, why couldn't it be somebody else?

**JIM:** It never is. It's always the one it kills you to hurt.

**SULAMAI:** Ef you ax me to let you go, I'll try. I could do it fer you, Jim—I could go away somewhere and never come back—Den ev'ything would be all right. Dere wouldn't be no mo' Sulamai, an' no mo' trouble.

**JIM:** Hush, honey, you know I can't give you up now. It's too late.

**SULAMAI:** Den what is we gonna do? Dat's how come I want you to go to de Pilgrims' meetin'. I tol' you I alwaus feel better when I hear Brother Moses talk. He 'splains ev'thing so lovely. An' Jim, you would understan' him much better din I kin. I ain' been fer enough in school to know all dem big words he uses. He talks *so* gran' 'bout love. It makes you feel lak we's doin' right 'stead o' wrong.

**JIM:** I feel like we doing right too—till I git 'roun' Pa an' Ella.

**SULAMAI:** But, Jim, maybe ef you would come an' hear 'im an' ax' 'im one or two questions, he could make you feel all right 'bout dat too. He is smart. You know he's from Oxnard University in England.

**JIM:** You mean Oxford, honey.

**SULAMAI:** Oh, is dat what it is? Anyhow, dere's where he's from an' he talks grander din Father Dean over at de white 'piscopal church. I know, 'cause I used to take keer o' Miss Dean's childun.

**JIM:** Didn't you tell me that this Brother Moses is very han'som, Sulamai?

**SULAMAI:** He's de finis' lookin' dark man I ever seen.

**JIM:** An' have *you* asked him any questions yet you said I could?

**SULAMAI:** No. I ain' never been close enough to 'im.

**JIM:** Well, why ain' you?

**SULAMAI:** *(suddenly rises and crosses D.R.)* Oh, go on, Jim. You yes' tryin' to signify. Tryin' to make me believe you's jealous.

**JIM:** *(crosses to her)* Well, I know Sulamai. That's all.

**SULAMAI:** *(sadly)* No, Jim. I wish sometimes I *could* think o' somebody else 'sides you.

**JIM:** *(pulls her to him)* But 'spose I wasn't here, baby. If it wasn't fer me—

**SULAMAI:** But you is here, Jim. Anyhow, I could never git dat close to Brother Moses—not as long as Elder Tongola is set-tin' dere, an' he's always dere.

**JIM:** Elder Tongola? He's the old prophet, ain't he?

**SULAMAI:** Ol? Ol's right. Looks lak he landed here wid Noah in de Ark. Dey say he is 'way pas' a hundred.

**JIM:** He mus' look terrible ugly. No wonder *you* can't go near him.

**SULAMAI:** No. It ain't dat. He ain't ugly at all. But he gives me de col' creeps. He don' mover nor make a soun'. He jes' sets dere all night an' looks an' looks an' looks at nothin'.

**JIM:** Maybe he's blin'.

**SULAMAI:** I ain' never heard nobody say so. You feel lak he's seein' ev'ything, his eyes is so live-lookin'. He looks lak he's done seed ev'ything under de sun an' is thinkin' 'bout all of it at de same time. His 'spression is lovely.

**JIM:** He is what they call a mystic seer.

**SULAMAI:** I could never go near 'im. I'd feel as if he was lookin' plum inter de bottom of my stomach—an' de truth is he never looks *at* nobody at all.

**JIM:** He mus' be wonderful. I'd love to see 'im. Didn't you tell me the other night that he ain't spoken for seven years.

**SULAMAI:** Yes, dat's what dey say in de meetin'.

**JIM:** He'd make a good husband for you, Sulamai. You could do all the talkin'.

**SULAMAI:** I don' feel lak no jokn' now. Oh, come on let's go to de meetin', Jim.

**JIM:** *(still trying to tease)* An' you ain't afeared I'll fall in love with his daughter or his granddaughter, you tol' me about?

SULAMAI: Who you mean, Mother Kanda? She's too ol' and Reba, her daughter, is—she's pretty but she ain' *lak* no regular woman. She is mo' lak a hant.

JIM: Like a hant?

SULAMAI: Yes. She jes' goes an' comes lak somebody walkin' in dey sleep. Wouldn't no man fall in love wid her. She ain' natural. But come on, Jim. You's jes' killin' time, Jim, to aggravate me. Come on. We can go through de railroad—out an' cross de backfield an' nobody'll see you, maybe.

JIM: *(suddenly serious again)* No. What's de use o' hidin'? Everybody in town gointer know it by dinnertime tomorrow, an' I don' care nothin' 'bout dat. It's only Pa I'm thinkin' of.

SULAMAI: Dat's jes' why you ought to go—to git your own min' made up. You jes' lak a sick man dat 'fuses to go see a doctor. Come on, honey. *(At this moment sounds of singing come from Hope Baptist Church, in the distance)*

JIM: No, no, Sulamai, I can't. I can't go. Listen to that song. It was my mother's favorite hymn. She sung it jest before she died. It seems like she's warnin' me herself not to go away from home. *(As* SULAMAI *comes nearer and touches him pleadingly)* No—I can't go tonight. I feel so bad about it.

SULAMAI: *Now* I *know* Brother Moses *is* right—what he said about sin.

JIM: *(catching at a straw)* What did he say 'bout sin?

SULAMAI: You know I can't 'splain it right, Jim. But it was some thin' lak dis. Sin ain' what you *do* but it's what you feel after you done done it. He say dat sin as a punishment God put on human bein's fer thinkin' dey was better den all de other creatures He made. An' den he said somethin'—I can't quite git it straight —somethin' 'bout de *sense* of sin an' de biographical urge.

JIM: No what he said is de *biological* urge.

SULAMAI: Yes, yes dat's it. Dem big words all soun' alike to me, dat's why I want you to go wid me an' I would understan' it so much better.

JIM: *(laughing)* But does this Brother Moses talk like that all the time? Don't he never talk simple.

SULAMAI: Yes—an' sometimes he don't talk a-tall. Jes' stan' dere wid his arms stretched up to dey sky an' it makes you feel so peaceful lak jes' to look at 'im. Oh, Jim, he's grand.

**JIM:** (*becoming very jealous*) He's sho' got you thinkin' so all right. I don't see how you managed to keep away from him all dis time. Sulamai, tell me the truth—ain't you never had no talk with this man alone?

**SULAMAI:** No, Jim. I ain't even tried. But Mother Kanda did tell me de other night dat if I could make up my min' to jine up wid de Pilgrims, she would 'range for me to have a talk wid Brother Moses so when dey moves on I could go 'long wid 'em.

**JIM:** Go along wid 'em? Look here, Sulamai, how come you ain't tol' me this befo'? So you thinkin' 'bout goin' with 'em, eh?

**SULAMAI:** Not yit, Jim. I couldn't 'cide nothin' till I seed what you was goin' to do. Well, I know I ain't got a chance to be nothin' in dis town, specially wid de Hope Baptis' people down on me. But over at de Pilgrims I feel lak I'm jes' as good as anybody else—so I been thinkin' ef I couldn't git you to go wid me, I would jine 'em an' go off. Den I'd be out o' yo' way.

**JIM:** But I don't want you to go, Sulamai. I want you here with me. Oh, we been happy together till these Pilgrims come.

**SULAMAI:** Not sho' 'nough happy. We have to slip an' dodge too much. An' den I feels so bad 'bout Miss Ella. You don't really b'long to neither one of us. I gotta have a man I kin have all to myself.

**JIM:** (*ironically*) So you're goin' off with this Brother Moses.

**SULAMAI:** Oh, Jim. How kin you talk so mean? Ain't I been beggin' you fer weeks to go wid us. Brother Moses wouldna never look at *me* nohow.

**JIM:** Oh, if you was aroun' him long enough he'd look at you all right. (*After a pause—crosses to hallway to get hat*) And I'm gonna fin' out what it is about him you's so crazy 'bout. I'm goin' over there jes' this once. Once can't do no harm, an' then I'll know.

**SULAMAI:** (*exultantly*) Hurry up. It's time to go now.

**JIM:** (*crosses back to L.*) Yes, I'd better befo' I change my min'. God mus' not intended me to be no preacher. I done put in all these years tryin' to be one an' now all I turn out to be is jes' a man.

**SULAMAI:** (*fiercely*) Yes, baby, (*Ring*) my man. Les go. (*Takes his hand and hurries off Right*)

(Curtain)

# ACT I

SCENE 2

    *Scene:* The Pilgrims of the New Day. Brother Moses' Meeting.

    *The general impression should be of something approaching voodoo—not too directly African, but with a strong African flavor. Since the cult is not designated by any familiar name, any feature may be introduced which serves to make the whole scene more striking without any chance of controversy or any possibility of offense to any existing religious group. There should be no suggestion of actual idol-worship or animal sacrifices, but rather references (in the chants) to Sun, Moon, Water, etc. joys of life with nature—joys of love. The whole betokens and partly expresses a religious attitude of joy and freedom toward life, in sharp contrast to the well-known spiritual joy of suffering which characterizes the more orthodox religious services of Negroes.*

    *To begin with, the scene is laid outdoors—a soft night with a moon. There are wild, low, soft chants, later louder with drums, possibly even guitars. Some individual demonstrations with solo dances and short ejaculatory speeches in "unknown tongues."*

    *At Rise: There are rude seats upstage center—a high one flanked on each side of lower one. All on a platform. People are scattered or standing in small groups talking as the curtain rises. From R. enters the* CYMBALIST *who strikes his cymbals together. As he does this, the* TOWNSPEOPLE *stop their chatter, and from R. and L. enter* TWO NOVITIATES *and a Gift Bearer. The participants are American Negroes getting back to nature worship. The* LEADER *comes from "no one knows where but is intelligent if not learned. He is a tall commanding figure with forceful presence and should speak a loose modern dialect full of roughly poetic expressions, somewhat in the manner of our sensational present-day Negro revivalists. He most likely wears a long robe and a head-dress resembling horns. The Crowd make way for* BROTHER MOSES' *party to approach the central elevated seats. Accompanying* BROTHER MOSES *is an extremely* OLD MAN, *bent and wrinkled, with long woolly white hair. This is* ELDER TONGOLA, *the African founder of the "New Day Pilgrims." He knows everything and looks it. Then, come* TWO WOMEN, *one quite old, tall, strong, who is* KANDA, *daughter of* ELDER TONGOLA *and looks like a powerful conjure-woman. The other is a tall slender black girl, gracefully clad in a long flowing robe. She is* REBA, *daughter of* KANDA *and completely under control of her mother and* ELDER TONGOLA. *Others in the little procession are two or three important looking men and several fantastically dressed women of middle age.*

ELDER TONGOLA *takes the middle seat.* BROTHER MOSES *sits on his right and* KANDA *on his left.* REBA *sits at the feet of* KANDA *and stares ahead of herself like a princess in a trance. The other attendants dispose of themselves in the remaining seats and, last of all,* TWO BLACK NEGROES *who are very tall, take their stand behind* ELDER TONGOLA'S *chair between him and his two neighbors.*

*When all are seated, the chanting stops. In the pause that follows,* BROTHER MOSES *rises majestically and begins his sermon.*

**MOSES:** *(sermon introduction)* Fellow Pilgrims of the New Day, in accordance with our regular custom, we will open our meeting with a brief outline of the origin, principles and purposes of our movement. Fellow Pilgrims, attend my words. *(Stir of preparing to listen, and after a pause)* Many thousands of years ago, there was on this earth a race of people who enjoyed the harmoniously manifested blessings of Nature, which always go hand in hand with the steady growth towards spiritual perfection. They had riches, wisdom and beauty. When they were removed from this globe, it was to make space for lower races with more elementary problems. The earlier inhabitants went on to higher planes. But, they have never lost interest in the welfare of this earth an' in every age some of these exalted beings has consented to take on human shape and live among men and try to guide their footsteps. *(Sighs of approval from the* HEARERS*)* To Us, the Bright Ones have sent Elder Tongola who for the past seven years has not lifted his voice in speech nor in song, but has expressed his will solely by means of thought. Even now, it is he who is telling me what to say —*his own* words that you are hearing through *my* voice. "Make ready for the coming of the New Day." It is you who must come and set them free with your high Gospel of Joy—you who must teach them the enduring spiritual qualities of laughter, dancing and song. For, from the accumulated torrents of your tears of sorrow, you have distilled the laughter which bespeaks the joy of living; the very chains that once bound your feet so securely have also taught them how to dance the rhythm which sets the Universe in motion; and out of the deep-throated cries of your most bitter anguish you have created the song that makes articulate the soul. The black man's God has never been a God of blood and malice. He has never meant that His children should suffer in His name. To know Him brings peace and joy and well-being. *(Recitative)* Elder Tongola says—"God is One"!

**CROWD:** God is One!

**BROTHER MOSES:** Elder Tongola says—"Nature is One"!

**CROWD:** Nature is One!

**BROTHER MOSES:** Elder Tongola says—"God and Nature and Joy is One"!

**CROWD:** God and Nature and Joy is One!

**BROTHER MOSES:** Let us be as one soul having many bodies!

**CROWD:** Let us be as one soul having many bodies!

**BROTHER MOSES:** And now. Fellow Pilgrims of the New Day, let us unite in singing that ancient and venerable Credo which Elder Tongola has taught us. The harmonious and rhythmic Ones have sent it—couched in the language and melodies of ten-thousand years ago. (BROTHER MOSES *leads the sections with a solo phrase in the ancient tongue, the* CONGREGATION *responds with answering phrases. There are suitable gestures and genuflections at appropriate places in the solemn music. Toward the end, there is a chorale-like section in broad sustained counterpoint finishing on three long, loud chords. Moon begins to rise from R.* BROTHER MOSES *proceeds)* (ELDER TONGOLA'S *message)* Fellow-Pilgrims, for the past seven years Elder Tongola has not lifted his voice in speech nor in song, but has expressed his will solely by means of thought. "Rise, Oh Black peoples of the earth! Tell all the nations what *you* have learned past the possibility of any forgetting. This is the command of Elder Tongola to you and this is the message of the Pilgrims of the New Day." *(End of Sermon—stir at finish)* According to our nightly custom, we now invite *any* who may feel the desire to help in this work, to present themselves as candidates. The older brothers and sisters will take them in charge and give them instructions as to the next stop in their probation. Come forward, children! *(A dozen or so people, all ages and sizes step up before the altar)* Tonight our celebration has a special significance. Elder Tongola has completed his task upon this earth. (JIM *and* SULAMAI *enter and come to the center. There is a stir in the crowd.* MOSES *motions* JIM *and* SULAMAI *back and they stand Stage L. Then* MOSES *resumes)* Very soon he will be recalled to activities on higher planes. *(Amazement in crowd)* But I shall continue to be his spokesman —through me you will always know the will of our Elder. (SISTER MATA *sees moon, rises and makes gesture toward it calling* MOSES' *attention to it.* JOBA *darts forward and makes obeisance to the moon)* Fellow-Pilgrims, behold the moon! Rising out of darkness, she is the eloquent symbol of our ideals and of our intentions. Let us welcome her with singing, dancing and Thanksgiving.

*Dance of the Full Moon*

*(a) Sister* MATA *begins a slow chant, which is taken up gradually by the people and works up into a*

*(b) Solo dance of* REBA. *At first slowly and with languid grace, gradually more speed and abandon. She keeps her attention mainly on* BROTHER MOSES *who watches her intently. The People chant, clap hands and gesticulate wildly.*

*(c) Dance of* YOUNG GIRLS. *Suddenly a band of young People rushes on and takes possession of the clearing.*

*(As they come on,* REBA *goes back to her place with arms outstretched to the moon. Drums and guitars swell the music of the chant, the dance grows wilder and wilder.* SULAMAI *draws nearer and nearer, fascinated by the beauty of the dancers and the changing rhythms of the strange music. Finally unable to control herself longer, she throws off her robe and hurls herself among the dancers. Fresh outbursts of enthusiasm from the crowd.* BROTHER MOSES *watches her greedily; at the wildest moment, the little band novitiates appear at the upstage entrances led by the* OFFICERS. JIM *towers above the crowd and can easily see* SULAMAI *in the frenzy of her dance. He notes* BROTHER MOSES' *attitude. Suddenly,* JIM *darts through the crowd, reaches* SULAMAI, *lifts her bodily almost to his shoulder and dashes off down stage left. The singing and playing and dancing never stop. There is only a moderate jolt in the music. A drummer is probably upset, a couple of dances jostled aside, some hands and practically all faces point in the direction of* JIM'S *exit, naturally, but the chanting and dancing do not stop. On the altar,* BROTHER MOSES *springs quickly to his feet as if with a sudden impulse to follow, but* KANDA *(who has been watching his interest in the new*

*dancer) puts out a restraining hand and gives him an indignant, questioning look.* REBA, *from her old position at* KANDA'S *feet, stares up at the other two with startled eyes. Only* ELDER TONGOLA *is completely unmoved and gazes straight ahead as he has done all through the scene. Perhaps he is blind. On this tableau—*

(Curtain)

## ACT II

SCENE 1

    *Scene:* The back porch of Sulamai's house in Toomer's Bottom.
    *Time:* It is evening, three days after the last scene.

    *At Rise:* BELLE *and* MAME *enter from right.*

**BELLE:** Come on, let's stop here at Mag's—that'll give me a chance to rest—'cause I sho' is tired.
    **MAME:** Au right—maybe if she ain't too tired, she jes' might come with us to the meetin'. *(Calls)* Mag—Oh—Mag.
    **MAG:** *(from within)* Yeah.
    **MAME:** Come on out chere.
    **MAG:** Be out there in a minute. (MAME *lights a cigarette, seats herself on a box at left.* BELLE *is arranging a great number of packages that she has carried on with her.* BELLE *is seated on a bench at* R. MAG *comes out of door)* Well, hello, hello. Gals, yo'all sho' lookin' good—Ain't seed you since de big dance down at de Elks Hall—didn't have a time dat night!
    **MAME:** You said it. *(all laugh)*
    **MAG:** Well, where yo'all been? Is *you* been buyin' out de town?
    **MAME:** Huh—dese days?
    **BELLE:** No, I ain't done bought out de town; but I sho' feels like I'm tryin' to tote it home. Whew! *(Pulls off her shoe)* We gonna have some fallin' weather too.
    **MAG:** *(sitting)* Yeah, my feet don't feel so good neither. I been standin' on 'em all day tryin' to finish Miss Dupree's ironin's. Sulamai's jes' left to take de cloe's home.
    **BELLE:** What you gonna do tonight, Mag?

**MAG:** Don' know nothin' to do. I sho' could stand a little good time de way I've been shovin' dat iron all day. What yo'all gonna do?

**MAME:** Me and Belle thought we might go over the Pilgrims' meetin'. Come along with us.

**MAG:** To de Pilgrims? Well, I ain't never been—Sulamai's so crazy 'bout 'em I been layin' off to go. But when night come, I'm jes' so tired, I jes' can't—

**MAME:** Oh, come on an' go, Mag. You works too hard. Everybody's been jes' flockin' over there since de big doin's day pulled off the other night.

**BELLE:** An' Mame says on our way we can stop by her house and wet our th'oats.

**MAME:** Yeah, Tom's back on his reg'lar run again and he's brought back some of that good Atlanta gin. Better come on an' go.

**MAG:** Well, I don't need no mo' 'suasion den dat—you know, good likker is scarce dese days.

**MAME:** How long is it gonna take for you to get ready? You know, if we don't soon start, we won't get a seat.

**BELLE:** And *Gawd* knows I sho' can't stan' up this evenin'.

**MAG:** Tain't gwine take me but a minute. I done had my bath—jes' slip on somepin! (MAG *has risen and walked toward the door.* SUE SCOTT *enters from left.* SUE *approaches the porch*)

**SUE SCOTT:** Good evenin' you'all.

**MAME:** Hello, Sue.

**BELLE:** How's everybody?

**SUE:** Dey's all well. Miss Mag, if Sulamai home?

**MAG:** No, Sulamai's gone to take Mis' Dupree's ironin' *and* she tole me to tell you whenever you come dat she ain't *never* home.

**SUE:** Das alright—you tell Sulamai, if she get somepin' and can't keep it—t'aint my fault.

**MAG:** (*starts to go after her*) You fresh little—

**MAME:** (*rises*) Oh, don't pay no 'tention to her—you know Sue.

**MAG:** I know she don't get 'side herself ever since she jined Hope Baptis'. Her and Sulamai growed up together right here in the Bottom and dey got along fine till Jim started comin' to see

Sulamai and never would go over to her house no more. Women is like dat.

**BELLE:** Den Sue's done a lot of talking too, you know, tryin' to skeer Jim off from Sulamai.

**MAME:** Everybody kin see her pint.

**MAG:** Well, I ain't heared nothin' 'bout dat, but I sho' wish somebody would do somepin' to skeer him off. I tell Sulamai every day of her life—ain't no good goin' to come of her foolin' wid dat man. He ain't got nothin' to give her and he can't marry her—good a wife as he's got.

**BELLE:** Day say now dat Sulamai is gwine jine de Pilgrims. She' so interested in some of de members over dere.

**MAME:** I heard dat too.

**MAG:** I hope she is interested in anythin' dat will take her min' off fum Jim. Dem two is 'bout to run me crazy. But lemme go on in here and slip on somepin' if I'm gwine wid yo'all. Be out in a minute. (MAG *enters the house and as soon as the door is shut,* BELLE *beckons for* MAME *to come and sit long-side her on the bench.* MAME *does so*)

**BELLE:** I don't believe she heard a thing 'bout it.

**MAME:** I don' believe she is.

**BELLE:** See, dat's what I always say, don't keer what the chilluns do's, der Ma and de Pa is always de las' ones to hear 'bout it.

**MAME:** And you know, Mag—she never could understan' Sulamai nohow. Dat gal takes after her Pa.

**BELLE:** *Pa!* And who is dat?

**MAME:** Gawd knows. Sh— (*They hear* MAG *coming out and pretend not to be gossiping*)

**MAG:** Well, I wan't so long, wuz I?

**BELLE:** No. Come on le's go 'cause I can't walk fast.

**MAME:** (*rises, takes a big bundle and hands it to* MAG, *then crosses to the box where she has left a small parcel that she picks up herself. As she is crossing, she says*) Here, here, Mag, take dis. You ain't totin' nothin'.

**BELLE:** (*rising and collecting her bundle, speaks to* MAG) And don' you lose dat, gal—dat's dat white empire gown dat I bought to wear to de Pullman Porter's Ball next week an' if you loses dat un, I sho' can't buy another un.

**MAME:** *(going off R.)* Not de way things is right thru here. I'm sho' glad dis month got 31 days—gimme one mo' day to make my rent.

**MAG:** *(laughs)* Oh, my Lawd—wait a minute—I mus' be losin' my min' 'fo' we even git to de Pilgrims. Lef' de light burnin', den come out and lock de door. Why Sulamai will be here any minute now—I got to leave de key. *(She goes up to the door and deposits the key under the mat)*

**MAME:** Oh, come on.

**BELLE:** Yes, 'cause it's gonna rain.

**MAG:** *(moving off with the other two)* Awright, I'm ready.

**MAME:** 'Cause dis Atlanta gin jes' won't wait. *(all leave stage R. laughing)* (MOTHER KANDA *comes on from the left, and she sees the three women leave. Then she approaches the door of the house, looking about as though she is not quite sure that it is the right house.* JIM *enters from left and approaches her)*

**JIM:** Why, who are you?

**KANDA:** *(she is startled for a moment, but recovers herself as she recognizes him)* You saw me three nights ago at our meeting. The Pilgrims of the New Day call me Mother Kanda.

**JIM:** But what are you doing here?

**KANDA:** I have come as a messenger from Elder Tongola. Sulamai must not come back to our meetings. Do you understand?

**JIM:** Yes, I think I do. I felt something was wrong the night I was there.

**KANDA:** And has been wrong ever since. If Sulamai succeeds in leading Moses into the Vale of Illusion, the results will be terrible.

**JIM:** What do you mean?

**KANDA:** You alone can save Sulamai. Take her back to your church—take her to another town. Take her anywhere, but you must hurry before Tongola takes her with him.

**JIM:** Why, you don't expect me to believe that—

**KANDA:** If you don't, then my warning has been in vain— here, take this, it is Tongola's last message—written by my daughter, Reba. Take it quickly, he is calling me. He is going tonight, at midnight—in a storm. (JIM *takes the letter and she hurries off R. as she goes)* Oh, Father, I must go to him. (JIM *stands for a moment* *looking after her, then gazes at the letter, opens it and reads it. He puts it into his breast pocket, then turns, goes to the door and knocks. As he knocks for the second time,* SULAMAI *enters from left, carrying the empty clothes basket, which she throws down behind the bench)*

**SULAMAI:** My, my, you's all primped up dis evenin'. Where you goin' lookin' so good?

**JIM:** I'm goin' to church—with Ella.

**SULAMAI:** Oh, Jim! An' I thought so sho' you was goin' wid me tonight to the Pilgrims. You been putting me off three days now.

**JIM:** I jus' can't make up my min' to go back there.

**SULAMAI:** I sho' wish you would go. I couldn't never enjoy our church no mo' lak I useter. Jim, I don' b'lieve you keer nothin' 'bout me a tall no mo'.

**JIM:** *(touches her for the first time during scene)* Don't say that, Sulamai. You know I *do* care about you.

**SULAMAI:** When I firs' tried to git you to go to de Pilgrims meetin', I thought you would fin' dat dat was de very place fer us to be happy together. 'Stid o' dat, you been actin' funny ever sence dat night you went.

**JIM:** *(sternly)* You know what happened, don't you?

**SULAMAI:** I know you grabbed me up an' run out o' de meetin' lak somethin' crazy, and when you *did* put me down, you gimme de devil 'bout dancin'.

**JIM:** It was outrageous.

**SULAMAI:** Out nothin'. *I* was jes doin' what de res' of 'em was doin'. Da's de way dey 'spress deyselves.

**JIM:** You sho' 'spressed yourself alright, an' Brother Moses looked as if he was seein' a woman for the first time in his life.

**SULAMAI:** Da's jes yo' 'magination, Jim. Brother Moses is done seen me at de meetin' plenty o' times befo'.

**JIM:** But he ever saw you dance befo'? Did 'e? *Did 'e?*

**SULAMAI:** *(sulkily)* No, I ain't never felt like dancin' befo'.

**JIM:** I thought so. A man don't look at a woman like that but once,—that is, not at the *same* woman.

**SULAMAI:** Aw, Jim, you jes 'specious an' evil. I ain't goin' to start nothin' wid Brother Moses. I wouldn't even dance again if you didn't want me to.

**JIM:** You ain't goin' to git a chance to—Read this. *(Gives her letter)*

**SULAMAI:** *(looking at letter. She crosses to bench L. and sits)* My Gawd! What funny writin'. Who's it from? *(Spelling to herself)* R–E–B–A—Reba! *(Nervously)* Here, Jim, you read it to me. I can' make out dat chicken-scratchin'.

**JIM:** *(reads letter aloud)* "Don't come back here and don't let Sulamai come back. Brother Moses and I have belonged to each other since childhood. My mother and grandfather have reared him to carry on our work, and they will not allow him to look at any other woman but me. Since the happenings of a few nights ago, there has been discord among us. If you return, you both will be destroyed. Elder Tongola has ordered me to say this to you. Farewell! *(Signed)*—Reba."

**SULAMAI:** *(after a moment of nervous silence)* You b'believe dat mess? *(Mockingly)* Her an' Moses done b'long to each other sence day was babies! Elder Tongola done ordered her to write dat! Elder Tongola ain't ordered her to do nothin' o' de kin'. Reba's jes' jealous, an' don't know how to he'p 'erse'f, dat's all.

**JIM:** *(pauses)* Well, what are you goin' to do about it?

**SULAMAI:** It ain't 'dressed to me. Other folks correspondence don' interest me.

**JIM:** It ain't addressed to you an' it wasn't delivered to you, but it sho' does *concern* you, an' if I was you I would pay some attention to it. 'Course, I know the biggest thing in yo' min' right now is to go back to de Pilgrims—especially since yo know they don' want you.

**SULAMAI:** Who don' want me? Ain't nobody had nothin' to do wid dat letter but Reba. Brother Moses didn't say for me not to come back, did 'e?

**JIM:** That's *jest* the trouble *now*. Moses *wants* you there and the rest of them are gonna keep you away from him anyway they can.

**SULAMAI:** An' if *you* go back wid me, Jim, dey can't think nothin'.

**JIM:** But, I'm not goin' back. I'm sick o' the whole mess.

**SULAMAI:** Sick? You's jes' scared.

**JIM:** Maybe I *am* scared? But ain't makin' myself the public scandal of the town on account of you? Ain't I comin' down here to Toomer's Bottom ev'y night to be wid you? Ain't I breakin' po' Ella's—

**SULAMAI:** *(crosses R to post and throws herself upon him, sobbing)* Oh, Jim, don't pay me no' min'. I'm so to' up, I don't know what I'm sayin'. Oh, Jim, I love you so. I can't give you up.

**JIM:** *(soothingly)* But, we are not givin' each other up. We can go on jes' as we've been.

**SULAMAI:** It can't be jist like we've bin, 'cause you gointer end up right back in Hope Baptis' an' I jes' can't stan' it dere no mo' wid— *(Bitterly)* —all dem ol' hellions snurlin' up dey noses at me lak I was a mangy, ol' she-dog, 'bout to fill 'em full o' fleas. I can't, Jim, I can't.

**JIM:** But I *got* to go, Sulamai. I promised Ella faithfully I was goin' with her tonight. An' I'm goin'. *(Crosses left to go)*

**SULAMAI:** Go on, then. *(Calls after him in a rage)* Good-night. Goodnight an' God bless you. Tell all dem prayer-prayin' hypocrites dat I made you late. Tell 'em you was down here in Toomer's Bottom wid Sulamai. Tell 'em I'm tired of 'em tryin' to hol' *you* up an' pin *me* down when none of dem ain't no better din I is. Tell 'em I started after you jes' to git even with dem an' I'll do it, by God, if it kills me. De nex' time dey lef' dey foot to kick me, dey'll have to kick us befo'. Jes' wait till dey see yo' Baby! *(Laughs hysterically and* JIM *at the beginning of* SULAMAI'S *last speech turns and stops still—looking at her—first in surprise and then in anger. He throws down hat and rushes back and seizes her roughly)*

**JIM:** *(fiercely)* So that's it. You accuse me of playin' with you an' all the time you was usin' me. An' now you come up with that lie—a baby. You know dey ain' no baby. Tell me— *(Shakes her)* tell me you're lyin'. *(Throws her to the ground)*

**SULAMAI:** *(weakly, but thoroughly enjoying her victory. She lies for a moment, then slowly, as she gets up)* Don't Jim. You hurts me. No, honey, I ain't lyin'. I wish I was—for yo' sake. I *is* goin' ter have a baby for you, de fust one I ever wanted. *(As she feels him relenting, she rushes into his arms)* Oh, God! We could be so happy—me an' you an' de baby—if we was only by ourselves.

**JIM:** Sulamai!

**SULAMAI:** I was scared to tell you befo', honey.

**JIM:** We've got to do something soon befo' everybody fin's out an' begins to talk.

**SULAMAI:** What kin we do, Jim? Oh, I feels so sorry for you. It doin' make no diffunce 'bout me.

**JIM:** There's a train out o' here at two o'clock, and honey you and I are going to take that train and go way up no'th.

**SULAMAI:** Jim, ain't dey no other way? I hates to go so far.

**JIM:** We *can't* stay 'roun' here.

**SULAMAI:** But, Jim, this is the only place I know. And I can't go away—dat is not now—not till after the baby is born.

**JIM:** It'll be no use then. That's why we're goin'.

**SULAMAI:** *(raging)* Da's why *you* goin'. I'm gointer stay right here—wid you or *widout* you. I'm gointer walk up an' down the street wid yo' baby in my arms, an' let dem ol' hens an' all dere ol' maid daughters see what happened to you, de darlin' o' dere hearts. I'll sho' 'em how good I is!

**JIM:** *(turning to go—coldly)* *You* don't love *me*, you don't even love yourself. All you want is power and revenge an' I'll feel sorry for you the night you go to bed with it. Goodnight. *(Thunder)*

**SULAMAI:** *(with rage of a loser)* Goodnight! Go on to church! You'll sho' have plenty to pray about.

**JIM:** Well, I'll be in my old church, sittin' by my old wife prayin' to my old God. If I jes' mus' be disturbed an' upset, I'll at least be among familiar things.

**SULAMAI:** Go on! You ain't much mo' din a year later. Some year!

**JIM:** That's alright. Ella'll be glad to see me whenever I come in. I jes' said I was gointer stop for a minute to pick up somethin' I had forgotten. *(*JIM *is taking stormy leaves of* SULAMAI. *She is in tears.* JIM *starts away but as he turns to hurl his last reproach he sees* BROTHER MOSES *approaching from opposite director. His curiosity gets the better of him, he stops and finally comes back.* MOSES *is saying to* SULAMAI*)*

**MOSES:** What's the matter, Sulamai?

**SULAMAI:** *(after a moment's embarrassment)* Oh—I didn't know you knowed my name, Brother Moses.

**MOSES:** Yes. I know your name—Sulamai. If I am intruding, I beg your pardon. *(*SULAMAI *looks anxious)*

**JIM:** No. Don't leave on my account. I was jes' goin' myself.

**SULAMAI:** *(very innocently)* No, Brother Moses. Please don't go. I'd like to talk to you a minute—if you got time.

**JIM:** *(with heat)* Here's the chance you been waitin' for. *(Glares at* SULAMAI, *then at* MOSES*)*

**MOSES:** *(to* SULAMAI*)* If I can help you, I shall be very happy.

**JIM:** *(cutting in)* She's listened to you too much already.

**MOSES:** Why, I don't know what you mean, Mister er—

**SULAMAI:** 'Scuse me, Brother Moses. I forgot you didn't know Jim—Ji—Rev. Jones. *(*MOSES *nods rather stiffly,* JIM *makes no sign at all)*

**MOSES:** *(to* SULAMAI*)* Perhaps Reverend Jones is referring to what you may have heard at our meeting.

**JIM:** Heard, seen and done! I was there, too.

**MOSES:** Being a minister yourself, you can understand, it is impossible to please everybody.

**JIM:** 'Specially when your congregation ain' nothin' but a crowd of curiosity-seekers.

**MOSES:** You shouldn't judge everyone's attitude by your own, Rev. Jones.

**JIM:** Any how, what I saw was scandalous—*(terrible)*—and I'll be glad when your whole crew is gone.

**MOSES:** *(indulgently)* Bro. Jones, I didn't stop here for a theological argument. They are apt to become so personal.

**JIM:** Well, I— *(rushes toward* MOSES*)*

**SULAMAI:** *(sweetly to* JIM*)* Oh, Rev. Jones. You musta forgot. You started to church twice—you must be gittin' awful late by now. De folk'll think you ain' comin'. *(*JIM *glances from one to the other, notices shadow of smile on both faces, turns on his heels and marches off)* *(*MOSES *and* SULAMAI *are silent a moment as they find themselves alone)*

**MOSES:** Sulamai, I'm afraid you have been cruel to your friend.

**SULAMAI:** You didn't hear what he was sayin' to me jes' fo' you come. In fac', he's been raisin' san' ever sence dat night I danced at de Pilgrims. An' den—den tonight—dere was somethin' else.

**MOSES:** Something else? What?

SULAMAI: *(picks up letter)* Des letter. Say, Brother Moses, did you know 'bout dat? *(Brother* MOSES *is silent)* Did Reba write it sho' 'nough an' is all dat true what was in it? Did Elder Tongola tell her to write it?

MOSES: *(slowly)* Elder Tongola told Reba to write it and it is true.

SULAMAI: *(sadly)* Den dey *don't* want me back dere sho' 'nough—de only place where I ever felt lak a real human. *(A little pause. Turns upstage away from* MOSES*)* An' say, Brother Moses, didn't you want me back neither?

MOSES: That's just it, Sulamai. I wanted you back too much.

SULAMAI: Den why can't I come back? You kin perteck me, can't you?

MOSES: I don't know, Sulamai. I can't explain it to you just now. I don't think you should come back. That is, not for a little while anyhow.

SULAMAI: Lord, what is de matter wid me? I ruins ev'ythin' I teches. You see, I wasn't borned jes' right fer dis here town. *(A little wildly) Dey*—dey won' gimme a chance.

MOSES: But this boy, Jim, will be nice to you again, as soon—as we're gone, then you will feel much better.

SULAMAI: But I had made up my min' to go back to de Pilgrims widout 'im.

MOSES: In spite of the letter?

SULAMAI: I would a gone back if ev'ybody else had said no—cepen *you.*

MOSES: *(tremblingly)* You would come anyhow—just on my authority?

SULAMAI: Ain't you de bigges' man over dere? You got to have a frien' *somewhere.* Jim's done quit me fer good an' now de Pilgrims don't want me. I ain't got nowhere to go. Please look at me, Brother Moses, look at me good—an' tell me why is it dat I always hurts people—'specially de people dat's de bes' to me, de very people I wants to love? *(Coming closer)* Kin you look at me an' tell me dat?

MOSES: *(turns his head away—confused)* No, Sulamai, I'm afraid I can't. Oh, what's the use? What's the use of lying to myself? *(Reaches out after her, but she steps back)* I can't leave as long as you stand there looking at me like that. I can't go back and make a fool of myself to the meeting and trying to talk to them with you in my thoughts.

**SULAMAI:** I didn't know you was thinkin' 'bout me that way a-tall.

**MOSES:** *(vehemently)* For the last three days I've done nothing *but* think about you—What shall I do? Sulamai, you don't know what you have done to me—to all of us! Oh, how can I make you understand? You see, in this work we are doing, the leaders—are supposed to have reached the stage wher they have outgrown the need of women. I thought I had reached that stage until the other night. Now, I can't go on until I have—

**SULAMAI:** *(proudly)* Washed yo' dirty clo'se wid me. Not if I know it, Mr. Moses. Ain't they women 'nough in de Pilgrims fer dat? *(Disgustedly)* An' I bin lookin' up to you all dis time. Oh, you men! An' what's gonna happen to *me* after *you* crawl back to de th'one? Da's what I wants to know?

**MOSES:** *(imploringly)* Oh, Sulamai! I don't want anybody but you. Come, go away with me. There is a train at two o'clock. Maybe we can both find a little happiness away from here—two pilgrims gone astray together.

**SULAMAI:** *(sarcastically—she is on familiar ground now and has lost all her awe)* Glory be! An't *I* gittin' good? All de boys want to stoop down from Heaven an' pick me up de same night. Want to take me away on de same train, too. *(Drops on bench)* *Gospel train* is right!

**MOSES:** *(sitting U.S. of her)* Sulamai, I mean it. You can have a fine house, a car, pretty clothes—everything. We can have all we want, if we can only get Elder Tongola's consent.

**SULAMAI:** *(bitingly)* Dat soun's awful good—an' might think it over—but for one thing. Why in de name o' Heab'n is you got to ax Elder Tongola? Has all de Pilgrim boys got to ax de Elder firs' 'fo' dey kin go to bed wid a woman? I never heard tell o'sich.

**MOSES:** Trust me, Sulamai, and tell me you'll go away with me, so I can speak to Father Tongola before it is too late.

**SULAMAI:** *(in a darker tone)* Well, it won't be necessary to bother 'im. Even if I wanted to go lak dat, I couldn't.

**MOSES:** Why, Sulamai?

**SULAMAI:** *(bluntly)* I'm gointer have a baby. A baby fer Jim. An' I'm gointer stay an' born it right here.

**MOSES:** But Jim can't marry you. If you go away with me, you will save him all that embarrassment. You know how his people would feel. What good would that do you?

**SULAMAI:** *(fiercely)* All de good in de worl'. I ain't anxious to hurt Jim. If it gits too hot fer him, he kin go away an' git out of it. Dat's about what he *will* do. But dem others—dem Hope Baptis' people. *(Rises and paces R.)* Won't dey love to see me struttin' up an' down de street ev'y day wid Jim's baby in my arms.

**MOSES:** *(follows her)* Have you thought how these people will hate you, and how they will look down on your baby? If they turn against Jim, they will turn against his baby, and treat it the same as they have treated you. *(Pause)* If they forgive Jim, they will love his baby and teach it to hate you when it grows up. In any case, there is nothing for *you* but hatred—begotten of your own hate.

**SULAMAI:** What kin I do? You can't help me now—'count of the baby.

**MOSES:** I won't mind about the baby, Sulamai. Won't it be yours too?

**SULAMAI:** *(pause)* You sho' is good.

**MOSES:** No, I must ask Father Tongola.

**SULAMAI:** Wait, Moses. I had my min' all made up to stay here an' you took all de pleasure out of it by showin' me how bad it would be. Now you 'bout 'suaded me to go wid you an' you gointer take all de joy out o' dat. How come you got to ax Elder Tongola? *(Peevishly)* You men is all jes' alak. Dere's always somepin' you love mo' down you do us p' women. Ain't dere a man nowhere what kin love me an' God, too?

**MOSES:** It is for *your* protection that I must talk to Father Tongola. Let me go now.

**SULAMAI:** Go on, an' I s'pose if he says "No," den you don't want me.

**MOSES:** *(sadly)* It would do no good for me to want you. We couldn't escape his judgment.

**SULAMAI:** *(flippantly)* Don't worry 'bout me. Worry 'bout yo'se'f. I ain't signed no papers wid no lodges. I might be skeered of Mother Kanda an' I might feel a little skittish 'bout Reba, but I ain' never gointer be 'fraid o' no dead m— *(Sudden flash and heavy thunder)*

**MOSES:** My God, child. Stop talking!

**SULAMAI:** *(frightened for a moment)* Jesus! Wasn't dat awful! I mus' go—I'm gittin' all nervous.

**MOSES:** Wait! You haven't told me where you'll meet me at midnight? (SULAMAI *pauses and turns. She is strongly attracted to the handsome black man, but is determined not to show it. She is baffled and angry to find that with both men of her choice, there is this same spiritual rival against which she is powerless—and power she must have. She determines to stake all on one throw of the dice. She realizes that she has lost her power over* JIM, *for the time being anyhow, so she will start in to tame this one from the beginning. She knows that he has wanted all through the conversation to touch her, but has not dared on account of his fear of* ELDER TONGOLA. *She wants a complete victory. She draws enticingly nearer and in a low tone she says)*

**SULAMAI:** Yes, I'll meet you—an' I'll go with you—only promise me one thing— *(Pauses)* Dat you don't ask *nobody nothin'*.

**MOSES:** *(aghast)* Little fool, you will destroy yourself.

**SULAMAI:** *(recklessly)* I don' give a damn. If you want me, you'll come fer me.

**MOSES:** Where?

**SULAMAI:** At de church.

**MOSES:** At the church?

**SULAMAI:** Sure, ain't you never had a date at a church befo'? At Hope Baptis' Church. I got some frien's I got to say goodbye to.

**MOSES:** Sulamai! (MOSES *makes a grab for her. She slips out of reach and runs toward exit left. Turns and calls back)*

**SULAMAI:** Pick me up at twelve bells, big boy. Don't be late! *(Exits, laughing)* *(Bright flash and roar—*BROTHER MOSES *stands looking at his hands as if they were strange to him)*

(Curtain)

## ACT II

SCENE 2

> *Scene:* Interior of Hope Baptist Church. Storm is brewing. Faint humming and sounds of prayer. Before curtain rises church is nearly dark.
> *Time:* Same evening as Scene 1.

*At Rise: Dim light discloses two people kneeling at mourners bench. A woman is prostrate on floor behind kneelers. In second pew a woman is sitting watching. She is swaying back and forth, humming an old spiritual. One or two people enter and take seats. The sexton enters and lights oil lamps on brackets along the walls and one on platform. More people come in. All are very solemn but exchange nods of greeting. As the older people come in to take their seats in the Amen corner, they drop on their knees for a moment of prayer before sitting. Gradually, they join in the song. The humming grows louder and takes on words.*

ELLA *enters; goes to seat in Amen Corner. She is easily known to be a person of some importance by the little stirs and glances all over the congregation. She sits and stares straight ahead as if afraid to look about.* REV. EBENEZER ALLEN, *the local preacher enters and takes upstage side chair on platform after kneeling for a moment. He then disposes of hat and cane rather pompously. He takes his place at the pulpit and "lines out" a hymn and this is the hymn:*

**REV. EBENEZER ALLEN:** Brothers and sisters, we will open our service by singing hymn number 289—Amazing Grace how sweet the sound that saved a wretch like me, I once was lost but now I'm found, was blind but now I see— *(The congregation rises for this hymn and sways to the rhythm of the music. During the singing of the first few lines, the church nearly fills with people. The* REV. SISTER LUELLA STRONG *(lady evangelist) arrives and takes other side chair on platform.* ELDER JONES *arrives, nods ceremoniously right and left on his way down the aisle and after kneeling, takes his place in the middle chair. The hymn continues. By now the church is quite full and the singing is quite important. At the close of this music,* ELDER JONES *"takes" the pulpit and addresses the congregation, as follows)*

**ELDER JONES:** Brothers, sisters and kind Christian friends, I am truly glad to see that so many have come out this evening in spite of the threatening aspect of the weather. This goes to show that the flame of the Holy Ghost is a hot and consumin' fire—not to be put out by a little rain—nor by a big rain, either.

**CONGREGATION:** Amen!

**ELDER JONES:** We are now nearin' the end of our fourth week of this protracted meetin', I'm sure you all have had a spiritual feas', an' durin' this time, quite a few sin-sick souls have heard the Sheperd's call an' turned their tired heads toward home.

**CONGREGATION:** Bless de Lord!

**ELDER JONES:** Fifty-four new converts have joined Hope Baptist Church in full membership and eighteen dear souls have been taken under "Watchcare." Much of the credit for this great harves' is due to the wonderful power of our beloved sister here on my left—the Reverend Sister Luella Strong. Sister Strong is one of the most eloquent speakers that ever took up the evangelistic work and she came all the way from Mobile to bring us the message, alternatin' with yo' humble servant. I am goin' to ask Sister Strong to lead us in a word o' prayer. *(Turning towards her)* Sister Strong, will you 'proach the Throne for us? *The* REVEREND SISTER LUELLA STRONG *is a big muscular-looking brown woman. Her appearance gives evidence of great physical, as well as spiritual strength—perhaps because of the decidedly masculine touches in her attire and general "get up." She rises rather ponderously, turns, kneels at her chair and begins to sing a well-known spiritual—joined gradually by the congregation)*

**SISTER STRONG:** *(song and prayer)*

Oh, Jesus, come dis-a-way!
Oh, Jesus, come dis-a-way!
You said you was a-comin', come dis-a-way.
You said you was a-comin', come dis-a-way.
Comin' in de lightnin'
Comin' in de thunder—etc., etc.

*(The song dies out into a hum and* SISTER STRONG *begins to pray)* All-wise an' strong-armed God, our heavenly Father, here 'tis once mo' an' agin we po', dyin' mortals of de moment's dus', knee-bowed an' body-bent, prostrate ourselves befo' Dy Throne. Befo' I further go, I want to thank you dat my las' night's lyin'-down was not in death an' my early-risin' was not befo' de judg-

men' bar. I thank you, Lord, dat my bed was not my coolin'—bo'd an' dat my kivver was not my windin'-sheet. We re'lize, Heav'nly Father, dat we is grave-yard travellers, judgment sons an' daughters—on our dusty march from a sin tryin' worl' to a never-endin' Glory. We thank you dat you have been a husban' for de widder, a father for de fatherless an' a mother for de motherless. Lo–o–ord God of Abraham, Isaac an' Jacob, if you turn Yo' face away from us po', he'pless sinners Ah, whithe–e—e–r, whither shall we go. But, Dow has' said, "Come unto Me, all ye dat are weary an' heavy-laden an' I will give you res'." Show us how to love one another. Bless de Shepherd o' dis flock dis evenin'. Strengthen him wid Dy Grace an' Dy Wisdom, so he kin be a Way-Shower an' a true Pathfinder to point out de road to Dy Eternal Salvation. *(Suddenly on a quieter tone)* An', now, Heav'nly Father, go wid us—stan' by us, an' when we come down to measure arms wid Death, when de piller is moved from under our head for de la-a-ast time an' death begins to work in de frame, —somewhere in Dy Kingdom, may we hear Yo' welcome Voice sayin': 'Well done, Dow good an' faithful servant.' May we look back on life well-spent in Dy service an' on befo' to a mornin' of everlastin' rejoicin'—worl' without en'—is de prayer of yo' unworthy servant. Amen!

**CROWD:** Amen! *(There is a moment of bustle, as kneeling members and* SISTER STRONG *regain their seats)*

**ELDER JONES:** *(Goes on with services)* Didn't yo'all enjoy that powerful prayer? The Rev'n Sister Strong is goin' ter be here with us all nex' week. I know all will be *sho'* to turn out an' hear 'er. An' now, I'm goin' to open the meetin' for testimonies an' expressions of religious determination. Now is the time for you young fledgelin' lam's to rise up an' tell what the Lord has done for you. Of course, we are always glad to hear from the older members, those warriors in the fiel',—true an' tried soldiers—battle-scarred heroes of many a bloody battle with Satan. Stan' up, children, an' testify 'cordin' to yo' faith. *(About eight or ten people get up and give short individual testimonies, interspersed with songs. These people are very varied and clearly-defined types. Old weather-beaten warriors from the Amen Corner—some withered and bent—others tall and thin—short and fat. There are a few young converts from the current revival—all telling lurid experiences of dramatic* *salvation involving weird visions, etc. The congregation punctuates with fervent amens and hallelujahs. There is much shouting and handclapping. For example,* BROTHER ABBALOM BROWN *is the first to start the ball a-rolling. He is an old veteran Christian. He rises majestically from his place in the Amen Corner and exhorts with lungs of leather in his song—"Done written Down-a-My Name")*

> **BROTHER BROWN:** *(sings)*
>
> Oh, Members Rise, oh, rise,
> An' don't you be ashame',—
> Jesus Chris' de Lam' o' God,
> Done written down-a my name.

*(The Congregation joins in lustily and the climax is very grand.* BROTHER BROWN *then goes into a brief personal testimony, finishing with a few words of advice and warning to the new converts)*

**MINNIE WILLIAMS:** *(she is a recent convert, stands and raises in song the question)* Is Dere Anybody Here Dat Loves My Jesus? *(Congregation joins—the song finishes and now* SISTER WILLIAMS *tells the story of her salvation. A few days ago she was the Town's leading "Sportin' 'oman.")*

**ELLA:** *(gives testimony)* Brothers an' Sisters, I *so* thank God dat I am able to git up an' stan' befo' yo'all dis evenin' to tell you what de Lord done for me.

**CONGREGATION:**

Amen!
Praise de Lord!

**ELLA:** *(after a pause)* Brothers an' sisters, dis ain' no stranger stanin' here talkin' to yo'all. Yo'all knows me an' you knows my pains an' burdens.

**CONGREGATION:**

True!
True!

**ELLA:** Brothers and sisters, yo'all knows my husban', and yo'all knows Jim is a good boy. Yo'all seen 'im borned an' raised right here in dis church. Ever sence 'e come back f'm school an' started prechin' de Word in dis here pulpit, he's been a shinin' light in de Master's vineyard—untell, untell about a year ago. *(There are sympathetic groans from audience)* Den de devil started workin' an' pullin' at Jim. He brought 'is temptation right into de church—'cause he couldn't ketch 'im nowheres else.

**CONGREGATION:** Amen! Amen! *(Intoning over humming chorus)*

**ELLA:** Sisters an' brothers, for de las' three days, *(I been)* not a meal have I et. Nothin' but a little bread an' water done passed my fevered lips. Fa-a-a-s'in an' pra-a-ayin' for my Jim. 'Tell dis mornin'—jes' fo' day—as I was cryin' out f'm de dep's of my mis'ry and despair, "How lo-o-o-ong, Oh Lord, How lo-a-ong, My god," suddenly—a bright light broke out all 'roun' me. An' I hear—a little voice—but I saw no man. An' de voice said, "Serva-a-ant, of servant, yo' cryin' an' groanin' done come up befo' de Lord for attention—an' dis very night, you shall have de answer to yo' prayer."

**CONGREGATION:** Glory be to God!

**ELLA:** *(quicker and louder)* Sisters an' brothers, when I heard dese words—I jumped out de bed, an' 'menced to walk de flo',—wavin' my arms an' shoutin' and cryin', "Hallelujah! Hallelujah! Glory an' Honor to de Lam' o' God forever!" *(Tremendous tumult of shouts in congregation—this dies out suddenly as* ELLA *continues, in low, calm tone, her narrative)* An' jes' den, I heard a soun' outside. It was Jim—jes' gettin' in.

**CONGREGATION:** Dar, Jesus!

**ELLA:** I was feelin' *so* good over my vision dat I spoke much sweeter din I mos'n' gin'ky does—even do' I knowed he was fresh from de chains o' Satan. I says to him—all sof'—lak, "Jim, honey, I was thinkin'—dat you might feel lak goin' wid me to meetin' tonight. De folks is all been axin' 'bout you." An' brothers an' sisters (God is so good), you know Jim 'greed so willin'—lak, I kno-o-owed t'want nothin' but de workin' o' de Holy Sperrit.

**CONGREGATION:** Amen!

**ELLA:** Well, long 'bout seven o'clock we started for de meetin'. Brothers an' sisters, dat was de happiest moment I spent sence de night me an' Jim was married—right here in Hope Baptis'. *(Pause, continues in lower tone)* But de devil is a snake in de grass. We got long by de crossroads, an' all of a sudden Jim stops —an' says: "Ella, yo go on. I done forgot somep'n." Well, I didn't say a word. I got so fulled up, all I could do was put my han' on 'is arm and stan' dere lookin' at Jim. He turned off down de lane.

How I got here, de Lord only knows. But here I is—an' Jim ain't come yit. *Pray* fumme, brothers and sisters—an' pray for my Jim. Somehow,—I feel kinder happy—I ain' giv' up hope it. For I done heard de voice dat cannot lie nor lead astray an' it said, jes' as plain as I am talkin' to yo'all, "*Tonight* yo' prayer will be answered. *Tonight!*" *(Even as* ELLA'S *voice dies away and while she is yet seating herself,* JIM *comes stalking down the aisle, ignoring the curious glances of the Congregation, and takes his seat beside* ELLA. *Someone "raises" a song and saves an embarrassing situation)*

**CONGREGATION:** *(sings)*

Oh, run little chillun, run!
'Cause de devil done loose in de lan'!
Oh, run on down to de Jerdon River,
Cover yo' face wid de fir-y piller,
Plant yo' feet on de *Rocks* of Ages,
'Cause de devil done loose in de lan'.

*(Throughout* ELLA'S *narrative,* ELDER JONES *has been sitting with his head leaned forward on his hand, as if in prayerful meditation. At the close of above song, he rises and begins his sermon)*

**ELDER JONES:** Folks, that sho' is a *gran'* song—a *mighty* song—an' how true how true! Chillun, when de devil pursues you an' you ain' got nowhere to hide—remember! Don' fall to de Eas', don' fall to de Wes', but fall in de middle of Jesus' breas'.

**CONGREGATION:**

Amen!
Amen!
Tell it!

**ELDER JONES:** *(continuing on a more formal tone)* We will take for the subject of our remarks this evin' a few verses from the fifteenth chapter of the Gospel accordin' to Saint Luke. About this time, Jesus was attractin' attention by a new doctrine he was teachin' an' there were always a crowd aroun' him tryin' to fin' some sort o' loophole to give him an argument. On this particular occasion, the scribes an' the Pharisees had been murmurin' against Him for receivin' sinners an' eatin' with 'em. So, accordin' to His usual method of instruction, He answered them with a parable. *(Reading from Bible)* "And he spake this parable unto them, saying, what man of you, having a hundred sheep, if he lose one of them, doth not leave the ninety and nine in the wilderness, and go after that which is lost, until he find it. And when he hath found it, he layeth it on his shoulders, rejoicing. And when he cometh home, he calleth together his friends and neighbors, saying unto them: 'Rejoice with me, for I have found my sheep which was lost.' I say unto you, that likewise joy shall be in heaven over one sinner that repenteth, more than over ninety and nine just persons, which need no repentance." *(Speaks again)* I want to call our *special* attention to the las' few lines:—'joy shall be in heaven over one sinner that repenteth.' Brothers an' sisters, you know what thet says to me. To me it says jus' this: That no matters what is it—whether people or animals or jus' things—it's the one that ought to be there an', for some reason, ain't, that right away becomes the most important. *(Soft merriment in crowd)* Sisters an' brothers—I want you to see how important *one* man, *one* thing can be if that's the one man or thing you need. Now there's another point to git out o' this parable. Brothers an' sisters, do you think, when the shepherd lef' the ninety and nine safe in the fol' an' went out in the chilly hills to fin' de po' little lam' that was lost—do you think he was so mad that he felt like jumpin' on the helpless creetur an' stompin' it half to death? No, indeed. The Scripture says, "and when he hath found it, he layeth it on his shoulder, rejoicing." *(Beginning to moan, and the Crowd is very responsive.* JIM *is visibly moved)* Brothers and sisters, Jesus is our Big Brother, watchin' over us all the time with His tender lovin' arms outstretched, ready to take two steps toward us if we'll take jus' one step toward Him. *(*JIM *bows his head forward on his hand)* O-o-o-o-h, chillun, His love is not like our love—given today an' taken back tomorrer. He is the same yistiddy, today an' forever. *(Louder thunder. At this point,* SULAMAI *enters the church—almost stealthily—and drops into a seat near the rear.* ELDER JONES *naturally sees her immediately—since he is facing the door. One by one, others become aware of her presence. Heads begin to turn, and glances are exchanged.* ELLA *shows no sign and* JIM'S *head is still bowed in prayer.* ELDER JONES *continues his sermon, but in a different vein. He is evidently annoyed by* SULAMAI'S *untimely appearance)* Brothers an' sisters, there is yet another point I want to bring to yo' attention this evenin'. A little further over in the same Gospel—we read: "Then said He unto the disciples, 'It is impossible but that offences will come; but *woe* unto him, through whom they come.' It were better for him that a millstone were hanged about his neck, and he be cast into the sea, than he should offend one of these little ones." Brothers and sisters, be careful in yo' dealin's with yo' fellow-man. *(Beginning to moan)* It may be that temptation has got to come, but don't you be the one to bring it. The Son of Man left His home in Glory knowin' that He was to be betrayed an' crucified, but that didn't make it no better for Judas. He threw down the thirty pieces of silver, the price of Jesus' blood, and went an' hanged himself to a tree. *(It is raining hard by now)* Oh, you hard-hearted men-sinners, that love to lead off young boys an' girls an' learn 'em to gamble an' drink liquor an' revel in the lusts of the flesh. Wo-o-o-, woe is you! *(*JIM *notices the change in the sermon and raises his head. He sees* SULAMAI*)* An', o-o-oh, you women, you ain't satisfied unless you are runnin' from one man to the other, who can't walk from yo' house to the sto' without smilin' yo' false smile up into some good man's face—try-y-y-yin' to lead him astray. *(The Congregation shows excited interest)* Oh-o-o-oh, you big-breasted daughters of Babylon, who have never even learned to respec' the sanctity of the marriage bed, but spen' yo' nights an' days plottin' and plannin' to git some woman's husban'. *(Shaking a menacing finger)* O-o-o-oh, you filthy spawn of Jezebel, you black bloodhounds of Satan, who ain't content to roam the streets by night, but bring the foul stench of yo' evil deeds right into the very Holy of Holies an' try to make God's house yo' crusin'-groun'. Wo-o-oh, woe, a *thousan' times* woe is you! *(Various heads begin to glance around at* SULAMAI *to see how she is "taking it." She naturally becomes extremely uncomfortable. Almost screaming, his finger shaking maledictions)* How do you think you gointer face a just an' angry God in that mornin'? *(Frantic cries from Crowd. Noises of rain and thunder steadily increasing, wild hum of moaning voices.* SULAMAI *can stand it no longer. She bursts into sobs and rushes from the church out into the dreadful storm)* Sinners! Don't fool yo'self—you can't escape the wrath o' God. You may run to the rocks, you may *crawl* under the mountains, you may sink yo'self to the bottom of the *boilin'* sea, but His long right arm will reach you out an' His righteous vengeance will mo-o-o-ow you down. I can hear Him sayin' on that mornin', while the sun burns into ashes an' the moon runs down in blood: "Depa-a-a-rt from me, ye cursed. depart into everlastin' fire, prepared for the devil an' his angels; where the worm dieth not an' the fire is not quenched. Prepare yo'selves to—" *(*JIM *has been growing more and more uneasy ever since he noticed that the sermon was being directed at* SULAMAI. *Now, thinking of her sobbing out in the storm, he dashes roughly out of the pew and down the aisle, out of the church in search of her. As he clears the door for exit,* ELLA, *almost in despair, rises slowly with arms outstretched to Heaven, sways a bit unsteadily and falls to her knees in her pew. Quite a bit of confusion in the congregation.* ELDER JONES *is disconcerted at this rather overwhelming effect of his sermon and for a moment expresses indecision. The father in him is struggling with the preacher. He quickly, fully gains control of himself and, lifting his hand for silence, asks the congregation to join him in a special prayer for* JIM. ELLA *is already praying audibly. Hand still up-raised)* Brothers an' sisters, we all know the painful situation that is present among us tonight. We also know the mighty power of heart-felt prayer. Fall on yo' knees with me an' let us storm the Throne of Grace in behalf of our errin' son and brother. Let us pray! *(He kneels at pulpit—facing the crowd, his face listed to Heaven. All the other members rise, turn and kneel at their seats. The younger ones lean hands forward on the bench-backs. With Congregation praying at same time. This is impossible to describe in words, as it soon becomes more music than anything else. There are groans, sobs, screams—all over an undercurrent of harmony with* ELDER JONES' *voice soaring above the whole in an impassioned plea to God to "Turn his boy around then and there, before it is everlastingly too late." The storm is at the height of its fury)* God of Love, God of Wisdom, God of Infinite Compassion, it is leanin' on Thy Word, throwin' ourselves on your promise that we come befo' Thee this evenin'. Lord, you know our trouble. You know it better than we do, for You sent it all from the beginning an' the en' is not yet. Lo-o-o-ord, you know our boy. You alone an' *only* You know what is in his heart. Help 'im, Father. Help 'im to stan', for if *you* desert him now, then there is nowhere we can turn for his salvation. Oh, Lord God Jehovah, for the sake of Yo' *own* dear son, look down into my achin' heart this evenin'. I have tried all these years to be a good an' faithful shepherd of Yo' sheep, an' now there's one lam', one precious lam', gone astray on the *mountain-side.* Lord give me the strength an' de wisdom to go out an' fin' 'im an' bring 'im back into Your fol'. Oh, Lord, it may be that in my human weakness, blinded by the pain in dis sufferin' father's heart, I have chosen the wrong way to work on this case, Lord, you who allowed a prostitute to dry Yo' feet with the hair of 'er head, have mercy on this little Magdalene, this po', helpless instrument of Satan. Show her the foolishness of her ways, Lord, an'— *(At this moment,* ELDER JONES' *prayer is interrupted by a noise at the door. The influence is that, as soon as he extends his prayer in Christian charity to include* SULAMAI, *it immediately becomes effective for* JIM. *The noise at the door is caused by* JIM'S *rushing in, bringing noises from the storm with him through the open door. He charges down the aisle, and throws himself on his knees at the mourners' bench, crying above all the noises:*

**JIM:** Pray for me! Pray for me, so I can find peace! *(Pandemonium breaks loose.* ELDER JONES *gives quieting signal once more and somebody starts a prayer-song. All are either kneeling or bowed and soon the whole church is singing)*

**CONGREGATION:** *(sings)*

*"Lord Have Mercy"*

Oh, Lord have mercy on me, on me,
Oh, Lord have mercy on me.
I'm gonna fall down on my knees
And I'm gonna face de risin' sun.
Oh, Lord, have mercy on me.

*(Through all is the sound of prayer and supplication—in shrill, high voices of old women, resonant, deep-throated tones from men, and, through all the roar of the storm. At the last verse, "Den we'll Drink Wine Together on our Knees," sung very softly,* JIM'S *voice is heard coming up stronger and stronger in prayer till, at the end of the verse, he rises with a shout and proclaims his regeneration. The Crowd jump to their feet with him and rushes forward and surround him.* JIM *starts off a bright joyful song.* ELLA *has thrown both arms about his neck and everybody presses forward to the open space in front of the benches. They literally push him into the pulpit with cries of "Tell it, boy, preach it! Help him, Jesus," etc.* ELDER JONES *and* ELLA *stand on the platform near him, their arms about each other and tears of joy streaming down their faces.* JIM *is singing his*

*salvation—leading the Crowd) (He leads Congregation in the song,
"Ser Glad," which is a corruption of "So Glad")*
**CONGREGATION:**

I'm ser glad, ser glad, newborn again,
Been a long time troubled wid my trials here below,
Free Grace! Free Grace! Free Grace, sinner,
Free Grace! Free Grace! I'm new-born again.

**JIM:** *(gives testimony. When song is finished* JIM *wishes to
speak, he waves for quiet, but gets only a comparative calm. He has
to shout over a tumult at first, but the people gradually grow more
and more still. He tells his story)* Brothers an' sisters, I am so happy
tonight. I am so glad to be back in my old place and it makes me
feel so good to see that you all seem to want me back. *(Cries of
assent from Congregation, then he continues on a suddenly quiet
tone)* Brothers an' sisters, I am not askin' you all to take me back
as I was befo', because I know I am *not* as I was befo'. I am an
older, stronger, wiser man. I have come to close grips with Satan
an' I believe I have won out. Pray for me, brothers an' sisters, pray
for me an' try me. I want you to join me in singin' dat ol' familiar
hymn that has never meant to me befo' what it means tonight.
*(Lines out hymn)*

Return, Oh, Holy Dove, Return
Sweet Messenger of Rest.

*(*JIM *leads the Congregation in singing these two lines and proceeds
to "line out" the next two)*

I hate the sins that made Thee mourn
And drove Thee from my brother . . .

*(A sudden silence—then* JIM *cries out, "*SULAMAI.*" She is standing in
the doorway; in the excitement no one has noticed her. She is standing dazed and fascinated by what she has seen. At the sound of his
voice, she comes to life, as all eyes are turned on her—she hesitates a
moment, then plunges through the crowd into the open arms of* JIM.
*A short embrace.* ELLA *closes her eyes. The Congregation is scandalized, but for a second only.* SULAMAI *breaks away, as suddenly and
rushes toward the door again! But three-fourths of the aisle, and a
terrific flash of lightning, together with a roar, she falls as one would*

*fall in such an event. She is in a comparatively empty place, as all the Congregation has pressed up around* JIM *in the pulpit)*

(Curtain)

*(Note: With the last flash of lightning,* BROTHER MOSES' *face may be seen at the window. With reminiscent strain of "New Day Pilgrims" music, offstage. Who is revenged, Jehovah, or* ELDER TONGOLA?*)*

# CONRAD SEILER

▼▼▼▼▼▼▼▼▼▼▼▼

During his first term in office President Franklin Roosevelt created the Work Progress Administration (WPA) to provide work and livelihood for the unemployed. The Great Depression had taken its toll on theatre artists, too, so Roosevelt included a Federal Theatre Project (FTP, 1935–1939) where actors, writers, designers, and so on, could practice their arts. Because segregation was still the "law" of the land, sixteen separate Negro units were formed in major cities, the majority in the Northeast.

Among the most widely touted of the FTP productions were Orson Welles' direction of the "Haitian voodoo" *Macbeth* (1936) and Shirley Graham's *Swing Mikado* (1939) with Gilbert and Sullivan music arranged by Gentry Warden in jazz tempo. The best FTP plays by African Americans included Hughes Allison's *The Trial of Dr. Beck* (1937), a story about a doctor who proposed making Black people white, and Theodore Ward's *Big White Fog* (1938), a family drama concerning the legacy of Marcus Garvey. The Great Depression had transformed the Art Theatre Movement into one of social problems and leftist politics, and this very social and political bent brought about its demise. The FTP suffered from charges by the Dies Committee on Un-American Activities that the federal government was funding immoral plays that promoted Communism and racial integration (one is reminded of Senator Helm's attacks upon the National Endowment for the Arts), and Congress refused to fund the project further. A specific example of the FTP's "threat to society" can be found in the history of the FTP at Cleveland. The following account is taken from *A History of the Karamu Theatre of Karamu House, 1915–1960* by Dr. Reuben Silver.

> At the Cleveland level, FTP activity was organized by K. Elmo Lowe, on the staff of the Cleveland Playhouse, as head, and with Rowena Jelliffe, director of Karamu, under him. Playhouse settlement became a cooperating arm of the Cleveland FTP, and a mixed group of white and Negro actors was organized in December 1935–January 1936. (The main Cleveland group was housed at the Carter Theatre in downtown Cleveland). This Karamu group was WPA #8118, popularly called "The Community Lab Theatre."
>
> The group mounted production, full-length and one-acts all through 1936, at Karamu and away: *The Big Top, United We Eat,* a sharecropper drama; *No Left Turn,* a short play on the social life of a Negro; *Peace on Earth,* the powerful Maltz-Sklar "agit-prop," and others. Tickets were free in order to stimulate theatre-going in these Depression times.
>
> In November 1936, WPA #8118 was dealt a low blow. Despite its integrated makeup and Karamu's interracial origins, Cleveland's FTP was ordered to segregate and re-form, with the added affront to the Negro performers that they be relegated to the State's Recreation Project and paid for "recreation" activity, not theatre work. The nineteen actors protested this arrangement as a slight to their abilities; they were dismissed and the Community Lab Theatre was abolished."

Although a second group of integrated players was later formed, it is possible to see that the "radical" content of plays like Conrad Seiler's *Darker Brother*, appearing in print for the first time in this volume, caused conservatives to call for the end of the FTP.

Conrad Seiler had already written two other challenging plays for FTP productions: *Censor* (1936) and *Sweetland* (1937). This latter was the story of Chet Jackson, who, decorated for bravery in the war, comes home to the Neill plantation. A "good nigger," he sees no injustice in the sharecropper's peonage and resents his wife's efforts to draw him into the sharecroppers' union. When his war-time buddy Sam is lynched as an agitator, Chet realizes that his place is in the union ranks. This play was produced at the Lafayette Theatre in Harlem, where it ran for six months.

Seiler's *Darker Brother*, although listed by the FTP, was not produced by them, but received its world premiere from the Gilpin Players at Karamu on March 16–27, 1938, using 14 men, six women, extras, plus a twelve-piece band. William Johnson, who had headed the radical WPA #8118 Community Lab Theatre played the lead role of Prayerful Johnson. He had previously played Dessalines in Langston Hughes's *Troubled Island*. Minnie Gentry, who many years later would star in Melvin Van Peebles's *Ain't Supposed to Die a Natural Death* on Broadway, played the role of the First Gold Star Mother.

*Darker Brother* begins like many "anti-lynch" dramas, a Black man facing a lynch mob who falsely accuse him of touching a white woman. While awaiting his fate, Johnson in prison fantasizes about a day when the tables are turned, when the Black man will govern the white. In his final moments, he articulates with a wild eloquence the hopes and aspirations of his people. In his imagined role as even-handed judge and President of the United States, he insists that he is innocent. Seiler skillfully blends the prison scenes with those of comic fantasy, maintaining a powerful sense of reality within the imaginary constructs. The ending is predictable and even terrifying.

An attentive reader will pick up allusions to *The Green Pastures* (1930)—the cigar smoking, the blowing of the bugle, etc. The original script contains very strong language for its time. Occasionally, Rowena Jelliffe, the play's director, has substituted "devil" for "bastard." The play's racial militancy is outstanding, greater even than Marita Bonner's call for revolution in *The Purple Flower*. One suspects that Seiler "got away with it" because the militancy occurs in the fantasies, which echo bits of old minstrel comedy; still, the militancy is there, and forceful, which may help explain why the play was never produced again.

The editors were not able to locate biographical information about the author, but Conrad Seiler was one of the very few African American playwrights of his time to use expressionism as a theatre form. *Darker Brother*, with the ambiguities of its title, is an African American satire written in the cynical tradition of Ambrose Bierce.

### References

Peterson, Bernard L., Jr. *Early Black American Playwrights and Dramatic Writers: A Biographical Director and Catalog of Plays and Broadcasting Scripts.* Westport, CT: Greenwood Press, 1990, p. 172.

# DARKER BROTHER

## Conrad Seiler

CAST

| | |
|---|---|
| PRAYERFUL JOHNSON | THIRD WHITE MAN |
| BURNTSIENNA HAWKINS | FOURTH WHITE MAN |
| SHERIFF | FIRST WAR MOTHER |
| PROSECUTOR | SECOND WAR MOTHER |
| FIRST CRAP SHOOTER | THIRD WAR MOTHER |
| SECOND CRAP SHOOTER | FOURTH WAR MOTHER |
| WHITE BOSS | NEGRO OFFICER |
| FIRST WAITER | CLERK |
| SECOND WAITER | BAILIFF |
| WHITE PROSTITUTE | WHITE WOMAN |
| FIRST WHITE MAN | PREACHER |
| SECOND WHITE MAN | MANAGER |
| FIRST DEPUTY | ATTENDANT |

WHITE AND NEGRO CROWDS, NEGRO POLICE, AND GUESTS, ETC.

SCENES

*Scene 1:* A prison cell.
*Scene 2:* At the levee.
*Scene 3:* The prison.
*Scene 4:* A dining car.
*Scene 5:* A street.

285

## SCENE 1

*Darkness. Silence. Then faint blue light, filtering through a small barred window high in a wall, reveals a prison cell. Most of the scene is indistinct, in deep shadow. A steel door is discernible. The cell is unoccupied . . . Suddenly, a scream is heard off, then a whimper like an animal in pain. Confused murmur. A door slams. Convulsive sobbing. Footsteps. The sobbing increases. The clatter of keys. The steel door swings open. Three white men—*THE SHERIFF *and two deputies—enter the cell with a handcuffed Negro—*PRAYERFUL JOHNSON. *His face is lacerated; his clothing, torn. He cries, gibbers. The evening light from the high aperture throws in sharp relief the steep door, the armed men, the agonized perspiring face of the Negro.*

**SHERIFF:** *(to one of the deputies)* Take 'em off, Jim! *(The deputy removes the hancuffs from* JOHNSON*)*

**JOHNSON:** *(crying)* I nevah done it, boss—fo' Gawd, I nevah done it! I nevah even seen dat woman!

**SHERIFF:** Shut up!

**JOHNSON:** Yo' gotta b'lieve me—I nevah touch her!

**SHERIFF:** You know you done it—you dirty rat! *(He hurls* JOHNSON *to the floor)*

**JOHNSON:** No—I nevah touch no white woman! I ain't a good for nothin' no'count. Fo' Gawd on high—I swears I nevah touch her! *(Indistinct shouting is heard off.* JOHNSON *listens, terror-stricken)* What dat? What's dat? . . . Boss, don't let 'em kill me! Dey'll shoot—dey'll burn me till I'se dead! Boss—boss—I'se only a hard workin' niggah. I ain't done nothin' to nobody! I'se inner-cent, boss! I'll tell de judge I'se innercent!

**SHERIFF:** Yeah? Well, mebbe you won't get no chance! *(To the deputies)* Come on boys, they'll be needin' us outside. That mob's a-growin', an' we gotta uphold the law. *(To* JOHNSON*)* You'll get yours—you black bastard! *(The steel door closes.* JOHNSON *is alone. He lies on the floor, whimpering)*

**JOHNSON:** Lawd, oh Lawd, ha' mercy on Praye'ful Johnson! I sho' needs yo' now. . . . I'se mighty low, Lawd. I has trouble fo' ce'tain. Yo' kin fix it ef anybody kin—please, Lawd. . . . I ain't sich a bad 'un no suh—yo' knows dat, Lawed. I ain't nevah swiped nothin' dat's wort' mo' 'an a dollar, an' I nevah love no woman dat don't b'long to me. It's de trut', Lawd. White men dey don't b'lieve me, 'cause I'se black. But yo' b'lieves me, Lawd, I knows yo' does. . . . I nevah seen dat white woman dey all talks 'bout. I nevah touch her, no suh. *(Shouting of the mob off.* JOHNSON *rises)* Heah dat? Yo' heah dat! Dey'se a-gonna kill me—sho' 'nough! Dey'se a-gonna kill me! I don't wanna die yit—no, Lawd, no! Don't let 'em git me, Lawd—Lawd!) *(He grips the steel bars of the door in his anguish; cries.)* I'se cold in dis heah place. I'se all tuckered out—most dead. Dey hurt mah wrists. I got blood on mah face—yeah, blood. Dey hit me. Dey done teared all mah clo'es—white trash, dat's what dey is—white trash! *(He walks back and forth, limping slightly, talking to himself.)* Oh, I jest knowed somet'in' was gonna happen when I lost dat rabbit's foot. Yeah, do mo'nin' when I finds out I says to mahself I says, "Pray'ful Johnson, yo' is in fo' it sho'." And I sho' is! *(Suddenly, he laughs, quietly at first, then with growing hysteria. Crescendo in mob cries off. The shouting becomes articulate: "Kill him!" "Kill the nigger!"—"Burn him!" A stone shatters the glass of the cell window and falls to the floor.* JOHNSON *stops laughing very abruptly, and cowers in fear.)* Don't let 'em git me! I knows dey wanna kill me! I ain't old 'nough to die! . . . Mercy, oh Lawd—mercy! *(Pause. The shouting subsides.* JOHNSON *speaks more quietly)* Mercy—mercy, dey ain't no mercy fo' de colo'ed people. Dis is white folks' worl'—ev'yt'ing b'long to white folks, Colo'ed folks dey ain't got nothin'. Dey'se de dirt under de feet: deyse de garbage outside de white folks' door. . . . God damn white trash! *(Pause.* JOHNSON *now stands motionless in the centre of the scene. The light from the window illumines his face, his eyes. Again he laughs, gibbers. Madness. Mob cries off. Again he stops laughing, quite abruptly, and then falls to his knees and speaks with peculiar intensity. There is an upsurge of shouting off—a sort of antiphonal response to* JOHNSON *prayer:)* Lawd, yo' made de heav'ns an' de eart', an' de waters in between. Yo' made de stars an' de flowers. Yo' is mighty powe'ful, Lawd, I knows yo' is. Yo' kin fix de whole worl' right—yes yo' kin, I knows yo' kin. De ol' worl' ain't right now, Lawd, no suh, she's in a awfu' mess. . . . Lawd, yo' gotta change all dis: yo' gotta give de colo'ed people a chance. Dey ain't had none, Lawd. Dey'se been slaves, layin' down. Now dey gotta stan' right up an' be men! . . . Lawd, yo' done said de weak was a-gonna 'herit de eart'. We'se weak, Lawd—all de colo'ed folks. We'se been weak long 'nough. Now we wanna be strong an' powe'ful—powe'ful lak yo' is! *(Pause.* JOHNSON'S *face is upraised. The mob cries diminish and then cease.* JOHNSON *rises slowly. The light from the window dims out)* Lawd, yo' heahs me? . . . Lawd, Lawd, is yo' dere? *(Silence. Very gradually, a preternatural ray of amber light appears from above and shines on* JOHNSON. *Then a deep voice booms forth from nowhere, speaking with a pronounced Southern accent)*

> **VOICE:** I is, Johnson!
>
> **JOHNSON:** *(ecstatically)* I knowed yo' was, Lawd! I knowed yo' was! . . . Lawd Lawd, will yo' stay roung a lil while and take care of Praye'ful Johnson, will yo'?
>
> **VOICE:** I will, Johnson!
>
> **JOHNSON:** An' will yo' take care of all de colo'ed folks?
>
> **VOICE:** I sho' will, Johnson!
>
> **JOHNSON:** Oh, t'ank yo', Lawd, t'ank yo'!
>
> **VOICE:** Yo'se welcome, Johnson!
>
> **JOHNSON:** Hallelujah! Praise de Lawd! *(Johnson stands in the shaft of light, his arms outstretched. On his face is the ecstasy of madness. The Lord's light dims. In the far distance, vague, dream-like, the shouting of the lynch mob. Darkness.)*

## SCENE 2

*The shouting of the mob in the darkness diminished still further and then blends with the languid singing of a score of Negro voices. The singing becomes louder as the shouting dies away. A weird, turquoise blue sky appears. In the foreground, the dark mass of a levee. Across the scene, left and right, in two symmetrical groups, are Negro workers, stripped to the waist. They are all going through the rhythmical movements of lifting imaginary bales or boxes, singing as they labor. Their patterned movements—all made together—are synchronized with the slow rhythm of their song. At the left, seated on a bale of cotton, is* PRAYERFUL JOHNSON, *dressed as in the prison cell. In the centre of the scene stands* THE WHITE BOSS *with a whip in his hand. As they work, the Negro's shadows are thrown against the sky. The shadow of* THE WHITE BOSS *dominates them all.*

**NEGROES:** *(singing)*

De right side o' Gawd, de right side o' Gawd—
We'se settin', settin' purtty on de right side o' Gawd;
de right side o' Gawd, de right side o' Gawd—
We'se settin', settin' purtty on de right side o' Gawd.
Waters caint drown us, an' fires cain't burn.
De guns dey cain't shoot us, an' ropes cain't hang—oh no,
    Lawd;
De right side O' Gawd, de right side o' Gawd—
We'se settin', settin' purtty on de right side o' Gawd.

**WHITE BOSS:** *(flipping his whip)* Come on, all of you, faster, faster *(The Negroes, still maintaining the same rhythm, quicken their movements.* JOHNSON, *seated on the bale, looks at the sky, smiles, chuckles to himself.* THE WHITE BOSS *crosses to him.)*

**JOHNSON:** It's a fine day, boss, ain't it?

**WHITE BOSS:** Don't you talk, big boy—work!

**JOHNSON:** *(smiling, unperturbed)* It's a fine day, white man.

**WHITE BOSS:** What in hell is that to you—work! *(*THE WHITE BOSS *lifts his whip menacingly. The Negro workers accelerate their rhythmic movements.* JOHNSON *remains on the bale.)*

**JOHNSON:** I sho' laks de days when dey'se fine. An' dey'se a-gonna be fine f'om now on, white man. *(The lights gradually grow dim.)*

**WHITE BOSS:** Damn you—get to work there! I told you to work! *(*JOHNSON *quietly slips down from the bale and faces* THE WHITE BOSS.*)*

**JOHNSON:** Did yo', white man? Well, ain't dat jes' too bad! S'ppose I don't wanna wo'k? S'ppose wo'k an' Praye'ful Johnson, dey don't lak each odder? S'ppose us Colored folks don't have to wo'k no mo? S'ppose we'se free—free! What 'bout dat, huh? *(*THE WHITE BOSS, *furious, raises his whip and is on the point of bringing it down full-force on* JOHNSON'S *head and shoulders, when, all of a sudden, there is a loud roll of thunder. Instantly,* THE WHITE BOSS' *arm freezes in midair, and he stands motionless, looking as though he was suddenly turned to stone.* JOHNSON *smiles,*

*but the Negro workers, with a simultaneous gesture, raise one arm
to their heads in trepidation.)* Don't yo' be skeered, brodders. He
cain't hurt yo' none. He ain't nobody now, he ain't. Jes' yo'
watch dis baby. (JOHNSON, *still smiling, takes the whip from* THE
WHITE BOSS, *whose arm remains in the air. The Negro workers lower
their arms. They are less afraid.)* What'd I tell yo'? *(To* THE WHITE
BOSS*)* Now yo' git to wo'k, white man—an' wo'k as yo' nevah
wo'ked in yo' life befo'. Come on—wo'k! (THE WHITE BOSS *comes to
life, and, in an attitude of fear, crosses upstage centre. As he does so,
his shadow thrown against the sky, diminishes until it is very small.)*
Us colo'ed folks is gonna take a long rest. (JOHNSON *and the Negro
workers sprawl on the ground.)* We sho' needs it. De Lawd's our
friend. He's helpin' us. Ain't yo' helpin' us, Lawd? Lawd, you res-
tin', too? I say, ain't you keepin' us, Lawd? *(Pause. The beam of
amber light appears again; and then the deep voice is heard from
nowhere)*

**VOICE:** I is, Johnson! *(The Lord's light dims out)*

**JOHNSON:** *(with increasing fervor)* Dis is de day o' retri-
bulation, white trash, when de colo'ed folks is all covered up wid
glory—praise de Lawd!

**NEGROES:** *(in unison)* Amen! Praise de Lawd! Praise His
glo'ious name!

**JOHNSON:** De whole worl's changed now!

**NEGROES:** Hallelujah!

**JOHNSON:** We'se a-comin' into our own!

**NEGROES:** Praise de Lawd!

**JOHNSON:** We'se boss now!

**NEGROES:** Hallelujah!

**JOHNSON:** *(rising, flipping the whip)* Git to wo'k, white
trash! Come on—git, damn yo'! *(The other Negroes rise and group
themselves at either side of* THE WHITE BOSS, *who moves faster and
faster.)*

**NEGROES:** *(pointing to* THE WHITE BOSS *jubilantly)* Git to
wo'k white trash.

**JOHNSON:** Hallelujah! *(The* NEGROES *sing "De Right Side
o' Gawd," but it is now a song of triumph.* THE WHITE BOSS *moves to
the rhythm of the winging. The shadows of the* NEGROES *against the
sky have become huge—*JOHNSON'S *shadow dominating. Darkness.
The singing seems to recede in distance. Then the shouting of the*

*lynch mob is heard, very faintly. It grows louder. The singing contin-
ues, but the other Negro voices drop out, one by one, until* JOHNSON *is
heard singing alone.)*

(Curtain)

## SCENE 3

*The light from the cell window appears, and the prison is visible
again.* JOHNSON *is discovered alone, standing in the same relative
position as in the previous scene. He is still singing. The light shines
on his face. The shouting of the mob continues.* JOHNSON *suddenly
stops singing and listens. His expression changes from elation to fear,
and then from fear to complacency.*

**JOHNSON:** Yo' cain't hurt dis boy no mo', white trash. De
Lawd's wid Praye'ful Johnson. No suh, yo' cain't shoot me nor
nothin'. An yo' cain't keep me where I doesn't wanna stay—no
suh. When I gits ready to leave dis heah ole place, I'se a-goin',
dat's all. De Lawd's mah friend, see? He don't lak de white trash
no mo'. He hates dem. An' He's a mighty powe'ful pusson. An'
when He gits His dander up, yo' jes' watch out. . . . See dat ole
iron door? It ain't nothin' to Him, no suh. An' He kin blow down
dese ole walls lak dey was paper. . . . Yo' show 'em, Lawd—jes'
show 'em. *(The light dims. The mob cries cease. silence. Then suddenly there is a whirring sound like a gust of wind or a giant's
breath, and the steel door falls—silently. Another gust, and the walls
go down.* JOHNSON *is seen, silhouetted against a deep-blue sky. Nothing else is visible.* JOHNSON *speaks with mounting rapture)* See dat?
He done it! No mo' walls! He let me out! Dey ain't no prison kin
hol' de Lawd's friend. I'se free now—free, yo' understan'? De
Lawd's by mah side. He kin do ev'ythin' He wants to. Yes suh,
He kin make me de biggest an' de bestest guy in de whole worl'.
. . . Praye'ful Johnson, yo'se a-gonna be Presiden' o' dese heah
United States—yes suh, President. What yo' think o' dat, huh?
Ain't it swell? An' yo' kin go wherevah yo' laks to go. Yo' feet
dey'se got wings. Yo'se a big man now, Praye'ful Johnson, an'
don' yo' evah forgit dat de Lawd done it all . . . Lawd! *(Silence)*
Lawd! *(No answer)* Where is yo'? *(Distant shouting of the lynch*

*mob. There is now a trace of anxiety in* JOHNSON'S *voice)* Where is yo', Lawd? *(Pause. The Lord's light appears)*

**VOICE:** I'se heah, Johnson!

**JOHNSON:** *(chuckling)* I reckoned I lost yo'. . . . Lawd— Lawd, I wants to be Presiden'.

**VOICE:** Okay, Johnson.

**JOHNSON:** An' I wanna go travelin' 'roun' in a train.

**VOICE:** What line yo' want, Johnson?

**JOHNSON:** De L. an' N's a good line.

**VOICE:** Yo' wish is done granted, Johnson.

**JOHNSON:** T'ank yo', Lawd, T'ank yo'.

**VOICE:** You's welcome, Johnson. *(Darkness. Mob cries. As they become fainter, a train is heard approaching. The noise increases until it seems that the train itself is passing in the darkness. Then the noise gradually diminishes)*

(Curtain)

## SCENE 4

*Darkness. A dinner gong is heard through the noise of the train, then a strident voice: "Last call for dinner!" Then a second voice— "Last call for dinner!" And then the two voices together: "Last call!"*

*A beam of light appears on a table in a moving dining car. At the table, loaded with comestibles of all kinds, sits* JOHNSON, *dressed in a Prince Albert and a silk hat, with medals on his bosom and a large cigar in his mouth. Out of the darkness appear two obsequious white* WAITERS. *One stands at either side of* JOHNSON. *With a simultaneous gesture, each strikes a match and lights* JOHNSON'S *cigar. The movements of* THE WAITERS *are more or less stylized)*

**JOHNSON:** *(looking at the food)* Yo' ain't forgot nothin'?

**1st WAITER:** *(bowing)* No, sir.

**JOHNSON:** Yo' sho?

**2nd WAITER:** Yes, sir.

**JOHNSON:** Le's see. Dere's sweet'taters, an' ham, an' fried chicken, an' chicken gumbo, an' corn-pone, an' red-hot biscuits, an' some pot licker—oh bo! Dat's what I calls service!

**WAITERS:** *(bowing together)* Yes, sir! *(*JOHNSON *puts his cigar aside and falls to eating)*

**JOHNSON:** I nevah been so empty, no suh—de li'le ribs is a-stickin' right to de backbone. *(Pause.* JOHNSON *wipes his mouth with his hand and looks up at the* WAITERS*)* Say, say, yo' knows who I is?

**1st WAITER:** No, sir—can't say as we do, sir.

**JOHNSON:** Yo' don't know who I is?

**1st WAITER:** No, sir.

**JOHNSON:** *(to the* SECOND WAITER*)* What 'bout yo'?

**2nd WAITER:** No, sir, I don't seem to know—

**JOHNSON:** Well, yo' sho' is ignerent.

**WAITERS:** *(bowing together)* Yes, sir!

**JOHNSON:** Look agin—look close. Dat's it. . . . Yo' don't know who I is?

**1st WAITER:** Sorry, sir— *(*JOHNSON *strikes an attitude)*

**JOHNSON:** I'se Johnson—Praye'ful Johnson!

**1st WAITER:** Not *Mr.* Johnson?

**JOHNSON:** Yeah—Mr. Johnson. I'se a pussonal friend o' de Lawd's.

**2nd WAITER:** Indeed!

**JOHNSON:** *(taking up his cigar)* Uhhuh. Me an' Him is great pals. He calls me "Johnson," de Lawd does.

**1st WAITER:** You don't say!

**JOHNSON:** He 'lected me President o' de United States.

**WAITERS:** President?

**JOHNSON:** Sho', Presiden'. Ain't yo' read 'bout it in de papers? . . . See dese heah medals? Dey'se de Presiden's medals.

**1st WAITER:** Now what do you think of that?

**JOHNSON:** Yeah. An' dat ain't all—no suh. De Lawd's a-payin' fo' dis li'le trip—yes suh, de Lawd hisself . . . Come on, show 'em, Lawd! *(Silence. Two beams of amber light appear from above. Then suddenly two bags of coins drop down.* JOHNSON *puffs away unconcernedly. The amber lights dim out. Each* WAITER *is about to pick up one of the money bags, and then hesitates)* Yo' kin take it. It's jes' a li'le tip fom de Lawd.

**WAITERS:** Oh, thank you, sir!

**JOHNSON:** Dat's pe'fec'ly a'right.

**1st WAITER:** It's all for us?

**JOHNSON:** Sho', me an' de Lawd kin 'ford it. *(While* JOHN-SON *is smoking, the two* WAITERS *whisper to each other across the scene and point to* JOHNSON*)* What yo' all sayin' to yo'self?

**1st WAITER:** *(embarrassed)* Oh, nothing, sir—nothing at all.

**JOHNSON:** Nothin'. It sho' didn't look lak nothin'.

**1st WAITER:** No, sir.

**JOHNSON:** Say, what you' wanna lie to me fo', white man? I seen yo' sayin' somethin'. What yo' say?

**1st WAITER:** It was only a little joke, sir—

**JOHNSON:** *(rising)* Damn yo' soul. What you' say?

**1st WAITER:** *(cringing)* We said—

**JOHNSON:** Come on!

**1st WAITER:** We said, "Mr. Johnson's a good sport, even if he is black.

**JOHNSON:** Yo say dat?

**1st WAITER:** Yes, sir—that was all, sir.

**JOHNSON:** Black—Black—sho' I'se Black. I'se your darker brother, white man.

**2nd WAITER:** That's just what we was saying—

**JOHNSON:** Black and I'se proud of it!

**1st WAITER:** Of course, sir.

**JOHNSON:** It's de color o' de night—it's de Lawd's color —Black! yo' ain't black, is yo'?

**WAITERS:** No, sir!

**JOHNSON:** *(with increasing emotion)* No, suh—course yo' ain't! Seems like de Lawd kind of run out of colors when he come to white folks. Yo' is de color o' worms when yo' lifts a stone ovah a pile of horse droppin's.

**WAITERS:** *(frightened)* Yes, sir.

**JOHNSON:** Yo'se jealous o' me, ain't you, white trash. I knows yo' is. Or maybe you think I'se a low down black boy without any raisin'. Well, das when you wrong. Mah mamie was a-livin with a good man, and I was born good. But yo'—yo' don't look like nothin' much to me. Look like all de strength gone out of you. Yo' is white bastards, git dat?

**WAITERS:** *(terrified)* Yes, sir!

**JOHNSON:** I hates yo' guts! Yo ain't no count. All yo' white devils ain't no count. White crackers ain't go no guts. I hates 'em. I reckon ain't none of you worth a damn. Yo' 'pressed we black folks. Yo' done took us out f'om de jungles, an' yo' makes us slaves to wo'k fo' yo'. Yo' treats us lak we was animals. Yo' kills us in yo' big ships. I knows yo' all, white devils. Mah gran' paw done tol' me. Yo' sleeps wid our gals, and dats how come de yellah folks walkin' 'round here, an' de chocolate colored folks an' all de no count low down trash. Yeah, yo'se all white bastards—I knows yo'. But de day o' wrat' is a-comin'—it's right heah now. Yes suh, dis ain't yo' world, understan'? An' de Lawd's done changed his politics. He don't lak white folks struttin' 'round like dey own de world. He's fo' de colored man, he done left yo' in de col'. Yo' nevah treats de Lawd right nohow, yo' white trash. Yo' nevah keeps de Comman'ments. Yo' preachers, dey ain't filled wid de Holy Spirit. Yo's is all white sepulchres an' hypocrites! (JOHNSON *takes out a large army revolver from his pocket*) See his heah gun? It's powe'ful strong, an' it kin send a white man to hell sooner 'an he kin open his mout'. (*To* THE WAITERS *who are panick stricken*) Fall to your knees. (*The light begins to dim*)

    **1st WAITER:** Oh, don't shoot, sir. Don't shoot.

    **2nd WAITER:** We never meant a thing!

    **1st WAITER:** Please—please, sir—

    **2nd WAITER:** Don't shoot us! Don't—

    **JOHNSON:** You' ain't white: yo'se yellah. Git up! Go on, get up! (*They do so trembling*) You' use to make we black folks wait on yo' hand and foot, didn't yo'? Yeah, in de ole days our folks cleaned yo' toilets, an' dey cooked yo' grub, an' dey et de leavin's, didn't dey? An' when dey wan't porlite 'nough to yo' an' asks yo' fo' what's a-comin' to dem, or when dey looks at yo' wommen, yo' shoots 'em an' yo' burns 'em, an' yo' strings 'em up till dey's dead . . . Dat's all ovah, white trash. We'se done come into our own. De Lawd's black now. He's wid de colo'ed folk, hallelujah! We'se de boss f'om now on, see? We'se took yo' place. Yo'se eatin' out o' our han's, and we'se a-gonna make yo' lake it. Reckon yo' git the idea, don't yo'? I'se jist givin' yo' some of you' own medicine, see. You said it was good for de black folks, so I'm goin' to try it out on you fo' lil while—till yo' gets the feel of it good, den maybe I'll kinda loosen up a bit later. Cose, I ain't sayin' fo' sho', but maybe. But it sho does me good to see yo' squirm. You're jist little white maggots, de lot of you. *(THE WAIT-ERS, inarticulate with fright, begin to back away)* Say, what yo' wanna run 'way fo'? Ain't skeered o' me, is yo'? Guess yo' doesn't lak mah company much. Well, I sho' is crazy 'bout yo'. *(THE WAIT-ERS again try to leave)* Who dere! I ain't through wid yo' yit, no suh. Yo' stay right where yo' is. I laks to see yo' mighty low. De lower yo' is, white trash, do higher is Praye'ful Johnson. Yo' use to make de black boys dance fo' yo'. Well, I kinda like a lil dancin' myself. Come on now, dance for Pray'ful Johnson. . . . Come on, white trash, li'le music an' yo' dance fo' me. . . . Dance—damn yo'! *(JOHNSON fires at THE WAITERS' feet. Whereupon THE FIRST WAITER takes out a harmonica and plays a jig, while his companion does a grotesque dance. JOHNSON laughs, shouts with glee. The noise of the train is heard. It becomes louder)* Come on, fastah, fastah, white trash! . . . What's a mattah, is yo' weak? Fastah! *(JOHNSON shoots again. Both WAITERS now dance to the accompaniment of the speeding train. JOHNSON laughs uproariously and fires his weapon once more. Blackout. He is heard shouting in the darkness)* Dance, yo' white buggah—dance! . . . Make it snappy! Come on, dat's de stuff! . . . Lawdy, Lawdy, yo'se funny! *(JOHNSON's laughter and the noise of the train become fainter as the shouting of the lynch mob is heard again.)*

## SCENE 5

(fade to black) *The shouting of the lynch mob diminishes and the train is heard again. Then a paean of welcome, beginning very softly and gradually increasing—with every word shouted in unison —comes out of the darkness: "Hurray fo' JOHNSON!"—Long libe de Presiden'!"—"Hurray!"*

*The cries are repeated in the same sequence, but louder, a brass band is heard. Then all sounds—the music, the shouting crowd, the oncoming train—blend together in one mad potpourri. Several beams of light gradually appear. Against a sky illuminated with a crimson light is the black silhouette of an old-fashioned locomotive, set at a crazy angle. A gleaming railroad track lies across the scene. At the right are two signal lights—red and green. A crowd of Negroes, right centre, are shouting while the Negro brass band con-tinues playing. Among the crowd is a welcoming delegation of black dignitaries, dressed in silk hats and frock coats with colored sashes.*

**CROWD:** *(in unison)* Hurray fo' Johnson!—Long lib do Presiden' ob de United States! Hurray! Hurray! *(All eyes are turned toward the left. The clatter of the train. Then the rear portion of a luxurious, gold-tinted Pullman, marked "*PRAYERFUL JOHNSON,*" slides into the scene. A white porter descends from the car with a stepping-block. The band plays. The crowd of Negroes shout hysterically and wave their hats, handkerchiefs and little American flags.* JOHNSON, *looking very grand and imposing, appears off the rear platform of the car. The white porter dusts him off. Pandemonium among the crowd the moment* JOHNSON *steps into view. All surge left)* Dere he is—Presiden' Johnson!—Hurray—Hurray! Who is Johnson! He's a'right!—Hurray! *(*JOHNSON, *hat in hand, smiles, bows)* Hurray fo' de Presiden'—hip—hip—hurray!—T'ree cheers fo' Johnson! *(*JOHNSON, *smiling, puts up his hand. Instant silence. The band stops playing)*

**JOHNSON:** Don't fo'git de Lawd, brodders.

**NEGRO:** T'ree cheers fo' Johnson an' de Lawd.

**CROWD:** Hurray!—Hurray!—Hurray!

**JOHNSON:** T'ank yo', brodders an' sisters, t'ank yo'. It sho' is a great pleasure to be wid yo' all, an' I 'preciates it—I sho' does. We'se a great race now fo' co'tain, an' wid Praye'ful Johnson as yo' Presiden', we'se a-gonna be greater.

**NEGRO:** Yo' said it, Mr. President.

**CROWD:** Amen!

**JOHNSON:** F'om now on dis is a black man's country. We'se a-gonna keep de whites in deir place.

**CROWD:** Dat's right—hallelujah!

**JOHNSON:** We'se a-gonna git Jestice at las'—all de colo'ed folks, yes suh. Ole Jestice was sho' late in comin', but she's right heah now. An yo' folks knows who's done it?

**NEGRESS:** Who, Mr. President?

**JOHNSON:** I'll tell yo' who's done it—de Lawd's de pusson what's done it.

**NEGRESS:** Long libe de Lawd!

**CROWD:** Amen!—Hurray!

**JOHNSON:** Brodders an' sisters, I wanna t'ank yo' agin. Yo' is mah people, an' it's sho' good to see yo' all—I t'ank yo'.

**CROWD:** Hurray fo' Johnson! Hurray fo' de Lawd! (JOHN-SON *steps down from the car. A negress holds up her child for* JOHNSON *to kiss. Storm of applause.* JOHNSON *again puts up his hand*)

**JOHNSON:** Jes' a minute, folks, jes' a minute! I wanna speak to de Lawd. *(Silence. The crowd freezes.* JOHNSON *looks upward, stretches out his arms. The light dims)* Lawd, Lawd, please show mah people yo' is satisfied wid 'em! Show 'em a li'le testimony, Lawd—jes' a li'le one! *(The Lord's light appears)*

**VOICE:** Okay, Johnson! Dey is right good people! *(Suddenly, a rain of money—coins, paper—falls over the crowd)*

**CROWD:** *(greatly excited)* Money f'om de Lawd! Rain o' gold! Look at dat, will yo'! Hurray fo' de Lawd!—Hallelujah! Long libe de Lord an' Presiden' Johnson!—Gawd bless 'em!—Hallelujah *(The Negroes go mad with joy. They scramble about, picking up the money, shouting, pushing. All participate—musicians, dignitaries, everyone.* JOHNSON *smiles, and, with the assistance of the white porter, steps up on to the rear platform of the car. Train noise. The car slides out of sight. Blackout. The shouts of jubilation become less distinct. Then the lynch mob is heard again)*

## SCENE 6

*Darkness. The shouting of the lynch mob increases. The prison cell becomes visible.* JOHNSON, *now in rags again, stands left—in the same attitude as at the end of the previous scene—smiling at the imaginary crowd.*

**JOHNSON:** T'ank yo', brodders an' sisters! Lawd bless yo' all! *(The mob off shouts more menacingly, then the noise recedes. The clank of lock and keys is heard.* JOHNSON *suddenly turns toward the steel door. His expression changes, as though he were now aware of reality.)* Who's dere? Who's dat? *(The steel door opens.* THE SHERIFF *and* THE PROSECUTOR *enter, accompanied by two deputies)*

**SHERIFF:** *(to the* PROSECUTOR*)* That's him!

**PROSECUTOR:** Johnson! Come here, Johnson! *(Johnson does not move.)*

**SHERIFF:** Johnson—damn rascal you.

**PROSECUTOR:** That's all right, Sheriff. Leave him to me. (THE PROSECUTOR *crosses to* JOHNSON, *who stares into space like a demented person)* I want to speak to you, Johnson. Just a few things I want to clear up. Now, you admit you assaulted the Collins woman—of course, you do.

**SHERIFF:** Johnson! I'll make him talk!

**PROSECUTOR:** Just a minute! (JOHNSON *speaks slowly, as if in a trance. He does not look at* THE PROSECUTOR)

**JOHNSON:** I nevah seen no Collins woman.

**PROSECUTOR:** Listen to me, Johnson. Lying ain't going to help you. We got the goods on you, see? Yesterday morning, about eight o'clock, you went to Mrs. Collins' home. You asked for some work. She said she didn't have any. She told you to go away. Then you got mad, and you grabbed hold of her and tore the clothes off her. Then she screamed, and you ran off.

**JOHNSON:** (as before) I nevah seen no Collins woman.

**SHERIFF:** You liar. I'll make you talk.

**PROSECUTOR:** I'll attend to this, Sheriff. (To JOHNSON) Look here, Mrs. Collins identified you. She said you looked like the one.

**JOHNSON:** I nevah seen—

**PROSECUTOR:** You'd better confess, Johnson, or that mob'll get you. You know what that means. They're out on serious business. We can't help you if you don't tell the truth.

**JOHNSON:** I nevah seen no Collins woman.

**PROSECUTOR:** *(changing his tone)* If you didn't do it, why did you hide in the bush when the Sheriff was looking for you? Answer me—why did you hide?

**JOHNSON:** I'se tellin' de trut'—I nevah seen dat woman.

**PROSECUTOR:** Don't keep on saying that!

**SHERIFF:** I told you he wouldnt say nothin'. . . . You're as guilty as hell, an' you know it—you black bastard. (THE SHERIFF *knocks* JOHNSON *to the floor, then kicks him.)*

**PROSECUTOR:** Come on, Sheriff.

**SHERIFF:** He knows he done it!

**PROSECUTOR:** It don't make much difference. We know it; Mrs. Collins said he was the one and the mob ain't gonna take much time askin' questions. Thought I might get some kind of a statement from him. It'd make things easier. But it's all right. *(Distant mob cries)* Say that crowd outside's getting mighty restless.

**SHERIFF:** Reckon they think justice is too slow; want to help along a bit.

**PROSECUTOR:** What about notifying the Governor?

**SHERIFF:** Notify the Governor for him? That's a good one! Say, the State saves money this–a–way—no board and lodgin's for 'em. *(He looks at* JOHNSON*)* You busy just now, Colonel?

**PROSECUTOR:** Why?

**SHERIFF:** Well, my cousin Alf just got a new case in from Mobile. It's sure swell stuff. Got a bottle in the office; it ain't been open yet. *(The steel door closes.* JOHNSON *is alone. Pause. He looks about the cell in a strange manner, then slowly rises. The light begins to dim.)*

**JOHNSON:** Yo' don't know who yo'se talkin' to, white man. Yo' cain't talk mean to me—no suh. I'se Praye'ful Johnson. I'se Presiden' o' dese heah United States. I'se a special friend o' de Lawd's, yo' understan'? *(With increasing fervor)* White trash, yo' listen to me now. I'se got de floor. Yo' cain't jedge de colo'ed man no mo', 'cause we'se jedgin' yo'—yo' heah. *(He screams)* We'se jedgin' yo'! *(Blackout. The shouting of the lynch mob)*

## SCENE 7

*Darkness. The mob cries gradually subside. Presently, a confused babble is heard—laughing, chattering; then the pounding of a gavel and* JOHNSON'S *voice, intoning.*

**JOHNSON:** *(in the darkness)* De Court o' Jestice is 'bout to commence! Keep quiet ovah dere! *(Coughing, scraping of chairs. Again the pounding of the gavel. Several beams of glaring white light gradually illumine a court room.* JOHNSON, *smoking a cigar, is discovered at the left, seated on a judge's bench. He is dressed in a judge's gown and a silk hat. Above the bench is a large picture, framed in gold, of a Negro dignitary in military uniform. The entire court personnel—the bailiff, the clerk, and the police— are black. At the back right, in the half shadow are the prisoners— some white, some Negro. The two races are segregated. Their features cannot be clearly discerned. The white prisoners include* THE PROSECUTOR, THE SHERIFF *and a strange white woman, who are handcuffed to one another. The court audience, right, is composed of a dozen Negroes of both sexes.* JOHNSON *continues after a brief pause)*

**JOHNSON:** Ev'body keep quiet! Now, stan' up—dat's it! Now, sit down! . . . Come on, court, we'se got heaps to do, we has. Who's de first what's to be jedged? Put up yo' hand. *(Two Negroes*—THE FIRST *and* SECOND CRAP SHOOTER—*raise their hands rather timidly)* Step up closer, boys. I ain't gonna hurt yo' none. What is yo' names?

**1st CRAP SHOOTER:** Joshua, yo' Honor.

**2nd CRAP SHOOTER:** Jeremiah's mah name.

**JOHNSON:** *(to the* CLERK*)* Put dat down. *(Kindly)* Dey'se nice names. What yo' heah fo', boys?

**NEGRO OFFICER:** Dey was caught shootin' craps, yo' honor.

**JOHNSON:** Dey was?

**NEGRO OFFICER:** Yes, suh.

**JOHNSON:** Shootin' craps—tst,tst,tst! Dat's too bad! What yo' say boys—guilty or not guilty?

**1st CRAP SHOOTER:** Seems lak we'se guilty, yo' Honor.

**JOHNSON:** Seems lak yo'se guilty? Don't yo' know ef yo' is?

**1st CRAP SHOOTER:** Yo, see, it's dis way, Jedge: de law 'ginst crapshootin' don't look no good to us.

**JOHNSON:** Dat so? What's de matter wid it?

**1st CRAP SHOOTER:** It's a'right fo' de white trash, but 'tain't right fo' us. *(To his companion)* Ain't dat de trut'?

**2nd CRAP SHOOTER:** It sho' is.

**JOHNSON:** *(after a pause)* Bot' o' yo' boys real colo'ed pussons?

**1st CRAP SHOOTER:** Yes, suh, we'se real.

**2nd CRAP SHOOTER:** Bet we is!

**JOHNSON:** No white blood in yo', is dere?

**1st CRAP SHOOTER:** No, suh, we'se pure colo'ed.

**JOHNSON:** *(meditatively)* Pure colo'ed. *(Pause)* Say, how much yo' play fo' in de crap game?

**1st CRAP SHOOTER:** Jes' two bits, yo' Honor.

**JOHNSON:** Dat's all?

**2nd CRAP SHOOTER:** Dat's all we has.

**JOHNSON:** 'Taint' no fun playin' fo' two bits.

**1st CRAP SHOOTER:** No suh, 'tain't much.

**JOHNSON:** Officer!

**NEGRO OFFICER:** Yes, Jedge?

**JOHNSON:** Officer, give dese boys a dollar—four bits apiece. (THE NEGRO OFFICER *takes the money from his pocket and distributes it as he is directed*) Guess dat'll fix yo' up.

**1st CRAP SHOOTER:** Yo'se a square shooter, Jedge!

**2nd CRAP SHOOTER:** Golly, I'll tell de worl'!

**CRAP SHOOTERS:** T'ank yo', Jedge!

**JOHNSON:** Dat's a'right, boys.

**1st CRAP SHOOTER:** An' we'se free?

**JOHNSON:** Sho' yo'se free. . . . Wait a minute. Officer, yo' got de bones dat b'longs to dese boys?

**NEGRO OFFICER:** Yes, Jedge, I got 'em.

**JOHNSON:** Den give 'em right back. (*Business*) Dat's all, boys.

**1st CRAP SHOOTER:** T'ank yo', Jedge!

**2nd CRAP SHOOTER:** T'ank yo'! (*The delighted crap shooters back off.* JOHNSON *turns again to the* NEGRO OFFICER)

**JOHNSON:** Say, don't you' 'rest no mo' colo'ed pu'sons fo' shootin' craps.

**NEGRO OFFICER:** No, Jedge.

**JOHNSON:** Yo' gotta draw de line somewheres.

**OFFICER:** Dat's right.

**JOHNSON:** An' let de line be colo'ed, see?

**NEGRO OFFICER:** Yes, Jedge.

**JOHNSON:** 'Specially when dey'se pure colo'ed.

**NEGRO OFFICER:** Yes, suh.

**JOHNSON:** Next! Next! Who's next? (THE WHITE PROSTITUTE *steps forward.* JOHNSON *speaks gruffly*) What she done?

**NEGRO OFFICER:** Prostitutin', yo' Honor.

**JOHNSON:** Bad?

**NEGRO OFFICER:** Terrible bad.

**JOHNSON:** How come, prisoner?

**PROSTITUTE:** (*arrogantly*) That's my business!

**JOHNSON:** I knows it is. Yo'se a first-class streetwalker. What's yo' name?

**PROSTITUTE:** Lilybelle.

**JOHNSON:** Nice name to be wasted on a no count gal like you. Yo'se pure white?

**PROSTITUTE:** I'm white, and I don't care who knows it!

**JOHNSON:** Is dat so? Lilybelle, yo' bettah shut yo' mout' an' stop 'criminatin' yo'self fo' nothin'.

**PROSTITUTE:** I'm not afraid of you.

**JOHNSON:** An' I ain't 'fraid o' 'yo, Lilybelle. Fifty bucks or fifty days fo' bein' white an' prostitutin'.

**PROSTITUTE:** I'll take fifty days—nigger!

**JOHNSON:** Oh, no yo' won't! Nine'y days an' nine'y bucks fo' insultin' de Jedge in de court! . . . Take dat woman away! (THE WHITE PROSTITUTE *is led off by two Negro policemen.*) Next! Next! Who's—? *(A young, comely Negress in a gaudy, tight-fitting dress steps forward.* JOHNSON'S *manner instantly changes. He rises, removes his hat, his cigar, smiles)* Mo'nin', sister!

**NEGRESS:** *(smiling)* Mor'nin', Jedge!

**JOHNSON:** Nice day, ain't it?

**NEGRESS:** Yeah—kinda—li'le warm.

**JOHNSON:** Won't yo' set down? *(Barking to* THE CLERK*)* Let de lady set down! (THE CLERK *jumps up with alacrity and gives the prisoner his seat)* What's yo' name, sister?

**NEGRESS:** Burn'sienna Hawkins.

**JOHNSON:** Ain't I seen yo' somewhere befo', Burn'sienna?

**BURNTSIENNA:** Mebbe yo' has. I been 'round good deal.

**JOHNSON:** Travels a lot, does yo'?

**BURNTSIENNA:** Yeah—f'om town to town.

**JOHNSON:** Yo' looks familiar. . . . What yo' come in dis heah court fo', Burn'sienna? (BURNTSIENNA *does not answer.*) Now don't yo' be bashful, sister, We'se all one big family heah—jes' one big fam'ly—ain't we boys? *(He turns to the court)*

**COURT:** *(together)* Yes, yo' Honor—jes on big fam'ly!

**JOHNSON:** Yo' see? Tell me, what yo' heah fo'? What yo' gone and done? *(The girl smiles, ill at ease, fidgets in her chair, but does not answer)* What's de charge, officer?

**NEGRO OFFICER:** Kinda bad, yo' Honor.

**JOHNSON:** Yeah? What is it? (THE NEGRO OFFICER *crosses to the bench.* JOHNSON *bends down.)*

**NEGRO OFFICER:** *(under his breath)* Prostitutin'!

**JOHNSON:** Mo' prostitutin'?

**NEGRO OFFICER:** Well, least wise, I has my 'spicions, Judge.

**JOHNSON:** Mah goodness! Seems lak dey's all doin' it! . . . What yo' gotta say fo' yo'self, Burn'sienna?

**BURNTSIENNA:** Nothin', Jedge—jes' nothin'.

**JOHNSON:** Yo' reckon yo'se guilty or not guilty?

**BURNTSIENNA:** I cain't tell.

**JOHNSON:** Dat ain't sense. Is yo' a bad gal—"Yes" or "No"?

**BURNTSIENNA:** *(smiling)* I s'ppose I'se bad.

**JOHNSON:** Why is yo' bad—nice lookin' gal lak yo'?

**BURNTSIENNA:** Well, yo' see, Jedge, I gotta live.

**JOHNSON:** Live—'course yo' gotta live. But cain't yo' find somethin' else to do?

**BURNTSIENNA:** I ain't got much experience in de odder trades. I knows dis one good.

**JOHNSON:** *(after a pause)* Say, Burn'sienna, how much money yo' got?

**BURNTSIENNA:** All de way f'om six bits to five bucks a t'row—'pends on de customer.

**JOHNSON:** I doesn't mean dat. I means, how much yo' got now—altogedder?

**BURNTSIENNA:** 'Bout ten dollars.

**JOHNSON:** Dat's all yo' has in de worl'?

**BURNTSIENNA:** Dat's all.

**JOHNSON:** 'Taint much.

**BURNTSIENNA:** No, suh.

**JOHNSON:** I doesn't lak to see a purtty gal lak yo' goin' dead wrong.

**BURNTSIENNA:** I doesn't lak it mahself, Jedge.

**JOHNSON:** Burn'sienna—

**BURNTSIENNA:** Yes, suh?

**JOHNSON:** Yo' evah takes on any white fellahs?

**BURNTSIENNA:** *(indignantly)* Does I look as bad as all dat?

**JOHNSON:** *(rising)* No, yo' doesn't. 'Cuse me, but dere's a lot o' fool questions dat eve'y jedge jes' gotta ask. *(JOHNSON jumps up on to the judge's desk and sits there)* Burn'sienna, come up heah. Come on right up. Dat's it—dat's it. *(BURNTSIENNA sits on the judge's desk beside JOHNSON)* Gimme yo' hand. . . . It's a soft li'le hand, ain't it? . . . Now listen to what I asks yo'.

**BURNTSIENNA:** I'se a listenin'.

**JOHNSON:** Will yo' try an' be a good gal ef I helps yo', will yo'?

**BURNTSIENNA:** *(smiling)* Mebbe.

**JOHNSON:** No, suh, dat ain't no answer. Yo' gotta say dat yo'll try and be good.

**BURNTSIENNA:** I'll try, Jedge.

**JOHNSON:** Yo' swear, Burn'sienna?

**BURNTSIENNA:** Sho', I swears. What yo' want me to say?

**JOHNSON:** *(to* THE CLERK*)* Bring de Book! *(A large Bible is brought forward)* Burn'sienna Hawkins, does yo' swear befo' de Lawd Hisself to try an' be a good gal?

**BURNTSIENNA:** Yeah, I does.

**JOHNSON:** Put up yo' right hand. *(*BURNTSIENNA *puts up her left)* Dat's it! Now swear.

**BURNTSIENNA:** I swears I'll try an' be a good gal—

**JOHNSON:** Befo' de Lawd.

**BURNTSIENNA:** I swears I'll try an' be a good gal befo' de Lawd—ef yo' helps me, Jedge.

**JOHNSON:** Amen! . . . Now yo' say dat.

**BURNTSIENNA:** Amen! *(The entire court stands)*

**COURT:** *(in unison)* Amen! *(*BURNTSIENNA *slips down from the judge's desk)*

**JOHNSON:** How much it cost yo' to keep yo'self pure, Burn'sienna?

**BURNTSIENNA:** I cain't say 'xactly, Jedge.

**JOHNSON:** Well, 'bout how much?

**BURNTSIENNA:** 'Bout t'ousand bucks.

**JOHNSON:** Yo' sho' dat's 'nough?

**BURNTSIENNA:** Yeah, up till next Christmas, mebbe.

**JOHNSON:** Ef I gits two t'ousand, reckon yo' kin put a li'le in de bank?

**BURNTSIENNA:** I guess I kin. I has no 'spensive habits no mo'. I turned 'way de la' one las' summer.

**JOHNSON:** Dat's fine. *(He stands upon the judge's desk and addresses the court)* Brodders, who wants to help dis heah gal to keep herself pure?

**COURT:** *(together, with enthusiasm)* We all wants to, yo' Honor!

**JOHNSON:** Dat's de spirit! Now how much is yo' willin' to pay? Come on, brodders, jes' yo' speak right up!

**NEGRO OFFICER:** One hundred dollars, yo' Honor! *(He gives the money to* JOHNSON*)*

**JOHNSON:** One hundred dollars! Dat's nice to start out wid. Who's de man dat'll make it five hundred? Five hundred dollars to keep Burn'sienna Hawkins 'way f'om sin!

**BAILIFF:** Five hundred! *(Business)*

**JOHNSON:** Gawd bless yo', brodder! . . . ain't dere nobody dat wants to give a t'ousand? 'Member, it's all fo' Burn'sienna 'case she's tryin' to be a good gal. . . . Where's de man wid a t'ousand?

**CLERK:** Right heah, Jedge! I cain't 'ford it, but it's fo' a good cause.

**JOHNSON:** Dat's de sen'iment! One t'ousand dollars! Gawd bless yo' all!

**COURT:** *(in unison)* Same to yo', Jedge!

**JOHNSON:** Now all de rest o' yo' folks give what yo' kin. Pass de hat, officer! *(*JOHNSON'S *top hat is passed around. All contribute liberally. One Negress in the court audience takes her money from her stocking.)* Burn'sienna Hawkins, come heah!

**BURNTSIENNA:** I'se heah, Jedge.

**JOHNSON:** In behalf o' dis court, I'se givin' yo' dis money to refo'm yo' allovah, an' make yo' a pure woman. *(He gives her his hat with the money)*

**BURNTSIENNA:** I'se ce'tainly 'bliged to yo'—to all o' yo'. I'll do mah ve'y best—I promise yo' dat.

**JOHNSON:** Dat's all yo' kin do, Burn'sienna. . . . Drop in agin, an' tell us how yo'se gittin' 'long.

**BURNTSIENNA:** I sho' will.

**JOHNSON:** You know I'se Presiden' o' dese United States on de side, an' ef dere's somethin' I kin do fo' yo'—jes' yo' whistle.

**BURNTSIENNA:** I will Jedge. *(She whistles a few notes, smiles)*

**JOHNSON:** Ef de temptations dey gits too strong fo' yo', jes' yo' come right back heah, I kin fix yo' up.

**BURNTSIENNA:** Dat's mighty sweet o' yo'. *(She stands very close to* JOHNSON, *who is seated on the judge's desk. As he bends down,* BURNTSIENNA *moves away)* Goo'bye, Jedge!

**JOHNSON:** Goo'bye, Burn'sienna.

**BURNTSIENNA:** *(turning)* Ain't yo' name Johnson?

**JOHNSON:** Yeah, dat's right—Praye'ful Johnson.

**BURNTSIENNA:** Mah uncle's name was Johnson, It's a purtty name, ain't it?

**JOHNSON:** I laks it. . . . Yo' name's kinda purtty too.

**BURNTSIENNA:** Well, goo'bye, Mr. Johnson!

**JOHNSON:** Goo'bye, Burn'sienna. Don't yo' sin no mo'.

**BURNTSIENNA:** I'se gonna try hard, Mr. Johnson. *(To the court)* Goo'bye, ev'body!

**COURT:** *(in unison)* Goo'bye, Burn'sienna! Come agin, Burn'sienna! *(*BURNTSIENNA *goes out. Pause)*

**JOHNSON:** *(dreamily)* Might nice kid.

**NEGRO OFFICER:** Sho' is—good lookin', too. . . . Did yo' see dem legs, Jedge?

**JOHNSON:** Yeah—say, yo' mind yo' own business! *(Lights begin to dim. Then, suddenly the cries of the lynch mob are heard.* JOHNSON *listens intently. His face becomes distorted with fear. He jumps down from the judge's desk and cringes on the floor—again the abject and pitiful figure of Scene 1.)* What's dat noise? What's dat noise?

**NEGRO OFFICER:** *(unconcerned)* Why, dat's de crowd otside o' de court.

**JOHNSON:** Crowd—what dey want?

**NEGRO OFFICER:** Dey'se a-waitin' to lay deir hands on dem white trash. *(He points to the group of handcuffed whites standing in the shadow—*THE SHERIFF, THE PROSECUTOR *and the strange* WHITE WOMAN. JOHNSON *slowly rises, as if in a daze.)*

**JOHNSON:** Who's dey?

**NEGRO OFFICER:** It's de rapin' case, yo' Honor.

**JOHNSON:** *(slowly)* Oh yeah—de rapin' case! *(His expression hardens. He crosses to the bench and sits down—once more a judge. His voice is gruff)* Lemme look at yo'! come on up heah! *(The whites slowly cross centre into the light)* I'se sho' glad to see yo' all, white trash. *(To* THE WHITE WOMAN*)* Who is yo'?

**WHITE WOMAN:** My name is Collins.

**JOHNSON:** *(slowly)* Collins . . . Collins—I knows yo' now! Even if I ain't ever seen ya before. Yo'se de bitch dat said I 'tacked yo'. Did yo' say dat?

**COLLINS:** I did.

**JOHNSON:** Yo' say I 'tacked yo'?

**COLLINS:** I do.

**JOHNSON:** Yo' is a Goddamn liar! *(To* SHERIFF *and* PROSE-CUTOR*)* Yo' say I 'tacked dis heah woman?

**SHERIFF AND PROSECUTOR:** *(together)* Yes!

**JOHNSON:** Den yo'se all Goddamn liars. Yo'se goddam liars and de Lawd's gonna pass out what's comin' to yo'. *(suddenly cringing again)* I nevah seen dis woman befo'. I doesn't know nothin' 'bout her. I nevah 'tacked her! Yo' don't believe me?

**SHERIFF AND PROSECUTOR:** *(together)* No!

**JOHNSON:** I teared de clothes off' her—you say dat?

**SHERIFF AND PROSECUTOR:** Yes!

**JOHNSON:** Yo' 'sinuate de Presiden' o' de United States is a liar?

**WHITES:** We do.

**JOHNSON:** *(screaming)* Yo' dirty white bastards! Take 'em out an' shoot 'em. Take 'em out!

**OFFICER:** Shall I use de lie detector on 'em, Judge?

**COLLINS:** No-no!

**JUDGE:** No, put 'em in the chain gang. *(Several officers take the white prisoners away. Silence. Then as* JOHNSON *slowly raises one hand to his face, the court audience slowly rises with one concerted movement—unreal as in a dream. A sudden fusillade of revolver shots offstage. Everyone stands motionless. The lights dim out. The shouting of the lynch mob in the darkness.)*

(Intermission)

## SCENE 8

*Darkness. The mob cries diminish and then cease.* JOHNSON'S *voice is heard, followed by the voices of* THE FIRST *and* THE SECOND CRAP SHOOTER.

**JOHNSON:** Come on, seben! Come on, sweetheart!

**1st CRAP SHOOTER:** Oh Luck, yo' gotta kiss papa!

**2nd CRAP SHOOTER:** Seben—seben—oh yo' honey chile! *(Lights gradually appear on the President's office. At the right, an imperial-looking chair on a dais. A few commanding portraits of Negro grandees—major-generals and statesmen—adorn the black drapes enclosing the room. Beside the chair, very splendidly attired, two Negro flunkeys are standing at attention. Kneeling on the floor near the dais, engrossed in their play, are* JOHNSON *and* THE FIRST *and* THE SECOND CRAP SHOOTERS—*the same Negroes who appeared in the previous scene.* JOHNSON *wears a frock coat and a top hat—a little awry over one ear. His presidential medals are very much in evidence. The three men are smoking cigaretttes.)*

**JOHNSON:** *(playing)* Dat's it, ole gal! Come on—come on!

**1st CRAP SHOOTER:** Yo' t'row, buddy. *(Ad lib for crap shooting.* JOHNSON, *in the heat of the game, removes his coat. A bell rings. The players ignore it. The bell rings again.* JOHNSON *looks up, disturbed.)*

**JOHNSON:** Mah goodness—dat bell! 'Tain't all a picnic bein' Presiden', I'll tell de worl'.

**1st CRAP SHOOTER:** I reckon 'tain't.

**JOHNSON:** *(without getting up)* I'se always 'sturbed when I'se got 'portant business. *(The bell rings a third time)* Yeah, what yo' want? *(A Negro* ATTENDANT *enters. He is most deferential toward* JOHNSON.*)*

**ATTENDANT:** Is yo' home, Mr. Presiden'?

**JOHNSON:** Who de hell wants to know?

**ATTENDANT:** It's de Jestice Club f'om Savannah.

**JOHNSON:** Jestice Club—dey'se colo'ed?

**ATTENDANT:** No, suh—

**JOHNSON:** Dey'se white?

**ATTENDANT:** Yes, dey'se white.

**JOHNSON:** Den I ain't home.

**ATTENDANT:** Yes, suh.

**JOHNSON:** Say, Randolph, dem white bums been heah befo', ain't dey?

**ATTENDANT:** Yeah, las' week dey was heah.

**JOHNSON:** How come?

**ATTENDANT:** Search me, Mr. Presiden'.

JOHNSON: Doesn't dey know 'tain't lawful to 'sturb de Presiden'? Doesn't dey know I'se a busy man?

ATTENDANT: I guess dey doesn't.

JOHNSON: Well, I can't see dem. Yo' jes' tell 'em to git while de gittin's good.

ATTENDANT: Yos, suh, I'll tell 'em.

JOHNSON: An' don't yo' come in heah agin, Randolph, fo' somethin' dat ain't portant. I'se busy, see?

ATTENDANT: Okay, Mr. President. (THE ATTENDANT *goes out*)

JOHNSON: Cain't be boddered wid no white trash—no, suh. . . . Come on, boys, le's git on wid de game. (*They begin to play again. The bell rings.* JOHNSON *rises in a passion*) Jesus Christ! Evah see de lak! (*Shouting*) Yeah, what's up? (THE ATTENDANT *enters*) What's a-matter now?

ATTENDANT: It's de same Jestice Club, Mr. Presiden'.

JOHNSON: Didn't I tells 'em to git?

ATTENDANT: Yo' did, but dey don't.

JOHNSON: What's dat? Say, I'll sho' hawl off an' mow 'em down, I sho' will—de dirty dogs!

ATTENDANT: Dey says dey jes' gotta see yo', Mr. Presiden'. Somethin' 'portant—matter life an' deat'.

JOHNSON: Cain't de Presiden' nevah have no peace?

ATTENDANT: It sho' don't look lak it, suh.

JOHNSON: I'se a powe'ful busy man, Randolph.

ATTENDANT: We all knows yo' is.

JOHNSON: What dey wanna see me 'bout?

ATTENDANT: Dey wouldn't tell me, but some o' dem was a- cryin'.

JOHNSON: Cryin'! Maybe—no, now watch your step, Mr. President. Do go gettin' soft now. The time ain't come to loosen up yet. They ain't had enough of their own medicine. . . . Well, de Presiden' ain't a-gonna see dem fo' mo'n five minutes—an' dat's de las' word. Yo' come back heah in five minutes an take dem away.

ATTENDANT: I'll do dat, suh. (*He crosses toward the exit*)

JOHNSON: Hey dere!

ATTENDANT: Yes, Mr. Presiden'?

JOHNSON: How many's comin'?

**ATTENDANT:** 'Bout five or ten.

**JOHNSON:** H'm! When yo' come back heah fo' dem, bring 'long de perlice wid yo'.

**ATTENDANT:** Yes, suh.

**JOHNSON:** Looks better, see? An' ef dere's some trouble, de perlice kin help out.

**ATTENDANT:** Dat's all, suh?

**JOHNSON:** Dat's all. 'Member, Randolph, yo' come back heah in five minutes.

**ATTENDANT:** Yes, Mr. President. *(THE ATTENDANT goes out)*

**JOHNSON:** *(yawning and stretching)* Lawdy, Lawdy, I'se tired. I got too much on mah mind. *(The two Negro crap shooters rise.* JOHNSON *crosses to them)* Say yo' boys step in de nex' room fo' ali'le while, will yo'?

**1st CRAP SHOOTER:** Sho'.

**JOHNSON:** Mebbe dey wants to tell me somethin' kinda private.

**1st CRAP SHOOTER:** Come on, Jerry.

**JOHNSON:** Yo'll find somethin' to drink in de pantry— swell stuff. *(Slowly, as if in a trance, he repeats the line he heard* THE SHERIFF *speak in the prison cell)* Mah cousin done brung some up f'om Mobile. *(Casually again)* Jes' help yo'self. I won't keep yo' long.

**2nd CRAP SHOOTER:** Take yo' time, Mr. Presiden'. Me an' Josh is feelin' kinda dry. *(The crap shooters go out.* JOHNSON, *assisted by the two Negro flunkeys, puts on his coat. The flunkeys brush him off)*

**JOHNSON:** Dat's 'nough! 'Tain't nobody o' no 'Portance. *(*JOHNSON *sits on the high-backed chair, looking very solemn and disagreeable. He still wears his top hat.* THE ATTENDANT *appears)*

**ATTENDANT:** *(announcing)* De Jestice Club o' Savannah! *(A delegation of four very obsequious white men enter, hats in hand. They bow to* JOHNSON*)*

**1st WHITE MAN:** *(effusively)* Ah, good mornin', Mr. President!

**2nd WHITE MAN:** Such an honor—!

**3rd WHITE MAN:** Such a great honor—!

**4th WHITE MAN:** So good o' you to see us!

JOHNSON: *(Gruffly)* What yo' all want?

1st WHITE MAN: It's about our race, Mr. President—

JOHNSON: Yeah, what's de matter wid it?

2nd WHITE MAN: As members o' the Justice Club o' Savannah, we wanna protest 'gainst the way the white people is bein' treated in this country.

JOHNSON: Ain't dis country good 'nough fo' yo'?

1st WHITE MAN: It ain't dat—

JOHNSON: Say, ef yo' don't lak it heah, den yo' kin go right back where yo' comes f'om.

1st WHITE MAN: You don't quite get us, Mr. President. The white race—our race—is sufferin' terrible.

JOHNSON: Oh yeah? Den I guess dat's what dey deserves.

2nd WHITE MAN: Mr. President, you can't believe that!

JOHNSON: Cain't I? Who say's I cain't?

2nd WHITE MAN: Why, they're lynchin' white men in this country—hundreds of 'em.

JOHNSON: Dat so? Who's lynchin' 'em? *(No answer)* Who's lynchin' em?

1st WHITE MAN: We don't wanna insult you, Mr. President.—

JOHNSON: Yo' cain't insult me none, white man. I'se so high 'bove yo', sometimes I doesn't know where yo' is. Who's doin' all dat lynchin'?

1st WHITE MAN: *(hesitantly)* The colored people—your people.

JOHNSON: Dey'se a-lynchin' white folks?

WHITES: *(together)* Yes, Mr.President.

JOHNSON: Say, ain't that nice? But den I reckon dey's doin' it fo' a mighty good reason.

WHITES: *(scandalized)* Mr. President!

JOHNSON: Mebbe yo' ain't perlite 'nough to de colo'ed folks. Mebbe yo' looks nasty at our wimmen. Yo' gotta know yo' place, see? An' ef yo' don't know it, we jes' gotta learn yo'.

2nd WHITE MAN: We wanna law 'gainst lynchin'.

JOHNSON: Yo' does, does yo'? Well, yo' cain't have none. It's all wrote down in de constitootion.

3rd WHITE MAN: But sure, Mr. President—

JOHNSON: Say, when I says "No," I means "No." Lynchin's too good fo' some o' yo'.

2nd WHITE MAN: The white people don't want Jimcrowin'—no discrimination. We gotta have free an' equal elections.

JOHNSON: Is dat all?

4th WHITE MAN: We wants equality!

JOHNSON: 'Quality?

WHITES: Yes!

JOHNSON: Say who de hell yo' think yo' is? Yo'm de equal o' de colo'ed folks? Don't make me laugh! . . . Look heah, white trash, de Lawd Gawd made de colo'ed people s'prerior, an' He made yo' what yo' is. An' what de Lawd's done, has gotta stay, see? It's all in de constitootion, an' yo' cain't change de law o' dis heah land. Dis is a black man's country. Ef yo' don't lak de way we'se a-runnin' it, yo' kin git right out.

1st WHITE MAN: But, Mr. President—

JOHNSON: Dey ain't no "buts." Yo' time's up.

2nd WHITE MAN: Mr. President—

JOHNSON: (*rising*) Yo heah what I says? Time's up. Git out! Go on—git!

1st WHITE MAN: Mercy, Mr. President—!

2nd WHITE MAN: Mercy!

JOHNSON: Mercy, nothin'! go on—out wid yo'!

3rd WHITE MAN: Listen, Mr. President—!

4th WHITE MAN: Have mercy for all the white folks!

WHITES: (*falling to their knees*) Mercy! Mercy! (*The delegation burst into tears.* JOHNSON *looks toward the exit used by* THE ATTENDANT, *and then takes out a large pocket watch. No* ATTENDANT. JOHNSON *rings a small dinner bell.* THE ATTENDANT *enters immediately with four burly, Negro policemen. The white men continue sobbing.*)

JOHNSON: (*to* ATTENDANT) Yo'se late.

ATTENDANT: Sorry, Mr. Presiden'—

JOHNSON: Yo' gotta be on de jump ef yo' wanna wait on de Presiden'. He's gotta have service.

ATTENDANT: Yes, Mr. Presiden'. (*The delegation weeps louder*)

**JOHNSON:** Dey'so whiners. Take 'em out! I cain't stand whiners. An ef dey evah comes round heah agin bodderin' de Presiden', I wants yo' to put 'em straight in de can.

**ATTENDANT:** Yes, suh. *(To the police)* Take 'em out! *(The white delegation, still sobbing, is unceremoniously bustled off by the Negro policemen.* JOHNSON *stands centre lost in thought. He speaks half to himself.)*

**JOHNSON:** What yo' tink o' dat! Dem white trash sho' gives me a pain!

**ATTENDANT:** Dat's too bad, suh. Don't let dem worry yo' none, dey ain't wort' it.

**JOHNSON:** What dey want anyway?

**ATTENDANT:** I don't know, suh.

**JOHNSON:** Ain't we got a Constitootion?

**ATTENDANT:** Sho' we has.

**JOHNSON:** Ain't it a good Constitootion?

**ATTENDANT:** De bes' in de country.

**JOHNSON:** White trash cain't have no rights dey ain't 'titled to. Dey oughta know deir place. What dey mean—pretendin' to be de equal o' de colo'ed people? *(Laughing)* dat's funny— gosh, dat's funny!

**ATTENDANT:** *(laughing)* It sho' is!

**JOHNSON:** Dey's plumb crazy, dat's de trut'!—bughouse! But they was pitiful now, wasn't they?

**ATTENDANT:** Sho' was. Makes you feel kinda bad, don't it?

**JOHNSON:** Yes, Maybe. No, now don't you go gettin' soft on 'em, Randolph. They ain't took their own medicine long enough yet.

**ATTENDANT:** Guess youse right, Mr. Presiden'.

**JOHNSON:** Don't you let in no mo' 'jectionable characters. I ain't got no time fo' white trash, understan'?

**ATTENDANT:** I understan', Mr. Presiden'.

**JOHNSON:** I reckon I ain't got time fo' nobody.

**ATTENDANT:** No, suh. Is dat all, suh?

**JOHNSON:** Yeah, dat's all. Go 'way now, Randolph. I'se got powe'ful lot to think 'bout. I ain't very comfortable in my mind with dis Presiden' business. Randolph, git along. I'se a busy man. *(*THE ATTENDANT *goes out.* JOHNSON *is lost in thought)*

**JOHNSON:** *(to himself)* Equal—equal—how dey git dat way? Insultin' we colo'ed folks. *(Pause. The bell rings violently.* THE ATTENDANT, *without waiting for* JOHNSON'S *leave, reenters in great excitement)* I told you I'se busy. What you mean comin' in heah lak dat?

**ATTENDANT:** 'Cuse me, Mr. Presiden' . . .

**JOHNSON:** What's a-matter? Why all de 'citment?

**ATTENDANT:** *(jubilantly)* It's de War Modders!

**JOHNSON:** Gold Star Mothers!

**ATTENDANT:** Yeah!

**JOHNSON:** Well, ain't dat a su'prise fo' yo'—Gold Star Mothers. Yo' tell 'em to come right up. Golly, I'se sho' glad to see dem! Say . . .

**ATTENDANT:** Yes, suh?

**JOHNSON:** Let de bugler know 'bout it, an' give dem a good li'le bugle—de bes' he got.

**ATTENDANT:** I'll tell him suh.

**JOHNSON:** Well, dis sho' is a su'prise! I ain't seen dem ladies fo' long time. . . . What yo' waitin' fo', Randolph? Tell de War Modders to come up—step on it!

**ATTENDANT:** Yes, suh—right away, suh! *(*THE ATTENDANT *goes out)*

**JOHNSON:** *(to the two Negro flunkeys)* Come on, fix me up good, an' don't let de years grow under yo' feet! . . . Where de hell's mah odder medals? No good bein' Presiden' widout plen'y o' medals. *(The flunkeys take out a handful of medals and a bright colored scarf from beneath the President's chair. The medals are pinned to* JOHNSON'S *chest)* Put some mo' ovah heah—dat's it, dat's it! Some mo' heah. Now put dat stuff 'roun me nice. *(The scarf is arranged)* Yeah, yeah—dis way li'le bit. . . . Now a li'le powder to take de shine off. Where's dat powder? *(A box of face powder and a large puff are produced)* Dere, dat's 'nough! Yo' got de glass? *(*JOHNSON *is provided with a hand mirror. He looks approvingly at himself)* Say, I sho' looks lak de Presiden' now! *(Bugle call off)* Golly, heah dey come! Put dis 'way—hurry up dere! *(The toilet miscellany disappear under the chair. Another bugle call.* THE ATTENDANT *appears)*

**ATTENDANT:** *(announcing)* De War Modders! *(Another bugle call, and the Negro War Mothers enter. Some are stout, some* *thin, others medium, but they are all beaming.* JOHNSON *crosses to them with outstretched hands)*

**JOHNSON:** Well, well, I'se sho' happy to see yo' all!

**WAR MOTHERS:** *(together)* An' we'se happy to see yo', Mr. Presiden'!

**JOHNSON:** *(shaking hands)* Ef it ain't ole Granny White-top! How is yo', how is yo', Granny?

**OLD NEGRESS:** I still got de rheumatiz, Mr. Presiden', but I cain't complain.

**JOHNSON:** Dat's fine! . . . well, well, an' heah's Modder Tildy! Say yo'se lookin' jes' as sweet as yo' evah was, an' not a day older dan sixteen—no, suh!

**ANOTHER NEGRESS:** *(embarassed)* Mr. Presiden'—!

**JOHNSON:** An' Sister Isabel, an' Aunt Emma—! Wel-come, welcome to yo' all! Yo'se sho' lookin' mighty good—all o' yo'!

**WAR MOTHERS:** *(together)* An' we'se a-feelin' mighty good, Mr. Presiden'!

**1st WAR MOTHER:** Yo'se lookin' real pert yo'self, Mr. Presiden'.

**JOHNSON:** I'se nevah felt better. . . . Well, so yo' is all git-tin' ready fo'de long trip, is yo'?

**WAR MOTHERS:** Yes, suh!

**JOHNSON:** An' yo'se gonna see yo' sons what give deir lives fo' deir country . . . Eve'ythin' a'right fo' de li'le journey? *(THE WAR MOTHERS exchange glances, but do not respond)* Ef it ain't, yo' Presiden's gonna make it right. Speak what's on yo' minds, ladies. Don't be skeered. De Presiden' he's de bes' friend yo' got.

**1st WAR MOTHER:** *(after a pause)* Ev'thin's a'right but one, suh.

**JOHNSON:** What's dat? Ain't de ship good 'nough? Den we'll git anodder.

**2nd WAR MOTHER:** No, de ship's fine, Mr. Presiden'—nevah seed no better.

**JOHNSON:** What's de matter, den? *(Prolongued pause)*

**1st WAR MOTHER:** *(slowly)* It's de company.

**JOHNSON:** De company—what's wrong wid de company?

**1st WAR MOTHER:** *(in a half whisper)* Dey'se white!

**JOHNSON:** White?

**1st WAR MOTHER:** Yes, suh—white wimmen!

**2nd WAR MOTHER:** Some o' de colo'ed folks'lowed it was a 'tentional insult—

**JOHNSON:** 'Tentional?

**2nd WAR MOTHER:** But we all knowed dat our Presiden' ain't gonna let it pass.

**JOHNSON:** *(vehemently)* I'll say de Presiden' won't let it pass! Where's de son-of-a-gun dat done sech a t'ing—white wimmens on de same ship wid our colo'ed modders—dat's sho terrible!

**WAR MOTHERS:** *(together)* Dat's jes' what we says!

**JOHNSON:** Ladies, I gies yo' mah word o' honor: de colo'ed folks an' de whites ain't gonna trabel togedder on dat boat—not while I is Presiden', no suh! *(He rings the bell)* Ef dey does it, it's ovah mah dead body—yes suh!

**4th WAR MOTHER:** Yo'se a good man, Mr. Presiden'.

**2nd WAR MOTHER:** An' we all loves yo'—bless yo' heart!

**WAR MOTHERS:** Gawd bless yo'!

**JOHNSON:** T'ank yo', ladies. I'se glad yo' got fait' in yo' Presiden'.

**2nd WAR MOTHER:** Dat's 'cause yo' b'lieves in jestice fo' all—de colo'ed 'specially. (JOHNSON *rings again.* THE ATTENDANT *enters)*

**ATTENDANT:** Yes, suh?

**JOHNSON:** Take dis down—ve'y 'portant.

**ATTENDANT:** Yes, Mr. Presiden'. (THE ATTENDANT *takes out a pencil and pad, and follows* JOHNSON *as he paces back and forth, dictating)*

**JOHNSON:** Is yo' ready?

**ATTENDANT:** Yeah.

**JOHNSON:** "F'om now on, de blacks an' de whites dey gotta trabel on diffrent boats—"

**1st WAR MOTHER:** Hallelujah!

**JOHNSON:** An' write dis what's a-comin' in great big letters—de biggest yo' knows.

**ATTENDANT:** Yes, suh.

**JOHNSON:** "De colo'ed War Modders is gonna take de finestest boat in de Navy. De odders takes what's left. Signed—Yo's truly, Praye'ful Johnson, de Presiden' o' dese United

States." Now yo' read dat las' to me out loud, so I knows yo' git it right.

**ATTENDANT:** *(reading)* "De colo'ed War Modders is gonna take de finestest boat in de Navy. De odders takes what's left. Signed—Yo's truly, Praye'ful Johnson, de Presiden' o' dese United States."

**JOHNSON:** Dat's it 'xac'ly. Now send de letter right off to de Navy 'Partment, special d'liv'ry.

**ATTENDANT:** Yes, suh. (THE ATTENDANT *goes out*)

**JOHNSON:** Dat'll settle de whole business, ladies.

**1st WAR MOTHER:** Oh, we'se evah so much 'bliged to yo', Mr. Presiden'!

**WAR MOTHERS:** *(together)* Gawd bless yo'!

**JOHNSON:** Yo'se all welcome, I'm sho'.

**2nd WAR MOTHER:** *(giggling)* Granny wants to know ef she kin kiss yo'.

**JOHNSON:** She sho' kin.'

**3rd WAR MOTHER:** She ain't nevah kissed no Presiden' befo'. *(The aged Negress kisses* JOHNSON. *He embraces her and kisses her in turn. General laughter)*

**4th WAR MOTHER:** I done tol' Granny dat de Presiden' ain't so diffrent dan de odder men—

**1st WAR MOTHER:** 'Course he's diffrent—he's jes' dat much nicer!

**3rd WAR MOTHER:** Dat's right, ain't it, ladies?

**WAR MOTHERS:** It sho' is! *(Laughter)*

**JOHNSON:** De Presiden' cain't cont'dict dat! *(more laughter)* An' jes' to show yo' how yo' Presiden' 'preciates all yo' done fo' yo' country, I wants to give yo' somethin' to 'Member me by —jes a li'le 'membrance. Heah yo' is, ladies! One fo' each o' yo'. *(He takes a number of medals from his own chest and pins one to each elated Negress)*

**ONE:** Oh, t'ank yo', Mr. President!

**1st WAR MOTHER:** Ain't dat won'erful!

**2nd WAR MOTHER:** He's de bestest Presiden' dis country evah has!

**3rd WAR MOTHER:** Yo' bet he is!

**4th WAR MOTHER:** Gawd bless de Presiden'!

**WAR MOTHERS:** Gawd bless him!

**JOHNSON:** Ef yo' cain't use dese heah medals yo'self, mebbe yo' kin hock dem an' git somethin' else.

**2nd WAR MOTHER:** Why, Mr. Presiden', how kin yo' talk lak dat!

**3rd WAR MOTHER:** Dat's purtty near blasphemy—ef anoder pu'son said it!

**4th WAR MOTHER:** Hurray fo' de Presiden'!

**WAR MOTHERS:** Hurray!

**1st WAR MOTHER:** We doesn't give des 'way fo' one million dollars, does we?

**WAR MOTHERS:** No, suh—nevah!

**1st WAR MOTHER:** Dat's how we all feels 'bout it.

**JOHNSON:** An' dat's a mighty fine sen'iment—might fine. I cain't tell yo' all what I feels—de words, dey jes' won't come! (JOHNSON *takes out a bandana handkerchief and blows his nose*)

**1st WAR MOTHER:** Bless yo', Mr. Presiden'! (*Other handkerchiefs appear. The Negresses wipe their eyes, sniff, blow their noses.* JOHNSON *rings the bell.* THE ATTENDANT *appears*)

**JOHNSON:** Tell dat bugler to give de ladies 'nodder good bugle. But he gotta give it wid mo' spirit dan de first time.

**ATTENDANT:** Yes, suh. (THE ATTENDANT *goes out*)

**1st WAR MOTHER:** Now we mus' say goo'bye to yo'. Yo'se a busy man and we'se busy wimmen, 'cause de boat's a-leavin' early in de mo'nin'.

**2nd WAR MOTHER:** And we's got to fry de chicken for de lunch baskets to take on de boat.

**3rd WAR MOTHER:** An' we got a lot o' packin' to 'tend to. T'ank yo', Mr. Presiden' fo' all yo' done fo' us. (*Bugle call off. Excitement, general hand shaking*)

**WAR MOTHERS:** Goo'bye! Goo'bye! De Lawd keep yo', Mr. Presiden'!

**JOHNSON:** De same to you', Ladies! Goo'bye. Goo'bye, goo'bye. Have a nice trip!

**WAR MOTHERS:** Goo'bye. (*Another bugle call.* JOHNSON *escorts the* WAR MOTHERS *across the scene.* THE FIRST WAR MOTHER *lingers behind until all her companions are gone. She eyes* JOHNSON *with tender maternal affection, not unmixed with embarrassment.*)

**1st WAR MOTHER:** Mr. Presiden' . . .

**JOHNSON:** Yes, sister?

**1st WAR MOTHER:** I guess I'll wait till we'se 'lone togedder. *(She looks at the two Negro flunkeys)*

**JOHNSON:** *(to the flunkeys)* A'right, boys, yo'se 'cuse till after dinner time. *(The flunkeys move slowly)* Git de hell outa heah! *(Exeunt the flunkeys)* What kin I do fo' yo'? Sit down, sister.

**1st WAR MOTHER:** Mebbe yo' don't want me to say it—

**JOHNSON:** 'Tain't bad as all dat, is it?

**1st WAR MOTHER:** *(after a pause)* Yo'se a handsome man, Mr. Presiden'.

**JOHNSON:** Dat's what dey all tells me.

**1st WAR MOTHER:** An' yo'se strong an' Gawd-fearin'.

**JOHNSON:** I hopes I is.

**1st WAR MOTHER:** *(after another pause)* Dere's a heap o' good wimmen in dis worl', Mr. Presiden'.

**JOHNSON:** I reckon dere is.

**1st WAR MOTHER:** Yo'se too good a man to stop where yo' is.

**JOHNSON:** Stop where I is?

**1st WAR MOTHER:** De Lawd said to de chillun o' Israel, "Be fruitful an' multiply."

**JOHNSON:** De Lawd said dat?

**1st WAR MOTHER:** He sho' did. An' yo' cain't multiply all by yo'self, Mr. Presiden'.

**JOHNSON:** I s'ppose yo' cain't.

**1st WAR MOTHER:** Dat's where de wimmen kin help yo'.

**JOHNSON:** Say dat's mighty nice o' yo'— (THE FIRST WAR MOTHER *crosses toward the exit, then turns and smiles)*

**1st WAR MOTHER:** Jes' yo' t'ink it ovah, Mr. Presiden'.

**JOHNSON:** I sho' will.

**1st WAR MOTHER:** An' 'member, we's all willin' to help yo'. . . . Go'bye, Mr. Presiden'.

**JOHNSON:** Goo'bye! (THE FIRST WAR MOTHER *is gone. The lights begin to dim.* JOHNSON *slowly crosses to the dais, sits down, picks up the dice left by the two crap shooters and throws them in an abstracted manner, while he speaks to himself)* De Lawd said to de chillun o' Israel, "Be fruitful an' multiply." *(Pause. Then Johnson smiles)* Dat's right! Dat's right! *(Blackout. During this brief interregnum between scenes, the faint cries of the lynch mob are heard again)*

## SCENE 9

*Darkness. The cries of the lynch mob recede, then commingle with the sounds of laughter, talking, clapping, and the clatter of glasses and crockery. Jazz music. Lights gradually appear on a cabaret. A crowd of gaily dressed Negroes are dancing to the "blues" played by an invisible orchestra. Two fawning white waiters—the same who served* JOHNSON *on board the train in Scene 4—scurry from table to table with bottles of liquor and other refreshments. One of the tables is decorated with festoons of flowers and more than the ordinary number of bottles. In the centre of the decorations is a placard reading: "PRESIDENTS TABEL—DONT TECH." All the guests are Negroes. Among them are members of the crowd in Scene 5, and the black court personnel of Scene 7 all in evening dress. The music stops. Applause, conversation, laughter. drinking among the Negroes at the tables. The dialogue of a Negro couple, seated at the left, is heard:*

**1st GUEST:** Oh, Lawsy, Chet! I nevah had a better time!

**2nd GUEST:** Ain't it hilarious!

**1st GUEST:** Dat music sho' makes de li'le feet trabel!

**2nd GUEST:** an' how! . . . Dis is a great night!

**1st GUEST:** I'll say! I jes' cain't wait to see de Presiden' git married! I hopes he gits a good woman.

**2nd GUEST:** Ef dere is one, he'll git her a'right. Leave it to de Presiden'.

**1st GUEST:** Chet!

**2nd GUEST:** Yeah?

**1st GUEST:** Why is de Presiden' gonna pick out a gal heah? Ain't dere no odder places?

**2nd GUEST:** De manager o' dis heah dump's got de bes' lookin' gals in de country. Dey're all fancy, A Number One's. *(The conversation of* THE FIRST *and* SECOND GUEST *becomes more intimate, and that of a second couple, seated at the right—a masterful looking, fat Negress and her rather diminutive, scrawny, male companion—becomes audible)*

**3rd GUEST:** Oh, come on dere, kiss me, Oggie! What's amatter, ain't I fascinatin' to yo' no mo'?

**4th GUEST:** 'Taint dat.

**3rd GUEST:** Is yo' skeered?

**4th GUEST:** No, 'course I ain't skeered.

**3rd GUEST:** What's amatter?

**4th GUEST:** I doesn't lak public ex'bitions, 'Lizabeth. Wait till we gits back home.

**3rd GUEST:** I cain't wait! Come on, funny man—kiss me!

**4th GUEST:** Heah, take 'nodder drink!

**3rd GUEST:** I doesn't want no drink, Oggie. I jes' want yo'.

**4th GUEST:** Say yo' keep yo' hands off'n me! Ain't yo' got no shame, 'Lizabeth?

**3rd GUEST:** No, I'se a ruint woman! *(The orchestra strikes up same tune)* Come on, Oggie, le's dance! *(The amorous Negress forces her reluctant swain to the floor, puts her arms about him, and they whisk off. Other Negroes dance . . . Presently, a well-dressed white couple enter the cabaret. They glance around curiously. One by one, the Negro couples stop dancing and stare at the whites with evident disapproval. The music continues, softly. The white couple cross the scene, look at the President's table, smile and seat themselves.)*

**DANCER:** *(To her companion)* Better call de Manager . . . Dis is sho' disgraceful. *(Several Negroes go out. Murmurs of protest from the crowd.)*

**CROWD:** What dey doin' in heah? De idea! At de President's banquet! Dey sh' got nerve! Did yo' ever see de lak? White trash! Dey oughta know deir place! Mah goodness, what dis worl' a-comin' to! *(The white couple remain seated, talking together, oblivious to the mounting antagonism around them.* THE MANAGER *enters, followed by several irate guests. He is the same person as* THE FIRST CRAP SHOOTER, *appropriately dressed for his new role.)*

**MANAGER:** Stop dat music! *(The music stops instantly.* THE MANAGER *with a lowering expression, crosses to the white couple)* Sy, yo' cain't stay in heah. We don't 'llow no whites. It's 'ginst de rules o' de house. Better git out right now. *(The white couple rise, smile uncomfortably and exeunt.)*

**CROWD:** Did yo' git dat look? Who dey t'ink dey is—'sociatin' wid decent colo'ed folks! White trash!

**1st GUEST:** De Manager oughta be keerful!

**MANAGER:** I'se sorry, people.

**2nd GUEST:** An' yo' oughta be. Ef dis happens agin, yo' stand to lose all yo' bes' customers.

**CROWD:** Dat's right!

**MANAGER:** It won't happen agin—I promise yo'. Yo' see, de doorman, he wasn't lookin'. He reckoned dey was colo'ed.

**3rd GUEST:** He's cockeyed! Why yo' have a bum lak dat 'round heah?

**4th GUEST:** Dat's it, 'Lizabeth! Lay him out!

**3rd GUEST:** Makes me boilin' mad—white trash in heah wid 'spectful colo'ed folks!

**MANAGER:** I'se awful sorry, people, but I tells yo' it won't happen agin . . . Have a drink on de house—come on, ev'ybody! I'll show yo' mah heart's in de right place! . . . Waiters, bring in de ve'y bes' yo' got! Music ovah dere—music! *(Music, drinking, dancing.* THE THIRD GUEST—*the amorous Negress—still holds her partner in firm embrace. . . . Suddenly, a loud bugle call is heard off.* THE MANAGER *crosses to the entrance and puts up his hand for silence. Music and dancing stop. The guests seated at the tables rise)*

**CROWD:** *(excitedly)* It's de Presiden'!—Jezzez, de Presiden's heah! Does I look a'right? *(Ties, vests, gowns, hair, faces are gone over)*

**MANAGER:** *(to the* FIRST WAITER*)* Ev'yt'ing ready?

**1st WAITER:** Yes, sir!

**MANAGER:** De gals in line?

**1st WAITER:** Yes, sir!

**MANAGER:** De Preacher heah?

**1st WAITER:** Yes, sir! *(Excited murmuring among the crowd. At the entrance,* THE MANAGER *stands on a chair and again holds up his hand)*

**MANAGER:** Ladies an' Gentlemen: Introdoocin' Praye'ful Johnson—de Presiden' o' de United States! *(THE MANAGER motions to the musicians off)* Nice, big chord, boys—come on, come on! *(The orchestra plays a fanfare of welcome. The crowd surges toward the entrance.* THE MANAGER *jumps down from the chair and pushes them back)* Stan' back, folks, stan' back! Give de Presiden' some room! Stan' back! *(To the musicians off)* Nodder chord, boys! *(Another fanfare from the orchestra, then the bugle, and* JOHNSON *enters—top hat, Prince Albert, cane, smiles, medals and all. He is* *the cynosure of all eyes. Applause, bows, courtsies. Handkerchiefs are waved)*

**CROWD:** Hurray fo' de Presiden'!—Hurray!

**MANAGER:** Dis is sho' a great honor, Mr. Presiden'! *(Indicating the special table)* Won't yo' have a seat?

**CROWD:** Speech!—Speech!

**JOHNSON:** *(clearing his throat)* Brodders an' sisters: *(Applause)* I'se glad to be wid yo' on dis great 'cassion. Yo'se mah people, an' I loves yo' all. *(Applause)* But yo' gotta 'cuse me dis evenin' f'om sayin' any mo', 'cause I got some 'portant matters on mah mind. T'ank yo' all, t'ank yo', an' Gawd bless yo'—ev'yone! *(Applause.* JOHNSON *sits down.* THE MANAGER *takes a box of cigars from* THE SECOND WAITER *and presents them to* JOHNSON. *He takes one, bits off the end, spits it out.* THE MANAGER *lights the cigar. Pause.* JOHNSON *smokes for a moment in silence. The crowd looks on)* Good cigar.

**MANAGER:** Oughta be, suh. It's a "Presiden' Johnson." *(*JOHNSON *puffs away. The crowd continues to gaze at him in respectful silence)*

**JOHNSON:** *(to the* MANAGER*)* De gals ready?

**MANAGER:** All ready, Mr. Presiden'.

**JOHNSON:** Where dey com f'om?

**MANAGER:** F'om George, Sout' Carolina, an' Alabama.

**JOHNSON:** Good-lookin'?

**MANAGER:** I couldn't find none better nowheres.

**JOHNSON:** Den le's go!

**MANAGER:** Right away, Mr. Presiden'! *(*THE MANAGER *motions off the musicians. They play. The crowd stands back.* THE MANAGER *crosses to the entrance and shouts)* Come on, come on! *(Then one after another, a dozen very personable Negro girls cross the scene—not unlike a beauty contest. They are all dressed in abbreviated dance costumes. Passing before* JOHNSON, *each girl turns completely around, like a modiste's model.* THE MANAGER *comments on his wares to their best advantage)* Nice hair, Mr. Presiden'! *(*JOHNSON *smokes, looks on critically, but he is noncommittal. Another girl appears. Again* THE MANAGER *supplies suitable praise)* Look, look at dat figure, will yo'! Ain't dey swell! *(The girl goes off. Still another enters)* Evah seen eyes lak dat? Look at dem legs—oh baby! Make any man happy! *(*JOHNSON *smokes in silence. The procession of girls* *continues. Presently,* THE WHITE PROSTITUTE—*the same woman as in Scene 7—enters like the rest.* JOHNSON *rises in sudden passion and knocks over his chair. Music stops. The guests, bewildered, look at one another.* THE MANAGER *is dismayed )* What's amatter, Mr. President'?

**JOHNSON:** *(furiously)* Dat woman's no good! Take her 'way! Take her 'way, damn yo'! *(*THE WHITE PROSTITUTE *is hurried off.)* What yo' mean bringin' her in heah?

**MANAGER:** I didn't know, suh—she's kinda goodlookin', an'—

**JOHNSON:** Goodlookin'—!

**MANAGER:** I t'ought de Presiden'—mebbe he lak white woman fo' change. Dey'se diff'ren'—

**JOHNSON:** *(with venom)* I hates 'em!

**MANAGER:** Yes, suh—I sees yo' does!

**JOHNSON:** I nevah wants to see 'nodder white woman, understan'?

**MANAGER:** Yes, suh.

**JOHNSON:** Dey cain't tell de trut'!

**MANAGER:** No, suh.

**JOHNSON:** *(bellowing)* Dey'se liars—liars, dey'se all damn liars! *(Pause.* JOHNSON *slowly sits down again. The Negro guests, intimidated by this outburst, stand about with open mouths)*

**MANAGER:** *(timidly)* Mr. Presiden'! *(No answer)* Mr. Presiden'!

**JOHNSON:** *(surlily, without looking up)* What yo' want?

**MANAGER:** Lemme show yo' de rest o' de gals. Dey'se good and dark—extra fancy—an' dey'se sho beautiful. *(*JOHNSON *does not answer.* THE MANAGER, *taking his silence for assent, motions to the musicians off. The same tune is played and more girls enter— all Negresses.* JOHNSON *hardly notices them. Then* BURNTSIENNA HAWK- INS—*the black prostitute of scene 7—now unbelievably lovely in her dance costume, passes across the scene like her predecessors.* JOHNSON *sits up, watches her intently; he smiles. She smiles in turn.* JOHNSON *rises. The orchestra plays pianissimo and then stops. The crowd looks on with greatest interest)*

**JOHNSON:** Say, ain't yo' Burn'sienna—Burnsienna Hawk- ins?

**BURNTSIENNA:** *(slowly revolving like a model)* Dat's me! An' ain't yo', Mr. Johnson?

**JOHNSON:** Dat's right! I ain't seen yo' fo' long time. How yo' been gittin' 'long?

**BURNTSIENNA:** Fine an' dandy. How 'bout yo'?

**JOHNSON:** Oh, I'se a'right. . . . Say, Burn'sienna—

**BURNTSIENNA:** Yes, Mr. Johnson?

**JOHNSON:** Is yo' pure now?

**BURNTSIENNA:** Sho' I'se pure. When I makes a promise, I keeps it.

**JOHNSON:** *(after a pause)* Yo' know—yo' know, I been T'inkin' lot 'bout 'yo.

**BURNTSIENNA:** *(smiling)* Yeah? I'se glad.

**JOHNSON:** Yo' is?

**BURNTSIENNA:** Sho', 'cause I been t'inkin' lot 'bout yo'.

**JOHNSON:** *(after another pause)* Livin' 'lone, Burn'sienna?

**BURNTSIENNA:** Yeah, all 'lone, Mr. Johnson.

**JOHNSON:** Dat's good. . . . Say, don't yo' nevah git lonely, spendin' de time all by yo'self?

**BURNTSIENNA:** Sometimes.

**JOHNSON:** What 'bout me helpin' yo' fill in yo' time?

**BURNTSIENNA:** Dat's kiddin', ain't it?

**JOHNSON:** No, it ain't. . . . Burn'sienna, yo' sho' looks good to me. I laks yo'—ev'y bit o' yo'. How does I look to yo'? *(He turns completely around)*

**BURNTSIENNA:** Mighty swell, big boy!

**JOHNSON:** I got somet'in serious to say to yo'?

**BURNTSIENNA:** Yeah?

**JOHNSON:** Evah read de Bible, Burn'sienna?

**BURNTSIENNA:** Why yo' ask me dat?

**JOHNSON:** De Lawd said to de chillun o' Israel, "Be fruitful an' multiply." I wants yo' to help me, Burn'sienna.

**BURNTSIENNA:** I'se a powe'ful good helper, Mr. Johnson.

**JOHNSON:** I wants yo' to marry me.

**BURNTSIENNA:** Marry yo'? Hell, I didn't know yo' means dat!

**JOHNSON:** Sho' I means it. What yo' say?

**BURNTSIENNA:** Well—

**JOHNSON:** Yeah?

**BURNTSIENNA:** Ef yo' was somebody else I'd say to yo', "Big Boy, be yo'self; Burnsienna's a free woman."

**JOHNSON:** But I ain't nobody else, Burn'sienna.

**BURNTSIENNA:** Den I say—

**JOHNSON:** What yo' say?

**BURNTSIENNA:** Yo' cain't turn de Presiden' down! (JOHNSON *puts his arm around* BURNTSIENNA)

**JOHNSON:** Honey gal! *(The embrace.* JOHNSON *turns to* THE MANAGER) Call de preacher—right 'way!

**MANAGER:** Yes, suh—right dis minute! *(Murmur among the crowd)*

**CROWD:** Dat's sweet, it sho' is!—She's de bes' lookin' o' de lot! She's a beaut! Smart li'le gal!—Dey'll make a fine couple!

**MANAGER:** *(at the entrance)* Rev'rend! Rev'rend! Come on in! Dey's waiting!

**3rd GUEST:** Hurray fo' de President' an' his woman!

**CROWD:** Hurray! Hurray!

**MANAGER:** Come on, Rev'rend! Make 'er snappy! (THE PREACHER *enters. He is the same Negro as* THE SECOND CRAP SHOOTER, *but he now wears a long ministerial coat, a proper collar, and carries a book. The talking among the crowd subsides. The musicians off play very softly)*

**JOHNSON:** I wanna git married right off.

**PREACHER:** Dat's mah speciality. *(turning to* BURNTSIENNA*)* An' dis is de fo'tunate young lady?

**JOHNSON:** Yeah, an' dis is de fo'tunate young man.

**PREACHER:** I'se mighty happy to heah dat de Presiden's gonna settle down fo' life. Yo'see, when de Presiden' does it, de odder folks dey'se anxious to do de same. An' dat's 'xac'ly what de Lawd wants.

**JOHNSON:** Better hurry up, Rev'rend. I'se a busy man.

**PREACHER:** I'se a-hurryin' all I kin. Yo' cain't push dese heah matters none, Mr. Presiden'. . . . Yo' got a ring? *(JOHNSON searches his pockets)*

**JOHNSON:** Where'd I put it? Doggone, I knows I had one! . . . Cain't we have de weddin' widout it? I'll git yo' nice one tomorrer.

**PREACHER:** No, suh, we cain't have no ceremony widout a ring. It's 'gainst de rules.

**MANAGER:** *(advancing)* Heah, yo' take mine, Mr. Presiden'. I ain't got no use fo' it no mo'.

**JOHNSON:** Yo' sho'?

**MANAGER:** Yeah, I doesn't 'spect to git married agin. I learned 'nough f'om mah firs' wife to las' till de trumpet blows. . . . Take it, Mr. Presiden'. (JOHNSON *takes the ring*)

**PREACHER:** Yo' want de long ceremony or de short one? De short cost mo'.

**JOHNSON:** *(Looking at* BURNTSIENNA*)* De shorter de better, Rev'rend!

**PREACHER:** I'll give yo' de ve'y bes' I has. . . . Take yo' hat off. (JOHNSON *does so*) Now put de ring on de bride. (THE PREACHER *opens the book*) Mr. Praye'ful Johnson, look at de bride; bride, look at de bridegroom. Mr. Prayeful Johnson, does yo' take dis heah woman to be yo' lawful wed' wife, to love her an' cherish her jes' as long as you kin?

**JOHNSON:** I sho' does.

**PREACHER:** Miss Burn'sienna Hawkins, does yo' take dis heah man to be yo' lawful wed' husban', to love him all de res' o' yo' life?

**BURNTSIENNA:** I does.

**PREACHER:** Den, yo'se married. Amen!

**CROWD:** Amen!

**PREACHER:** Dat's all dere is to it. Now I kisses de bride. Now yo' kin kiss togedder. (THE CROWD *murmur their approbation. The music stops*)

**JOHNSON:** Burn'sienna—

**BURNTSIENNA:** Yeah, Praye'ful?

**JOHNSON:** Burn'sienna, I feels lak I was in heaben, settin' on de right side o' Gawd! *(They kiss again and embrace)*

**CROWD:** Hallelujan!—Hurray fo' de firs' lady in de land!— Long libe de Presiden' an' his wife!—Hurray! (THE PREACHER *stands on a table and shouts*)

**PREACHER:** Come on, folks! Le's all sing, "De Right Side o' Gawd!" Ready le's go! (THE PREACHER *beats time while the crowd sing jubilantly—widout accompaniment—swaying in the rhythm of the song. Then, led by* JOHNSON *and his bride, and still singing,* THE CROWD *circle in couples in and out around the tables in grotesque processional)*

**ALL:** *(sing)*

De right side o' Gawd, de right side o' Gawd—
We'se settin', settin' purtty on de right side o' Gawd;
De right side o' Gawd, de right side of Gawd—
We'se settin', settin' purtty on de right side o' Gawd.
    Waters cain't drown us, an' fires cain't burn,
      De guns dey cain't shoot us, an' ropes cain't hang—oh
        no, Lawd!
    De right side o' Gawd, de right side o' Gawd,
    We'se settin', settin' purrty—

*(Suddenly, a terrific smash is heard off, as though a door were being smashed in. Instantly the singing stops. Everyone freezes in an attitude of fear. The lights begin to dim.)*

**JOHNSON:** *(Motionless)* What's dat? Who's dere?

**BURNTSIENNA:** I'se 'fraid! I'se 'fraid!

**MANAGER:** Jeesez, It's de cops! Quick, git dat licker!

**CROWD:** *(motionless)* It's de cops! *(Another loud smash. No one moves. The lights go out. Screaming in the darkness. Then* JOHNSON'S *voice is heard.)*

**JOHNSON:** Burn'sienna—Burn'sienna! Where is yo'? Burn'sienna! Don't yo' be 'fraid! Dey cain't hurt yo' none. I'se de Presiden' heah! I'se a friend o' de Lawd's! . . . Burn'sienna! *(Pistol shots, then the shouting of the lynch mob. The shouting becomes louder and more distinct.)*

**SHOUTING:** "Kill him!"—"Kill the God-damn nigger!"— "Git out o' this, Sheriff, or you'll git hurt!"—"Where is them keys?—Fork 'em over!"—"We're gonna git that black son-of-a-bitch!"—"Kill Him!"—"Burn the bastard!" "Burn him!"

## SCENE 10

*Darkness. The cries of the lynch mob become still louder—frenzied, insane. Gradually the prison cell is discovered in vague evening light. Through the grated window high in the wall can be seen an uncertain reddish glow.* JOHNSON *stands centre; he is again dishevelled, dressed in rags.*

**JOHNSON:** Burn'sienna! . . . She ain't heah! . . . Burn'sienna. . . . Dat's a'right. Dey cain't hurt her none. Dey cain't hurt me, no suh. Mah feet's got wings, dey has. I'se de Lawd's man. *(The shuffle of running feet is heard off. Then confused forms are visible in the corridor beyond the steel door. Furious pounding off.)* Keep 'way f'om me, white trash, keep 'way! I'se de Lawd's man—de Lawd's man! . . . Where is de Lawd—where is He? I ain't seen Him fo' long time! . . . Is yo' dere, Lawd? I needs yo' bad! Lawd, it's Praye'ful Johnson! . . . Lawd, is yo' dere? *(*JOHNSON *speaks louder and louder, until he is almost shrieking. He falls to his knees, stretches out his arms. Pause. The noise of the lynch mob recedes, then stops. The Lord's light appears, shining on* JOHNSON. *And the deep voice is heard again, as from afar:)* I is, Johnson!

**JOHNSON:** (smiling) Yo' always where I wants yo', Lawd. I'se a-comin' up to yo' now, Lawd. I'se tired o' dis heah place. You see Lawd, you and me's got a lot of plannin' to do. Things ain't goin' good at all down here, Lawd. You and me's got to start all over on dis business.

**VOICE:** Come on up, Johnson. You and me's got to have a long talk. *(*JOHNSON, *looking upward ecstatically, slowly rises. As the Lord's light dims out, Negro voices are heard off, singing very softly. "De right side o' Gawd." Then the shouting of the lynch mob; the shouting increases and the singing is no longer heard. From the corridor several voices suddenly shout above the rest of the mob)*

**VOICES IN THE MOB:** There he is! There's the nigger. Smash that door. Come on boys, smash it. *(The cell door is broken in. Part of the lynch mob pours into the cell)*

**VOICES:** Burn the black bastard! He'll touch a white woman, will he! Kill him! Burn the nigger! Burn him! *(*JOHNSON *is beaten to the floor, then the mob drags him off. Again the receding cries blend with the distant singing of the Negro chorus. The cell is empty. The red flow through the window is transmuted into a whirling flame of crimson and yellow—the fire from the stake. The noise of crackling wood. On the opposite wall, the bar of the cell window throws an elongated shadow of a cross against a background of flame. Suddenly, a rapid succession of revolver shots, then a scream. Then instant silence . . . and a shadow on the wall, and then darkness.)*

(Curtain)

# Langston Hughes
## (1902–1967)
▼▼▼▼▼▼▼▼▼▼▼▼

Langston Hughes had a special relationship with Karamu Theatre. Born in St. Louis, Hughes early in life moved to Cleveland, where he attended Karamu programs and classes; after he left Ohio, he kept in touch with the director, Rowena Jelliffe, and the Gilpin Players, who produced a number of his plays, including the premieres of *When the Jack Hollars* [sic] (1936), *Troubled Island* (1936), and *Joy to My Soul*. In an interview with Reuben Silver of Karamu, Hughes said:

> It is a cultural shame that a great country like America, with twenty million people of color, has no primarily serious colored theatre. There isn't. Karamu is the very nearest thing to it.
>
> My feeling is not only should a Negro theatre, if we want to use that term, do plays by and about Negroes, but it should do plays slanted toward the community in which it exists. It should be in a primarily Negro community since that is the way our racial life in America is still. . . . It should not be a theatre that should be afraid to do a Negro folk play about people who are perhaps not very well-educated because some of the intellectuals, or "intellectuals" in quotes, are ashamed of such material[1]

By 1940, according to Hughes's biographer Arnold Rampersad, "Langston consigned all his skits and sketches, divided into three classes—Negro Social, Negro Non-Social, and white—to his agent, who had alerted him that Cafe Society, a novel interracial cabaret founded in New York by Barney Josephson, was planning a revue. Hughes sent twenty skits, collectively titled *Run, Ghost, Run.*" He also sent a copy to Karamu; there is no record that the revue was staged there or anywhere. Three of those skits appear here in print for the first time, and these three may have been produced by the Suitcase Theatre, a group which he and Louise Patterson had formed in Harlem. Although *Don't You Want to Be Free?* was always the main attraction at the Suitcase Theatre (135 performances), at different times Hughes added to the program a short satirical skit: *Limitations of Life*, or *Little Eva*, as well as those appearing in this volume.

In the 1930s, Hughes saw theatre as a tool for social change, one benefiting not only African Americans, but all poor people. A glance at the provocative anthology *Good Morning Revolution* (1973), edited by Faith Berry, will remind the reader how radical Hughes was. Even as late as 1961, he had not given up his vision that theatre could make a difference in the real world. He told Reuben Silver at Karamu:

"I don't see why it [theatre] couldn't have such agit-prop plays if one wanted them or needed them. . . . writers are starting to realize that there are so many social problems that need to be stated forcefully and strongly, and social material has not been fashionable since the McCarthy era because it has been dangerous to use it. But I think now, there is a going into it again." While he was in Los Angeles in 1961, he attended the "sit-in" musical *Fly, Blackbird* and praised its revolutionary spirit.

As the Great Depression transformed the Art Theatre Movement into one of social dramas and leftist politics, Hughes wrote the four plays in this section. Though he put them in circulation in 1938, the skits stem from earlier inspirations. *Scarlet Sister Barry* originates from a Pulitzer Prize novel *Scarlet Sister Mary* (1928). H. L. Mencken had advised the author, a white southern woman named Julia Peterkin, to refuse the Pulitzer because the fiction committee was "entirely devoid of critical talent and ability." She, of course, accepted the prize. In a 1930 adaption of the Peterkin novel by Daniel Reed, Ethel Barrymore appeared on Broadway in blackface to play Mary, a "scarlet" Negro woman who bears eight illegitmate children. Rose McClendon, star of

*Porgy* (1927), kept a scrapbook of all the scathing reviews, which she shared with Hughes. He may have written his satire shortly after, but he apparently did not circulate his sketch until later.

*Scarlet Sister Barry* presents a famous white actress whose face is made-up half-black, half-white. The setting is the "Realm of Art." In a few short pages, Hughes lashes Ethel Barrymore's performance, and he even gets in a dig or two at *Showboat* (1927).

*The Em-Fuehrer Jones* is the happy confluence of a satire of Eugene O'Neill's *The Emperor Jones* (1920), and Hitler's embarrassment at Jesse Owens's triumph over the Aryan race at the Berlin Olympics in 1936. Two years later, Joe Louis floored the German boxer Max Schmeling three times in the first round of the world's heavyweight boxing match. Other contemporary references include the Yorkville marches of the German-American Bund, the communists, and the Jews.

*[America's] Young Black Joe*, although interspersed with dialog, is basically a song. On March 22, 1941, Hughes wrote Arna Bontemps: "Young Black Joe" is my favorite work after 20 years of creating! So I want to see it get launched in the world. His frequent comments in letters to Bontemps confirm his enthusiasm. "'Young Black Joe,' our song is catching on all over the South. Fisk has asked to use it for commencement." Later, he wrote, "I just got a letter from [Melvin] Tolson, too, saying 'America's Young Black Joe,' is to be sung all over down there." Again, he wrote, "You didn't by any chance hear 'Young Black Joe' sung anywhere down South, did you? Letters tell me it is getting around. And Robbins is now interested in publishing it. Hope that goes through."[2] It didn't. Music publisher Edward B. Marks turned it down, too. After the war and Joe Louis's eventual loss of the world's heavyweight boxing crown, the song and the skit became "lost" to Americans.[3]

In Paris in August of 1938, Hughes began to write *The Organizer (De Organizer), A Blues Opera in One Act*, an anthem dedicated to organizing the Black cotton pickers of the South. James P. Johnson would compose the music. (The score, except for "The Hungry Blues," has been lost). The opera, much like Clifford Odet's *Waiting for Lefty*, begins with workers waiting for the Organizer, the man who will lead the sharecroppers out of deadly and deadening physical slavery and its dire poverty. Mid-play, the Organizer arrives, bringing his message. The Overseer attempts to break up the meeting.

*The Organizer* was performed at Carnegie Hall in 1940 as part of an International Ladies' Garment Workers Union convention, which may have been its solo stage production. CBS then considered it for a radio production, but finally stated that it was "too controversial for us to give it an emotional treatment on an essentially dramatic show."

## NOTES

1. James V. Hatch and Leo Hamalian, eds., "Langston Hughes, Playwright. Interview by Reuben and Dorothy Silver, 1961," *Artist and Influence* XIII (New York: Hatch Billops Collection, Inc., 1994).

2. Charles H. Nichols, ed., *Arna Bontemps/Langston Hughes Letters 1925–1967* (New York: Dodd, Mead, 1980).

3. The name of Charles Leonard appears on the script as the co-author.

## REFERENCES

Hatch, James V., and Leo Hamalian, eds. "Langston Hughes, Playwright. Interview by Reuben and Dorothy Silver, 1961." *Artist and Influence* XIII. New York: Hatch-Billops Collection, Inc., 1994.

Rampersad, Arnold. *The Life of Langston Hughes.* Vol. I. New York: Oxford University Press, 1986.

# SCARLET SISTER BARRY

## Langston Hughes

CAST

### ONE ACTRESS AND HER VOICES

*Time:* Oh!
*Place:* Realm of Art

*The scene is a velvet back drop.* THE ACTRESS, *who is blond and pale on one side, brown-skin and colored on the other, in race and make-up half and half, emerges from the center folds of the curtain, her white side foremost. She strikes a posture.*

**ACTRESS:**

Dear public: In my time
I've played everything
From Juliette to the Twelve Pound Look—
Now I want to play a Negress
From a Pulitzer Prize book.
Of course, you know it runs the danger
Of being slightly declassé,
But the First Lady of Our Theatre

By permission of Harold Ober Associates and the estate of Langston Hughes.

Has a right to do just what she may.
I've visited the South, of course,
A day or two at a time—
So my Negro dialect naturally
Is perfectly sublime.
Thus, as Scarlet Sister Mary,
I now propose to show
How the First Lady of this Stage portrays
Even a Negro.
Listen:

*(Singing as she turns her dark side to the audience)*
Way down upon de
Swanee Ribber!
*(Steamboat whistle)*
Oh, river! Ah hear his gentle voice calling me, Lula Mae!—
Cherio, Lula Mae!—His voice says, Lula Mae, Lula Mae, here's
July!

July de 4th? says I.
Naw, your husband, July.
What do you want, July? says I.
You know what I want, honey.
Un-huh! You been gwine—gone—going-go—gone too
long, July.
Ah ain't been no whar but down de ribber, honey.
*(Steamboat whistle. She sings)*
Way down upon de Swanee Ribber!
But July, me, your little Bright Skin's been waitin' for you.
You got a dark way of showing it.
*(As she half turns around)*
You two-faced hussy!
Oh, July!
You betrayed me while I been away, Lula Mae!
*(Whistle)*
But you left too soon, July. You didn't even wait to see if our
chile would be a little blond or a little brunette.
What did you name our chile, Lula Mae?
I didn't name it after you, that's shure!
Who did you name it after, then?
I named him after his father.

Who was his father?

You think I'd a-named him what I did if I'd a-knowed who his father were?

What did you name him, Lula Mae?

I named him—Mark.

Mark who?

Question Mark!

*(Cymbals)*

Lawd-a-mercy, Lula Mae! I'm goin' away agin.

*(Whistle)*

Cherio, July!

*(Singing)*

You're ole Man Ribber,

So jest keep rollin' along!

*(She waves farewell. The curtain falls and rises to great applause off stage.* THE ACTRESS *finishes acting and turns her white side to the audience again. She bows profusely)*

Thank you, folks! Thank you! The Greatest Lady of Our Theatre thanks you.

*(Moving toward the wings she recites)*

Now, in my role of Scarlet Sister Barry,

I've proven I could show

How a great artiste like me portrays

Even the Negro!

Goodbye! . . . Goodbye!

(Curtain)

# YOUNG BLACK JOE

## Langston Hughes

### and

## Charles Leonard

CAST

> JOE
> TRAINER
> A NAZI REPORTER
> REPORTERS

> *Place:* Interior of a prize fighter's dressing room. Lockers, rub-down table, bench.
> *Curtain:* In the darkness sound of bell ringing as cheers of boxing audience die down. Over the mike the voice of THE ANNOUNCER is heard.

**ANNOUNCER:** The winner—Joe Louis! *(Wild cheers from crowd. Light go up and* YOUNG BLACK JOE *followed by his* TRAINER, MANAGERS, *and a crowd of* REPORTERS, *enters his dressing room. Babble of voices as reporters with note books try to get a statement from* JOE*)*

> **REPORTERS:**

> Another knockout!
> Boy, what you did to that Fritz!

By permission of Harold Ober Associates and the estate of Langston Hughes.

What do you say about this one?
How was he—a pushover this time?
Who are you going to fight next—another Heinie?
C'mon, Joe, give us some copy.
Yes, c'mon. We got to make the early edition.

**REPORTER:** What's your statement, Joe?
**JOE:** Just another lucky night.
**REPORTER:** Ah, c'mon. Say more than that.
**NAZI:** You can't expect an African to talk. Hitler was right when he says in *Mein Kampf* only Aryans have brains.
**JOE:** Huh? What you mean, Mister?
**NAZI:** As a reporter for the Berlin *Taggeblatt*, I might waste a few words on you in my cable. What's your name?
**JOE:** Who?
**NAZI:** Don't you understand nothing? Your name.
**JOE:** Joe.
**NAZI:** Oh, Old Black Joe! (*NAZI laughs curt laugh*)
**JOE:** You got me wrong, Mister. (*His talk flows gently into a song*)

Why, don't you know—
I'm America's young black Joe.
Most times good natured, smiling and gay,
Sky is sometimes cloudy, but it can't stay that way.
"I'm comin', I'm comin'"
But my head *ain't* bendin' low.
I'm walking proud, I'm speaking outloud—
America's Young Black Joe!

(*REPORTERS get busy with their note books, taking down his words as the NAZI, in high dudgeon, glares at JOE a moment and walks out. The others grin an encourage JOE to go on as one cries out in amazement*)
**REPORTER:** Boys, Joe's talking.
**TRAINER:** Preach it, Joe, and I'll say "Amen." (*JOE continues his song*)
**JOE:**

This is my own, my native land
And I'm mighty glad that's true.
Land where my fathers worked

The same as yours worked, too.
So from every mountain side
Let freedom's bright torch glow—
Standing hand in hand with democracy,
I'm America's Young Black Joe.
*(He speaks to the music)*
Now, you-all keep your notebooks out
And take down some names I know.
I don't want you to think I'm the only one—
Even if I am Young Joe.
There's Henry Armstrong, three titles to his name,
Beat everybody his size in the fighting game.
For in sports it's blow to blow
With America's Young Black Joe.
In the stadium Kenny Washington in a football suit—
Run, pass, kick, tackle, and block to boot.
For on the gridiron I've got plenty to show—
Has America's Young Black Joe.
Don't forget the track men like Ellerbee—
Who runs "up North" for Tuskegee.
And Jessie Owens with his laurel wreath
Certainly made old Hitler grit his teeth.
Man! Look at those dark boys streaking by,
Feet just flying and heads held high!
Looky yonder at Metcalf! Edwards!
Johnson! Toland! Down the field they go!
Swift and proud before the crowd—
America's Young Black Joe!
*(He turns to the* REPORTERS*)*
Now, I ain't trying to boast nor nothing like that,
But I just want to tell you what I know for fact.

**REPORTERS:**

That's right, Joe!
O.K., boy!
You're talking democracy now!

**TRAINER:** Lincoln said, "Of the people, for the people, and by the people!" Yes, he did! (JOE *steps forward as the curtains* *close leaving the crowd behind them.* JOE *stands alone in his bronze manhood and manliness)*

**JOE:**

I'm America's young black Joe.
Manly, good natured, smiling and gay,
Sky sometimes cloudy, can't stay that way.
"I'm comin', yes, I'm comin'."
*(Spoken out of the past)*
I ain't forgot you, slavery-time folks, way back
younder in them days before the war. I know how
you bore them slavery chains. I know how you
struggled. I know what freedom meant to you. Now,
I'm gonna guard it!
*(sings)*
So my head *ain't* bendin' low!
I'm walking proud, speaking up outloud—
America's Young Black Joe.

# THE ORGANIZER
## A Blues Opera in One Act

JAMES P. JOHNSON AND
LANGSTON HUGHES


CAST

> THE ORGANIZER, *Baritone*
> THE WOMAN, *Contralto*
> THE OLD MAN, *Bass*
> THE OLD WOMAN, *Soprano*
> BROTHER DOSHER, *Tenor*
> BROTHER BATES, *Tenor*
> THE OVERSEER, *Bass*

> *Place:* Interior of a cabin on the backward plantation in the South. Night. Lanterns and flashlights. The room is full of ragged sharecroppers, men and women.

**WOMEN:** Where is that man?
**MEN:** He ought to be here now!
**CHORUS:** De organizer! Organizer!
**WOMEN:** Where is that man?
**MEN:** He ought to be here now!
**CHORUS:**

De organizer! Organizer!

By permission of Harold Ober Associates and the estate of Langston Hughes.

Where is that man? He ought to be here now!

**OLD WOMAN:** Brother Dosher, it's gettin' late.
**DOSHER:** Sit down, sister, you got to wait.
**OLD WOMAN:**

Brother, I'm tired o' waitin'.
He ought to be here now.

**DOSHER:**

You might be tired o' waitin'
But we's got to wait anyhow!
You didn't get your freedom in a day.
We can't get a union by hurryin' this a way.

**OLD WOMAN:** Well, then, where is that man?
**CHORUS:** He ought to be here now.
**BATES:** Yes, where is that man?
**CHORUS:** He ought to be here now.
**BATES:**

Organizing a union is all right,
But damn if I can organize all night!

**OLD WOMAN:** Yes, where is that man?
**CHORUS:**

He ought to be here now!
The good Lawd knows,
He ought to be here now.

**BATES:** Yes, he ought to be here now!
**DOSHER:**

Don't worry! He'll be here.
He's a sharecropper, too,
Just like me and you.

**OLD MAN:** Sharecroppers!
**OLD WOMAN:** Sharecroppers! . . . Oh!
**CHORUS:**

Plantin', plowin', hoein'!
Gettin' up early in de mornin'.
Plowin', plantin', hoein'!
Out in de fields at dawnin'.

Always watchin' cotton growin'.
Plowin', plantin', hoein'!
Wonder where that cotton's goin'?
Plantin', plowin', hoein'!
Wonder where my life is goin'?
Plowin', plantin', hoein',
Wonder where my life is goin'?

**OLD MAN:**

Just poor sharecroppers,
That's all we is:

**CHORUS:** Plantin', plowin', hoein'!
**DOSHER:**

Just poor sharecroppers, yes!
But we ain't gonna be always.
We gonna get together
and end these hongry days.
Folks, I've got them hongry blues—
And nothin' in this world to lose.
People's tellin' me to choose
    'Tween dyin',
      And lyin',
        And keepin' on my cryin'—
But I's tired o' them hongry blues.
Listen! Ain't you heard de news?
There's another thing to choose:
A brand new world, clean and fine,
Where nobody's hongry and
There's no color line!
A thing like that's worth
Anybody's dyin'—
Cause I ain't got a thing to lose
But them dog-gone hongry blues!

**OLD WOMAN:**

I done washed so many clothes
My hands is white as snow.
Done got to de place that I
Don't want to wash no more.

I'm goin' up to heaven,
Say, good Lawd, here am I!

**BATES:**

But, Sister Mary, de Lawd's gonna say:
You can't come in here till you die.

**CHORUS:** You can't come in here till you die!
**OLD WOMAN:** Well, I've got them hongry blues.
**CHORUS:** But nothin' in this world to lose!
**DOSHER:**

Folks, ain't you heard de news.
There's another thing to choose:
A brand new world, clean and fine,
Where nobody's hongry and
There's no color line—
A thing like that's worth
Anybody's dyin'—

**CHORUS:**

Cause we ain't got a thing to lose
But them dog-gone hongry blues!

**OLD WOMAN:** Where is that man? He ought to be here
now.
**OLD MAN:** Yes, where is that man?
**BATES:** Where is that man?
**OLD MAN:** Maybe I better go and take a look once more.
**DOSHER:** Shade de light, brother, 'fore you open de door.
**OLD WOMAN:** Yes, shade that light, so's the boss won't
see.
**BATES:** And when you hits de pike, walk quietly.
**OLD MAN:**

I'll walk quietly.
But that man, which way'll he come?
From de East or from de West?

**DOSHER:**

He's comin' from de West,
Where de Union's best.

*(A* WOMAN'S *voice giving the password outside)*
    **WOMAN:** Jerico!. . . . Jerico!
    **CHORUS:** Shsss-sss-ss-s! Who can that be?
    **WOMAN:** Jerico!
    **DOSHER:** One!
    **WOMAN:** Jerico!
    **DOSHER:** Two!
    **WOMAN:** Jerico!
    **DOSHER:**

Three!
Then she's due to be!
Open de door, let's see.

*(The* OLD MAN *opens the door. The* WOMAN *enters, bringing leaflets.)*
    **WOMAN:** Folks, it's me!
    **DOSHER:**

Yes, she's due to be!
She brings us news about that man.
And something here for us in her hand.

    **CHORUS:** Strange woman, where is that man?
    **OLD WOMAN:** That organizing man?
    **CHORUS:** Yes, where is that man?
    **WOMAN:**

That man is comin' by a secret way.
That man is comin' all alone.
That man is like Little David
What threw that mighty stone—
Cause he's de organizer!

    **CHORUS:** He's de organizer! He's de organizer!
    **WOMAN:**

That man, he travels on de wings of song.
He travels on de air.
He travels like a cloud by night.
That man is everywhere—
Cause he's de organizer!

    **CHORUS:** He's de organizer! Organizer!

**WOMAN:**

He's gonna help us build a union,
Build it of white and black,
Cause de people that works in de fields all day
Is tired of de landlords on our back.

**CHORUS:** Yes, we's tired of de landlords on our backs.
**WOMAN:**

Folks, I bring you leaflets!
Folks, read 'em well.
This little bit of paper here's
Got a lot to tell.
It says:
Ten thousand bales of cotton to de landlord!
How much was ours?
Ten thousand acres of cane to de big boss!
How much was ours?
How can we get them things
That should be ours?
Here, take this little leaflet, folks,
And read it well.
This little bit of paper's got
A lot to tell.

**OLD MAN:** What does it say?
**CHORUS:** How can we get them things that should be ours?
**OLD WOMAN:** Which is de way?
**BATES:**

Them things we plant and plow and hoe for
Underneath these southern skies?

**DOSHER:** How can we make a living?
**WOMAN:** Organize!
**CHORUS:** Organize! . . . Organize!
**OLD WOMAN:** This here little leaflet says, Organize!
**CHORUS:**

Organize! . . . Organize!
O–R–G–A—N–I–Z–E!
O–R–G–A—N–I–Z–E!

**OLD MAN:** Who ever wrote this paper sure must be wise!

**CHORUS:** Cause this here little leaflet says ORGANIZE!

**OLD WOMAN:** But where is our man?

**BATES:** Yes, where is that man?

**OLD MAN:** Maybe something's happened to our man?

**OLD WOMAN:** Woman, now you tell us where is that man?

**WOMAN:**

He'll be here soon.
He travels on de air.

**DOSHER:**

He travels like a cloud by night.
That man is everywhere.

**WOMAN:** He'll be here.

**OLD WOMAN:** He's your man?

**WOMAN:** Yes, he's my man. I love him, too.

**OLD WOMAN:** But ain't you scared for your man? Ain't you?

**WOMAN:**

No, he'll be here soon. He's coming to you.
He's helping us all. And I can't be selfish
About him. Of course, sometimes I miss him because
My man's an organizer.
My man's an organizer.
He moves from place to place.
I guess I wouldn't be human
If I didn't miss his loving face.
So I admit:
Sometimes I'm lonely when he's gone away,
But I keep thinking there will come a day.
When this man of mine will do
All the things he's wanted to,
And the better world he's dreamed of will come true.
Then what will it matter all these
Days we've spent apart,
There'll be a future bright with joy
Blooming in my heart,

All the poor folks in the world
Will be poor no more,
For my man's an organizer and
That's what he's working for.
And although I'm lonely when he's gone away from me,
Tomorrow he'll be with me and tomorrow we'll be free,
You and I, my man and me, we'll be free!

**OLD WOMAN:**

I believes you. You sure do love 'im.
But when's he comin' here.

**OLD MAN:** We can't wait! It's gettin' late!
**BATES:** We got to go. Where is that man?
**WOMAN:** Listen! (*A* MAN'S *voice heard without giving the password*)
**ORGANIZER:** Jerico! . . . Jerico!
**DOSHER:** Now, I reckon you'll stay.
**BATES:** Yes, I'll stay! Get out o' my way.
**ORGANIZER:** Jerico!
**DOSHER:** One!
**ORGANIZER:** Jerico!
**DOSHER:** Two!
**ORGANIZER:** Jerico!
**DOSHER:**

Three!
It's de organizer! Glory be!

**CHORUS:**

It's de organizer! Yes, it's he!
It's de organizer! Thank God a-Mighty!
It's de organizer! Lawd! De Organizer!
Thank God a-Mighty! It's de organizer!

(*The door opens and the* ORGANIZER *enters*)
**DOSHER:** Jackson, where you been so long?
**ORGANIZER:** I been organizing.
**DOSHER:** Where you been organizing?
**ORGANIZER:** Been way cross Mississippi organizing.
**DOSHER:** Who you been organizing?

**ORGANIZER:**

I been organizing black folks!
And organizing white folks!
And organizing peoples on de land!
I been tellin' everybody
In de cotton and de cane fields,
Been tellin' everybody they's a man!

**OLD MAN:** And de white folks, what they sayin'?
**ORGANIZER:**

De poor white folks is with us.
De rich white folks is mad.

**WOMAN:** But, baby, how you feelin'?
**ORGANIZER:** Lawd, I'm feelin' mighty glad!
**CHORUS:** Mighty glad! Mighty glad!
**ORGANIZER:** Oh, I'm feelin' mighty glad! (*As he mounts
to a box to speak*)
**CHORUS:**

De organizer's here and
We's feelin' mighty glad!
Mighty glad! Mighty glad!
Yes, de organizer's here and
We feelin' mighty glad!

(Mighty glad! Mighty glad! *continues softly as the* WOMAN *lifts her
voice in praise and love*)
**WOMAN:**

Oh! Ma man is like John Henry.
Ma man is big and strong.
Nothin' in this world can scare him.
Nothin' makes my man do wrong.
Yes, ma man is like John Henry.
He's a hero in de land.
And folks deep in troubles
Comes lookin' for ma man.
Yes, they comes lookin' for ma man,
Cause ma man is like John Henry 'cept he's
Put his hammer down.
Now, just like John Henry, he

Goes from town to town.
Oh! Ma man is like John Henry, but he
Don't drive steel no more.
What ma man is doin' now is
Organizin' de poor—
And when he gets done organizin' we
Can take this world in hand.
Cause ma man is like John Henry and
John Henry was a man!

**CHORUS:**

John Henry was a man, Lawd!
John Henry was a man!

**ORGANIZER:**

Folks, you is hongry!
Folks, you need bread!
What you gonna do, folks?

**CHORUS:** Get mad! Get mad!
**ORGANIZER:**

Folks, that ain't de way!
Folks, that ain't right.
The way to get what we all need's
Unite! . . . Unite!
You don't get mad at de rain, do you?
You don't get mad at de sun?
Ain't no use to get mad then
At a big boss with a gun!
De rain you stores in cisterns.
De sun gives de berries their juice.
De union can take any old boss
And turn him every way but loose!
When we got a big strong union, folks,
A union of black and white,
There'll be more difference in this old South
Then there is twixt day and night.
So to organize is right!

**CHORUS:** Yes, to organize is right!

**ORGANIZER:**

Sharecroppers all over Dixie,
Farmhands and tenants as well,
De union is de only way
To free ourselves from hell.

**CHORUS:**

To free ourselves from hell!
Yes, to free ourselves from hell!

**ORGANIZER:**

Then Brother Dosher, take de chair,
And let's get de meetin' started here.

**OLD WOMAN:** Yes, let's get de meetin' started here.
**OLD MAN:**

Brother Dosher, I wants de floor.
I has a word to say.

**DOSHER:**

Wait a minute, Brother John,
Till de meetin's underway.

**OLD MAN:**

Well, when de meetin's underway,
I has a word to say. And it is this:
The sooner we on this plantation organizes,
the better, because the way things is going now,
if we don't organize, we is gwine to get put off,
and if we get put off we's got no place to go,
and no work, and to get relief is hell, and I
don't want relief nohow! I likes to work, so let's
get together and organize and pertect ourselves
and these here fields and this here state and our
country, because. . . .

*(Loud shots are heard outside)*
**OLD WOMAN:** Uh-oh! That's de overseer!
**BATES:** De overseer!
**DOSHER:** Put out that light!

**ORGANIZER:**

Keep quiet! Don't run!
Let him in if he knocks!
We might as well face him now
And tell him what we've made up our minds to.

**CHORUS:** Face him! Tell him! Yes, that's true! *(A commanding voice is heard outside)*

**OVERSEER:**

You John! . . . You Mary!
You must think I can't see that light!
You'll hold no meeting here tonight!

**OLD WOMAN:** That's de overseer!

**OVERSEER:**

You-all croppers think you're wise,
Sneaking off to the woods to organize!
*(Knocking loudly)*
Open up that door!

**OLD MAN:** Come in, if you want to come in!

**OVERSEER:** *(kicking in door)*

I'll come in all right!
What's going on in here tonight?—

**ORGANIZER:** We's organizing!

**OVERSEER:**

What? . . . That's a damned disgrace!
You'll have no union on this place!
Don't you know the landlord don't allow no organizing
    here?

**CHORUS:** What?

**OVERSEER:**

The landlord don't allow no organizing here!
I've got my whip and I've got my gun—
And you'll get no organizing done!
The landlord don't allow no organizing here!

**CHORUS:**

But there's gonna be some organizing here!
Yes, there's gonna be some organizing here!
We don't care what de landlord don't 'low,
We gonna organize anyhow.
There's gonna be some organzing here!

**OVERSEER:** What? What's that? What's that I hear?
**CHORUS:** We said there's gonna be some organizing here.
**ORGANIZER:**

In spite of your whip
And in spite of your gun,
We gonna get some organizing done!

**CHORUS:**

There'll be some organizing here!
Yes, there'll be some organizing here!

**OVERSEER:**

Who are you dogs? Say!
Who's talking back to me?

**CHORUS:**

Look in Alabama, man, and you will see!
Look in Mississippi! Look in Tennessee!
Take a look at Dixieland and you will see!

**ORGANIZER:** *(lighting up his own face with a flash-light)*
Take a look at me! *(Others light up their faces, too, until the* OVER-
SEER *is surrounded by a sea of faces glowing in the night)*
**OTHERS:**

And me!
And me!
And me!

**OVERSEER:** *(cracking his whip angrily)*

But I said there'd be no organizing here!
I mean there'll be no organizing here!

**CHORUS:**

You may crack your whip!
You may shoot your gun—
But we's made up our minds
To get some organizing done.

**OVERSEER:** I said NO! *(He shoots four times. Quickly, the* SHARECROPPERS *surround him and take his gun)*

**ORGANIZER:**

All the bullets in the world
Can't shoot me!

**OTHERS:**

Nor me!
Nor me!
Nor me!

**CHORUS:**

We're four million croppers
Determined to be free!
Be free!
Be free!
Be free!

**OLD MAN:**

Mary, take that gun and put it on de shelf.
*(to the* OVERSEER*)*
If you want to 'tend this meeting,
You behave yourself!

**ORGANIZER:**

We've got too much business here tonight
To be interrupted by outsiders
Who want to start a fight.
Brother John, while you're over in that corner,
Bring the flag along.

**OLD MAN:**

I will.
This here flag I carried at San Juan Hill.
My son followed it in France when he was killed.

**ORGANIZER:**

It's your flag, Mister Overseer,
And my flag, too.
So listen what us croppers have
To say to you:

**VOICE:** I've chopped de cotton all my life long,
**CHORUS:** So to want a little freedom now can't be wrong.
**VOICE:** I've worked in de sun all day long.
**CHORUS:** So to want a little freedom now can't be wrong.
**VOICE:** I've plowed with old Jennie all my life long.
**CHORUS:** To want a little freedom now can't be wrong.
**VOICE:** I got up at sunrise all my life long.
**CHORUS:** To want a little freedom now can't be wrong.
**VOICE:** Plowing, planting, hoeing, all life long.
**CHORUS:** To want a little freedom now can't be wrong.
**OVERSEER:**

You-all say *freedom?*
Don't look at me.
I work for the landlord, too.
I ain't free!

**WOMAN:**

Then take this little leaflet.
Read it and be wise.
If you want to be free,
Organize!

**CHORUS:**

Organize! Organize!
If you want to be free,
Organize!

**OVERSEER:** How many's in this union?
**CHORUS:** Everybody here!
**OVERSEER:** I'm going back and tell the landlord.
**OLD WOMAN:** Huh! We don't care!

**ORGANIZER:**

All we want is, be sure to get it right!
Tell him we organized a UNION here tonight!

**CHORUS:** Yes, we organized a union here tonight!
**OVERSEER:** Lemme out of here! *(He rushes out)*
**CHORUS:** We organized a union here tonight! *(Everybody dances, joins hands, exultant with joy. Happy movement. Large signs are lifted,* SHARECROPPER'S UNION*)*
**MEN:** Fight! . . . Fight!
**WOMEN:** Right! . . . Right!
**CHORUS:** We organized a union here tonight!

(Curtain)

# THE EM-FUEHRER JONES

## Langston Hughes

CAST

### THE EM-FUEHRER
### A NEGRO BOXER
### VOICES

*Time:* Maybe Someday
*Place:* The Black Forest
*Scene:* A forest at night. Quite dark except for a will-o-the-wisp light that follows the Em-Fuehrer.

*The* EM-FUEHRER *has a little mustache, and a bang of hair over his forehead. He is Aryan (so he says). He wears a uniform, a few medals, an officers' cap, and high boots. He goosesteps. He heils! He doesn't want the world or himself to know he is afraid, but to tell the truth, he is lost in a great black forest.*

EM-FUEHRER: *(goosestepping)* Heil!
VOICES: *(echoing very faintly)* Heel!
EM-FUEHRER: Heil!
VOICES: Heel! Heel!

By permission of Harold Ober Associates and the estate of Langston Hughes.

**EM-FUEHRER:** *(angrily)* Heil! Ich habe gesaght, Heil!

**VOICES:** *(clearly now)* Heel! Heel! Heel!

**EM-FUEHRER:** Vas ist das? Dat can't be Aryan voices! Dat can't be my crowd. Vere is dis, anyhow? Heil!

**VOICES:** Heel! Heel! Heel! Heel! Heel! *(Tom-toms begin to beat)*

**EM-FUEHRER:** Mussolini! Cut out that Ethiopian racket! *(Tom-toms louder)* I don't like it! That's Non-aryan! Heil!

**VOICES:** *(with savage joy)* Heel! Heel! Heel! Heel!

**EM-FUEHRER:** Vat is dis? How come I hear dos voices? Shut up! Shut up! I must be off mein road to Roumania. I must be off. Vere ist the road? *(He goosesteps and sights)*

**VOICES:** He's off! He's off! He's off! Ru-maniac! Ru-maniac! Maniac! Maniac! *(Sudden footsteps running like the crunching of track shoes)*

**EM-FUEHRER:** Ah-ha! I know! I'm at the Olympics! Heil! . . . But who's that running? I can't see. It's too dark. Who's that in the dark?

**VOICES:** Jesse! Jesse! Jesse!

**EM-FUEHRER:** Jesse who? Jesse vat?

**VOICES:** Jesse Owens! Jesse Owens! Jesse Owens!

**EM-FUEHRER:** Ach! Non-aryan! Stop him! Non-aryan! *(Footsteps and tom-toms grow louder)*

**VOICES:** Heel! Heel! Heel!

**EM-FUEHRER:** Heil! Stop him, I say. *(Pleading)* Jesse, vat you doing running after me? You got your laurel wreath, so stop it, I say! *(Footsteps continue)* I don't want to race with you. These boots hurt my feet. Oh! Wait a minute! Lemme take 'em off! *(Sits on ground and removes boots)* What's this I'm Schmelling? Something's Schmelling! *(Sniffs his boots)*

**VOICES:** Joe Louis! Joe Louis! Joe Louis! *(Leaps up and throws his boots aside)*

**EM-FUEHRER:** Mein Gott! Non-aryan! Schmelling, heil!

**VOICES:** Heel! Heel! Heel! Heel! *(Loud laughter)*

**EM-FUEHRER:** Lemme get away from here! Vat way is Berlin? It must be there. *(Begins to goosestep, then to trot, later run)*

**VOICES:** Gefullterfish! Gefullterfish! Gefullterfish!

**EM-FUEHRER:** *(drawing back)* Mein Gott! I can't go there! that's the Bronx! *(Unbuttons coat)* A map! A map! My Reich for a map! *(Takes out a map from inner pocket)* Where is Yorkville? Where is the Bund Hall? Where is Mein Kampf?

**VOICES:** Camp! Kampf! Camp! Kampf!

**EM-FUEHRER:** Stop it! Stop it! Vait till I get my gang together. *(Calling)* Chamberlin! Chamberlin! Oh, Chamberlin! *(Tom-toms louder and louder)* Daladier! Daladier! Dala . . . dier!

**VOICES:** Hey! Hey! Hey! Hey! *(The drums beat now in mocking jazz rhythm)*

**EM-FUEHRER:** Mein gott! Where ist Mein Kampf? *(He begins to take off his clothes piece by piece as he runs and casts them away. First his hat, then his coat, then his shirt, and undershirt. He has a swastika tattooed on his back and on his chest, very large, blue-black. The tom-toms and the mocking voices continue)*

**VOICES:** Oi-yoi-yoi! Oi-yoi-yoi! Oi-yoi-yoi!

**EM-FUEHRER:** *(stopping with sudden command)* Em-Fuehrer! Hold on to yourself! An Aryan never gets scared! Be proud! Proud! Vat's the matter? Are you lost? My map's no good —but maybe I'll try the stars. *(Looks up)* Oh, no! I mustn't look at the stars!! Einstein invented the stars. They're Non-aryan!

**VOICES:** Oi-yoi-yoi! Oi-yoi-yoi!

**EM-FUEHRER:** Shut up! If you don't, I'll hold a plebescite and get even with you! Whee, it's so hot! Lemme get off this shirt! If the sun would just come up, maybe even a dictator could see. *(A red sun rises in the East)* Mein Gott! Not that sun! That's red! *(Suddenly screams)* Ow-oo-o! The Bolsheviki! Bolsheviki! *(Backs hastily up against a cactus and yells in pain)* Aw-wwww-www-ww- w! *(Turns and salutes the cactus)* Heil! *(Suddenly drooping)* Oh, I thought it was Goering! Where's Goering, Goebbels, Goering? Don't lemme go primitive! Heil! Lemme pray! Oh! Lemme pray! *(Falls on his knees)* Wotan! Wotan! Wotan!

**VOICES:** Ave Maria! Ave Maria! *(He leaps to his feet)*

**EM-FUEHRER:** Catholics! Catholics! Lemme out of here!

**VOICES:** Go! Go! Go! Go!

**EM-FUEHRER:** Go where? Go where? Go where?

**VOICES:** Goebbels! Goebbels! Goebbels!

**EM-FUEHRER:** Lemme out of this black forest! Black! Black! Wah, black! Fritz Kahn, I'm coming! I'm coming to America! *(Pistol shots. Loud drums. Fire and flares. The* EM-FUEHRER *leaves the stage and runs wildly into the audience. Suddenly the house lights come on. The drum stops. He looks around and collapses in the aisle)* Mein gott, Non-aryan! *(An enormous Negro youth in boxing togs with a Joe Louis ribbon across his chest comes down the aisle, picks the* EM-FUEHRER *up by the seat of his pants, and drags him back across the stage in full light. At the wings, the colored boy stops and speaks triumphantly into a microphone)*

    **BOXER:** Ah guess it was dat punch to de ribs dat got him!

    (Blackout)

# SHIRLEY GRAHAM
## (1896–1977)
▼▼▼▼▼▼▼▼▼▼▼▼

Shirley Graham's professional career as a playwright and director changed course dramatically after her marriage to W. E. B. Du Bois in 1951 while he was campaigning to ban nuclear weapons. When he was indicted for his role in the world peace movement, Graham identified herself fully with his cause and accompanied him to Ghana, where he became a Ghanaian citizen and she became active in television and education. Following his death in 1963, she devoted herself to pursuing his vision of an international community free of racism, classism, and sexism. She was writing a book about the women of China under the rule of Mao when she died on March 27, 1977, in Beijing.

Graham was born in Indianapolis, Indiana, to a mother of Cherokee blood who raised four sons and daughters, and a minister who encouraged his children to love African history and to venerate all forms of life. It was in her father's African Methodist Episcopal Church that Graham first sang spirituals, conducted the choir, and learned to play the piano and the organ. She remembers that one of her childhood heroes, Frederick Douglass, about whom she would later write a book, visited her grandfather's farm allegedly carrying with him the sword of Toussaint L'Ouverture.

After completing her early education at Lewis and Clark High School, in Spokane, Washington, she worked for the government during World War I and then at the navy yard in Seattle, where she met and married Shadrach T. McCanns in 1921. She relied on her musical skills to provide the extra money they needed to raise two sons, Robert and David. The couple was divorced in the mid-1920s, and when her brother was appointed principal of a mission college in Monrova, Liberia, Graham accompanied him as far as France. She studied music at the Sorbonne and met many Blacks from Senegal and Martinique who introduced her to African music. Her brother, an American diplomat who had gone into the Liberian jungle, taught her authentic rhythms and rituals that she would use later in *Tom-Tom*, a highly successful musical play.

When she returned from Paris, Graham taught music at Morgan State College (1929–1932) and continued her studies in musicology at Oberlin College. During this period, she began to write plays. She sent a copy of the one-act play *Tom-Tom* to Russell and Rowena Jelliffe's Gilpin Players (later renamed the Karamu Players) in Cleveland, hoping that they would accept it into their repertory. At the time, the Jelliffes could not accommodate her, but in the spring of 1932, when producer Lawrence Higgins asked them if they could unearth a black opera for his ambitious summer program called *Theatre of Nations*, Mrs. Jelliffe remembered the script of *Tom-Tom*. Graham was encouraged to transform it into a musical pageant. Higgins gave her a hotel room and a piano. Within three months, she had expanded the one-act into a sixteen-scene, three-act opera ready for a June 30 premiere at the Cleveland Stadium.

Following the success of this vehicle, Graham lectured and performed at Black colleges and sorority gatherings between 1932 and 1935. She completed a master's thesis entitled "The Survival of Africanism in American Music" at Oberlin and, according to Kathy Perkins, gained stature in the musical world of her people as a historian and composer. During her summers, she attended Columbia University and taught at the Washington Conservatory of Music.

In 1935, Graham was appointed head of the Fine Arts Department at Tennessee State College in Nashville. Disheartened by the lack of facilities at the school, she importuned W. E. B. Du Bois for assistance. He replied that she had students and she had brains, that was all she needed. Shortly afterward, as she was about to accept a position at Talladega College in Alabama, she heard that the Negro unit of the Federal Theatre Project in Chicago was about to disband for lack of interest. She vigorously opposed the decision, and as a result, she was invited by Hallie Flanagan, director of the Federal Theatre of America, to take it over.

In the next years, Graham designed, wrote, and composed musical scores, organized classes and administered a lively program of musical dramas at the Princess Theatre. Notable among her FTP Chicago successes were a production of Theodore Ward's *Big White Fog*; a family comedy, *Mississippi Rainbow*; and *Little Black Sambo*, a children's play by Charlotte Chopenning (with music by Graham), which people lined up around the block to see at the roomier Great Northern Theatre, where the troupe had moved. She also had a hand in a syncopated version of Gilbert and Sullivan, *The Swing Mikado*. Its great success, paradoxically, encouraged Broadway's Mike Todd to imitate the Graham show and open *The Hot Mikado* across the street, starring the great Bojangles Robinson.

Graham decided that she needed to sharpen and expand her talents with a Rosenwald Fellowship in creative writing at Yale University. She moved away from musicals towards straight plays, and between 1938 and 1940 wrote five dramas: *Dust to Earth*, a three-act tragedy about black coal miners reminiscent of *Black Damp* (produced at Karamu Playhouse); *It's Morning*, about a mother whose daughter is being sold into slavery (directed by Otto Preminger at Yale in 1940); the piece included in this volume, *Track Thirteen*, a radio play about train porters and their superstitions (produced at Yale over WICC Radio and published in *Yale Radio Plays*, Boston: Expression Press, 1940) and *Elijah's Raven*, a comedy produced in 1941 by the Gilpin Players, the Florida A&M Players, and Atlanta University Summer Theatre. Graham also wrote the music for and danced in the Yale Drama School production of *The Garden of Time* by classmate Owen Dodson.

Graham hoped that Broadway would call her, but no producer was prepared to mount even a proven success like her *Tom-
Tom* in the uncertain theatre conditions of prewar New York,
though there was talk about doing so. From 1940 to 1941, Graham directed a troupe at the YWCA in Indianapolis and assumed
similar duties with the USO in Fort Huachuca in Arizona.
Because she protested against the racial discrimination at the
camp, she was accused of "rabble rousing" and dismissed from her
position. She next joined the NAACP in New York as a field secretary and became increasingly involved with civil rights issues. She
also began writing biographies of black heroes such as Phyllis
Wheatley, Frederick Douglass, George Washington Carver,
Booker T. Washington, and Benjamin Banneker. The book that
brought her international notice was *Paul Robeson, Citizen of the
World*, published in many languages. She also wrote about Gamal
Abdul Nasser, the Egyptian leader of the 1960s, and completed a
protest novel set in South Africa called *Zulu Heart*. She later
became the founding editor of *Freedomways*, an important issues-
oriented magazine. To date, only four of Graham's plays for theatre and only one musical composition have seen publication
(*Tom-Tom* appears in *Roots of African American Drama* [Detroit:
Wayne State University Press, 1991]). Writing about the oblivion
to which her works have been consigned, Kathy Perkins says in
"The Unknown Career of Shirley Graham" (*Freedomways* 25, no.
1 [1985]), "Few Blacks have succeeded simultaneously as a writer, composer, conductor, and director. To achieve success in just
one of these areas would have been noteworthy for a Black
woman during Graham's time. To have achieved in all of these
areas deserves acclaim and appreciation."

Radio in the 1940s provided an entirely new field for dramatists like Graham. Writing for radio, they had to learn how to suggest place, time, and action by words alone, accompanied only by
the use of impressionistic sound and music. This medium offered
Black dramatists the opportunity to bring their daily lives into the
living rooms of America and show how Black people viewed the
outside world.[1] In 1944, Richard Wright put together a series of
radio programs on the life of a black family, but they remained
unproduced except for a partial presentation on Radio Hamburg,

Germany. Graham was the first African American woman playwright to respond to the challenge of radio.

In *Track Thirteen*, produced in 1940 on WICC in New Haven, despite the familiar cops-and-robbers plotline and the near-stereotypes of porter and conductor, Graham dramatizes the typical trials and often comic tribulations of Black employees on a railroad train speeding across the continent, With equanimity and patience, they respond to the often absurd demands of the passengers, who bring babies, animals, and stolen bonds aboard. Usually the butt of racist jokes, Speck and his colleagues sound dignified and responsible next to the passengers, who appear incapable of caring for themselves.

Although Graham showed a flair for pithy radio dialogue and a wicked eye for the foibles of the white middle-class, most Americans were not prepared to accept the role-reversal that gives *Track Thirteen* so much of its vitality. After this experiment with radio drama, Graham chose to return to her first love, the stage.

## NOTE

1. William Robson wrote one of the first Black radio plays, *An Open Letter on Race Hatred*, about the Detroit race riots of 1943. It was published in *Theatre Arts* of September 1944. Also, Richard Wright's story, *Fire and Cloud*, was adapted for radio by Charles O'Neill. It appears in *American Scenes* (1941). Roi Ottley's "The Negro Domestic" was broadcast on WMCA in New York in the series called *New World A-Coming* (1944). And Langston Hughes took a crack at radio with *Booker T. Washington in Atlanta*, published in 1945, but apparently found it an infertile field for his talent.

## REFERENCES

Brown-Guillory, Elizabeth. "Shirley Graham Du Bois" *Black Women in America*. Brooklyn, NY: Carlson Publishing, 1993, 357–58.

Perkins, Kathy. *Black Female Playwrights*. Bloomington: University of Indiana Press, 1990.

_____ "Shirley Graham." *Dictionary of Literary Biography* 76. Detroit: Gale Research, 1988, 66–75.

# TRACK THIRTEEN
## A Comedy for Radio

SHIRLEY GRAHAM

CAST

| | |
|---|---|
| WOMAN | 3RD MAN |
| CLERK | CONDUCTOR |
| RED CAP | ENGLISHMAN |
| MAN | TOM |
| ELIZABETH | MOTHER |
| FRANCES | JONES |
| NEWSBOY | DRUNK |
| PORTER | 1ST CALIFORNIAN |
| SPECK | 2ND CALIFORNIAN |
| 1ST MAN | DR. LOCKE |
| 2ND MAN | VOICES |

**ANNOUNCER:** *La Salle Station, Chicago, crouching like a huge, blinking spider in the very heart of that hub city, sending its curving tentacles of steel north, south, east and west and drawing to itself those queer, uprooted bits of humanity called travelers. Day and night they weave back and forth beneath the dome of the depot, restless, tossed here and there, eyes gleaming with the spirit of adventure or shrinking back within themselves, furtively searching for some familiar port. A clerk at the Information Desk casts a weary*

By permission of David G. Du Bois.

*eye at the great clock high on the frescoed wall. The hands point to one minute to ten.*

**SOUND:** Railroad Station

**LOUDSPEAKER:** Omaha—Cheyenne—Ogden—Reno—Sacramento—Berkley—Oakland and San Francisco. Train number 27, on track 13, leaving at 10:25. Omaha—Cheyenne—

**WOMAN:** Right here, porter. Er—mister!

**CLERK:** *(tired voice)* Yes, madame?

**WOMAN:** Where do I get my train?

**CLERK:** Where are you going, madame?

**WOMAN:** *(confidential)* Out to spend the winter with my daughter. You know, she isn't so well and. . . . *(Fade)*

**LOUDSPEAKER:** Train number 27, on track 13, leaving . . .

**REDCAP:** *(eager)* Redcap, mister?

**MAN:** No.

**REDCAP:** Take your bag, mister?

**MAN:** Yes—10:25 to Frisco.

**REDCAP:** Right this way. What car?

**MAN:** *(snapping)* Here's the ticket. *(Footsteps)*

**WOMAN'S VOICE:** *(tense)* Come on, Elizabeth! That's our train.

**ELIZABETH:** *(anxious)* Are you sure, Frances?

**FRANCES:** Didn't he say "track 13" and isn't he going to San Francisco? Come on!

**ELIZABETH:** Well, we don't want to get on the wrong train. After all our planning and—

**NEWSBOY:** Extry! Extry! Read all about daring robbery—Ace Kelly slips through net! Paper, lady?

**ELIZABETH:** Shall I get one? Sounds exciting!

**FRANCES:** Heavens, no! We're going away for a rest. Here's track 13, and here's the train.

**ELIZABETH:** My goodness, what a long train! Let's see where's our ticket?

**FRANCES:** That man's probably going to the same car.

**NEWSBOY:** *(in distance)* Extry! Extry!

**ELIZABETH:** *(alarmed)* What if we follow him into the wrong car? What if we get in the wrong berth? Frances, imagine it! There we'd be all undressed and in bed, and in the middle of the night—in the middle of the night, mind you, some strange man would draw back the curtains and—

**FRANCES:** Stop being silly! The porter'll see that we get the right berth. Here he is. Porter, is this the car for San Francisco?

**PORTER:** Yes, *mam*. What berth, mam?

**ELIZABETH:** Lower 5. And be sure you—

**FRANCES:** Sh-sh-sh-sh! Elizabeth!

**PORTER:** Let me take your bags. Watch the step. Now, right this way. *(Sounds are muffled)*

**ELIZABETH:** *(whispering)* Isn't it quite. The berths are all ready.

**PORTER:** Here's the switch for your lights. Would you care to have the fan on?

**NEWSBOY:** *(outside)* Extry! Extry!

**FRANCES:** We'll ring if we need you.

**MAN'S VOICE:** Porter!

**FRANCES:** That's the man we were following.

**ELIZABETH:** Sh-sh-sh-sh! He's in the next berth.

**PORTER:** Yes, sir.

**MAN:** What's that extry?

**PORTER:** Something 'bout a bank being held up. Like a paper, sir?

**MAN:** Don't bother. Thought it might be important. Oh, porter, I may receive a telegram before the train leaves—Frederick Lock's the name. Dr. Frederick Lock.

**PORTER:** Yes, sir. I'll see that you get it at once, sir.

**NEWSBOY:** *(dying away)* Extry! Extry!

**ELIZABETH:** *(whispering)* I wonder who he is. Must be important.

**FRANCES:** I'm not interested. Well, we're on our way! *(Door opens and shuts. Outside Platform sounds: Rolling baggage trucks, hissing steam, voices in distance, hurrying feet on cement, etc.)*

**VOICE:** Hi there, big boy!

**PORTER:** Hello, Speck! How's every little thing in the diner?

**SPECK:** Oh, rollin' long, boy, rollin' long. Nothing to do till breakfast. Like these night trains. Gives a fellow a chance to get a little rest 'fore tha grind starts.

**PORTER:** Yah! And I know you needs it after two nights in Chicago.

**SPECK:** *(modestly)* Well, Ah won't say Ah do and Ah won't say Ah don't. Course, us native sons do pretty well along the boolevards.

**PORTER:** *(sarcastically)* Native sons of what? Say, fellow, if any of them Californians hear you callin' yo'self a native son they'll run you in the middle of the sunset and lock the Golden Gate, they'd . . . *(softly)* Here come passengers!

**VOICE:** *(approaching—big, booming and with a mighty Western roll)* Yes, sir! I sure am glad to be getting back to God's country. Yes, sir, where I can breathe. I tell you these Eastern cities choke a man's lungs.

**2nd VOICE:** *(equally booming)* Cramp you! Can't stretch my legs—always scared I'll kick over something. Last time I was in St. Louis—

**1st MAN:** Don't tell me! I know! Now, my wife says—

**2nd MAN:** Ain't it the truth! Those gals eat it up! Must "go east" to buy dresses from Marshall Fields and hats on Michigan Avenue—

**1st MAN:** Market Street's good enough for me any time. Say, where you gonna find such stores?

**2nd MAN:** Or such traffic?

**1st MAN:** Or skyscrapers?

**2nd MAN:** And food! Say, my stomach's tied up in knots!

**1st MAN:** Don't say a word! Mouth's lined with seal skin! But twenty-four hours in that California sunshine—

**2nd MAN:** That air right off the bay—

**1st MAN:** Oh! boy, *California here I come!* *(Fade)*

**PORTER:** Well, native son, why didn't you join the chorus?

**SPECK:** Say, look like we're gonna have a full house.

**PORTER:** Sure does! Most of my lowers taken.

**SPECK:** Them words listen good to me! Say, las' trip that diner might as well been a ice wagon in Greenland. Honest, we had to dump so much stuff when we got to Frisco folks thought we was a WPA Project!

**PORTER:** Well, move out of my path, dark boy, I gotta strut my stuff. *(Fade)*

**WOMAN'S VOICE:** *(with rising indignation)* I won't do it! I simply won't. If this is the kind of service this road offers—I'll go to the manager! I'll sue the company!

**CONDUCTOR:** *(in strained voice)* I'm sorry, madame! We'd be happy to accomodate you, but it's absolutely against the rules.

**WOMAN:** Rules! Rules! What are rules to Mimi? Poor, innocent little Mimi!

**CONDUCTOR:** But madame, your dog will be well taken care of in the baggage car, I assure you.

**WOMAN:** Never! Mimi sleeps on my bed every night of her life. Are your berths any better than my bed? Mimi's certainly clean. Here, let me put her up against your face and see for yourself. *(Dog gives nasty, yelping bark.)*

**CONDUCTOR:** *(hurriedly)* Oh! no—er—I don't for a minute doubt that your dog is clean. It's just the sleeping car rules. Now, the porter will take it and make up a nice, soft bed in the baggage car—I'm sure he has an extra cot—and—Porter! Porter! Where is the fellow?

*(Dog begins weedy, angry barking.)*

**WOMAN:** Is muvva's little baby mad? Po' 'ittle girl. Nassy man wants take baby way from muvva. Don't cry! Um-um-um.

**CONDUCTOR:** *(desperate)* Porter!

**PORTER:** Yes, sir!

**CONDUCTOR:** *(choking)* Where the—Where have you been?

**PORTER:** Settling a couple of passengers in the drawing room, sir.

**CONDUCTOR:** *(mollified)* Oh! Well, here's a lady who needs your most expert service.

**WOMAN:** *(haughtily)* I don't need his services at all.

**CONDUCTOR:** Now, madame, if you'll let the porter take your—er—dear—little dog, you can rest assured it is in the most competent hands. This is one of our smartest men. I believe he's studying right now to be a vet. Isn't that so—er—Wilson?

**PORTER:** *(astonished)* A—um—yes, sir!

**WOMAN:** I'll cancel my reservation. I'll—But, I've got to be in Reno by the 10th. I'll have to submit to this tyranny. It's another case of man's cruelty to poor weak woman. Oh! Mimi! We'll have to suffer together. *(Sharply)* Porter, are your hands clean?

**PORTER:** Yes, mam, I—

**WOMAN:** Mimi will probably bite you, and she mustn't contract any germs! Wash your hands every time you handle her. Oh! my poor 'ittle, bitsy—

*(Dog yelps frantically)*

**CONDUCTOR:** Hurry, Porter. Only five minutes more. Come this way, madame, I'll show you to your berth.

**WOMAN:** Tyranny! That's all it is.

**CONDUCTOR:** Here we are—lower 12.

**WOMAN:** *(gives a screech)* What! My berth! Here at the very end of the car, right over the wheels? Let me see that ticket. "Car 23, lower 12." *(Bitterly)* I might have known! Another one of that man's tricks to humiliate me. He planned for me to lie on the rails all the way out to Reno and bump up and down until I was black and blue!

**CONDUCTOR:** But, madame—

**WOMAN:** Nobody knows like a husband how to torture the woman he has promised to love and cherish. I should have expected something like this. *(Imitating man's voice)* "Don't worry yourself about the details, Maxine, I'll get your ticket and make all arrangements." Even reminded me how pleasant Reno is in the fall! *(Snapping)* Well, we'll have to change this right away.

**CONDUCTOR:** I'm sorry, madame, the—

**WOMAN:** Now what?

**CONDUCTOR:** This car is practically full. Unless you'd like an upper?

**WOMAN:** *(almost beside herself)* An upper! Oh! how you men stand together! It's shameful! It's disgraceful! Men! How I hate them all! I . . .

**REDCAP:** 'Scuse us, lady.

**CONDUCTOR:** If you would let the passenger by. These aisles are so narrow.

**WOMAN:** I should say they are. I can see nothing—

**MAN'S VOICE:** *(real Oxford accent)* Pawdon me, steward, but is the boy stowing my luggage properly?

**REDCAP:** *(nonchalant)* Car 23, lower 10. Here's the ticket.

**CONDUCTOR:** That's quite right, sir.

**ENGLISHMAN:** Right ho, it is, then. Here you are, fellow.

**REDCAP:** Thank you, sir.

**CONDUCTOR:** The observation car is just three cars back, sir, if you don't care to retire.

**ENGLISHMAN:** *(curious)* Observation?

**CONDUCTOR:** A combination reading and smoking car.

**ENGLISHMAN:** Oh! I see. *Take a look. (Fade)*

**WOMAN:** *(drawing in her breath)* Oh! He sounds just like Leslie Howard!

**CONDUCTOR:** Um-um-um. Now, let me see—Maybe, I could exchange berths—

**WOMAN:** *(still breathless)* Did you read the labels on his bags? I could see them.

**CONDUCTOR:** No, I didn't. If you will just—

**WOMAN:** Right here, in a berth next to mine! Undoubtedly an English nobleman. He's probably traveling incognito!

**CONDUCTOR:** I'll change you to—

**WOMAN:** Oh! really, I mustn't put you to any trouble. A real traveler must be willing to put up with trifling inconveniences. I'm sure you've managed everything beautifully. Just settle my things right here. Where is my book? I think I'll read a while in the observation car before going to bed. *(Sweetly)* goodnight! *(Fade)*

**CONDUCTOR:** Well, I'll be—What a—

**PORTER:** Everything all set, Captain?

**CONDUCTOR:** I *hope* so. Phew! Come on outside. I need air!

*(Doors open and shut. Sounds on platform come up)*

**CONDUCTOR:** Hello, cookie! Well, I guess I'd better check. *(Fade)*

**SPECK:** What's he looking so flust'rated about?

**PORTER:** *(thoughtfully)* You know, Speck, there's one thing worrying me.

SPECK: Boy, was you sittin' right beside St. Peter strummin' yo' harp, You'd be worryin' cause you didn't have no raincoat in case it stormed!

PORTER: *(slowly)* Do you know what track this train is standing on this minute?

SPECK: Track 15, where it always stands for this trip.

PORTER: Is that so? Well, cast your eyes over to that train leaving for Seattle at midnight.

SPECK: *(a slow whistle)* That *is* on fifteen. Then what track is this?

PORTER: I reckon you can count.

SPECK: No! No! It can't be—Don't tell me—Ned, this must be 17! No, there's seventeen over there—Oh, Lawd have mussy! We're rollin' out on *13!*

PORTER: Something's bound to happen.

SPECK: *(in a hollow voice)* Sweet angels of light! *(Crying baby approaching.)*

PORTER: And here comes trouble right now!

YOUNG MOTHER: Let me take her, Tom. Hush, darling.

TOM: That's all right, sweetheart. She'll stop in a minute.

PORTER: I'll help you, Lady. Watch the step.

TOM: Thank you, Porter.

MOTHER: Lay her down. Here we are, precious.

TOM: See, I'm putting the baby's things here on this shelf. You've got the entire section so you won't be crowded. Do be careful, won't you?

MOTHER: Don't worry about us.

OUTSIDE: All aboard! All aboard!

TOM: Goodby, darling. I'll speak to the porter as I go out. Ring for him whenever you need anything.

MOTHER: Good-bye, Tom.

TOM: Porter!

PORTER: Yes, sir.

TOM: Please see that my wife has every attention. The baby's pretty young. It'll take extra time, but—here. *(There is the sound of rustling paper)*

PORTER: Thank you, sir. . . . *(Voices calling "goodbye"!)*

PORTER: Hotziggatidog! This ain't bad luck!

**SPECK:** Hump!

**PORTER:** Hump nothing! Gaze on this greenback.

**SPECK:** Five dollars! Well, dat's what Ah calls a *white* man!

**CONDUCTOR:** *(Sharply—at distance)* Wilson!

**PORTER:** Yes, Mr. Jamison.

**CONDUCTOR:** Step here, back in these shadows.

**SPECK:** *(sotto)* Um-um! Ah'd better scram! *(Sound of stumbling)*

**PORTER:** Oh! I'm sorry.

**HEAVY VOICE:** Okay, you couldn't see me.

**CONDUCTOR:** This man's from headquarters. He wants to see you.

**PORTER:** Me?

**CONDUCTOR:** Go ahead, Jones, you can trust him. I'll hold the train a minute.

**JONES:** Here's the dope. We were tipped off today that Ace Kelly was traveling west—

**PORTER:** *(weakly)* Ace—Kelly!

**JONES:** *(sharply)* Hush! Yes, the bank robber. He's got that half million in bonds. So far, we've got nothing but a blank. Today we picked up a clue. The fellow he shot is dying. Kelly's desperate. Everything pointed to this train. I've been watching but it's been no good. Your conductor suggests several of you fellow acting as spotters.

**PORTER:** What does he look like?

**JONES:** No telling. He walked out of Joliet a month ago right under the guard's nose. He's a smart man. There's a five thousand dollar reward. Keep your eyes peeled and your mouth shut.

**PORTER:** But if I don't know what he looks like what can I do?

**JONES:** Get Ace Kelly, and remember, he's a killer!

**SOUND:** *(All A-board! Al-l-l A—boar—rred!)*

**DRUNKEN VOICE:** Hey, wait a minute! Wait jus' a minute!

**JONES:** Here comes your last passenger. I'll get a look at his face as you help him on. Might be Ace! Well, so long and good luck! *(Fade)*

**PORTER:** Shut my mouth!

**DRUNK:** Das right, porter, nice boy!

**REDCAP:** Here's his ticket, Upper . He's tight, but I guess harmless. Almost fell out his taxi. (*All aboard! Sound of train starting*)

**PORTER:** Come on, mister. Where's that—lean on me! Watch out, the train's starting! Suffering catfish! Might be—Oh, Lawdy!

**DRUNK:** What's at you're saying, Porter? (*Doors slamming, train getting up speed*)

**PORTER:** We're all right now. Steady! There! Sit here till I fix your berth.

**DRUNK:** Nice man, ver' nice man! Have a lil' drink.

**PORTER:** Sh-sh-sh-sh! People are sleep! You'll wake them.

**DRUNK:** Com' on, have a lil' drink, George. All same to me. Come on, George—Thash your name, ain't it—George?

**PORTER:** No, it's Ned.

**DRUNK:** Ned! Can't be. (*reflectively*) Ned! Oh, well! What's difference! Anyhow, have lil' drink—George—uck!—Ned!

**WOMAN:** *Porter!*

**PORTER:** Sh-sh-sh-sh! Be quiet. I'll be right back. (*Hurried footsteps*)

**PORTER:** Yes, mam?

**WOMAN:** Can't we have a little less noise in here?

**PORTER:** Yes, mam, I'll see to it, mam. (*Bell rings*)

**MAN:** Porter!

**PORTER:** Yes, sir.

**MAN:** Will we be in San Francisco on time?

**PORTER:** I'm quite sure we will, sire.

**LOWER 12:** (*sweetly*) Oh, Porter, did you find a good bed for Mimi?

**PORTER:** Yes, mam.

**LOWER 12:** Then I think I'll retire. (*Bell rings*)

**MAN:** Porter, is there a presser on this train?

**PORTER:** I'll take them, sir.

**WOMAN:** Porter, this pillow's much too thick.

**PORTER:** Yes, mam. I'll get you another. (*Bell rings long and persistently*)

**MAN:** Porter!

**PORTER:** Excuse me, sir, I'll have to answer my bell.

**WOMAN:** Porter!

**DRUNK:** *(calling)* Ish my berth ready, Porter. Come on, hav' a— *(Baby starts to cry. The bell is ringing without ceasing)*

**MAN:** Hey, Porter!

**PORTER:** *(groaning)* I knowed wasn't no good gonna roll offa Track Thirteen! *(Fade) (Train up and out)*

**ANNOUNCER:** Westward, across the plains of Illinois, the Overland Limited thunders its way through the night. The click of wheels and strain of iron rises upon a peak of sound with each shrill whistle. Far back in car 23 all is peace and quiet. Like old Mother Hubbard, Porter Wilson has succeeded in putting all his children to bed within their curtained cubicals. The lights are dimmed and swaying portals assume queer shapes along the aisle. Someone is snoring contentedly. It is nearly one o'clock. *(Sound of snoring and muffled train noise. Suddenly, there is a sharp telegraphic beat of some hard object on steel. "Tat-tat, tat, tat, tat-tat-tat." Silence. The sound is repeated and then, upon a wooden object comes "Tat, tat, tat, tat")*

**ELIZABETH:** *(urgent whisper)* Frances! Frances! Wake up!

**FRANCES:** Eh, what? Oh! Elizabeth, lie down. What do you want?

**ELIZABETH:** I heard something queer. *(Pause)* I don't hear it now. Oh! what's the matter?

**FRANCES:** *(awake)* Something bumped against our curtains. Sh-sh-sh!

**ELIZABETH:** I'm going to peep out.

**FRANCES:** Don't. Probably somebody on his way to the—

**ELIZABETH:** I don't see why anybody would be sending ahead wireless messages for that! Darn, did you fasten all these buttons?

**FRANCES:** I certainly did. Elizabeth, stop that!

**ELIZABETH:** *(tense)* Frances, the curtains are billowing out along the sides as if somebody's creeping along under them. Oh! Stop jerking me!

**FRANCES:** I'll jerk your head off if you don't get it back in here and mind your own business. I'd better ring for the porter.

**ELIZABETH:** No, wait. Let's see—

**FRANCES:** Sh-sh-sh-sh!

**MAN'S VOICE:** *(hoarse whisper)* You can't get off at Omaha. Watching every train.

**2nd VOICE:** I gotta get through.

**1st VOICE:** Stay on. It'll be easier further out. Better drop the stuff.

**2nd VOICE:** You're crazy.

**1st VOICE:** O.K. I've warned you. Now, it's your funeral.

**2nd VOICE:** Cut it! Any bulls on board?

**1st VOICE:** Not that I know of.

**2nd VOICE:** I'm getting up early in the morning and look things over. Might get some ideas. *(Bell rings in distance)*

**2nd VOICE:** Duck! The porter.

**FRANCES:** I'm going to call him!

**ELIZABETH:** Wait a minute! Let's listen!

**PORTER:** Number 12? You rang, madame?

**LOWER 12:** Yes—oh—Porter, did the gentleman in Lower 10 leave a call for morning.

**PORTER:** No, he didn't, mam.

**LOWER 12:** He didn't say anything about—breakfast?

**PORTER:** Not to me.

**LOWER 12:** Oh, dear! Well, I suppose I'll be getting up. Nothing like starting the day with a substantial meal. Er—a—porter, English people do eat breakfast, don't they?

**PORTER:** I reckon so, mam.

**LOWER 12:** You may call me at eight-thirty. It will be too utterly ridiculous if he doesn't— *(Fade)*

**FRANCES:** *(calling)* Porter!

**PORTER:** Yes, mam.

**ELIZABETH:** Miss Clark wanted another blanket, please, porter.

**PORTER:** Yes, mam, right here, mam. Anything else?

**ELIZABETH:** No, that's all. Thank you!

**FRANCES:** Elizabeth!

**ELIZABETH:** Now, don't "Elizabeth" me! You were going to spoil everything. Snap out the light. We're getting up early. Nothing like being on the spot when things happen. Goodnight, darling. *(Train rumble comes up, whistle blows. Door opens and shuts and we hear subdued voices and throaty laughter together with the brush and snap of shoe polishing)*

**RICH DRAWL:** Shine, baby! Lemme see mah face!

**2nd VOICE:** T'ain't possible in no black shoe! Ha! Ha! Ha!

**PORTER:** Here's a tan shoe you might try!

**1st VOICE:** Hi, Ned, everything tucked in?

**PORTER:** Yep! All's quiet for the night. Jiminy! No! I'd better go back and take a look at that young souse. Hold everything, fellows, won't be a minute. *(Sound of door)*

**2nd VOICE:** Don't rush! Bad for you!

**3rd VOICE:** You know, I can look at a man's shoes and tell you a good many things about him.

**1st VOICE:** Hump! Such as . . . ?

**3rd VOICE:** Well, take these shoes Ned just left here— Hand 'em over. Um-um-um-um-um—Something funny 'bout these shoes!

**2nd VOICE:** *(sarcastic)* Just like we 'spected!

**3rd VOICE:** No, it's a fact. Look here! They're expensive shoes, but they're old shoes, yet' they're hardly worn at all. The person who owns these shoes ain't been wearin' 'em. Must a been in a hospital, the pen or—

**1st VOICE:** A jail-bird, em! Oh, you Mr. Charlie Chan! *(Door bursts open)*

**2nd VOICE:** Ned! What's tha matter?

**PORTER:** He's gone!

**SEVERAL:** Gone? Who?

**PORTER:** The drunk! Thought first he might of rolled out. No sign of him—not in the corridors. Just gone!

**2nd VOICE:** *(sarcastic)* Shows you don't know a dead drunk when you see one. If he was bad as you said he couldn't climb down from an upper berth and—

**PORTER:** *(agonizing)* Man, don't talk to me! What I'm thinking would send cold chills down your back and make bristles on your head stand straight up! I speck he wasn't drunk a-tall! *(Fade)* *(train whistle)*

**ANNOUNCER:** Well, it's morning. I don't hear any birds chirping. In fact, I doubt if there are any birds out here in Iowa, because, you see, there aren't any trees. The roar and whistle of the trains seems to have diminished as if all this open space swallows it up. Within Car 23 there is much rustling of curtains and many grotesque bumps appear along the aisle. The porter, all starchy fresh almost collides with the Englishman as he rounds the corner—

**PORTER:** Oh! Excuse me. Good morning, sir. You're up early.

**ENGLISHMAN:** Wanted to have a look around. All this view one sees from the window is rather amazing, you know—so much space.

**MAN:** *(calling)* Porter!

**PORTER:** Good morning, Dr. Locke. Hope you rested well.

**DR. LOCKE:** Shan't complain. You did your best in settling that noisy young man. Make any trouble during the night?

**PORTER:** I didn't hear a sound. *(Interested)* Did you?

**DR. LOCKE:** Thought I heard him tossing a bit this morning.

**PORTER:** *(surprised)* This morning? Is he—Why, I thought—

**DR. LOCKE:** What is it?

**WEAK VOICE:** Porter!

**DR. LOCKE:** Ah! There he is now—probably under the weather.

**WEAK VOICE:** *(irritated)* Couldn't we have a little less talkin' round here? Say, Porter, can you get me a little fixer?

**PORTER:** I'll see, sir. What would you like?

**WEAK VOICE:** Anything. How the hell did I get up in this stuffy hole?

**PORTER:** *(sotto voice)* That's what I'm wondering!

**WEAK VOICE** What'd you say? Speak up, my head's got a buzzing.

**DR. LOCKE:** I'll go on up to the front of the car out of the way.

**PORTER:** Breakfast is being served.

**DR. LOCKE:** Thank you. Hump! Oh! pardon me.

**1st CALIFORNIAN:** *(heartily)* That's all right, mister. Can't move round here without bumping into somebody. Don't let that worry you. See you're going my way. Well, well! Here's somebody beat us up. Don't blame you for staring like that out the window. We're getting into God's country.

**ENGLISHMAN:** I beg your pardon?

**1st CALIFORNIAN:** Out where the west begins. You know, "Out where the skies are a little bluer, out where hearts are a little truer." Never were truer words spoken! First trip?

**ENGLISHMAN:** Indeed. I am seeing your wonderful country for the first time.

**1st CALIFORNIAN:** You don't say. You're an Englishman, arn't you? Always tell 'em by their dialect. By Jimmy! Let's celebrate. Didn't I hear the porter call this other gentleman a doctor?

**DR. LOCKE:** I am Dr. Locke.

**1st CALIFORNIAN:** Well, I want you and this English gentleman to have breakfast with me. Know you're an Easterner. Want to break you all right in to Western hospitality. Ah, here's Mac. Glad you've come. Just invited these two gentlemen to have breakfast with us.

**2nd CALIFORNIAN:** Sure thing! Won't be California food yet, but we're on our way.

**ENGLISHMAN:** Really, I don't know—I—

**1st CALIFORNIAN:** Not a word. My name's Bill Jennings, and this is my friend, Allen McArthur. And we've met doc, here. Come on, let's put on the feed bags. Nothing fancy 'bout us. Just good, one hundred percent Americans. No fuss— *(Fade)*

**ELIZABETH:** Come on, let's have breakfast, too.

**FRANCES:** Elizabeth, you're being perfectly ridiculous— trying to shadow those men.

**ELIZABETH:** Frances, we heard one of them say last night he was going to get up early and look around. Well—

**FRANCES:** How do you know it was one of them.

**ELIZABETH:** Do you see any other men up? Come on! *(Fade)*

**PORTER:** Lawd! Is one of them men—Ace Kelly? *(Train whistles. Train up and out)*

**CONDUCTOR:** *(walking)* Train pulling into Omaha Station. Twenty minutes wait. Passengers wishing to leave train may do so. No more stops until we reach Cheyenne.

**MOTHER:** Porter! What time do we reach Cheyenne?

**PORTER:** Eight o'clock tonight.

**MOTHER:** Oh, then I'll have to buy baby's milk here. Can you get it for me? You'll have to find a dairy. Grade "A," raw milk. They have only pasteurized milk on the train.

**PORTER:** I'll do my best, mam.

**MOTHER:** Please. I must have it. *(Train stopping. Doors opening)*

**1st CALIFORNIAN:** Shall we stretch the legs a bit?

**ENGLISHMAN:** Bully idea! *(Station sounds)*

**MAN:** *(in distance)* Hey there, Porter! *(Nearer)* Where are you going?

**PORTER:** Errand for passenger.

**MAN:** Just a minute. Where's your conductor?

**PORTER:** There he is.

**MAN:** Call him!

**PORTER:** Mr. Jamison!

**CONDUCTOR:** What's the trouble?

**MAN:** Fellow says he's going on errand for passenger. What about it?

**CONDUCTOR:** What's the errand, Wilson?

**PORTER:** Lady with baby wants some "raw" milk!

**CONDUCTOR:** Doesn't the diner have it?

**PORTER:** She say I gotta find a dairy.

**MAN:** Guess it's all right, but I'll have to go with you.

**CONDUCTOR:** Sorry, Wilson. We're all under surveillance. They've got the G-men down to meet us. Certain Ace Kelly's on board. If he doesn't get off they're boarding the train and searching it as soon as we leave.

**PORTER:** You don't think *I'm* Ace Kelly!

**G-MAN:** Big boy, we arn't *thinking!* We wantta know. Come on, if you need that milk.

**PORTER:** Yes, sir. *(Fade) (Station noises. All aboard! All aboard! Doors slam, train gathers speed and gradually establishes a regular momentum)* Phew! Lemme get offa my corns for one minute. Sweet rest! *(Bell rings)* Doggone! Now, who wants what?

**CALL:** *(monotonous)* Lunch is now being served in the dining car. Last call for lunch! *Last call* for lunch! *(Fade)*

**LOWER 12:** Porter, has Mimi had her lunch?

**PORTER:** Yes, mam, I fed her myself.

**LOWER 12:** Then, Mr. Terry, since you insist, we'll go out and get a bite, just a bite.

**ENGLISHMAN:** I shall be delighted, I'm sure.

**LOWER 12:** Flatterer! I know you think we American women quite superficial. English women have *brains*, but we— *(Fade)*

**MOTHER:** Porter, I hate to be so much trouble, but I don't know what to do with this bag of baby's er—a—er—

**PORTER:** Yes, I know.

**MOTHER:** They're damp and I'm wondering if there's some place you could hang them for me. I just haven't any idea. *(Bell rings)*

**PORTER:** All right, mam. There's the conductor ringing for me. Leave the bag where I can get it and I'll see what I can do.

**MOTHER:** That's fine!

**DR. LOCKE:** Always in a hurry, eh, porter?

**PORTER:** Did you enjoy your lunch, doctor?

**DR. LOCKE:** Fine food, fine service. I can look forward to some quiet reading now.

**WOMAN:** What a sweet baby. But, aren't you going to lunch.

**MOTHER:** No, I believe not. I can hardly take her with me and—

**WOMAN:** Do let me keep the baby for you. I'd love to.

**MOTHER:** Sure you wouldn't mind.

**WOMAN:** Mind! I should say not. Here, let me take her to my seat. Precious little thing! Hurry, you'll be late.

**MOTHER:** It's awfully sweet of you. I'm leaving this bag for the porter. He'll get it.

**WOMAN:** I'll tell him. Run along. *(Train rumble comes up —Whistle sounds)*

**VOICE:** *(tense, low)* Keep looking out the window. Don't say anything. I'll lean over your shoulder. They're searching the train. You gotta get rid of that stuff. *(Gasp and sudden movement)*

**VOICE:** I'm doing some fast thinking. See that bag over there? Nobody's in the seat, car's almost empty. I can push 'em under the baby's things. Give 'em here. *(Sound of rustling paper)*

**VOICE:** I'll go over and be looking out the window. *(Door slams)*

**FRANCES:** We'll be crossing the Salt Lake about eight-thirty in the morning.

**ELIZABETH:** I'm sure you brought your "See America First" *(Low)* Frances, what's that man doing over there?

**FRANCES:** Oh, he's just looking out the window. *(Fade)*

**VOICE:** *(low)* It's done. Had to take a few pieces out to make room in the bag. Got 'em under my coat. I'll get rid of them right now. Keep your eye on that bag! *(Train rumble comes up. Door slams, footsteps)*

**ENGLISHMAN:** Oh! porter, there you are. Where is seat twelve? The lady left her mantle. I came back for it.

**PORTER:** Right here, sir.

**ENGLISHMAN:** Right you are! *(Fade)*

**WOMAN:** There's the bag, porter. The baby's mother left it for you.

**PORTER:** Yes, mam, I'll take it right now. *(Train rumble comes up. Door slams and noises on outside platform crossing from car to car, footsteps)*

**DRUNK YOUNG MAN:** Porter! That bag!

**PORTER:** Well, sir, hope your headaches gone. Why! What's the matter? Are you ill?

**DRUNK:** No—yes—*(Laughs)* Guess my head's still swimming. I'm seeing double. Ha! Ha! Thought you had two bags in your hand. Funny, isn't it?

**PORTER:** Yes, that is funny. You see, I have only one.

**DRUNK:** Yes, I see. I—I—think I'm going to be sick! *(Fade) (Door slams. Rumble of train as porter goes through several cars, opening and shutting doors, faint suggestion of voices, outside platform)*

**VOICE:** *(sharp)* Stop there. Where are you going? Oh! It's you. What is it this time? Well, I'll be a—Are you running a nursery? Just left you with a milk bottle and here you come, unless my eyes deceive me, toting a rubber bag of baby's most intimate clothing.

**PORTER:** That's it, chief. The mother's awful young—Didn't know what to do with 'em.

**G-MAN:** You know, there are times I don't like my job, but at that I think I'd like yours less. Proceed, general. The line is open.

**PORTER:** Thanks, chief. *(Door opens and shuts upon comparative quiet)* High there, Speck!

**SPECK:** What yo' say, big boy? What yo' doin' way up here?

**PORTER:** Now, Speck, don't give me none of your mouth. I just want a little space. I thought—maybe—behind one of those boilers—er—in a corner of—

**SPECK:** *(ominously)* What have you got in that bag?

**PORTER:** Listen, Speck, I'd put 'em in my locker, only there's no room, and in the heat out here they'll soon be dry, and—

**SPECK:** What have you got in that bag?

**PORTER:** Diapers.

**SPECK:** Diapers!

**PORTER:** Diapers. . . . See! I'll zip the bag and dump 'em out. *(There is the tearing sound of the zipper, followed by a soft thud and a great hustling of paper)*

**SPECK:** That's mostly paper.

**PORTER:** *(puzzled)* She said—What *is* all this? Let's see! *(Rising roar of train. Something like a clap of thunder—absolute silence and then a choking gasp!) (Whisper)* Speck!

**SPECK:** Is yo' seein' a ghost?

**PORTER:** Speck!

**SPECK:** Catch yo' breath, boy. Yo' is pale as a lily. An' when yo' get's pale it's painful!

**PORTER:** It's—it's—the bonds! The half million dollars they're looking for!

**SPECK:** Talk sense! You're making sounds, but dey don' mean a thing.

**PORTER:** The bank robber! They're searching the train right now. They think he's on here.

**SPECK:** Bank robber! You mean to sit dar and tell me you jus' dumped out of des here bag the bonds what was stole from dat bank in Chicago?

**PORTER:** That's just what I believe.

**SPECK:** Then, boy, yo' can melt away like a cough drop on mah tongue. I ain't even curious.

**PORTER:** But, Speck—

**SPECK:** Don't "but" me, big boy. Jus' gather up them pieces of paper and fade offa my horizon.

**PORTER:** But that woman isn't the thief. She put diapers in this bag. Somebody hid the bonds here. Speck, we could capture him!

**SPECK:** What you mean "we"? Now, listen! Much as Ah needs money Ah ain't never makin' no date with the undertaker to get it.

**PORTER:** Come on, be a sport. Look, I'll roll these bonds up in this dirty coat and stuff it up here. Then, I'll take the bag back to the car and put it in my locker. We're in the middle of the prairie, going sixty miles an hour. Ace Kelly ain't going to leave this train without his bonds if he can help it!

**SPECK:** Oh, Lawd! This is the fus time Ah ever invited Mister Trouble to step right up an' kiss me! *(Fade) (Train rumble comes up and fades)*

**ANNOUNCER:** Meanwhile back in the car the G-Men have arrived.

**G-MAN:** Sorry, Madame, but no one may leave the car right now.

**LOWER 12:** Why! What do you mean? Mr. Terry and I are going to the—

**G-MAN:** Sorry, Have to wait a few minutes. Conductor will explain.

**1st CALIFORNIAN:** What is it? Mac? What's wrong?

**MAC:** Can't go to the smoker. Don't understand.

**CONDUCTOR:** Will everyone come this way, please. I have something very important to say.

**VOICES:** My goodness, what's wrong.

Is it a hold-up?

What did he say?

**CONDUCTOR:** Folks, I'm asking everyone to be very calm and patient. We want to handle this thing with common sense.

**1st CALIFORNIAN:** Well, mister, get to the point.

**CONDUCTOR:** I will. We have reason to suspect that there is a dangerous criminal on board. *(Woman screams)* Now, lady, nobody's going to harm you. He's trying to get away. If possible, we want to prevent that and we want to recover what he has stolen. If you'll all just be seated right where you are these two men will go through your baggage.

**LOWER 12:** I shan't allow it.

**CONDUCTOR:** Sorry, but we must. Nothing will be disturbed.

**ENGLISHMAN:** I must say! This is most extraordinary!

**DR. LOCKE:** Only the course of the law, sir. We must assist the law in its efforts to apprehend criminals.

**FRANCES:** Now, you see, Elizabeth!

**ELIZABETH:** I see even more than that. *(Whisper)* After what we heard last night we *know* the criminal is in *this* car.

**FRANCES:** Oh! *(Train fades out)*

**ANNOUNCER:** Well, of course, nothing was found in Car 23. But gone was the jovial fellowship of the morning. The utter flatness of the surrounding, drab plains offered little for cheerful diversion; dinner hour came and passed with a certain staid dignity and now grayness is falling over the landscape and within the car lights are snapped on. The baby is fretting.

*(Train in)*

**YOUNG MAN:** Porter, you know I'm getting off at Cheyenne.

**PORTER:** Oh! Thought you were going through.

**MAN:** I was so tight last night, guess you didn't notice my ticket. It's Cheyenne.

**PORTER:** Sorry, sir. Can I brush you off? We're almost in. *(Sound of whistbroom)* Live out here?

**MAN:** My folks do. Going home for a visit. Here you are!

**PORTER:** Thank you, sir. I'll take your bags. *(Rumble of train coming to stop. Whistle blows)*

**VOICE:** *(gruff)* You're a fool to get off here. Know you'll be shadowed.

**WHISPER:** Sure, I'll be shadowed, but I'd be a bigger fool to stay on. My job was to warn you. I'm finished. *(Train pulling into station)*

**1st CALIFORNIAN:** Here we are a few miles nearer home. Cheyenne is growing to be quite a town.

**2nd CALIFORNIAN:** Won't be long now!

**ELIZABETH:** Frances, that young man is getting off!

**FRANCES:** Will they let him go? He might be—

**ELIZABETH:** Nobody's stopping him. Oh, look at that nice old lady who met him. *He* couldn't be Ace Kelly!

**FRANCES:** There's our nice porter talking to one of his friends. *(Outside platform sounds, baggage trucks, etc. etc.)*

**PORTER:** Speck, I'm disappointed. There goes the fellow I thought might be Ace Kelly.

**SPECK:** Humph! How you know he ain't.

**PORTER:** I don't believe Ace Kelly would walk off from half million without even trying to get it. I wouldn't.

**SPECK:** Dey say Ace Kelly's a smart man, an' a smart man know when to quit. *You* ain't smart.

**PORTER:** Well, I'm going to try a little scheme tonight. If it don't mount to nothing I just lose a little sleep. *(Sound: All aboard! All aboard!)* So long, see you later!

**SPECK:** Maybe! *(Train fade out)*

**ANNOUNCER:** Once more our porter has transformed the train coach into a corridor of curtained bedrooms. The passengers are quiet and subdued, retiring early. Lady in Lower 12 has not even asked about Mimi. She seems worried. The porter moves to and fro in a strangely ominous calm. He watches his time carefully. When he is sure every passenger is in his berth, he stops in front of the section containing mother and baby and speaks with deep earnestness.

*(train in)*

**PORTER:** Madam! I'm so sorry!

**MOTHER:** Why, what's the matter?

**PORTER:** This bag you gave me. I clear forgot it. When the G-Men came in, I stuffed the bag in my locker and just now saw it.

**MOTHER:** Well, I—

**PORTER:** Let me leave it here on your shelf till I finish my other work. I'll come right back and get it.

**MOTHER:** I hate to put you to so much trouble, but I do need—

**PORTER:** I'm sure sorry I forgot it. *(Train rumble comes up)*

**ENGLISHMAN:** I say, porter, can you dim the lights. This day has been rather exhausting.

**PORTER:** Yes, sir. Just a few minutes, sir.

**ANNOUNCER:** The Overland Limited goes thundering through the night. Car 23 sways rhythmically, lights almost out and shadows thick and pulsing. It is very still. Not even the sound of a snore, the billowing curtains weave a —

*(Loud scream by a woman! Hard, falling object. Sound of a struggle, babble of voices. Baby begins to cry violently)*

**VOICES:** Lights! Lights!

**PORTER:** I got him! *(More screams, "Hold him," running feet, shouts, blows, door slamming)* Stop him! He's getting away. Lawd! I pulled off his head!

**CONDUCTOR:** All right, Wilson. We've got him. That's his wig you're holding.

**1st CALIFORNIAN:** Dr. Locke!

**VOICES:** It's Dr. Locke!

Is he a robber?

How awful!

**MOTHER:** *(hysterically)* He was climbing in my berth!

**G-MAN:** Kelly! You old scoundrel!

**ENGLISHMAN:** I can't believe it!

**1st CALIFORNIAN:** Ought to be horsewhipped!

**PORTER:** No, no! He was just trying to get the diaper bag. He couldn't, cause it's pinned down.

**CONDUCTOR:** The diaper bag?

**PORTER:** Yes, sir. He thought the bonds were in it.

**G-MAN:** What?

**PORTER:** Yes, sir, but they're not. I took 'em out!

**CONDUCTOR:** You—WHAT?

**PORTER:** I wrapped 'em in an old coat and stuck 'em in my locker.

**G-MAN AND CONDUCTOR:** What?

**PORTER:** I'll get them for you.

**ENGLISHMAN:** Most extraordinary!

**MOTHER:** *(crying)* Porter!

**PORTER:** Yes, mam.

**MOTHER:** He spilt the baby's milk!

**PORTER:** *(quietly)* Yes, mam. I'll see what I can do, mam.

*(Blend and up. Leave music)*

**ANNOUNCER:** Well, we have the bonds and Ace Kelly, but no milk! And the Overland Limited rolls along over track 13.

(Curtain)

# APPENDIX:
## DOCUMENTS RELEVANT TO
## THE LOST PLAYS
## OF THE HARLEM RENAISSANCE

▼▼▼▼▼▼▼▼▼▼▼▼▼▼▼▼▼▼▼▼▼▼▼▼▼▼▼▼▼

## INTRODUCTORY NOTE

In 1926, from March through November, Jessie Fauset, literary editor of *The Crisis*, the official organ of the NAACP, published responses to seven questions she had posed to Black and white theatre artists. Herself a member of the "Talented Tenth," she had perceived that in the popular novels, stories, and plays of her time, the authors, some Black but mostly white, exploited the stereotypes of "low life" Negroes.

Seventy years later, "Black" Hollywood films elicit the same questions. Although Fauset focused on the single issue of class, her questions resonate with other issues of the period. The following documents are intended to provide various popular points of view in the twenties. The first eight documents concern social issues: By what racial designation should people of color call themselves? What was woman's place in the home, the market, the voting booth, the arts? The remaining twelve documents address issues of the theatre: How should a Negro theatre be conceived, and what would be its function in society? What kinds of plays should it mount, and how could its artistic standards be improved? The debates of the twenties echoed on into the thirties and forties.

# 1. THE NEGRO IN ART: HOW SHALL HE BE PORTRAYED?

## Jessie Fauset

1. When the artist, black or white, portrays Negro characters, is he under any obligations or limitations as to the sort of character he will portray?

2. Can any author be criticized for painting the worse or the best characters of a group?

3. Can any publisher be criticized for refusing to handle novels that portray Negroes of education and accomplishment, on the ground that these characters are no different from white folk and therefore not interesting?

4. What are Negroes to do when they are continually painted at their worst and judged by the public as they are painted?

5. Does the situation of the educated Negro in America with its pathos, humiliation and tragedy call for artistic treatment at least as sincere and sympathetic as *Porgy* received?

6. Is not the continual portrayal of the sordid, foolish and criminal among Negroes convincing the world that this and this alone is really and essentially Negroid and preventing white artists from knowing any other types and preventing black artists from daring to paint others?

7. Is there not a real danger that young colored writers will be tempted to follow the popular trend in portraying Negro character in the underworld rather than seeking to paint the truth about themselves and their own social class?

---

First published in *The Crisis*, June 1926.

## 2. WHAT ARE WE, NEGROES OR AMERICANS?

## J. A. Rogers

In the June issue of *The Messenger*, W. A. Domingo, discussed the subject, "What are We, Negroes or Colored People?" J. A. Rogers, author of "From Superman to Man," and other works is following up Mr. Domingo's able discussion with this article—*Editor.*

### ORIGIN

Just what is a Negro? Where and how did the term originate? Is it a term of honor or reproach? These are some of the phases it is necessary to discuss.

The modern use of the term, Negro, dates back to 1442, when Anton Gonsalves, lieutenant of Prince Henry the Navigator, on a trip to the coast of Guinea brought back six captive natives from that region to Spain, a step which resulted in the African slave trade.

These natives were black in color, or *negro*, in the Spanish or Portuguese languages. *Los negros* (the blacks); *los blancos* (the whites). From Spain these *negros* were taken to Cuba as slaves, and later to English-speaking America, where the word, *negro*, was used, later to replace "blackamoor" and "Ethiopian," the former English words for black men.

The whole history of the word, Negro, except for the last sixty-one years is then associated with slavery. In other words, with things, with

First published in *The Messenger*, August 1926.

chattels, having no rights that "the white man was bound to respect." It is important to remember this.

## SCIENTIFIC USE

Later, the word with a capital "N" was to find its way into scientific language, and acquire, perhaps, a slight measure of dignity. Johann Blumenbach (1752–1840), first of the great anthropologists, and perhaps, even at this late day, the greatest of them all, in founding the study of Man, as a science, divided the human race into five varieties, one of which he called, Negro. Blumenbach, it is important to note, was very careful to point out that his division was a purely arbitrary one, that there was, in reality, hundreds of varieties, which blended one into the other by "insensible and imperceptible" degrees; and, that when the last word had been said on the subject that there was but one race—*the human race*. Blumenbach did his work with the thoroughness of the German scientist, as those who will read his "Anthropological Treatise," will see.

In this book he stated in no uncertain terms his opinion that the Negro, then in the very depths of enslavement in the New World, was the biological equal of the other four varieties. And Blumenbach was in a position to know as he had a whole library filled with literary, scientific, and philosophical treatises by European Negroes, many of whom had been graduated with honors from the leading universities. The European Negro has throughout received better treatment then the African or the one in the New World. Negro slavery was abolished in Europe finally in 1773, Portugal being the last place to have Negro slaves.

Compare the thoroughness, the painstaking work, and the knowledge of the Negro as well as that of the other varieties, by this great master with that of the long line of quacks that have followed him as Madison Grant, Lothrop Stoddard, Putnam Weale, Earnest Sevier Cox, R. W. Shufeldt, Henry Fairfield Osborne, and a score of others. Verily a descent from Olympus to a mud puddle!

In Blumenbach's own words:

"Finally I am of opinion that after all these numerous instances I have brought together of Negroes of capacity, it would not be difficult to mention entire well-known provinces of Europe, from out of which you would not easily expect to obtain off hand such good authors, poets, philosophers, and correspondents of the Paris Academy; and on the other hand there is no so-called savage nation known under the sun which has so distinguished itself by such examples of perfectibility and original capacity for scientific culture, and thereby attaching itself so closely to the most civilized nations on earth, as the Negro."

## PRESENT STATUS

To limit now the discussion to the United States. After the black man had been a slave for two hundred and forty-four years, during which his color and physiognomy had been so changed that within his ranks almost every type under the sun could be found, and every disgrace and ignominy known to the baseness of human nature had been heaped on him, not the least of which was the white man's religion and his doctrine of superiority, at bottom the same, he was set free to become five years later a full-fledged citizen of the United States, *on the books.*

There was much opposition to this, as is known, but it was nothing singular from the standpoint of ignorance and illiteracy. The bulk of the Southern whites were in the same state that the mountaineers of Tennessee and North Carolina are now. Indeed, if the word of Olmsted, author of "The Slave States," and others, is to be taken, the masses of the poor whites were below the free Negroes and the slave domestics. The only asset of these poor whites was the empty honor of possessing the same color as the top dog. Hence, if these whites could be citizens, anyone else, in common justice, could be.

## AMENDMENTS TO THE CONSTITUTION

Citizenship and suffrage, as it ought to be well-known, were conferred by the Fourteenth and Fifteenth Amendments to the Constitution. Since it is certain that comparatively few Negroes have read them, it is well to quote them here:

Art. XIV says in part: *"All Persons, born or naturalized in the United States and subject to the jurisdiction thereof, are citizens of the United States, and of the States wherein they reside. No State shall make or enforce any law which shall abridge the privileges or immunities of citizens of the United States."*

Art. XV. *"The right of citizens of the United States shall not be denied or abridged by the United States or by any State on account of color, race, or previous condition of servitude."*

## WHEN IS A NEGRO A NEGRO?

As the term, Negro, stands today it is fully as undefinable as electricity. A white-skinned person who is legally a white man in North Carolina can be legally a Negro in the adjoining state of Virginia; one legally white in Virginia will be classed as black in Oklahoma; the same person legally white in Oregon will be legally black in North Carolina; the whole definition for America being as uncertain and crotchety as an old maid. Each state acts according to its prejudices, or clearer yet, the exploitable possibilities of the "Negro."

Many contend that the term, Negro, is one of opprobium. There can be no doubt that it is. It was founded on slavery and forced degradation. Further, in many of the Southern States, as in South Carolina, Louisiana, and Georgia and those states, in which the population is so mixed that the imputation is likely to be true it is as libellous to call one, supposedly white, a Negro, as to call him a horse-thief, pimp, or crap-shooter. Some years ago a newspaper in South Carolina, in reporting a story, accidentally called a supposedly white man, colored. The judge in awarding him damages uttered this remarkable bit of legal wisdom: " . . . . if one race be inferior to the other socially the Constitution of the United States cannot put them on the same plane." In North Carolina a man recently brought suit when called Negro.

At the mere mention of the word, Negro, particularly in white newspapers, fully ninety percent of the population of the United States, regardless of color, experience a feeling of repulsion, except in certain instances, such as when it comes to telling what the "Negro" has done for the country. Hence the just contention of those who insist the term is a debasing one. As to the word, nigger, there is really no difference, except that custom has made it so. Apart from the fact that the majority of "Negroes" refer to themselves as "niggers," that word, is only the slip-shod pronunciation, as "sah," for "sir." It is certain that the perverters of the word had no added insult in mind.

The objectors to the word, Negro, as was said, are right, but when they suggest some other word as "colored," Ethiopian, Ethican, Afro-American, Race-man, they but constitute themselves killers of time, and diverters from the main issue, the getting of one's rights. For it is not the name but the treatment that hurts. Anglo-Saxon, Christian, Yankee, Irish, and a host of other names were once terms of reproach. When the social, that is, the economic standing of the possessors of those names had improved, the terms also acquired dignity. With loss of economic standing names also lose their standing as Greek, Spaniard, Turk, Italian. Call the black man white, and the white man black; reverse the terms, Negro, and, Caucasian, and with treatment unchanged it will make no difference.

And the worst part of it is that the proscribed is bound to use, some time or another, the opprobious name, given by the oppressor. For instance, in the South the "Negro" is forced by law into separate places labelled for him. In describing himself in legal documents in every state in the Union, and even in the departments conducted by the United States Government itself he is compelled to describe himself as "Negro" or "colored," as in marriage licenses, criminal proceedings, naturalization proceedings, Federal positions, census reports. Although the Constitution of the Federal Government, itself, declares that he is a citizen, yet the government goes to the length of denying this by writing him down as "Colored" or "Negro" in the census reports. It is noteworthy, in this respect that it is only those incapable of becoming citizens, who are thus enumerated separately, as Indians, Chinese, Japanese. Those of other nationalities as, Italians, Jews, Greeks, Germans, provided they are native-born are never mentioned as such. If not born here they are all classified as foreign-born whites. In short, though the Federal government calls the so-called Negro, a citizen, it classifies him as an alien, or rather something betwixt and between, that something, as I will later show being still a slave, to a certain degree of the white man.

Because this is so the Supreme Court of the United States, final voice of the Federal government, always with an eye to the preservation of property rights has been notorious in its decisions as to what is justice for the black man—an old story dating from the Dred Scott decision to the present segregation affair in Washington, D. C.

Although forbidden by the Constitution to make or enforce any bill, based on color, these injunctions, to every state south of the Mason-Dixon line and some north of it are but so many scraps of paper. "Negroes" are forced to pay the same taxes, the same railroad fare, poll-tax, bound to the same contracts, in short the same civic obligations as the white man. But when it comes to getting returns for his harder-earned dollar he gets less, anywhere from seventy-five to twenty cents, and in the matter of education sometimes as low as five cents to the dollar.

On a recent trip to the South I rode from Wilmington, N. C., to Richmond on an old wooden jim-crow car placed between a modern steel baggage car, and steel coach for the whites. In a collision the colored coach, if one can dignify it by that name, would have been crushed to tinder. Further, the conductor, the railroad employes, and the news "butcher" pre-empted eight places while passengers stood. The toilet room of the colored women happened to be nearest the baggage car, so employees on that car used it. Further the colored car is always placed ahead, so that in case of a head-on collision, the "Negroes" will get killed first. This, by the way, is about the only instance in the South where the black man goes first; in jim-crow street cars he rides in the rear. Yet there is an impartial fare for both. This, of course, is only a very minor incident. This article is pianissimo.

In all of these jim-crow states a Negro may ride in the white coach provided he is in the employ of some white person or is a prisoner. Hence, if all Negroes travelled as servants or as convicts, there would be no jim-crow cars.

Sufficient has been said in answer to the query at the head of this article to prove that in actuality, and regardless of what the Constitution may say we are not Americans, but "Negroes" or "colored" as the census reports define us. By and large we have not even the rights of the alien, even those aliens incapable of becoming citizens. With my own ears I heard the terrific fight put up, by ministers of the gospel in the Virginia senate last February to keep Chinese, Japanese and other Asiatics from being jim-crowed in conveyances and public places, and they won. A so-called race integrity bill which passed the house ingeniously declared that the bill would not affect those persons "who by the Constitution of the United States are *ineligible* to become citizens of the United States," meaning Asiatics. Think of that! Chinese, Japanese, and Mexicans ride where they please in the South.

Then there is the Indian, a ward of the nation, and living on the reservation. He pays no taxes but when he comes among the whites, with the saloons now illegal, he may go where he pleases. No segregation for him. The same holds true of any European who touches these shores. There is no segregation for a German, though he made a thousand American widows in the last war: There is segregation for the "Negro" veteran, though he saved a thousand from becoming widows, unless he is travelling as valet for the German.

The sole purpose of segregation is to preserve the status of slave and master—to so arrange it that the "Negro" will have a back-door entrance to everything.

Nor, as was said, is the Federal Government any stricter in the enforcement of the law than the states. Washington, D. C., is under the direct rule of the President and Congress, yet but for the jim-crow car one might well be in Mississippi.

But after all the Negro has been taught on the subject of citizenship, the above will sound incredible. Am I at no time a citizen, he will ask. Yes, there are times when he is not only a citizen, but he is compelled to be, and this holds true of the most barbarous of the Cracker states as of the Northern ones. When it comes to paying taxes, to service in the draft, to defense of the country as in case of foreign invasion, in short in all those things that make for the white man's benefit, he is a one hundred percent citizen. In those that makes for his own benefit, he is only a Negro. In things that make for the white man's benefit the United States is to the Negro, a nation; in things that make for his own benefit, it is a race or tribe, and he an alien in it.

In the awarding of citizenship he has received most of the bitter and little of the sweet, which makes one wonder what those who declare he shouldn't have been made a citizen, have to kick about.

The white workers sometimes call themselves, wage-slaves. The Negro, by and large, is only that in all its sinister implications. There are some above this grade, yet they also are all times subject to attack by the mob and gratuitous insult by the meanest whites.

Baron d'Estournelles de Constant of the French Senate made a study of the Negro in the America and aptly summarized it when he said the American Negro is "freedman not a citizen." Still many Negroes fondly believe themselves citizens. These remind one of the story of the man who had a large fortune and lost it, following which he lost his mind. In this state he fancied he had got it back again, and was content as before. Many a lunatic behind bars is quite happy in the belief that he is Napoleon or Jesus Christ.

In one or two spots as New York, Boston, Minneapolis, and Chicago, the Negro is given a slight measure of citizenship, but compared with that accorded the French Negro it is a joke.

\* \* \* \*

When is the Negro a citizen: In matters of duty. As Stephenson in "Race Distinctions in Law" has demonstrated, the Negro is still largely white man's property.

You realize, then, that this is no question of philanthropy, or of general interest. It is urgent, imperative. If there is to be any of that stuff, which the constitution calls the inalienable right to life, liberty and the pursuit of happiness,—if there is to be any left to our children we must fight for it here, and that right soon. We see the need. Now it becomes for us either,—a fight,—or,—a compromise.

In conclusion, in order to make it unnecessary for you to question me on this, I expect you would like to know where I think this fighting program, which I advocate, will lead in the future. To my mind there is only one goal in all these discussions of race-values, race-destinies, and race-relations, and that goal is to break down all barriers, prejudice, and discrimination due to color and race. We must hold for our fundamental conviction the single standard of manhood by their *deeds* shall you know men, not by the texture of their hair, nor the color of their faces; nor yet their wives, nor their grandfathers, but by their *works*. We must strive toward a society wherein the workers are hired and fired on their individual merit.

I am no prophet, nor the son of a prophet, and I have no gift of divinations. I cannot tell whether or not this means breaking down that delicate and fragile thing called Racial Integrity. I don't care. I am much more concerned with the perpetuation of the most useful tools of society, and the most beautiful arts of civilization, than I am interested in the appearance of the folks who shall carry these treasures down the years.

## 3. WHAT ARE WE?

### George S. Grant

The respect of his fellow-citizens is the citizen's birthright.

When through circumstances not created by himself, this birthright is threatened or taken away, it becomes his duty as well as his privilege to use all lawful means to restore unto himself intact this right which is lost or threatened.

A title which is neither contemptuous, or ridiculous, is an essential part of this birthright.

The word "negro" used to designate a certain group of American citizens is a contemptuous term; resembling in sound and structure the more opprobious epithet, "nigger." The associations brought up by one are easily recalled by the other and aside from its ethnological incorrectness make it an unfit term with which to classify American citizens.

The misplaced word, "colored," used to designate this group is ridiculous; grammatically absurd, it also inevitably calls to mind the comic, the grotesque, which never demand respect.

The term BLACK AMERICANS fills a long felt want. The argument for it begins with the fundamental assertion that we are not Negroes (niggers) or colored people (culled fellahs) but Americans; if it is necessary to distinguish us from the white Americans, then we are BLACK AMERICANS; not all of us are black, not all of white people are white, but "black" and "white" are used here to classify rather than to describe.

---

First published in *The Messenger*, October 1926.

**401**

It logically follows that as Americans we were entitled to the same treatment that other Americans are; no more, no less than the white Americans.

Here we see the subtle danger of the nicknames which have been given us by the whites and to which most of our group cling. As negroes we may be jimcrowed, disenfranchised; as colored people we may be segregated, discriminated against; but against Americans such methods are clearly seen to be unjust, unpatriotic and unwise.

This clinging by us to the nicknames which harm us is explained by our aversion to the word "black." This aversion may be explained in turn by analysing three fallacies which form its basis; first, the false motion of white purity and black impurity, which takes its root in popular religious conception of white divinities, angels, etc., and black devil demons, etc. Springing from this false notion we find this idea (as expressed in the song, "Wash me and I shall be whiter than snow"), developing, growing until it permeates all the literature and thoughts of the Western civilization until it is very common and habitual to speak of "black thoughts," a "black evil countenance," etc.

The second false notion is the idea that beauty is somehow connected with skin color to the credit of lighter shades. This notion depends somewhat upon the first and is the result of the unceasing propaganda of the Western civilization.

The third false notion is the idea that because a people of a certain racial type occupy a position of economic and political power and control, they are inherently and potentially superior.

This last fallacy is the most difficult to correct, because, to the average mind the immediate experience assumes an importance out of all proportion to its real value; seeing the white people occupying most of the important positions, controlling most of the wealth and power, we are apt to forget that other races have at various times been at the lead in civilization—we are disposed to overlook the ease and celerity with which other races assimilate and IMPROVE upon the arts and sciences of the Western civilization; we are prone to look upon a phase of civilization and call it civilization itself.

By adopting the term "BLACK AMERICAN" we will avoid the nicknames which furnish a large part of the excuse for attempts to impose upon us different and inferior treatment and conditions; also as the whole machinery of education and publicity in the United States is designed and operated to build up respect and romantic idealism around the word "American," by merely including that term in our group name, we inevitably appropriate the effect of that propaganda.

By voluntarily choosing the logical mark which distinguishes our group from the group of White Americans, we endow both it and ourselves with a dignity, which reinforced by the development of economic, cultural, and political strength will operate to dispel the fallacious idea of white purity. white beauty, and white superiority.

# 4. THE NEGRO-ART HOKUM

## George S. Schuyler

Negro art "made in America" is as non-existent as the widely advertised profundity of Cal Coolidge, the "Seven years of progress" of Mayor Hylan, or the reported sophistication of New Yorkers. Negro art there has been, is, and will be among the numerous black nations of Africa; but to suggest the possibility of any such development among the ten million colored people in this republic is self-evident foolishness. Eager apostles from Greenwich Village, Harlem, and environs proclaimed a great renaissance of Negro art just around the corner waiting to be ushered on the scene by those whose hobby is taking races, nations, peoples, and movements under their wing. New art forms expressing the "peculiar" psychology of the Negro were about to flood the market. In short, the art of Homo Africanus was about to electrify the waiting world. Skeptics patiently waited. They still wait.

True, from dark-skinned sources have come those slave songs based on Protestant hymns and Biblical texts known as the spirituals, work songs and secular songs of sorrow and tough luck known as the blues, that outgrowth of ragtime known as jazz (in the development of which whites have assisted), and the Charleston, an eccentic dance invented by the gamins around the public market-place in Charleston S. C. No one can or does deny this. But these are contributions of a caste in a certain section of the country. They are foreign to Northern Negroes, West Indian Negroes, and African Negroes. They are no more expressive

Reprinted by permission from *The Nation*, June 16, 1926.

or characteristic of the Negro race than the music and dancing of the Appalachian highlanders or the Dalmatian peasantry are expressive or characteristic of the Caucasian race. If one wishes to speak of the musical contributions of the peasantry of the South, very well. Any group under similar circumstances would have produced something similar. It is merely coincidence that this peasant class happens to be of a darker hue than the other inhabitants of the land. One recalls the remarkable likeness of the minor strains of the Russian mujiks to those of the Southern Negro.

As for the literature, painting, and sculpture of Aframericans—such as there is—it is identical in kind with the literature, painting, and sculpture of white Americans: that is, it shows more or less evidence of European influence. In the field of drama little of any merit has been written by and about Negroes that could not have been written by whites. The dean of the Aframerican literati is W. E. B. Du Bois, a product of Harvard and German universities; the foremost Aframerican sculptor is Meta Warwick Fuller, a graduate of leading American art schools and former student of Rodin; while the most noted Aframerican painter, Henry Ossawa Tanner, is dean of American painters in Paris and has been decorated by the French Government. Now the work of these artists is no more "expressive of the Negro soul"—as the gushers put it—than are the scribblings of Octavus Cohen or Hugh Wiley.

This, of course, is easily understood if one stops to realize that the Aframerican is merely a lampblacked Anglo-Saxon. If the European immigrant after two or three generations of exposure to our schools, politics, advertising, moral crusades, and restaurants becomes indistinguishable from the mass of Americans of the older stock (despite the influence of the foreign-language press), how much truer must it be of the sons of Ham who have been subjected to what the uplifters call Americanism for the last three hundred years. Aside from his color, which ranges from very dark brown to pink, your American Negro is just plain American. Negroes and whites from the same localities in this country talk, think, and act about the same. Because a few writers with a paucity of themes have seized upon imbecilities of the Negro rustics and clowns and palmed them off as authentic and characteristic Aframerican behavior, the common notion that the black American is so "different" from his white neighbor has gained wide currency. The mere mention of the word "Negro" conjures up in the average white American's mind a composite stereotype of Bert Williams, Aunt Jemima, Uncle Tom, Jack Johnson, Florian Slappey, and the various monstrosities scrawled by the cartoonists. Your average Aframerican no more resembles this stereotype than the average American resembles a composite of Andy Gump, Jim Jeffries, and a cartoon by Rube Goldberg.

Again, the Aframerican is subject to the same economic and social forces that mold the actions and thoughts of the white Americans. He is not living in a different world as some whites and a few Negroes would have us believe. When the jangling of his Connecticut alarm clock gets him out of his Grand Rapids bed to a breakfast similar to that eaten by his white brother across the street; when he toils at the same or similar work in mills, mines, factories, and commerce alongside the descendants of Spartacus, Robin Hood, and Erik the Red; when he wears similar clothing and speaks the same language with the same degree of perfection; when he reads the same Bible and belongs to the Baptist, Methodist, Episcopal, or Catholic church; when his fraternal affiliations also include the Elks, Masons, and Knights of Pythias; when he gets the same or similar schooling, lives in the same kind of houses, owns the same makes of cars (or rides in them), and nightly sees the same Hollywood version of life on the screen; when he smokes the same brands of tobacco and avidly peruses the same puerile periodicals; in short, when he responds to the same political, social, moral, and economic stimuli in precisely the same manner as his white neighbor, it is sheer nonsense to talk about "racial differences" as between the American black man and the American white man. Glance over a Negro newspaper (it is printed in good Americanese) and you will find the usual quota of crime news, scandal, personals, and uplift to be found in the average white newspaper —which, by the way, is more widely read by the Negroes than is the Negro press. In order to satisfy the cravings of an inferiority complex engendered by the colorphobia of the mob, the readers of the Negro newspapers are given a slight dash of racialistic seasoning. In the homes of the black and white Americans of the same cultural and economic level one finds similar furniture, literature, and conversation. How, then, can the black American be expected to produce art and literature dissimilar to that of the white American?

Consider Coleridge-Taylor, Edward Wilmot Blyden, and Claude McKay, the Englishmen; Pushkin, the Russian; Bridgewater, the Pole; Antar, the Arabian; Latino, the Spaniard; Dumas, *père* and *fils*, the Frenchmen; and Paul Laurence Dunbar, Charles W. Chesttnut, and James Weldon Johnson, the Americans. All Negroes; yet their work shows the impress of nationality rather than race. They all reveal the psychology and culture of their environment—their color is incidental. Why should Negro artists of America vary from the national artistic norm when Negro artists in other countries have not done so? If we can foresee what kind of white citizens will inhabit this neck of the woods in the next generation by studying the sort of education and environment the children are exposed to now, it should not be difficult to reason what the adults of today are what they are because of the education and environment they were exposed to a generation ago. And that education and environment were about the same for blacks and whites. One contemplates the popularity of the Negro-art hokum and murmurs, "How come?"

This nonsense is probably the last stand of the old myth palmed off by Negrophobists for all these many years, and recently rehashed by the sainted Harding, that there are "fundamental, eternal, and inescapable differences" between white and black Americans. That there are Negroes who will lend this myth a helping hand need occasion no surprise. It has been broadcast all over the world by the vociferous scions of slaveholders, "scientists" like Madison Grant and Lothrop Stoddard, and the patriots who flood the treasury of the Ku Klux Klan; and is believed, even today, by the majority of free, white citizens. On this baseless remise, so flattering to the white mob, that the blackamoor is inferior and fundamentally different, erected the postulate that he must needs be peculiar; and when he attempts to portray life through the medium of art, it must of necessity be a peculiar art. While such reasoning may seem conclusive to the majority of Americans, it must be rejected with a loud guffaw by intelligent people.

[*An opposing view on the subject of Negro art will be presented by Langston Hughes in next week's issue.*]

## 5. The Negro Artist and the Racial Mountain

## Langston Hughes

One of the most promising of the young Negro poets said to me once, "I want to be a poet—not a Negro poet," meaning, I believe, "I want to write like a white poet"; meaning subconsciously "I would like to be a white poet"; meaning behind that, "I would like to be white." And I was sorry the young man said that, for no great poet has ever been afraid of being himself. And I doubted then that, with his desire to run away spiritually from his race, this boy would ever be a great poet. But this is the mountain standing in the way of any true Negro art in America—this urge within the race toward whiteness, the desire to pour racial individuality into the mold of American standardization, and to be as little Negro and as much American as possible.

But let us look at the immediate background of this young poet. His family is of what I suppose one would call the Negro middle class: people who are by no means rich yet never uncomfortable nor hungry—smug, contented, respectable folk, members of the Baptist church. The father goes to work every morning. He is a chief steward at a large white club. The mother sometimes does fancy sewing or supervises parties for the rich families of the town. The children go to a mixed school. In the home they read white papers and magazines. And the mother often says "Don't be like niggers" when the children are bad. A frequent phrase from the father is, "Look how well a white man does things." And so the

First published in *The Nation*, 1926. Reprinted by permission of Harold Ober Associates and the estate of Langston Hughes.

word white comes to be unconsciously a symbol of all the virtues. It holds for the children beauty, morality, and money. The whisper of "I want to be white" runs silently through their minds, This young poet's home is, I believe, a fairly typical home of the colored middle class. One sees immediately how difficult it would be for an artist born in such a home to interest himself in interpreting the beauty of his own people. He is never taught to see that beauty. He is taught rather not to see it, or if he does, to be ashamed of it when it is not according to Caucasian patterns.

For racial culture the home of a self-styled "high-class" Negro has nothing better to offer. Instead there will perhaps be more aping of things white than in a less cultured or less wealthy home. The father is perhaps a doctor, lawyer, landowner, or politician. The mother may be a social worker, or a teacher, or she may do nothing and have a maid. Father is often dark but he has usually married the lightest woman he could find. The family attend a fashionable church where few really colored faces are to be found. And they themselves draw a color line. In the North they go to white theaters and white movies. And in the South they have at least two cars and a house "like white folks." Nordic manners, Nordic faces, Nordic hair, Nordic art (if any), and an Episcopal heaven. A very high mountain indeed for the would-be racial artist to climb in order to discover himself and his people.

But then there are the low-down folks, the so-called common element, and they are the majority—may the Lord be praised! The people who have their nip of gin on Saturday nights and are not too important to themselves or the community, or too well fed, or too learned to watch the lazy world go round. They live on Seventh Street in Washington or State Street in Chicago and they do not particularly care whether they are like white folks or anybody else. Their joy runs, bang! into ecstasy. Their religion soars to a shout. Work maybe a little today, rest a little tomorrow. Play awhile. Sing awhile. O, let's dance! These common people are not afraid of spirituals, as for a long time their more intellectual brethren were, and jazz is their child. They furnish a wealth of colorful, distinctive material for any artist because they still hold their own individuality in the face of American standardizations. And perhaps these common people will give to the world its truly great Negro artist, the one who is not afraid to be himself. Whereas the better-class Negro would tell the artist what to do, the people at least let him alone when he does appear. And they are not ashamed of him—if they know he exists at all. And they accept what beauty is their own without question.

Certainly there is, for the American Negro artist who can escape the restrictions the more advanced among his own group would put upon him, a great field of unused material ready for his art. Without going outside his race, and even among the better classes with their "white" culture and conscious American manners, but still Negro enough to be different, there is sufficient matter to furnish a black artist with a lifetime of creative work. And when he chooses to touch on the relations between Negroes and whites in this country with their innumerable overtones and undertones, surely, and especially for literature and the drama, there is an inexhaustible supply of themes at hand. To these the Negro artist can give his racial individuality, his heritage of rhythm and warmth, and his incongruous humor that so often, as in the Blues, becomes ironic laughter mixed with tears. But let us look again at the mountain.

A prominent Negro clubwoman in Philadelphia paid eleven dollars to hear Raquel Meller sing Andalusian popular songs. But she told me a few weeks before she would not think of going to hear "that woman" Clara Smith, a great black artist, sing Negro folksongs. And many an upper-class Negro church, even now, would not dream of employing a spiritual in its services. The drab melodies in white folks' hymnbooks are much to be preferred. "We want to worship the Lord correctly and quietly. We don't believe in 'shouting.' Let's be dull like the Nordics," they say, in effect.

The road for the serious black artist, then, who would produce a racial art is most certainly rocky and the mountain is high. Until recently he received almost no encouragement for his work from either white or colored people. The fine novels of Chesnutt go out of print with neither race noticing their passing. The quaint charm and humor of Dunbar's dialect verse brought to him, in his day, largely the same kind of encouragement one would give a sideshow freak (A colored man writing poetry! How odd!) or a clown (How amusing!).

The present vogue in things Negro, although it may do as much harm as good for the budding colored artist, has at least done this: it has brought him forcibly to the attention of his own people among whom for so long, unless the other race had noticed him beforehand, he was a prophet with little honor. I understand that Charles Gilpin acted for years in Negro theaters without any special acclaim from his own, but when Broadway gave him eight curtain calls, Negroes, too, began to beat a tin pan in his honor. I know a young colored writer, a manual worker by day, who had been writing well for the colored magazines for some years, but it was not until he recently broke into the white publications and his first book was accepted by a prominent New York publisher that the "best" Negroes in his city took the trouble to discover that he lived there. Then almost immediately they decided to give a grand dinner for him. But the society ladies were careful to whisper to his mother that perhaps she'd better not come. They were not sure she would have an evening gown.

The Negro artist works against an undertow of sharp criticism and misunderstanding from his own group and unintentional bribes from the whites. "Oh, be respectable, write about nice people, show how good we are," say the Negroes. "Be stereotyped, don't go too far, don't shatter our illusions about you, don't amuse us too seriously. We will pay you," say the whites. Both would have told Jean Toomer not to write *Cane*. The colored people did not praise it. The white people did not buy it. Most of the colored people who did read *Cane* hate it. They are afraid of it. Although the critics gave it good reviews the public remained indifferent. Yet (excepting the work of Du Bois) *Cane* contains the finest prose written by a Negro in America. And like the singing of Robeson, it is truly racial.

But in spite of the Nordicized Negro intelligentsia and the desires of some white editors we have an honest American Negro literature already with us. Now I await the rise of the Negro theater. Our folk music, having achieved world-wide fame, offers itself to the genius of the great individual American Negro composer who is to come. And within the next decade I expect to see the work of a growing school of colored artists who paint and model the beauty of dark faces and create with new technique the expression of their own soul-world. And the Negro dancers who will dance like flame and the singers who will continue to carry our songs to all who listen—they will be with us in even greater numbers tomorrow.

Most of my own poems are racial in theme and treatment, derived from the life I know. In many of them I try to grasp and hold some of the meanings and rhythms of jazz. I am as sincere as I know how to be in these poems and yet after every reading I answer questions like these from my own people: Do you think Negroes should always write about Negroes? I wish you wouldn't read some of your poems to white folks. How do you find anything interesting in a place like a cabaret? Why do you write about black people? You aren't black. What makes you do so many jazz poems?

But jazz to me is one of the inherent expressions of Negro life in America: the eternal tom-tom beating in the Negro soul—the tom-tom of revolt against weariness in a white world, a world of subway trains, and work, work, work; the tom-tom of joy and laughter, and pain swallowed in a smile. Yet the Philadelphia clubwoman is ashamed to say that her race created it and she does not like me to write about it. The old subconscious "white is best" runs through her mind. Years of study under white teachers, a lifetime of white books, pictures, and papers, and white manners, morals, and Puritan standards made her dislike the spirituals. And now she turns up her nose at jazz and all its manifestations—likewise almost everything else distinctly racial. She doesn't care for the Winold Reiss portraits of Negroes because they are "too Negro." She does not want a true picture of herself from anybody. She wants the artist to flatter her, to make the white world believe that all Negroes are as smug and as near white in soul as she wants to be. But, to my mind, it is the duty of the younger Negro artist, if he accepts any duties at all from outsiders, to change through the force of his art that old whispering "I want to be white," hidden in the aspirations of his people, to "Why should I want to be white? I am a Negro and beautiful!"

So I am ashamed for the black poet who says, "I want to be a poet, not a Negro poet," as though his own racial world were not as interesting as any other world. I am ashamed, too, for the colored artist who runs from the painting of Negro faces to the painting of sunsets after the manner of the academicians because he fears the strange unwhiteness of his own features. An artist must be free to choose what he does, certainly, but he must also never be afraid to do what he might choose.

Let the blare of Negro jazz bands and the bellowing voice of Bessie Smith singing Blues penetrate the closed ears of the colored near-intellectuals until they listen and perhaps understand. Let Paul Robeson singing "Water Boy," and Rudolph Fisher writing about the streets of Harlem, and Jean Toomer holding the heart of Georgia in his hands, and Aaron Douglas drawing strange black fantasies cause the smug Negro middle class to turn from their white, respectable, ordinary books and papers to catch a glimmer of their own beauty. We younger Negro artists who create now intend to express our individual dark-skinned selves without fear or shame. If white people are pleased we are glad. If they are not, it doesn't matter. We know we are beautiful. And ugly too. The tom-tom cries and the tom-tom laughs. If colored people are pleased we are glad. If they are not, their displeasure doesn't matter either. We build our temples for tomorrow, strong as we know how, and we stand on top of the mountain, free within ourselves.

# 6. The Negro Woman and the Ballot

## Alice Dunbar-Nelson

It has been six years since the franchise as a national measure has been granted women. The Negro woman has had the ballot in conjunction with her white sister, and friend and foe alike are asking the question, What has she done with it?

Six years is a very short time in which to ask for results from any measure or condition, no matter how simple. In six years a human being is barely able to make itself intelligible to listeners; is a feeble, puny thing at best, with undeveloped understanding, no power of reasoning, with a slight contributory value to the human race, except in a sentimental fashion. Nations in six years are but the beginnings of an idea. It is barely possible to erect a structure of any permanent value in six years, and only the most ephemeral trees have reached any size in six years.

So perhaps it is hardly fair to ask with a cynic's sneer, What has the Negro woman done with the ballot since she has had it? But, since the question continues to be hurled at the woman, she must needs be nettled into reply.

To those colored women who worked, fought, spoke, sacrificed, traveled, pleaded, wept, cajoled, all but died for the right of suffrage for themselves and their peers, it seemed as if the ballot would be the great objective of life. That with its granting, all the economic, political and social problems to which the race had been subject would be solved. They did not hesitate to say—those militantly gentle workers for the vote

First published in *The Messenger*, June 1927.

—that with the granting of the ballot the women would step into the dominant place politically, of the race. That all the mistakes which the men had made would be rectified. The men have sold their birthright for a mess of pottage, said the women. Cheap political office and little political preferment had dazzled their eyes so that they could not see the greater issues affecting the race. They had been fooled by specious lies, fair promises and large-sounding words. Pre-election promises had inflated their chests, so that they could not see the post-election failures at their feet.

And thus on and on during all the bitter campaign of votes for women. One of the strange phases of the situation was the rather violent objection of the Negro man to the Negro woman's having the vote. Just what his objection racially was, he did not say, preferring to hide behind the grandiloquent platitude of his white political boss. He had probably not thought the matter through; if he had, remembering how precious the ballot was to the race, he would have hesitated at withholding its privilege from another one of his own people.

But all that is neither here nor there. The Negro woman got the vote along with some tens of million other women in the country. And has it made any appreciable difference in the status of the race?

Unfortunately statistics are not available to determine just how the additional vote has affected communities for the better. The Negro woman was going to be independent, she had averred. She came into the political game with a clean slate. No Civil War memories for her, and no deadening sense of gratitude to influence her vote. She would vote men and measures, not parties. She would scan each candidate's record and give him her support according to how he had stood in the past on the question of the race. She owed no party allegiance. The name of Abraham Lincoln was not synonymous with her for blind G. O. P. allegiance. She would show the Negro man how to make his vote a power, and not a joke. She would break up the tradition that one could tell a black man's politics by the color of his skin.

And when she got the ballot she slipped quietly, safely, easily and conservatively into the political party of her male relatives.

Which is to say, that with the exception of New York City, and a sporadic break here and there, she became a Republican. Not a conservative one, however. She was virulent and zealous. Prone to stop speaking to her friends who might disagree with her findings on the political issue, and vituperative in campaigns.

In other words, the Negro woman has by and large been a disappointment in her handling of the ballot. She has added to the overhead charges of the political machinery, without solving racial problems.

One or two bright lights in the story hearten the reader. In the congressional campaign of 1922 the Negro woman cut adrift form party allegiance and took up the cudgel (if one may mix metaphors) for the cause of the Dyer Bill. The Anti-Lynching Crusaders, led by Mrs. Mary B. Talbot, found in several states—New Jersey, Delaware, and Michigan particularly—that its cause was involved in the congressional election. Sundry gentlemen had voted against the Dyer Bill in the House and had come up for re-election. They were properly castigated by being kept at home. The women's votes unquestionably had the deciding influence in the three states mentioned, and the campaign as conducted by them was of a most commendable kind.

School bond issues here and there have been decided by the colored woman's votes—but so slight is the ripple on the smooth surface of conservatism that it has attracted no attention from the deadly monotony of the blind faith in the "Party of Massa Linkum."

As the younger generation becomes of age it is apt to be independent in thought and in act. But it is soon whipped into line by the elders, and by the promise of plums of preferment or of an amicable position in the community or of easy social relations—for we still persecute socially those who disagree with us politically. What is true of the men is true of the women. The very young are apt to let father, sweetheart, brother or uncle decide her vote. The next in years prefer not to take the thorny path of independence because it involves too many strained relations in the church or social club. Being human and gregarious, she follows along the line of least resistance, and rightly dubs politics a bore.

Whether women have been influenced and corrupted by their male relatives and friends is a moot question. Were I to judge by my personal experience I would say unquestionably so. I mean a personal experience with some hundreds of women in the North Atlantic, Middle Atlantic and Middle Western States. High ideals are laughed at, and women confess with drooping wings how they have been scoffed at for working for nothing, for voting for nothing, for supporting a candidate before having first been "seen." In the face of this sinister influence it is difficult to see how the Negro woman could have been anything else but "just another vote."

All this is rather a gloomy presentment of a well-known situation. But it is not altogether hopeless. The fact that the Negro woman CAN be roused when something near and dear to her is touched and threatened is cheering. Then she throws off the influence of her male companion and strikes out for herself. Whatever the Negro may hope to gain for himself must be won at the ballot box, and quiet "going along" will never gain his end. When the Negro woman finds that the future of her children lies in her own hands—if she can be made to see this—she will strike off the political shackles she has allowed to be hung upon her, and win the economic freedom of her race.

Perhaps some Joan of Arc will lead the way.

# 7. THE NEGRO WOMAN IN THE PROFESSIONS

## Anna Jones Robinson

Twenty years ago the woman engaged in the practice of a profession was a rare creature. Seventy-five per cent of the women graduating from professional schools never actually pursued the practice of their professions, either because discouraged too quickly by the opposition and difficulties of pioneer work or because the duties of marriage made impossible the career for which they had been trained.

The small number of women who persisted in spite of obstacles have had a great measure of success. This has come because of the very real interest in their work, and love for the profession which they have chosen. They have not tried to avoid the drudgery or uninteresting details upon which any real success must be founded. Indeed this attention to small details has helped many women to climb to very responsible positions such as executive in large business enterprises. Women with legal training and real ability are eagerly sought to prepare briefs and to take charge of certain classes of cases in law firms because of their very careful work and attention to details which are often most lightly passed over by men.

Twenty years ago the professions entered by women were limited. With the exception of teaching, which up to the present has always been regarded as a field for which women were particularly fitted, there was very little representation. Medicine was regarded with most favor, with dentistry a close second. In all three of these professions the woman

---

First published in *The Messenger*, July 1923.

could still live a more or less secluded life and was not required to go forth into active competition with men engaged in the same work. The woman physician or dentist could count on a certain number of people who would seek her out because of real ability, and because they preferred a woman doctor or dentist.

To-day, although teaching, medicine and dentistry still hold first places, we find women successfully engaged in professions which require active competition with men. We have women lawyers, journalists, architects, interior decorators, designers, accountants and women in various other professions which keep them always before the public and require that they match their wits with men who have the advantage of a longer period of time.

The struggle has not been an easy one. Prejudices and conventional ideas about woman's place in the home have been great hindrances. First among the obstacles to be overcome was the attitude of the professional schools, some of which, even to-day, refuse to admit women to their classes, notably among them, Columbia University Law School, in the City of New York. However, once admitted to the school, the woman has had very little difficulty. Her mentality is unquestioned, and indeed the few women in the classes are usually among the best students and sometimes carry off the highest honors. Once graduated, her troubles begin. She must now rub shoulders and match wits with men, some of whom welcome her as a fellow-practitioner, ignoring difference in sex, while others refuse to take her seriously, either ignoring her whenever possible or else seeking to hold her up to ridicule when she makes some mistake due to her inexperience. Happily, this class of professional men are in the minority, the majority being willing to treat her as they would any young man just entering upon his professional career. If the woman is big enough to refuse to accept any favors or special consideration just because she is a woman, and is willing to give the best that is in her to her work, there is no reason why she should not be successful.

If success is measured by financial gain, medical women are the most successful professional women, for they, as a whole, are earning more money than women in other professions, and medicine is one of the few professions in which women receive the same remuneration as men. But this may be accounted for by the longer experience which women have had in this science. Ever since Hygeia, the daughter of Aesculapius, was associated with her father and presided over his temple, devoted to the sick at Epidaurus, women have never been wholly debarred from the profession, although in many countries and at various times, much has been done through prejudice to exclude them from the study and practice. Dentistry is a branch of the medical profession in which women have had about seventy years experience. The proportion of women in the profession is smaller, but each year sees greater numbers taking up the work.

The first woman lawyer in this country graduated from the University of Michigan fifty-one years ago. It has been estimated that there are to-day 1,500 women who have been admitted to practice law in the various states. However, a large number of those who have been admitted and are entitled to practice, do not follow their profession, but do other work in secretarial, executive or business fields, using their legal training merely as an aid to advance themselves in these fields. It may be safely said that the number of women actually practicing law in the country to-day, is perhaps less than one-half of the number who have been admitted to the bar. The financial returns to the woman lawyer are not always large. A lawyer man or woman, often begins work with a salary of $25 or $30 a week. The rest is entirely dependent upon the individual, but it may be said that very few women have made more than $6,500 a year and the average earnings are between $2,000 and $2,500. On the whole these amounts do not compare unfavorable with the amounts earned by men. A few years ago it was reported that among 15,000 lawyers in New York City, the average earnings were $1,500. However women lawyers who have persisted have been able to build up very lucrative practices and to obtain all the work they can handle. Then too, the woman lawyer is compensated for lack of financial success, but the very great opportunity afforded her in the practice of her profession, to render service to the community, to make her influence felt, and to set an example of the very finest type of citizenship.

In this new freedom of woman, the Negro woman is only excelled by her white sister in numbers. In all the large centers of the country where there is a large Negro population can be found the colored professional woman, a credit to her profession and an influence for good in her community.

The Negro woman has always had her share of responsibility, even when confined to the home, and so has carried with her into these new fields a spirit of independence which has prevented her from being guilty of playing on sex when up against competition with men.

Women who have had special training in various lines have always been willing and eager to do service in their community. This is especially true of the Negro woman. In any movement for the social betterment and happiness of her people, the Negro woman of the professions is always among the first, anxious to give her time, services and money to help a worthy cause. Her aid is lent without any selfish motive and her interest in politics is impersonal, and stimulated by an honest desire to improve the social and economic conditions of her people and community.

The opportunities and possibilities open to the Negro woman in the professions for self-development and service to her people are as yet unexplored, and as more of them enter the field with this idea in mind, their influence cannot but be felt and seen in the improved condition of their community. For the reason young women who have the desire and ability should be encouraged and aided in every way possible in their efforts to attain a profession, and the community which encourages its young women, will be well repaid by receiving unselfish and devoted service at all times.

# 8. THE NEGRO WORKING WOMAN: WHAT SHE FACES IN MAKING A LIVING

## Mary Louise Williams

My working career started a few years back in a small city in New York State, with a high school education. After graduation, being filled with the enthusiasm of youth, I naturally turned my thoughts to "something different."

I applied to several offices for employment, seeking even as inferior a position as addressing envelopes. At every place I met with disappointment. None felt they could use colored help in that capacity.

By this time I felt somewhat like a peacock who had looked at his feet. Now, I worked around at odd jobs and housework until one day I received a surprise.

Through the kind intercession of the Vice-President of a manufactory I was given an opportunity in its perfume department. I was to act as forelady and stock clerk. I made good. The management, being so well pleased, doubled my salary after a year's service. No question of color ever arose. In the course of a few more months I was walking home with a co-worker and met my mother. Naturally I was proud of her and wanted my friends to meet her. At the corner, as had been our habit, we separated. Next morning I was summoned to the office. You can imagine my surprise upon finding my services were no longer needed. Mr. Vice-President softened it as best he could: "There is no fault with your work, but the girls will not work with a Negro. We would

First published in *The Messenger*, July 1923.

gladly keep you if we could, but it is better to lose one girl than to lose twenty."

On another occasion I answered an advertisement in the paper worded thus: "Wanted: a young colored girl, high school graduate preferred. Apply Dey's Department Store." I dressed with care expecting to find at least a saleslady's opening. Just picture for yourself my chagrin upon learning they desired a bootblack in the ladies' rest room! The reason they wanted an educated girl was to keep their wealthy customers from coming in contact with objectionable Negroes. I had no chance to refuse the job because Mr. T. said I looked too much like a Caucasian and he could not use me. He finally hired a high school graduate who had trained two years for a teacher. Is it not a pity that a colored girl must be educated to qualify as a bootblack?

Finding no real openings for me in the clerical line, I turned my attention to shop work. I did this for three reasons. First, it gave me more time for myself than housework. Second, I received a more liberal reward per hour for my services. Third, it placed me on a more equal basis with the other workers although I needed no education other than to read and write. At this work I made just enough money to make both ends meet and sometimes I had to stretch pretty hard to do so, especially when we had a holiday. Naturally I received a little less pay than the white workers. The difference in pay was due possibly to the open shop. In this city there is no colored garment workers' union and the white unions do not take the Negro in. In the shops the Negro has no chance of advancement.

I heard so much about Cleveland. I went there and found conditions more favorable, due probably to the fact that the Negro himself was more enterprising. Here I found a Negro Vaudeville employing all Negro help. There were also colored doctors, lawyers. clubs, hotels, rooming houses, ice cream parlors, drug stores, and restaurants. These were all using colored help. The Phyllis Wheatly Home and the National Association for the Advancement of Colored People took an active part in placing girls in suitable positions. Still there were many girls uncared for.

I happened to be one of these and took a job to wash glasses and silver in a white hotel. I found hotel conditions here very much as they were at home. Though we ate the same food as the whites, we ate at the dishwashers' table, men and women eating together. Here I worked nine hours a day for forty dollars a month. Out of this I paid carfare twice a day, for one meal a day, four dollars a week for a room, and one dollar for laundry. This left me very little for the pleasures of life. I was about discouraged when the assistant steward was taken up in the draft. After this the head steward had quite a job to keep this place filled. So I braved the lion in his den and the result was I became the assistant. It was really a man's job. I had to take care of the storeroom and coolers, also to keep track of the cost of keeping up the various parts of the hotel. I probably would be there yet only peace was declared and with it came the return of the former assistant steward. This position afforded me so many luxuries of life that it showed me what a joy work would be to the Negro woman if given a position and salary instead of a job and wages.

Being a little homesick I returned. Somehow I expected to see conditions changed. With the exception of a few elevator operators, girls to dust china and furniture, two or three girls to rearrange stock behind white salesladies, and a few more women working in shops, I found no change. Oh, yes, I found three women working as salesladies, but as these were "passing" they mean less than nothing in the history of the Negro Woman.

Not being able to find anything that pleased me I turned my attention to canvassing. Even now I feel loathing for this work. If I called at the front door I was directed to the rear. In many instances the door was shut in my face before I could make my errand known. Others treated me well, but that expression of incredulity upon seeing a Negro agent spoke louder than words. Some business men would give me an audience, sometimes with an order. Others received me with so much attention I felt they thought my magazines were only a camouflage.

And since there is a general tendency to expand the field of her operations, manual and mental, let us say with Longfellow:

> Out of the shadow of night
> The world moves into light,
> It is daybreak everywhere!

## 9. "RACHEL" THE PLAY OF THE MONTH: THE REASON AND SYNOPSIS BY THE AUTHOR

### Angelina W. Grimké

Since it has been understood that "Rachel" preaches race suicide, I would emphasize that that was not my intention. To the contrary, the appeal is not primarily to the colored people, but to the whites.

Because of environment and certain inherent qualities each of us reacts correspondingly and logically to the various forces about us. For example, if these forces be of love we react with love, and if of hate with hate. Very naturally all of us will not react as strongly or in the same manner—that is impossible.

Now the colored people in this country form what may be called the "submerged tenth." From morning until night, week in week out, year in year out, until death ends all, they never know what it means to draw one clean, deep breath free from the contamination of the poison of that enveloping force which we call race prejudice. Of necessity they react to it. Some are embittered, made resentful, belligerent, even dangerous; some are made hopeless, indifferent, submissive, lacking in initiative; some again go to any extreme in a search for temporary pleasures to drown their memory, thought, etc.

Now the purpose was to show how a refined, sensitive, highly-strung girl, a dreamer and an idealist, the strongest instinct in whose nature is a love for children and a desire some day to be a mother herself —how this girl would react to this force.

First published in *The Competitor*, January 1920.

The majority of women, everywhere, although they are beginning to awaken, from one of the most conservative elements of society. They are, therefore, opposed to changes. For this reason and for sex reasons the white women of this country are about the worst enemies with which the colored race has to contend. My belief was, then, that if a vulnerable point in their armor could be found, if their hearts could be reached even if only a little, then, perhaps, instead of being active or passive enemies, they might become, at least, less inimical and possibly friendly.

Did they have a vulnerable point and, if so, what was it? I believed it to be motherhood. Certainly all the noblest, finest, most sacred things in their lives converge about this. If anything can make all women sisters underneath their skins it is motherhood. If, then, the white women of this country could see, feel, understand just what effect their prejudice and the prejudice of their fathers, brothers, husbands, sons were having on the souls of the colored mothers everywhere, and upon the mothers that are to be, a great power to affect public opinion would be set free and the battle would be half won.

This was the main purpose. There is a subsidiary one as well. Whenever you say "colored person" to a white man he immediately, either through an ignorance that is deliberate or stupid, conjures up in his mind the picture of what he calls "the darkey." In other words, he believes, or says he does, that all colored people are a grinning, white-toothed, shiftless, carefree set, given to chicken-stealing, watermelon-eating, always, under all circumstances, properly obsequious to a white skin and always amusing. Now, it is possible that this type is to be found among the colored people; but if the white man is honest and observant he will have to acknowledge that the same type can be duplicated in his own race. Human nature, after all, is the same. And if the white man only cared to find out he would know that, type for type, he could find the same in both races. Certainly colored people are living in homes that are clean, well-kept with many evidences of taste and refinement about them. They are many of them well educated, cultivated and cultured; they are well-mannered and, in many instances, more moral than the whites; they love beauty; they have ideals and ambitions, and they do not talk—this educated type—in the Negro dialect. All the joys and sorrows and emotions the white people feel they feel; their feelings are as sensitive; they can be hurt as easily; they are as proud. I drew my characters, then, from the best type of colored people.

Now as to the play itself. In the first act Rachel, loving, young, joyous and vital, caring more to be a mother than anything else in this world, comes suddenly and terribly face to face with what motherhood means to the colored woman in the South. Four years elapse between the first and second acts. Rachel has learned much. She is saddened, disillusioned and embittered. She knows now that organized society in the North has decreed that if a colored man or woman is to be an economic factor, then he or she must, with comparatively few exceptions, remain in the menial class. This has been taught her by her own experience, by the experience of her brother, Tom, and by the experience of John Strong, the man she loves. She has learned that she may not go to a theater for an evening's entertainment without having it spoiled for her since, because of her color she must sit as an outcast, a pariah in a segregated section. And yet in spite of all this youth in her dies hard and hope and the desire for motherhood. She loves children, if anything, more than ever. It is in this act that she feels certain, for the first time, that John Strong loves her. She is made very happy by this knowledge, but in the midst of her joy there comes a knocking at the door. And very terribly and swiftly again it is brought home to her what motherhood means, this time to the colored woman in the North. The lesson comes to her through a little black girl and her own little adopted son, Jimmy. Not content with maiming and marring the lives of colored men and women she learns this baneful thing, race prejudice, strikes at the soul of little colored children. In her anguish and despair at the knowledge she turns against God, believing that He has been mocking at her by implanting in her breast this desire for motherhood, and she swears by the most solemn oath of which she can think never to bring a child here to have its life blighted and ruined.

A week elapses between Acts II and III. During this time Rachel has been very ill, not in body, but in mind and soul. She is up and about again, but is in a highly over-wrought, nervous state. John Strong, whom she has not seen since she has been sick, comes to see her. She knows what his coming means and tries unsuccessfully to ward off his proposal. He pleads so well that, although she feels she is doing a wicked thing she finally yields. Just at the moment of her surrender, however, the sound of little Jimmy's heartbreaking weeping comes to her ears. She changes immediately and leaves him to go to Jimmy. Every night since Jimmy has undergone that searing experience in the previous act he has dreamed of it and awakens weeping. With that sound in her ears and soul she finds that she cannot break her oath. She returns and tells John Strong she cannot marry him. He is inclined, at first, not to take her seriously; but she shows him that this time her answer is final. Although her heart is breaking she sends him away. The play ends in blackness and with the inconsolable sounds of little Jimmy weeping.

## 10. PRESCRIPTION FOR THE NEGRO THEATRE

### Carl Van Vechten

Since that summer, four years ago, when *Shuffle Along* aroused so much enthusiasm among paying theatregoers, producers have made a consistent effort to repeat the success of that Negro revue. *Put and Take, Oh Joy, Strut Miss Lizzie, How Come, Runnin' Wild, Liza, Dixie to Broadway, The Chocolate Dandies,* and *7–11* are the titles of the most conspicuous of these pieces, not one of which won the popularity of its celebrated forerunner, although a few attracted an ephemeral attention.

Latterly, the lack of public interest in these African frolics has become so pronounced that it has come to be believed along the upper stretches of Seventh Avenue and in the dusky section of Tin Pan Alley that any Negro musical show is now foredoomed to certain failure and faces are long and features are glum as a result. It might be well, therefore, to study some of the causes contributing to the apathy of the admirers of this exotic form of entertainment, an apathy which has been the direct occasion for this false psychological reaction among the entrepreneurs.

In the first place it is an error to take it for granted, as so many of those recently initiated into the titillations of these agreeable buffooneries are prone to do, that *Shuffle Along* was the first notable Negro revue. A little inquiry by those born too young to be privy to the facts would easily elicit the information that Bert Williams and George Walker, for

First published in *Vanity Fair*, 1925. Reprinted by permission of the estate of Carl Van Vechten.

many seasons in many vehicles, were greeted with applause on both sides of the Atlantic and showered with dollars and sovereigns. The name of Ernest Hogan may be forgotten, but in his day he was a comedian of parts who starred at the head of his own company. Bob Cole is dead, but Rosamond Johnson is very much alive to remind us that the popular team of Cole and Johnson once existed. In 1913, J. Leubrie Hill produced his *Darktown Follies* at the Lafayette Theatre and rewon an audience which had been captivated thirteen years earlier by Williams and Walker, but which, through Walker's death and Williams's subsequent abandonment of his troupe in favor of vaudeville, had been deprived of a suitable opportunity to express its approval of these Ethiopian carnivals. The *Darktown Follies*, if I remember rightly, continued its run in the heart of Harlem and was not delivered over to a Broadway house, but Broadway flocked to the Lafayette and Florenz Ziegfeld bought three songs from this revue for the coeval edition of his own Follies.

Moreover, apparently it has also been forgotten that the musical shows of Williams and Walker, Ernest Hogan, and J. Leubrie Hill had their own imitations which soon faded into that obscurity which has gathered in the majority of the successors of *Shuffle Along*. As a sympathetic witness who has attended these Negro diversions for twenty-five years, I may state that the reason for the occasional public apathy is perfectly clear to me: these entertainments are built upon a formula which varies so little in its details that only once in five years or so, after the customers have forgotten the last one, is it possible to awaken interest in a new example, and only then when there is an exceptional cast or especially tuneful music. It is well to keep in mind that Bert Williams was a comedian almost of the first rank, a perfect artist within his limitations, who would have made a name for himself anywhere; he might have enjoyed a considerable career had he relied solely on his pantomimic gifts. For a decade, after the demise of his troupe, he was a leading figure in the music halls and in the Follies. George Walker, too, was inimitable in his own line, that of portraying the smartly dressed, Negro swell, prancing with heaved chest, while his wife, Ada Overton Walker (later, I believe, she became Aida, perhaps responding to the urge of some insistent numerologist), was a singer and dancer of personal magnetism and far from negative talent. If J. Leubrie Hill's company included no such stars, his show boasted three or four good tunes and he exhibited a plethora of ingenuity in his staging of the intricate dancing numbers. *Shuffle Along* possessed not only a score which set the town to whistling and the phonographs to whirling, but also a cast which included [Noble] Sissle and [Eubie] Blake, [Flournoy] Miller and [Aubrey] Lyles, and Gertrude Saunders, the latter eventually supplanted by Florence Mills. These performers have since separated to head their own respective companies.

Aside, however, from the music of *Shuffle Along* and the talent of certain of the principals, no new element was introduced to give a kick to the connoisseur of such shows. The dancing of the chorus was a delight, but the dancing in any Negro revue is always *hors de concours*. All the old stuff was strutted, together with the fulsome imitation of white revues which has come to be such a discouraging feature of these entertainments. One of the hits of this piece was a tune in the moth-eaten, sentimental ballad form, "Love Will Find a Way." The innumerable encores allotted at every performance to "I'm Just Wild about Harry" were occasioned by a strutter who maneuvered his chest and buttocks after the manner made famous by George Walker. Any one who had ever enjoyed the privilege of observing George Walker negotiating the cakewalk would not have been very much excited over the modest prowess of his successor. The customary cavortings in overalls and bandannas, clog dancing on the levee, also were in evidence. All Negro revues open either the first or second act with a levee or a plantation scene.

Further, the comedians blacked their faces and carmined and enlarged their lips. This is a minstrel tradition that seems to die hard, even with colored minstrels. Bert Williams, who had a very light complexion, may have had some excuse for following this tradition, although, personally, I do not believe that he had. For it to be followed blindly, unthinkingly, by practically every comedian in the Negro theatre is worse than an absurdity. In the end it will amount to suicide.

This is not the only unworthy tradition perpetuated by *Shuffle Along* and its less vital successors. The tendency which is likely to have the ultimate effect of destroying the last remnants of general public interest in these revues is the persistent demand, on the part of the producers, for light chorus and dancing girls. The girls latterly on exhibition are so nearly white that what with the injudicious application of whitening and the employment of amber illumination (together with the added fact that all of them have straight, and many of them red or blonde hair), there is nothing to distinguish them from their sisters in the *Scandals* or *Artists and Models* save their superior proficiency in the Charleston.

In professional agility and vitality these girls must be the envious despair of many a Ned Wayburn. Nor can it be said that the Negro stage is lacking in more highly skilled talent. I could name fifty exceptionally clever colored actors, singers, and dancers, some of them as yet undiscovered save by cabaret habitués. . . . But these performers do not write the revues, much less produce them, and it is in these two departments that weakness is betrayed, for as yet no Negro has written or produced a revue which indicates that any original thought has been expended on the job.

Awaiting the appearance of a dusky Charlot or a chocolate Ziegfeld, permit me to offer a few hints to prospective purveyors of Negro revues. First and last: advertise for a dark chorus. I don't think it will be necessary to look for "chocolate to the bone" cuties. Indeed, a fascinating effect might be achieved by engaging a rainbow chorus: six black girls, six "seal-browns," six "high Yellas," and six pale creams. With the proper costumes, and a director capable of contriving appropriate evolutions and groupings, it is impossible to set a limit to what might be done with this human palette of color. In case, for some reason, this scheme is found impracticable, as many dark girls as possible should be engaged. There are certainly many Negroes who prefer dark girls; white people who go to Negro shows expect to see them and are disappointed when they don't. Seek beauties who can dance and sing, and see that the lightest is about the shade of strong coffee before the cream is poured in, and I guarantee that your show will be a success even if you throw in all the old stuff, the cemetery scene with the ghost, the moon song rendered by the tenor who doesn't know what to do with his hands, and the "I want to be in Dixie," or the Mammy, or the cotton-bale song. It might be well, however, to eliminate these stale features also, together with the repulsive liver-lips and cork complexions of the comedians. I believe, if I were a Negro and it were my profession to make people laugh, that I could parade my material as successfully without these childish adjuncts as with them. At any rate it would be a welcome relief to see somebody make the attempt.

Let me offer a few more suggestions as substitutes for the discarded features. Why doesn't some sapient manager engage Bessie Smith, "the empress of the Blues," or Clara Smith, "the world's greatest moaner," to sing the Blues, not Blues written by Sissle and Blake or Irving Berlin, but honest-to God Blues, full of trouble and pain and misery and heartache and tribulation Blues like "Any Woman's Blues," "If You Only Knowed," or "Nobody Knows the Way I Feel Dis Mornin'":

> I feel like I could scream an' cry dis mornin',
> I feel like I could scream an' cry dis mornin',
> I feel like I could scream an' cry,
> But I'm too downhearted an' I'd rather die;
> Nobody knows the way I feel dis mornin'.
> I even hate to hear yore name dis mornin',
> I even hate to hear yore name;
> I could kill you quicker than an express train:
> Nobody knows the way I feel dis mornin'.

To hear Clara Smith sing this song is an experience that no one, who has had the privilege, will soon forget. Her voice, choking with moaning quarter tones, clutches the heart. Her expressive and economic gestures are full of meaning. What an artist! Yet I do not think she has ever appeared in one of the first-class revues, although her phonograph records are famous wherever disks of Blues are bought.

On the streets of Harlem this summer, or even on Broadway during the theatre hour, you may have encountered a crowd of pickaninny ragamuffins dancing the Charleston for baksheesh. These gamins are so proficient and skillful in varying their steps, their appearance is so picturesque, that no sooner do they begin their exhibition of terpsichorean virtuosity than a large crowd collects. Has it occurred to any Negro producer that this scene on the stage would create a riot of enthusiasm in his auditorium? It has not. Nor has he arrived at the conclusion that an hysterical camp-meeting number with a chorus singing evangelical Spirituals would probably cause so great a gathering to assemble before his box office that it would be necessary to call out the police reserves.

The reproduction of a scene in an authentic Negro cabaret, such as Small's (if it could be reproduced), would be another excellent plan. Naturally it would not bear the slightest resemblance to the cabaret scene ordinarily exhibited on the stage. The difficulty would not be to match the ebullient entertainers, or the dancing waiters, or the eccentric jazz band, with its mad drummer, who might all be transplanted successfully in person, but to recapture the spirit of the frequenters of the resort as they go through the paces of the Black Bottom, the Hey Hey, the Scronch, and the gestures of the Itch and Picking Cherries, and all the other gestures and paces that accompany the insane tappings of the drum, the moans of the hatted trumpet, and the harmonious thumping of the piano. And if the comedian of the troupe could not get a laugh occasionally by admonishing certain couples in the crowd to "get off that dime," he would do less than the saturnine floor managers of the real cabarets.

For the culmination of my spectacle—which might include a scene in Strivers' Row, as the block of yellow brick houses designed by Sanford White on 139th Street between Seventh and Eighth Avenues is so reasonably dubbed by the Negroes who do not live there, and a scene in a typical Harlem beauty parlor, the humor of which would not have to be exaggerated—I offer a wild pantomimic drama set in an African forest with the men and women as nearly nude as the law allows. There, in front of a background of orange-tinted banana fronds and amethyst palm leaves, silhouetted against a tropical blue sky divided by a silver moon, the bucks, their assegais stabbing the sky like the spears of the infantry in Velásquez's *Las Landas,* and their lithe-limbed, brown doxies, meagerly tricked out in multihued feathers, would enact a fantastic, choreographic comedy of passion.

The scenes in this ideal revue should riotously contrast one with the other, now relying on a picturesque realism for their effect, now on a chromatic, colorful arrangement of rhythm and form. It is unfortunate that Léon Bakst was never invited to stage such a revue, but there are other designers, Miguel Covarrubias for one—who would seize such an opportunity gratefully.

I have spoken above about the regrettable imitation of white revues in the Negro musical shows already staged. To be perfectly fair, I should state that practically all the dancing and a good share of the musical rhythms now to be seen and felt on the white stage have been raped from the Negro. The white producer, however, quite intelligently steals the best features of the Negro stage, while the Negro producer is content to take over the stalest features of the white stage. No white dancers, however, can hope to rival the Negro in those special dances which are peculiarly his own and which make even his poorest shows exciting whenever they occur, just as no Negro can ever hope to make a favorable impression with such a number as "Apple Blossom Time in Normandy." If the Negro will stick to his own, embellishing it and displaying some originality in his treatment of it, I predict that he will be able to evolve with the talent at his disposal—where in the world else are there two dancers to compare in their specialties with Eddie Rector and Bill Robinson?—a type of entertainment which will be world-famous instead of the fad of a few people for a few moments. The ideal director will not harbor an exclusive taste for yellow gals and it will be easy for him to sacrifice liverlips, burnt cork, sentimental ballads warbled by anemic tenors, bandannas, basses who sing "Old Black Joe" and "Georgia Rose," in fact all the tiresome clichés that at present prevent the Negro revues from raising the roof.

## 11. The Negro in Dramatic Art

### Raymond O'Neil

There are two peoples in the modern world possessing in marked degree fresh and strong potentialities for artistic creation—the Russians among Europeans and the Negroes among the conglomeration of racial and national groups which go to make up the United States.

The similarity between the gifts and accomplishments of these two peoples is striking and easily endures a severe scrutiny. They are most pronounced in folk expression. The Russians possess dance forms which in variety and expressiveness are equalled in the contemporary world only by those of the Negro. There is wanting only some outstanding synthetic and sophisticated intelligence to carry the Negro's dance forms to the height of artistic development to which the Ballet Russe carried those of their own land.

In folk music both peoples have expressed themselves in manners which are unrivalled in their diversity and in the poignancy and truthfulness of their interpretation of human emotions, from reckless jollity to most tragic sorrow.

Another resemblance between Russian and Negro is discernible in the effort each makes to decorate his living quarters. Those who know the carved and brightly painted exteriors of houses of the Russian peasant or of the small town dweller are at no loss to understand and appreciate the spirit that has led the Negro to paint in bright colors and decorate with vivid curtains the little vegetable stands, soft drink parlors

First published in *The Crisis*, February 1924.

**433**

and barbecue restaurants he has built in the poorer sections of Negro quarters. Wherever he has had to take the white man's expressionless and ugly dwelling or store he has generally let bad enough alone but whenever he has had the opportunity of building for himself a small dwelling or business place there has almost invariably gone into it an original feeling for form and decoration which is both charming and hopeful.

Yet it is in the theater where the Negro and the Russian show their most pronounced artistic kinship. Strangely enough it needed the performances of the Moscow Art Theater Company in the United States to emphasize this fact and to point the way to a still more significant conclusion which is that the resemblance between the Negro and the Russian in artistic expression is based upon an almost identical attitude towards life and a sensuous manner of living it.

By means of the Moscow Art Theater the Russians have brought the ugly duckling of theatrical representation to a degree of fidelity towards actual life and to a degree of beauty that no other national group has attained. Even American critics have penetrated to this fact. They have written thousands of columns in praise of this company in which are set forth scores of ingenious hypotheses in an effort to explain the freshness, richness and vitality of the Russian theater's presentations.

Yet not a commentator has touched upon the basic and simple reason which is the Russian's sensuous acceptance of life. For him all the senses exist to be exercised, delectified and developed. His nature is warm and his emotions are many, varied and responsive. Always is he saying "yea" to life sensuously, even to the paradoxical extent of finding pleasure in tears, sorrow and the contemplation of death.

With all these qualities the Negro is likewise richly endowed. He too is gifted with a sensuous nature. He loves life and he lives life with the sensuous and the emotional parts of him constantly exposed to it. As with the Russians these sensuous qualities are the springs of the Negro's creative potentialities. Developed, refined and brought under a constantly more subtle and sophisticated intellectual control they predicate possibilities in creation and expression that give one a warm joy merely to contemplate.

It might be shown with not a great amount of difficulty that nations and peoples have created beauty in direct proportion to their capacity for extracting sensuous enjoyment from life. Those people who have not been gifted with responsive sensuous natures pretty generally have had a sad art and a still sadder life.

Consider for a moment the plight of the non-Negro American. Through the greater part of his national history he has been the object of a steadily played stream of restrictions and prohibitions which have had as their object the paralyzing and extirpation of his sensuous nature and emotions. Being mostly Anglo-Saxon, hence possessing sensuous and emotional qualities none too robust at the best, he surrendered to the assault upon him with scarcely a protest. The result has been a nation of individuals who receive less fun, pleasure and inspiration from clouds, flowers and birds than any other group of civilized beings.

In his own image the good one hundred per cent American has set up his art. By an elaborate system of automatic precautions he has seen to it that it shall not return to him more of emotion than he himself possesses or that unexpectedly it shall not impinge upon a sense or feeling which may be merely sleeping. Thus it comes that in his teeming land of plenty the normal white, Protestant, Nordic American lives without a music of his own, without more than occasional pieces of painting or sculpture, with a literature just emerging from the nursery, and with a stage reflecting a life as hollow and painful as a drilled-out aching tooth. Frequently he sends up his voice to the effect that as soon as he is through with this "development-of-a-country business," he will turn his attention to art. Certainly, he suggests, with a note of pride and an overtone of contempt in his voice, a working people cannot be expected to produce an art as they labor.

In this he is unaware that another people have been working at his side in the same land, who, through suffering a heavy handicap of political and economic disabilities, have been producing an art as they worked. And here again is a pleasant resemblance between the Russian and the American Negro. They have both dwelled and worked in areas undeveloped or in the process of development and as they have worked they have taken time to gaze upon clouds, to listen to birds, to smell flowers and to regard the bodies and souls about them. And doing this they have been impelled to sing, and dance, and play and in this spontaneous glorification of the senses and the objects the senses apprehended they have created an art, each in his own image.

These arts are twins in that they are rich and warm and sensuous, leaving none of the senses neglected. They are lithe and soft and round and gentle. Understanding much, they forgive everything that is human. They spring from the earth, a well manured earth, and hold their blossoms straight up into the sky. They are wistful, lender, straightforward as a child and they are robust, passionate, sensuous as a youth. And always they are human, all too human.

Negro and Russian arts possess these qualities because their creators possess them. That ability sensuously to comprehend life and to enjoy in and for itself the act of living has been the basis of Russian vitality and richness in the arts and has been the basis of what the Negro so far has created. Upon it can be forecast his pregnant future. An Evelyn Preer and a Charles Gilpin, to consider only the theatre, are no mere accidents. They are the product of a mode of living and are the precursors, undoubtedly, of many more distinguished products of that mode.

As the Russians guarded their arts as much as they could from Westernization, so will the Negro have to guard his from one hundred per cent Americanization. Particularly must he be on his guard against the white friends of his art who will urge its development in the direction of their prejudiced imagination. A very great advantage which Negro art has enjoyed has been white contempt or indifference towards it, qualities which are rapidly changing now to interest and to eventual commercial and intellectual exploitation. Many people who love art for the strength it gives to man are hoping that the Negro will be able to resist this evil white pressure with the same flexible strength with which he has resisted so much other evil from the same source. For there is nothing more precious in America today than the creative potentialities that the Negro indubitably possesses.

## 12. THE HOPE OF A NEGRO DRAMA

## Willis Richardson

Is it true that there is coming into existence in America a Negro Drama which at some future day may equal in excellence the American Negro Music? If the signs of the times do not point to such a thing, we must change their direction and make them point the right way; we must have a Negro Drama.

There is no doubt that the Negro has a natural poetic gift; neither is there any doubt that a dramatist is fundamentally a poet; therefore, in order to help towards this, something may be done if some of our numerous poets will consent to rest from their usual labors for a while and lend a hand towards the writing of Negro plays. There need be no groping for subject matter. Here is a wealth of material, a mine of pure gold. I know of no field which is richer for the purpose of so democratic an art.

But to attain this end, to obtain the wealth of this mine, will require diligent toil—the honest sweat of the brain. As Sir Arthur W. Pinero says in reference to playwriting generally: "When you sit in your stall at the theater and see a play moving across the stage, it all seems so easy and natural, you feel as though the author had improvised it. The characters, being, let us hope, ordinary human beings, say nothing very remarkable, nothing, you think—thereby paying the author the highest possible compliment—that might not quite as well have occurred to you. When you take up a playbook (if you ever do take up one), it strikes you

First published in *The Crisis,* November 1919.

as being a very trifling thing—a mere insubstantial pamphlet beside the imposing bulk of the latest six-shilling novel. Little do you guess that every page of the play has cost more care, severer mental tension, if not more actual manual labor, than any chapter of a novel, though it be fifty pages long."

When I say Negro plays, I do not mean merely plays with Negro characters. Dramatizations of Harriet Beecher Stowe's "Uncle Tom's Cabin" and Gustave Flaubert's "Salammbo" did not make Negro plays, although they had important Negro characters. Miss Grimke's "Rachel" is nearer the idea; still even this, with its Negro characters, is not exactly the thing I mean. It is called a propaganda play, and a great portion of it shows the manner in which Negroes are treated by white people in the United States. That such a work is of service will be acknowledged by anyone who will examine many of the plays of Shaw, Galsworthy and Brieux. Still there is another kind of play; the play that shows the soul of a people; and the soul of this people is truly worth showing. Mr. Ridgley Torrence, with the aid of Mrs. Norman Hapgood and Mr. Robert E. Jones, has accomplished it. "Granny Maumee," "The Rider of Dreams" and "Simon, the Cyrenian" are Negro plays; and we can never thank Mr. Torrence enough for such an excellent beginning of a movement we hope to continue. Miss Mary Burrill in "Aftermath" has also written a fine play; and these two examples prove the richness of the subject matter.

An excellent model, and one by which we ought to profit, is the case of the Irish National Theater, the history of which may be learned elsewhere. My point is this: that with no richer material, and among a population of less than five millions, the Irish have built a national drama, encouraged and sustained playwrights, who are respected the same as are the other members of their profession in larger countries, and trained a company of actors who have made a decent living by their work on the stage. Had it not been for the Irish Theater, perhaps such names as Synge, Yeats and Lady Gregory, Ervine, Colum and Murray would never have been known among the world dramatists. As it is, they stand high and are honored. This being the case, what ought the Negro Drama in the United States be capable of among a population of fundamentally artistic people, which twice outnumbers the population of Ireland?

The Negro has some natural ability for fine acting on account of his skill in imitation and on account of the mellowness of his voice. Take the sharp Caucasian "I" and compare it with the mellow "Ah" of Negro dialect. The "I" prolonged for a second changes to the sharper "E"; but the "Ah" prolonged continues its mellow sound unchanged. A similar difference may be seen in comparing the Caucasian "my" with the "ma" of Negro dialect. But even with these two assets to fine acting—mimicry and mellow tone of voice—there are yet other things necessary for the making of the finished actor; and not least among these other things is skill in interpretation. Skill in interpretation is more the fruit of long and careful training than it is a gift of nature. This being the case, it naturally follows that if the Negro actor is given long and careful training, he will make his mark on the stage.

Mr. George Jean Nathan in his volume, "Mr. George Jean Nathan Presents," has a chapter called "The Black Art" in which he pays many compliments to the Negro actor. One of the things he says is that the Negro is better fitted to play Shakespearean parts than the Caucasian, because the sweetness of the Negro tones is so well suited to the poetry of Shakespeare. Mr. Nathan hates to acknowledge it, but he thinks that the part of Othello should always be played by a Negro actor, since a Negro actor is as well fitted for that part as a white actress is fitted for the part of Desdemona. These are very encouraging things, but Mr. Nathan spoils the book by trying to be funny. He says words to the effect that we are all "porters, waiters and cooks"; and at some place in the chapter he goes so far as to call us "coons." And as I was reading his book, I was thinking that among these "porters, waiters and cooks" perhaps there were some with a little vision, a few ideas and a sufficient knowledge of dramatic technique to make plays out of the interesting things in the lives of these "porters, waiters and cooks."

I am very sure that all those broad-minded people who are intelligently interested in the welfare and development of the Negro race in America will be delighted when we shall be able to send a company of Negro Players with Negro plays across our own continent; and those intelligent people who have never been interested in us will surely give us a second thought when we send our Negro Plays and Players to show hitherto unknown things to the artistic peoples of Europe.

## 13. Steps Toward the Negro Theatre

### Alain Locke

Culturally we are abloom in a new field, but it is yet decidedly a question as to what we shall reap—a few flowers or a harvest. That depends upon how we cultivate this art of the drama in the next few years. We can have a Gilpin, as we have had an Aldridge—and this time a few more—a spectacular bouquet of talent, fading eventually as all isolated talent must; or we can have a granary of art, stocked and stored for season after season. It is a question of interests, of preferences:—are we reaping the present merely or sowing the future? For the one, the Negro actor will suffice; the other requires the Negro drama and the Negro theatre.

The Negro actor without the Negro drama is a sporadic phenomenon, a chance wayside flower, at mercy of wind and weed. He is precariously planted and still more precariously propagated. We have just recently learned the artistic husbandry of race drama, and have already found that to till the native soil of the race life and the race experience multiplies the dramatic yield both in quality and quantity. Not that we would confine the dramatic talent of the race to the fence-fields and plant-rooms of race drama, but the vehicle of all sound art must be native to the group—our actors need their own soil, at least for sprouting. But there is another step beyond this which must be taken. Our art in this field must not only be rescued from the chance opportunity and the haphazard growth of native talent, the stock must be cultivated beyond the demands and standards of the market-place, or must be safe

First published in *The Crisis*, December 1922.

**440**

somewhere from the exploitation and ruthlessness of the commercial theatre and in the protected housing of the art-theatre flower to the utmost perfection of the species. Conditions favorable to this ultimate development, the established Negro Theatre will alone provide.

In the past, and even the present, the Negro actor has waited to be born; in the future he must be made. Up till now, our art has been patronized; for the future it must be endowed. This is, I take it. what we mean by distinguishing between the movement toward race drama and the quite distinguishable movement toward the Negro Theatre. In the idea of its sponsors, the latter includes the former, but goes further and means more; it contemplates an endowed artistic center where all phases vital to the art of the theatre are cultivated and taught—acting, playwriting, scenic design and construction, scenic production and staging. A center with this purpose and function must ultimately be founded. It is only a question of when, how and where. Certainly the time has come; everyone will admit that at this stage of our race development it has become socially and artistically imperative. Sufficient plays and sufficient talent are already available; and the awakened race consciousness awaits what will probably be its best vehicle of expansion and expression in the near future.

Ten years ago it was the theory of the matter that was at issue; now it is only the practicabilities that concern us. Then one had constantly to be justifying the idea, citing the precedents of the Irish and the Yiddish theatres. Now even over diversity of opinion as to ways and means, the project receives the unanimous sanction of our hearts. But as to means and auspices, there are two seriously diverse views; one strenuously favoring professional auspices and a greater metropolitan center like New York or Chicago for the Negro Theatre; another quite as strenuously advocating a university center, amateur auspices and an essentially educational basis. Whoever cares to be doctrinaire on this issue may be: it is a question to be decided by deed and accomplishment—and let us hope a question not of hostility and counter-purpose, but of rivalry and common end.

As intended and established in the work of the Department of the Drama at Howard University, however, the path and fortunes of the latter program have been unequivocally chosen. We believe a university foundation will assure a greater continuity of effort and insure accordingly a greater permanence of result. We believe further that the development of the newer forms of drama has proved most successful where laboratory and experimental conditions have obtained and that the development of race drama is by those very circumstances the opportunity and responsibility of our educational centers. Indeed, to maintain this relation to dramatic interests is now an indispensable item in the program of the progressive American college. Through the pioneer work of Professor Baker, of Harvard, the acting and writing of plays has become the natural and inevitable sequence, in a college community, of the more formal study of the drama. Partly through the same channels, and partly as a result of the pioneer work of Wisconsin, college production has come to the rescue of the art drama, which would otherwise rarely get immediate recognition from the commercial theatre. And finally in its new affiliation with the drama, the American college under the leadership of Professor Koch, formerly of North Dakota, now of the University of North Carolina, has become a vital agency in community drama, and has actively promoted the dramatization of local life and tradition. By a threefold sponsorship, then, race drama becomes peculiarly the ward of our colleges, as new drama, as art-drama, and as folk-drama.

Though concurrent with the best efforts and most significant achievements of the new drama, the movement toward Negro drama has had its own way to make. In addition to the common handicap of commercialism, there has been the singular and insistent depreciation to stereotyped caricature and superficially representative but spiritually misrepresentative force. It has been the struggle of an artistic giant in art-engulfing quicksands; a struggle with its critical period just lately safely passed. Much of this has been desperate effort of the "bootstrap-lifting kind," from the pioneer advances of Williams, Cole, Cook, and Walker, to the latest achievements of "Shuffle Along." But the dramatic side has usually sagged, as might be expected, below the art level under the imposed handicap. Then there has been that gradual investment of the legitimate stage through the backdoor of the character role; the hard way by which Gilpin came, breaking triumphantly through at last to the major role and legitimate stardom. But it is the inauguration of the Negro art drama which is the vital matter, and the honor divides itself between Burghardt Du Bois, with his "Star of Ethiopia," staged, costumed, and manned by students, and Ridgley Torrence, with his "Three Plays for a Negro Theatre." In the interim between the significant first performances and the still more significant attempts to incorporate them in the Horizon Guild and the Mrs. Hapgood's Players, there was organized in Washington a Drama Committee of the N.A.A.C.P. which sponsored and produced Miss Grimké's admirable pioneer problem-play, "Rachel," in 1917. Between the divided elements of this committee, with a questionable paternity of minority radicalism, the idea of the Negro Theatre as distinguished from the idea of race drama was born. If ever the history of the Negro drama is written without the scene of a committee wrangle, with its rhetorical climaxes after midnight—the conservatives with their wraps on protesting the hour; the radicals, more hoarse with emotion than effort, alternately wheedling and threatening

—it will not be well-written. The majority wanted a performance; the minority, a program. One play no more makes a theatre than one swallow, a summer.

The pariah of the committee by the accident of its parentage became the foundling and subsequently the ward of Howard University. In its orphan days, it struggled up on the crumbs of the University Dramatic Club. One recalls the lean and patient years it took to pass from faculty advice to faculty supervision and finally to faculty control; from rented costumes and hired properties to self-designed and self-executed settings; from hackneyed "stage successes" to modern and finally original plays; and hardest of all progressions, strange to relate, that from distant and alien themes to the intimate, native and racial. The organization, under the directorship of Professor Montgomery Gregory of a Department of Dramatics, with academic credit for its courses, the practical as well as the theoretical, and the fullest administrative recognition and backing of the work have marked in the last two years the eventual vindication of the idea. But from an intimacy of association second only to that of the director, and with better grace than he, may I be permitted to record what we consider to be the movement's real coming of age? It was when simultaneously with the production of two original plays or, race themes written in course by students, staged, costumed, and manned by students, in the case of one play with the authoress in rôle, there was launched the campaign for an endowed theatre, the successful completion of which would not only give the Howard Players a home, but the Negro theatre its first tangible realization.

As will already have been surmised from the story, the movement has, of course, had its critics and detractors. Happily, most of them are covered by that forgiveness which goes out spontaneously to the opposition of the short-sighted. Not they, but their eyes, so to speak, are to blame. Rather it has been amazing, on the other hand, the proportion of responsiveness and help that has come, especially from the most prominent proponents of the art drama in this country; names too numerous to mention, but representing every possible section of opinion—academic, non-academic; northern, southern, western; conservative, ultramodern; professional, amateur; technical, literary; from within the university, from the community of Washington; white, black. Of especial mention because of special service, Gilpin, O'Neil, Torrence, Percy Mackaye, DuBois, Weldon Johnson, and the administrative officers of the University; and most especially the valuable technical assistance for three years of Clem Throckmorton, technical director of the Provincetown Players, and for an equal time the constant and often self-sacrificing services of Miss Marie Forrest in stage training and directing, services recently fitly rewarded by appointment to a professorship in the department. But despite the catholic appeal, interest and cooperation it is essentially as a race representative and race-supported movement that we must think of it and that it must ultimately become, the best possible self-expression in an art where we have a peculiar natural endowment, undertaken as an integral part of our higher education and our suit of culture.

The program and repertoire of the Howard Players, therefore, scarcely represent the full achievement of the movement; it is the workshop and the eventual theatre and the ever-increasing supply of plays and players that must hatch out of the idea. The record of the last two years shows in performances:

1920–21—
"Tents of the Arabs"—Lord Dunsany.
"Simon the Cyrenean"—Ridgley Torrence.
"The Emperor Jones"—Guest performance with Charles Gilpin at the Belasco; student performance at the Belasco.
Commencement Play, 1921–22—
"The Canterbury Pilgrims"—Percy Mackaye. Repetition of first bill in compliment of the delegates to the Washington conference on Limitation of Armaments.
"Strong as the Hills" (a Persian play)—Matalee Lake.
Original Student Plays—
"Genefrede,"—a play of the Life of Toussaint L'Ouverture—Helen Webb.
"The Yellow Tree"—DeReath Irene Busey.
Commencement Play—
"Aria de Capo"—Edna St. Vincent Millay.
"The Danse Calinda"—a Creole Pantomime Ms. performance— Ridgley Torrence.

A movement of this kind and magnitude is, can be, the monopoly of no one group, no one institution, no paltry decade. But within a significant span, this is the record. The immediately important steps must be the production of original plays as rapidly as is consistent with good workmanship and adequate production, and the speedy endowment of the theatre, which fortunately, with the amateur talent of the university, means only funds for building and equipment. I am writing this article at Stratford-on-Avon. I know that when stripped to the last desperate defense of himself, the Englishman with warrant will boast of Shakespeare, and that this modest Memorial Theatre is at one and the same time a Gibraltar of national pride and self-respect and a Mecca of human civilization and culture. Music in which we have so trusted may sing itself around the world, but it does not carry ideas, the vehicle of human understanding and respect; it may pierce the heart, but does not penetrate the mind. But here in the glass of this incomparable art there is, for ourselves and for the world, that which shall reveal us beyond all propaganda on the one side, and libel on the other, more subtly and deeply than self-praise and to the confusion of subsidized self-caricature and ridicule. "I saw Othello's visage in his mind," says Desdemona explaining her love and respect: so might, so must the world of Othello's mind be put artistically to speech and action.

*Stratford-on-Avon, August 5, 1922*

## 14. KRIGWA PLAYERS LITTLE NEGRO THEATRE: THE STORY OF A LITTLE THEATRE MOVEMENT

## W. E. B. Du Bois

It is customary to regard Negroes as an essentially dramatic race; and it is probably true that tropical and sub-tropical peoples have more vivid imagination, are accustomed to expressing themselves with greater physical and spiritual abandon than most folk. And certainly, life as black and brown and yellow folk have known it is big with tragedy and comedy. The home life of Africans shows this natural dramatic tendency; the strides of the native African, the ceremony of home and assembly, the intense interest in music and play, all attest to this.

In America, on the other hand, the road to freedom for the Negro lay through religious organization long before physical emancipation came. The Negro church gave the slave almost his only freedom of spirit and of the churches that came to proselyte among the slaves, only those were permanently successful which were strongly tinged with Puritanism, namely: the Baptist and the Methodist. These churches frowned upon drama and the play, upon the theatre and the dance; and for this reason the American Negro has been hindered in his natural dramatic impulses.

Today as the renaissance of art comes among American Negroes, the theatre calls for new birth. But most people do not realize just where the novelty must come in. The Negro is already in the theatre and has been there for a long time; but his presence there is not yet thoroughly normal. His audience is mainly a white audience, and the Negro actor has, for a long time, been asked to entertain this more or less alien

First published in *The Crisis*, June 1926.

446

group. The demands and ideals of the white group and their conception of Negroes have set the norm for the black actor. He has been a minstrel, comedian, singer and lay figure of all sorts. Only recently has he begun tentatively to emerge as an ordinary human being with everyday reactions. And here he is still handicapped and put forth with much hesitation, as in the case of "The Nigger," "Lulu Belle" and "The Emperor Jones."

In all this development naturally then the best of the Negro actor and the most poignant Negro drama have not been called for. This could be evoked only by a Negro audience desiring to see its own life depicted by its own writers and actors.

For this reason, a new Negro theatre is demanded and it is slowly coming. It needs, however, guiding lights. For instance, some excellent groups of colored amateurs are entertaining colored audiences in Cleveland, in Philadelphia and elsewhere. Almost invariably, however, they miss the real path. They play Shakespeare or Synge or reset a successful Broadway play with colored principals.

The movement which has begun this year in Harlem, New York City, lays down four fundamental principles. The plays of a real Negro theatre must be: 1. *About us.* That is, they must have plots which reveal Negro life as it is. 2. *By us.* That is, they must be written by Negro authors who understand from birth and continual association just what it means to be a Negro today. 3. *For us.* That is, the theatre must cater primarily to Negro audiences and be supported and sustained by their entertainment and approval. 4. *Near us.* The theatre must be in a Negro neighborhood near the mass of ordinary Negro people.

Only in this way can a real folk-play movement of American Negroes be built up. Even this building encounters certain difficulties. First, there is the problem of the plays. Five years ago there were practically no plays that filled the specifications noted. Already, however, this situation has begun to change on account of the prizes offered by *The Crisis* magazine and other agencies and for other reasons. There are available today a dozen or more plays of Negro life worth staging and the quantity and quality will increase very rapidly as the demand grows. The problem of actors is the least of the difficulties presented. In any group of colored people it is possible to get an unusual number of persons gifted with histrionic ability. The only trouble comes when effort is made to select the actors from limited groups or exclusively from among social acquaintances or friends. The third difficulty, that of a suitable playhouse, is real and must be worked out as circumstances permit. There are usually halls that can be used temporarily. Now and then a church is liberal enough to house a play.

In the New York movement, advantage is being taken of the fact that in the center of Harlem there is a branch of the New York Public Library which has in its basement a lecture room. The administration of this library has in the last few years changed from an attitude of aloofness from its Negro surroundings, and even resentment, to an attitude which recognizes that this library is serving a hundred thousand Negroes or more. It specializes on books which Negroes want to read; it subscribes to their periodicals and has lectures and art exhibits which attract them.

Some time ago Miss Ernestine Rose, the Librarian, suggested that a Little Theatre movement be started in connection with this library; but other activities interfered. This year the library authorities expressed their willingness to help equip a small and inexpensive stage in the lecture room and a group of 30 persons interested in such a theatre has been organized.

Foremost among these is Charles Burroughs. Charles Burroughs was trained in the college department of Wilberforce and at the School of Expression in Boston and has been a dramatic reader for many years for the Board of Education in New York City. He has been unusually successful in training actors as was shown by his training the groups which gave the pageant, "The Star of Ethiopia," in New York, Washington, Philadelphia and Los Angeles.

In the Harlem Little Negro Theatre the library authorities built the stage and dressing rooms and furnished the lighting equipment. The players group furnished the curtain, the scenery, gave the plays and secured the audiences. Three one-act plays were selected, for the initial experiment. Two were tragedies by Willis Richardson: "Compromise," which was published in *The New Negro*, and "The Broken Banjo," which took the first prize in *The Crisis* Contest of 1925. The third, "The Church Fight," by Mrs. R. A. Gaines-Shelton, is a comedy which took the second prize in *The Crisis* Contest of 1925. A cast of 20 persons was required and they rehearsed faithfully. Louise Latimer, assisted by Aaron Douglas, painted the scenery and on May 3, 10 and 17 the plays were given before full houses averaging 200 persons at each performance.

The success of the experiment is unquestioned. The audiences were enthusiastic and wanted more. The price of admission to membership in the group which gave the right to see the performances was only 50 cents and the total expense of staging the plays, not counting expenditures by the Library, was about $165 while the returns were something over $240. The players not only perform plays but they welcome other groups under easy conditions to come and use their playhouse under their patronage.

A second K. P. L. N. T. is being organized in Washington, D. C., and it is hoped the movement will spread widely.

# KRIGWA PLAYERS

## LITTLE NEGRO THEATRE

An attempt to establish in High Harlem, New York City, a little Theatre which shall be primarily a center where Negro actors before Negro audiences interpret Negro life as depicted by Negro artists; but which shall also always have a welcome for all artists of all races and for all sympathetic comers and for all beautiful ideas.

A. DOUGLAS

*At their Playhouse*
**Basement of the 135th Street Branch, New York Public Library**

# A LITTLE NEGRO THEATRE

Today, as the renaissance of art comes among American Negroes, the theatre calls for new birth. But most people do not realize just where the novelty must come in. The Negro is already in the theatre and has been there for a long time; but his presence there is not yet thoroughly normal. His audience is mainly a white audience and the Negro actor has, for a long time, been asked to entertain this more or less alien group. The demands and ideals of the white group, and their conception of Negroes, have set the norm for the black actor. He has been a minstrel, comedian, singer and lay figure of all sorts. Only recently has he begun tentatively to emerge as an ordinary human being with everyday reactions. And here he is still handicapped and put forth with much hesitation, as in the case of "The Nigger," "Lulu Belle" and the "Emperor Jones."

In all this development naturally then the best of the Negro actor and the most poignant Negro drama have not been called for. This could be evoked only by a Negro audience desiring to see its own life depicted by its own writers and actors.

For this reason, a new Negro theatre is demanded and it is slowly coming. It needs, however, guiding lights. For instance, some excellent groups of colored amateurs are entertaining colored audiences in Cleveland, in Philadelphia and elsewhere. Almost invariably, however, they miss the real path. They play Shakespeare or Synge or reset a successful Broadway play with colored principals.

The movement which has begun this year in Harlem, New York City, lays down four fundamental principles. The plays of a real Negro theatre must be: *One: About us.* That is, they must have plots which reveal Negro life as it is. *Two: By us.* That is, they must be written by Negro authors who understand from birth and continual association just what it means to be a Negro today. *Three: For us.* That is, the theatre must cater primarily to Negro audiences and be supported and sustained by their entertainment and approval. *Fourth: Near Us.* The theatre must be in a Negro neighborhood near the mass of ordinary Negro people.

Only in this way can a real folk play movement of American Negroes be built up.

## *Our Playhouse*

The **Krigwa Players Little Negro Theatre** is a free stage. It has been equipped by the joint effort of the Public Library and the Players. It will be further decorated by colored artists. Any one who has a play or any group which wishes to give a play is invited to use the playhouse, under certain easy conditions which the Library and the Players will formulate. We hope by plays, lectures and informal social gatherings to make this room a place of wide inspiration for all dark people everywhere and for all their friends.

*Season of 1926*
MONDAYS, MAY 3, 10 and 17, at 8:30 p.m.

# COMPROMISE
### A Play in One Act, from "The New Negro,"
*by* Willis Richardson
#### Characters

| | |
|---|---|
| Jane Lee | Eulalie Spence |
| Aleck Lee | William G. Holly |
| Annie Lee | { Mrs. Philitus Joyce |
| | Doralyne Spence |
| Ruth Lee | { Catherine Johnson |
| | Helen Lankford |
| Ben Carter | Joseph Steber |

# THE CHURCH FIGHT
### A *Crisis* Prize Play in One Act
*by* Mrs. Ruth Ada Gaines-Shelton
#### Characters

| | |
|---|---|
| Brother Ananias | Richard J. Huey |
| Sister Sapphira | Laura Smith |
| Sister Instigator | Ethel Bennett |
| Brother Investigator | Harlan A. Carter |
| Sister Meddler | Andrades Lindsay |
| Sister Experience | Ardelle Dabney |
| Brother Judas | John S. Brown |
| Sister Take-It-Back | Mrs. Marian King |
| Sister Two-Face | Mrs. Estelle Anderson |
| Parson Procrastinator | Ira DeA. Reid |

# THE BROKEN BANJO
### A *Crisis* Prize Play in One Act
*by* Willis Richardson
#### Characters

| | |
|---|---|
| Emma | Lilla Hawkins |
| Matt | Charles Burroughs |
| Sam | William Trent Andrews, Jr. |
| Adam | { Frank L. Horne |
| | R. Oscar Flanner |
| Police Officer | Myles A. Paige |

# THE KRIGWA PLAYERS

### THE CABINET
W. E. B. DuBois, Chairman, 69 Fifth Avenue, New York

Charles Burroughs    Frank L. Horne

Zora Neale Hurston    Louise Latimer

### MEMBERS

Laura Smith

Zora Neale Hurston

Harlan A. Carter

Aaron Douglas

Frank L. Horne

Margaret C. Welmon

Eulalie Spence

William G. Holly

James P. Holbrook

Louise Reba Latimer

Mrs. Estelle Anderson

R. Oscar Flanner

Mrs. Philitus W. Joyce

Ira DeA. Reid

John S. Brown, Jr.

Ernestine Rose

Myles A. Paige

Minnie Brown

Mrs. Daisy Reed

Dorothy Peterson

Harold Jackman

Mr. and Mrs. William Andrews

Gladys Hirst

Mr. and Mrs. George Cuffee

Charles Burroughs

Andrades Lindsay

Richard J. Huey

Catherine Johnson

W. E. B. DuBois

Lilla Hawkins

Dr. Ardelle Dabney

Ethel Bennett

Joseph Steber

Thomas Moseley

Helen Lankford

Mrs. Marian King

Augustus Granville Dill

Anyone wishing to join the Krigwa Players can do so by complying with certain simple conditions. Please write the cabinet.

# 16. PAYING FOR PLAYS

## W. E. B. Du Bois

We have published *The Crisis* in a number of plays and shall publish more. Most of them are adapted to amateur production. We would like to have them produced. But we have laid down the rule: Anyone who wishes to produce a play printed in *The Crisis* may do so upon payment of $5. Of this money $2.50 goes to the author and $2.50 to *The Crisis*. To our surprise there has been almost unanimous objection; and that shows the singular attitude of our people toward artists and writers. Plumbers, carpenters and bricklayers we pay without question; the workman is worthy of his hire. But if a man writes a play, and a good play, he is lucky if he earns first-class postage upon it. Of course, he may sell it commercially to some producer on Broadway; but in that case it would not be a Negro play or if it is a Negro play, it will not be about the kind of Negro you and I know or want to know. If it is a Negro play that will interest us and depict our life, experience and humor, it cannot be sold to the ordinary theatrical producer, but it can be produced in our churches and lodges and halls; and if it is worth producing there it is worth paying for. It seems to us that $5 is not an exorbitant charge. Of course, what is going to happen is that a number of our loyal friends are going to steal these plays, reproduce them without paying for them, and ask us impudently what we are going to do about it. And we can assure them pleasantly that we are not going to do anything. If they can stand that kind of encouragement for Negro artists, we presume we can.

First published in *The Crisis*, July 1926.

## 17. Main Problems of the Negro Theater

## Theophilus Lewis

Numerous signs indicate an awakening desire for Negro drama. This desire, like most mass impulses, is incoherent, confused and incapable of giving itself clear expression. It will always remain so. The desire for drama is a desire for beauty, and to expect Negro laymen to express that desire in definite terms is to expect them to be wiser than the members of any other race has ever been or are ever likely to become. To express the desire clearly and beautifully is the function of critics and artists. The critic's business is to reduce it to terms of ideas. The artist's work is to translate it into satisfying forms of beauty.

The work of the artist is of incomparably greater importance. While the critic can be helpful to the theater and drama he is not essential to the development of either. But the artist, who in this instance is the dramatist, is the only worker in the theatre who contributes anything of permanent value. When the other workers in the theater—actors, directors, producers, designers—have provided the dramatist with a suitable vehicle for his work, when they have made the theater a medium in which he can function freely and effectively, they have done the most they can do.

Too often these minor workers think of themselves as its principal factors. The actor is especially prone to consider everything in the theater of secondary importance to himself and frequently he persuades the laity

First published in *The Messenger*, July 1927.

to accept him at his own value. When that happens drama suffers and the laymen are cheated out of the very thing they want.

The first problem of the Negro theater, then, is the problem of drama. I mean it is the first problem in importance, not necessarily in sequence. The other problems, in the order of their importance, are acting, the audience and the ways and means of production. For the sake of emphasis I will repeat them.

> Drama
> Acting
> Audience
> Production

After recognizing that its principal reason for existence is to encourage drama the Negro theater must deal with the special problems peculiar to Negro drama. One of these is the problem of definition. There must be a clear understanding of what the term Negro drama means. To the judicious and disinterested outsider the term appears to explain itself, but among the workers in the theater there are no disinterested persons and only a few judicious ones. As acting is a comparatively easy art to master while drama is among the hardest the actor develops much faster than the playwright. In the embryonic period of the theater the former is always superior. This is the present condition in the Negro theater. Since the actor wants to keep before the public in better playing parts than Negro playwrights, in their present stage of development, are able to write, it is to the colored actor's interest to maintain that Negro drama consists of plays about Negro life or plays interpreted by colored actors. In self defense the dramatist must deny this, holding that Negro drama can be nothing else but a body of plays written by Negro authors.

It is an easy task to raise the question above logical dispute. Negro drama, reduced to a simple statement, is what the dramatist claims it is: the body of plays written by Negro authors. The kind of life represented in the play is immaterial. The scene may be in Norway or Spain and the characters presumably natives of one or the other country; nevertheless it will be a Negro play if it is the product of a Negro's mind. *Hamlet* is not a Danish play nor is *The Merchant of Venice* an Italian play. Both are English plays. The *Phaedra* of Euripides is Greek, while the *Phaedra* of Racine is French. And why? Because Euripides was able to endow his characters with indigenous habits of thought and feeling while Racine's Greeks, as Georg Brandes says, "are courtly Frenchmen from the salons." A play is a work of art and an artist always impresses the stamp of his mind and personality on his creation. To maintain that Negro drama consists merely of plays about Negro life, regardless of who writes them, is to alter the accepted meaning of terms.

After grasping the fact that the demand for Negro drama, reduced to a plain proposition, is a demand for plays written by Negro authors the next problem our theater must face is how to encourage colored playwrights in such a way that they may pass through the period of apprenticeship quickly and begin to produce mature plays as early as possible. Our definition virtually compels our theater to meet this problem by organizing itself as a national theater. That is, it must isolate itself and address its appeal exclusively to colored audiences.

I am tempted to say that the success or failure of the Negro theater depends on an accurate analysis of its potential audience. Its size, its economic status, how to get it into the theater and how to hold it there are matters of vital importance. In Harlem, which is and probably will remain the center of dramatic activity, the population will hardly supply an audience of more than ten thousand. And that number will not be immediately available. The sophisticated and prosperous classes cannot be included in the potential audience until Negro playwrights become efficient craftsmen. While Negro drama is in the crude and experimental stages they will continue to patronize Broadway theaters. Another class which cannot be counted on for immediate support is the considerable number of people whose inertia prevents them from doing anything until after a conspicuous social movement has begun to flow in its direction. After these classes have been eliminated, the actual audience immediately available for the Negro dramatic theater will hardly exceed five thousand.

The size of this audience at once determines the business policy of the theater, compelling frugal financing and low operating budgets. Its size also determines the production policy while its culture level limits the dramatic policy. As a week's run will be sufficient to exhaust the audience the management will be compelled to adopt a repertory system of production. Not many people care to see a play a second time and not many plays are worth seeing twice. Plays will have to be changed frequently, the better ones placed in the permanent repertory of the theater while the rest are discarded. This will be good for both actors and dramatists. Rapid changing of parts will increase the versatility of the former while turning plays out fast will develop the technique of the latter.

Finally the culture level of the audience must be considered. As most of its members will be persons educated by the movies it goes without saying that the spoken drama they will like at first must be full of thrills and sensations. The first effective repertory will consist of broad farces, sensational melodramas and breath-taking mystery plays. Once the audience has been won, higher forms of drama can be judiciously inserted in the repertory as a means of educating the audience.

The theater never deliberately plans the route of its progress. Like most other human institutions it advances by a trial and error method.

This is because the majority of the workers in the theater are specialists who never bother to study the institution as a whole. Still they are bound to follow the line of least resistance. If they are fortunate enough to adopt the wise policy first the Negro theater will advance rapidly. Failure will nullify every other course and force them to eventually take the right direction. It is hard to see how that direction can be other than a repertory system developed in each of the large centers of population, leading to an exchange of companies which will knit the detached units together in a National Negro Theater. This theater may or may not be housed in impressive buildings, but it will surely consist of compact organizations of actors and auxiliaries sensitive to the cultural demands of the race. The dramatist will be at home in it and able to work with comfort and assurance while he proceeds with the idealization of race character which in the last analysis is the real meaning of Negro drama.

# 18. VARIATION 0137 OF MONOLOGUE NO. 8

Theophilus Lewis

In spite of the conscientious efforts of the world's best minds to keep them down, bogus ideas about art and artists are everlastingly bobbing up to impede and embarrass sensible men and women engaged in creative work. These spurious notions seem to be as hard to conquer as vermin in a hotel kitchen, for they are no sooner subdued in one form than they reappear in some gaudier and more seductive guise, just as pestiferous as ever to the judicious and just as attractive to the multitude. Perhaps the most formidable of these protean fallacies is the art for art's sake humbug, a piece of hokum which reveals itself in numerous doctrines which appear contradictory on the surface though all of them lead to the conclusion that art is something wholly detached from life, like Christian Science or J. A. Rogers' views on the Negro problem. The truth, of course, is just the reverse. Instead of being hauled down out of airy nothingness art is extracted from the very core of life. This is why the highest art, no matter how thoroughly it is refined and perfumed, never quite loses the odor of viscera and bowels.

The raw material of art is the way men live, its production is the result of their imagination, and its function is to satisfy their spiritual hunger. Since its final and efficient causes are immanent in the acts and wants of people, it follows that genuine art can be produced only by men with a sound understanding of the nature and processes of life. The mentally near-sighted and emotionally anaemic cannot produce art; they can

---

First published in *The Messenger*, February 1927.

only produce imitations. This does not mean a man must be 100 per cent sagacious in order to produce sound art. It simply means he must possess a sure insight into the essentials of human motivation and behavior. In non-essential matters it won't hurt him if his mind is prone to run wild; indeed, for all I know, it may be a help to his imagination. The story of the Nativity is fiction; the idea that children cherish illusions with greater intensity than grown folks is full of error, and the views of Judge Gary on labor conditions are sheer nonsense, but a man may accept all those beliefs as gospel truth and still be able to paint good pictures, compose fine music or write poignant drama. But if he believes in two dimensional space or that marrying a loose woman to a man who loves her will automatically put a padlock on her personality and evermore prevent her from saying yes—if he believes things like that, it shows his mind is out of contact with reality at vital points; he is either incapable of making accurate observations or lacks sufficient imagination to grasp the meaning of what he observes. And without the ability to see straight and think straight a man cannot perform the function of an artist. The best he can make of himself is a pretty good business man or perhaps a fair to middling instructor in philosophy.

As an example of a presumably good pedagogue gone wrong I point to Massa Paul Green, and if anybody wants to know why I say so I submit his play, *In Abraham's Bosom,* the current offering at the Provincetown Playhouse. Massa Paul may be a wow in the business of initiating young crackers in the mysteries of Kant, Hegel and Spinoza, but when he turns from books to life he is no more capable of making clear observations than I am of reading the Rosetta stone. Being unable to see life in its true perspective, he just naturally can't produce sound drama. I am aware, of course, of the loud hosannas a chorus of Broadway critics, led by the mellifluent Barrett H. Clark, are chanting in praise of Massa Green, but that only means a playwright can get away with murder if he is shrewd enough to call his play a treatment of Negro life. Once the leading character is identified as a mulatto the Park Row boys throw Aristotle, Hazlitt, Lessing and the rest out of the window.

In *Abraham's Bosom* consists of two shorter plays spliced together. This would be a difficult undertaking even if both plays were similar in structure and theme. The fact that he has attempted to combine two organically different types of plays in one shows just how well Massa Green understands the art of the dramatist. The basis of drama, as William Archer has pointed out, is character. Every worthwhile play is built around the way some distinctive man or woman struggles with some problem of life. Now every individual has one character. not *two*. A man may be mercurial or he may be steadfast in his purposes, but he cannot be both. Each of the two plays Marse Paul has attempted to weld in one is constructed around a different type of temperament. The Abraham of the first play is a man of extravagant dreams but with no heart for the prolonged, gruelling struggle which is the price of success. As soon as the fight gets hot he deserts the barricades and seeks the solace of Cytherea. The Abraham of the second play is a doggedly persistent man who won't turn aside from what he has set his hand to do till the Butcher cuts him down. For him defeat is merely the prelude to rallying his forces for another offensive. After repeated reverses, perhaps, he ceases to believe in victory, but he can't stop hoping and fighting for victory. At least that is the kind of man Massa Green tried to make him. He didn't near succeed, of course, but he did make him definite enough to be incompatible with the Abraham of the first play. Which is a structural weakness sufficient to make the play break down from internal strain.

The play is not only mechanically weak; it is constructed of rotten material. One of the implications of the first play is that an erotic temperament and a lack of stamina go together. I suspect Massa Green attaches a racial significance to this, but since he doesn't say so I won't charge him with it. The thing is unsound on broader human grounds. Any of the illiterate field workers Massa Paul has so assiduously watched suffer could have told him that when a man went into the woods with a girl it didn't necessarily mean he intended to devote the rest of his life to going in the woods. Surely he must have read enough history to know that among the greatest geniuses you find the greatest lovers—examples: King David and his son King Solomon, Napoleon, Du Maupassant, Lord Byron and Catherine the Great. Equally untenable are the conclusions Massa Paul draws from the fact that the Negro masses are frequently indifferent and even hostile to blessings of education. Here he does imply special significance, and here, too, not only his conclusions but his facts are at fault. Instead of being indifferent to learning, Negroes, next to Jews, are perhaps the most enthusiastic supporters of education in the world. Their passion for education actually amounts to a weakness, so much so that one can collect good graft by visiting the smaller churches and posing as an indigent college student. The preacher will invariably pass the plate for the benefit of the seeker after learning and frequently he will waive his rake-off. Besides, when it comes to sending their own children to school white people are just as negligent as blacks; if they were not it would not have been necessary to decorate every code in Christendom with a compulsory school law. Lack of space prevents me from pointing out other numerous instances where Massa Green has mistaken the obvious for the actual and other places where he has attempted to palm off mere irrational behavior for authentic Negro character. Indeed, to rid the play of its imbecilities would be to destroy every essential of its structure.

In certain minor ways Massa Paul has achieved a modicum of success. He has accurately observed how workingmen go about eating their lunch, how sick people move themselves in bed, and how a poverty stricken woman acts when somebody steals her last fifty cents. But such accurate observation of everyday conduct alone does not constitute good drama. If it does then a *Daily News* photograph of Jack Dempsey is superior art to a George Bellows lithograph.

What the play lacks in dramatic interest is to a great extent made up for by the Provincetown's staging and casting. In spite of the Negro's much vaunted "natural" ability to act, the premier honors in the present production go to L. Rufus Hill, a white man. A word will suffice to describe his performance. It was excellent. Next in line, in the order named, come F. W. Wilson. Thomas Mosley, Rose McClendon, Armithine Lattimer and R. J. Huey. All did well. Mr. Julius Bledsoe, the big song and spiritual man, was cast as the hero, or, since the critics insist that the play is a tragedy, the protagonist. Having had a role in two plays, Mr. Bledsoe is now an actor of note. That is to say he interprets all the undulations of feeling in the same note. Even if he sings that way I am convinced that he can sing better than he can act.

\* \* \*

## THE SPENCE FAMILY PASSES IN REVIEW

An infant theater, like an infant industry, needs protection. With this fact in mind, I am inclined to look hack on the opening performance of the second season of the Krigwa little theater with a tolerant eye. Quite a number of gaucheries got into this performance; they did amusing tricks with the lights and curtains and various actors forgot their lines and had to be prompted from behind the scenes. But one makes allowances for this amateurishness as one makes allowances for the awkwardness of a child learning to walk.

Reading the program I see Ardelle Dabney, Charles Burroughs and William Holly each cast in two plays. This is a happy augury. Learning two or more parts simultaneously and rapidly switching from one role to another will develop versatility and the result will be the players will become actors and not mere types. This is just the kind of actor material the Negro theater requires for the chances are ten to one it will have to rest on a repertory basis.

Some of the acting can be applauded without reservation. The performance of William Jackson would be good acting on any man's stage, and Ardelle Dabney, while she wasn't so good in "Mandy," came back with rattling good work in "Her." Margaret Forster, Olga Spence and

Menta Turner reached an even higher level. Mrs. Forster surpassed the other two in precision and assurance but it would be hard to say which of the three possesses more of the latent stage poetry which needs only a modicum of experience to express itself in really fine acting. I hope it won't be long now before they will be playing before 10,000 people a week.

Aside from individual honors, the trophy for the highest number of points scored goes to the Clan Spence. They contributed two plays and two actresses to the evening's entertainment, a decided plurality of the program. Master Galton used to say genius runs in families.

# 19. NEGRO ART PLAYERS IN HARLEM

## Eulalie Spence

We have with us the Negro Art Theatre Players, onetime amateurs, gone professional. For the next few weeks they are being generously featured by the management of the Lincoln Theatre, in the very heart of old Harlem.

The first week they presented no other classic than "The Rider of Dreams" by Ridgeley Torrence. The cast, including Hemsley Winfield, Ardelle Mitchell Dabney, Albert W. Patrick and Melvina Dabney, strove earnestly, if ineffectually, to put the play across, and we, on the other side of the footlights, did try our very hardest to grasp the meaning of it all, but with no measure of success.

Right here and now, I want to congratulate the Lincoln audience for its fine sportsmanship. After the hurly burly of the typical Lincoln program, the curtain rose upon the Negro Art Theatre Players. The play was never once within the grasp of the players, with the possible exception of Albert W. Patrick as Uncle Williams. This Lucy was not the fervent, bitter, brooding creature that the playwright had created, but merely the scolding mother, the vaguely discontented wife. We did not sense the suffering of the woman struggling against the illusive vagaries of her husband's nature, desperately determined to be honest at any cost. There was no poignancy, no sharp-edged emotion. We wanted to feel and we couldn't. . . . Frustration. . . . And what of Madison? What of this-rider of dreams? Never once were we permitted to ride with him, to

---

First published in *Opportunity*, December 1928.

know this big, over-grown boy, to love him, to pity him, to feel his dream and share it. When Madison soared on the wings of his dream, we remained behind striving earnestly to understand his words which was no easy task, for Hemsley Winfield's enunciation is rather less than perfect. There was no lyrical note to the dream of Madison, which, by the way, was very much shorter than Torrence wrote it. And so, not understanding the dream, we failed to understand "The Rider of Dreams."

I have seen the play on three separate occasions and it can be a very moving drama, indeed. I need not criticise the stage direction, nor the stage "guitar" that was not a guitar, nor the conversion of Booker, the small son, into a girl, but only that we missed our emotion and a chance to see a very splendid characterization.

First presented to the Hapgood Players at the Garrick Theatre in New York City on April 14, 1917. "The Rider of Dreams" won immediate acclaim and will always take its place in every noteworthy collection of Negro plays.

To the Negro Art Theatre Players I can only wish better success in their next presentation, "Cooped Up" by Eloise Bibb Thompson.

## 20. A CRITICISM OF THE NEGRO DRAMA AS IT RELATES TO THE NEGRO DRAMATIST AND ARTIST

### Eulalie Spence

Yes, we have our colored artists. We have our Robeson, Rose McClenndon, our Wilson and various others who have reached an undeniable place of prominence in the realm of the theatre. And we have had our Florence Mills.

Even the most casual theatre-goer to-day is familiar with one or more of these stars in the theatrical firmament. But alas, the same cannot be said of the Negro dramatist.

Negro drama does not of necessity include the work of the Negro dramatist. Strictly speaking, Negro drama is any drama or theatrical production which essays to portray the life of the Negro. Where, then, is the Negro dramatist?

Who are the writers that have provided the vehicle for Gilpin, Robeson, Rose McClenndon and Bledsoe? Frankly, yet reluctantly, too, we may name them, and never a Negro will be found among them. Suppose there had been no *Emperor Jones*, and no *Porgy*, no *In Abraham's Bosom* and no *Show Boat*? What then? Ask the Negro artist, he knows.

Some there are who have shuddered distastefully at these plays; been affronted by Paul Green, degraded by Du Bose Hayward, and misunderstood by Eugene O'Neill. But ask the Negro artist if he is grateful to these writers. He will tell you. And ask the Negro dramatist what he feels about it. If he is forward-thinking, he will admit that these writers

First published in *Opportunity*, June 1928.

465

have been a great inspiration; that they have pointed the way and her-
alded a new dawn.

The drama, more particularly, the American drama, is from twenty
to thirty years behind the novel and short story in point of subject matter. There is almost no subject to-day that cannot be discussed with the
most revolting detail between the covers of a book. If there are any who
doubt this, let them read *Home to Harlem* by Claude McKay. Not so
with our drama. Here we have elected to be squeamish, and perhaps
advisedly so. Nevertheless, this does not imply that the theatre has not
made enormous strides ahead. The drama has developed a new technique, new ways and means, a new genius of mechanism and a new
direction.

Unfortunately, almost everyone thinks that he can write a play.
Writers will grant the poet his form and the novelist his; the essayist his
mould and the writer of short stories his. However, when it comes to the
play, why—one merely takes one's pen in hand and presto! we have Dialogue! I have seen plays written by our Negro writers with this caption:
To Be Red. Not Played!

A play to be read! Why not the song to be read not sung, and the
canvas to be described, not painted! To every art its form, thank God!
And to the play, the technique that belongs to it!

Here it is then that our Negro dramatists have failed to reach a
larger and more discriminating public. They have labored like the archi-
tect who has no knowledge of geometry and the painter who must struggle to evolve the principles of perspective.

May I advise these earnest few—those seekers after light—white
lights—to avoid the drama of propaganda if they would not meet with
certain disaster? Many a serious aspirant for dramatic honors has fallen by
the wayside because he would insist on his lynchings or his rape. The
white man is cold and unresponsive to this subject and the Negro, himself, is hurt and humiliated by it. We go to the theatre for entertainment,
not to have old fires and hates rekindled.

Of course, if we have a Shaw or a Galsworthy among us, let him
wander at will in the more devious by-paths of race dissection. Let him
wander wheresoever he will—provided he has no eye for the box-office.
For even as far-famed a dramatist as Galsworthy could not keep his
recent play, *The Forest*, more than a very limited time on the London
stage. Why? It dealt with propaganda, and as beautifully written and
staged as it was, it had to be withdrawn.

What, then, is left to the Negro dramatist? Let him portray the life
of his people, their foibles, if he will, and their sorrows and ambition and
defeats. Oh, yes, let us have all of these, told with tenderness and skill
and a knowledge of the theatre and the technique of the times. But as

long as we expect our public, white and colored, to support our drama, it were wise to steer far away from the old subjects.

A little more laughter, if you please, and fewer spirituals!